CANADIAN TELECOMMUNICATIONS LAW

ESSENTIALS OF
CANADIAN LAW

CANADIAN TELECOMMUNICATIONS LAW

DIMENSIONS IN A DIGITAL AGE

ROBERT G. HOWELL

Professor
Faculty of Law
University of Victoria
British Columbia

Canadian Telecommunications Law
© Irwin Law Inc., 2011

Published in 2011 by

Irwin Law Inc.
14 Duncan Street
Suite 206
Toronto, ON
M5H 3G8

www.irwinlaw.com

ISBN: 978-1-55221-055-0
e-book ISBN: 978-1-55221-192-2

Cataloguing in Publication data available from Library and Archives Canada

The publisher acknowledges the financial support of the Government of Canada through the Book Publishing Industry Development Program (BPIDP) for its publishing activities.

We acknowledge the assistance of the OMDC Book Fund, an initiative of Ontario Media Development Corporation.

Printed and bound in Canada.

1 2 3 4 5   15 14 13 12 11

TO MY MOTHER

(1914–2009)

SUMMARY
TABLE OF CONTENTS

DETAILED
TABLE OF CONTENTS

ACKNOWLEDGMENTS

From the initial conception of a need for a work that would encapsulate, explain, and analyze the dynamic technology-driven changes that were, and still are, reforging the dimensions of the law and policy applicable to telecommunications to the final product you are now reading, the completion of this book has been stretched out over a long period of time. As a consequence, most of the final content is entirely new or is reflective of earlier research efforts only in broad categorization.

   Circumstances over the last three years have, however, allowed an intensity of resources and effort that has enabled this work to be completed. It is to this period that my primary acknowledgements relate. Financially, two research grants totalling $10,000 (2008 and 2009) from the Foundation for Legal Research were instrumental in enabling completion by allowing the engagement of research assistance over a sustained period of time. I am very appreciative of these awards from the Foundation. I also thank the University of Victoria, Faculty of Law, for making research assistance available to the extent that funding permitted over shorter periods of time each year. Additionally, during the years of operation of our International Intellectual Property Law program (2002–07) the research assistance in implementation of that program ran parallel with many aspects of my research for this book so that research could be utilized for cross-purposes. My assistants also had some time, at least prior to the commencement of courses, to focus specifically on my research. Finally, my own personal financial contribution has been significant.

From a human perspective, I would first acknowledge and thank my secretary, Gail Rogers, who attended efficiently and without complaint to many handwritten drafts of my manuscript for all of the text and nearly all of the footnotes comprised in this work. Gail became my secretary in 2004 and therefore the bulk of the typographical work has fallen to her despite earlier work by my former secretaries. Secondly, there are my research assistants. I particularly thank Shane Sackman (2009–10) and Roland Hurst (2008–09), who provided intensive summer research and continued throughout the intervening academic years. More periodic attention was provided by Megan Shaw, Micah Weintraub, Kevin Nakanishi, Jason Glabb, Anna Johnston, and Christopher Funt. Thirdly, my assistants in the International Intellectual Property Law program were Claire Abbott (2002–03), Ryan Stammers (2004–05), and Lydia Zucconi (2006–07). I am grateful to all for their valuable research efforts and for the tedious work of checking or finding detailed footnote references.

I also acknowledge the assistance of researchers from earlier years. There were a number and their efforts provided me with a foundation to undertake this work. I make particular mention of Steve McKoen. He and I worked together in the late 1990s when I was preparing course-related materials to teach telecommunications law and policy for the first time, while also considering the dimensions a work of this nature might involve. The historical features and early aspects of regulatory and deregulatory analysis trace their origin to course-related material prepared at that time. The years have also meant that I have called on the services of our Law Library's reference librarians on numerous occasions and their help has always been cheerfully provided.

Finally, from the beginning of my interest in telecommunications, through to relatively recent times, I have benefited from discussions with Dr. Peter F. Driessen, Department of Electrical and Computer Engineering/School of Music and Department of Computer Science (cross-appointments) at the University of Victoria. Peter provided the occasional guest "engineering perspectives" lecture to my telecommunications law students and he and I enjoyed several dinners at the University Club involving engineering/law dialogue on telecommunications and a variety of related topics, especially intellectual property.

PREFACE

Few areas of law and policy have seen change so dramatic and encompassing as telecommunications. Historically contained as an administrative and regulatory subject of telecommunications (telegraph and telephone) and broadcasting (radio, television, and cable) under the encompassing guidance and control of the Canadian Radio-television and Telecommunications Commission (CRTC), telecommunications law and policy were, almost overnight, reborn and restructured. Or perhaps left scattered and unstructured, or "unbundled" — an appropriate pun. It was not simply the controlled deregulation from monopoly to competition in telephone communications, nor the convergence of broadcasting and non-broadcasting service providers, that deregulation facilitated. The media have changed and with them the regulatory focused subject area.

Deregulation of both long-distance and local telephone markets has become so encompassing of competition policy that a now significantly economically focused role for the CRTC in this context is challenged by the Competition Bureau as within its jurisdiction, requiring a relationship to be established between these agencies. By contrast, regulation continues for broadcasting in the traditional media of radio, television, and cable retransmission of signals of a network origin, together with direct-to-home (DTH) satellite broadcasts. For the latter, the requirement of a signal receiving and decoding device affords a measure of governmental control. Yet the market share of these traditional media is challenged, and regulatory capacity diminished, by the new media of digitized Internet communications in various manifestations, including Facebook, MySpace, YouTube, both wired and wireless, within desktop, laptop, and hand-held personalized devices. The historical categories of point-to-mass and point-to-point converge in these media, giving users the ability to select and personalize communication signals, broadcast or otherwise.

While digitized Internet communications are susceptible to broad political control over service providers and search engines to prevent access to services, the medium is largely decentralized, uncontrolled, and substantially anonymous in an everyday practical, economic, and governmental sense. Only an organized, sustained, and expensive effort of surveillance and access to Internet protocols through servers and search engines can provide authorities with details of individual usage. Necessarily, such information can emerge only after the individual activity has occurred, and as such is antithetical to regulatory control in a traditional sense. Other, more general areas of law must now be asserted in lieu of regulation to establish a legal infrastructure in which to operate.

The choice of what to encompass within "telecommunications" law becomes, essentially, one of demarcation. Traditional media – telephone (wired and wireless), radio, television, cable, and DTH satellite communications – remain core components, even as they integrate and converge with other media in the milieu of digitization. Yet the nature and breadth of digitization has juxtaposed other areas of law and imbued them with substantial significance and relevance to telecommunications as a whole. This trend is reflected in this book. I have chosen subject areas that involve a substantial telecommunications-related content or which are linked with telecommunications in some systemic sense.

Chapter 1 discusses constitutional and historical features of telecommunications law and policy. Before digitized communications, constitutional determinations concerned primarily the extraprovincial scope of the media and service providers, in order to remove them from provincial legislative and regulatory jurisdiction. They paid little attention to content and did not distinguish between medium and content. This relatively uncomplicated approach, if applied to the Internet, and particularly with respect to content, would cause most subject areas to fall within federal jurisdiction. Such a situation is, of course, politically and pragmatically impossible. Instead, the scope and diversity in application of the Internet calls for constitutional flexibility and a broader analysis within existing principles applicable to subject areas that encompass both federal and provincial jurisdictions.

Chapter 2 builds directly upon the historical features and details the regulatory (or deregulatory) position of telephone (point-to-point) telecommunications and of broadcasting (point-to-mass) under the federally enacted *Telecommunications Act* (1993) and the *Broadcasting Act* (1991), respectively. The chapter is a major component of this work, presenting internal convergences between these media and service providers as well as establishing a core from which both convergence and divergence occur with the new digitized media to reflect the now wider embrace of telecommunications in the twenty-first century.

Chapter 3 considers the organizational structure of Internet governance, including domain name allocation. An analysis of dispute arbitration with respect to conflicting domains is not included, this being now substantial and separately identifiable from a systemic coverage of the medium itself. However, an analysis is offered of fledgling developments, largely from the United States, concerned with providing relief from interference with the medium. Additionally, consideration is given to aspects of trademark infringement focused on features unique to the medium, such as the use of meta-tags in search engine listings or the use of trademark law, perhaps inappropriately, to afford relief from interference with the medium and the information encompassed within it. Of course, trademarks may be infringed in all media of telecommunications. As such, infringement is a matter for coverage in trademark law, not telecommunications law.

Many of the features in Chapter 3 are closely related to those in Chapter 4, concerning an analysis of privacy concerns within a context of digitized telecommunications media. While certainly not textually limited to digitized contexts, the federal *Personal Information Protection and Electronic Documents Act* (2000) (*PIPEDA*) was encouraged by, and is influential in, these contexts in both micro and macro situations. In a transactional sense, *PIPEDA* and copyright law are at the core of digitized file sharing, a process born of cyberspace and Internet communications technology. In broader contexts, it is the Privacy Commissioner, applying principles of *PIPEDA* and the process envisaged by this legislation, who is taking a lead, nationally and internationally, in working and negotiating with new media global entities such as Facebook and Google, to ensure that the benefits of these tools may be realized without substantial loss of privacy and personal information.

Chapter 5 addresses copyright in its application to radio, television, cable, and Internet-related media. While always inherently relational to communications, with nuanced development with respect to radio, television, and cable, copyright and telecommunications reached a substantial conjuncture once technology enabled the conversion of visual and aural expression to digital format. The challenge in the 1980s was the application and scope of copyright protection, and the ability of enforcement, with respect to computer technology in a "desktop" environment in business and industry. Momentously, this merged in the 1990s with Internet-related communications technologies. The ensuing battle over the scope and extent of copyright protection and the means of enforcement in a globalized world has given an entirely new dimension to society's perspectives on telecommunications media. The ability to share expression, information, and science in decentralized communications is pitted against the requirement of honouring by exclusivity, or at least remuneration, the attainment of reward by the creators and intermediary suppliers of content. The providers of media sit uncomfortably in between these factions. In many jurisdictions they have become the focus of enforcement by rights holders, yet service providers have contractual and privacy-related obligations to their users. In Canada, as elsewhere, the debate in these respects is heavily polarized, with little prospect of consensus resolution. Two legislative attempts have been made (2005 and 2007) to provide more comprehensive and effective copyright protection and to implement World Intellectual Property Organization (WIPO) treaties from 1996 that seek to achieve this in an electronic and digitized environment. Both attempts have lapsed in the House of Commons, given the circumstances of minority government and frequent federal elections (2006 and 2008) that have ensued since 2004. A third attempt is before the current Parliament.

My coverage concludes in Chapter 6 with a treatment of the principles of private international law (PIL) (conflict of laws) with an emphasis on telecommunications but also analyzing the dramatic restructuring of Canadian PIL that has continued unabated since the 1990s. One principal objective is to modernize PIL in order to facilitate international business transactions reflective of the global marketplace. This is evident particularly in transborder dealings between Canada and the United States. As in other contexts, telecommunications brings a nuance to PIL, but overall reflects the general dynamics of the area. The reach of telecommunications in all media is such that issues of jurisdiction, choice of law, and recognition and enforcement of extraterritorial judgments are of immediate relevance in international transmissions. In 2004, the Supreme Court of Canada applied the principal jurisdictional test of PIL (the "real and substantial connection" test) to extraterritorial Internet-related communication transmissions of musical works for the purpose of establishing Canadian jurisdiction over such transmissions even though the signals may originate from extraterritorial sources and servers.

The future portends major change. The federal *Telecommunications Act* (1993) and *Broadcasting Act* (1991) in the medium term are likely to be integrated into one enactment that will reflect the convergence of media and service providers.

Yet some things do not change. Despite the revolution in telecommunications media, broad political dimensions and diversities within Canadian society are seemingly preserved. This presents just one reason why the historical component of this work is important. The political lines drawn contextually with radio transmissions in the 1930s and '40s are entirely the same as those of today: Canadian versus foreign ownership, Canadian versus foreign content, Canadian competition versus foreign competition, and the protection versus non-protection of Canadian cultural industries are all as contentious as ever.

As far as possible in these subject areas, the law in this work is current to mid-April 2010, though some later references have been included.

FOREWORD

When I started practising transportation law in 1966, the bible was H.E.B. Coyne's 1948 edition of the *Annotated Railway Act*. Telegraph and telephone services were heavily regulated in fewer than twenty sections of the *Railway Act*, which consisted of a total of 460 sections. The focus was on regulating interference by telegraph and telephone lines with railways and highways. Rates and tolls were regulated in much the same way as railway freight rates. Radio and television was entirely separate. Technological change was hardly on the radar screen. Today, that environment seems like it belongs in the Stone Age. By comparison to the context of today, it was the Stone Age.

We live in an entirely different telecommunications world today. The historical distinctions between the traditional broadcast and non-broadcast sectors of the telecommunications industry are blurring. Deregulation and changing technologies have resulted in complex challenges for regulators, carriers, broadcasters, consumers, and content creators. Telecommunications technologies are changing at an extraordinarily rapid pace: the technologies used five years ago are often obsolete when compared to those used today. The impact of these changes is further increased when one takes into account the controlled deregulation of the telecommunications industry that has occurred over the last few decades. All of this change has resulted in new issues to challenge the legal community.

Robert Howell's *Canadian Telecommunications Law* makes an extremely valuable and, importantly, an up-to-date contribution to the body of knowledge surrounding telecommunications law in these times of rapidly changing technology and deregulation.

Changing telecommunications technologies have led to a trend in which other subject areas of the law have become increasingly relevant to telecommunications. Professor Howell's work is particularly significant because it includes discussion of these other subject areas of the law linked to telecommunications law. *Canadian Telecommunications Law* includes discussion of such subjects as competition law, trademarks, privacy, copyright, and conflicts of law as they relate to telecommunications.

The first chapter of this work provides the reader with the necessary historical and constitutional framework surrounding telecommunications law in Canada. The chapter introduces the discussion of the regulation of content, the Internet, privacy, and jurisdictional issues. This part of the work is important in that the historical policy issues surrounding Canadian content and ownership are still at play and are relevant in the modern context.

The regulatory scheme governing telecommunications is discussed in the second chapter of this work. Valuable commentary is provided with respect to the dramatic developments and restructuring occurring in the telecommunications industry, and the effect this is having on the relevant legal and policy framework. Professor Howell notes how new Internet-related technologies allow Canadians to bypass the traditional media and delivery platforms of both broadcast and non-broadcast telecommunications. Convergence between broadcast and non-broadcast telecommunications is also discussed. Of particular interest is Professor Howell's prognosis with respect to Canadian content and ownership requirements for carriers and content providers in light of the changes brought about by advances in technology.

A discussion of modern telecommunications law would not be complete without a consideration of the interrelated subjects of trademark law, privacy law, and copyright law, which are the focus of the third, fourth, and fifth chapters of this work. Professor Howell's discussion of trademark issues pertinent to Internet domain names is informative. He notes the risks to personal privacy and challenges posed to protecting intellectual property inherent in the new telecommunications technologies. Readers will find Professor Howell's discussion of the unique regulatory challenges posed by changes to telecommunications technologies to be of special interest. Worthy of note is Professor Howell's discussion about the successes of the federal Privacy Commissioner dealing with privacy concerns involving social networking and the Google Street View service. In addition, valuable discussion is provided about the importance of copyright law in balancing the protection of and access to information in light of modern telecommunications technologies.

Increasingly, modern telecommunications activities, both social and commercial, have an international component, and in particular, a Canada-US–cross-border aspect. *Canadian Telecommunications Law* concludes with an instructive discussion on the subject of conflict of laws and the influence that changes in telecommunications have had on this subject. Professor Howell notes how telecommunications technologies are substantially contributing to the globalization of trade and business. This not only adds jurisdictional and enforcement demands, but has also added subjects such as intellectual property rights and privacy that have had little influence on historical conflicts of laws theory and practice. Readers will find the discussion of conflict of laws in the context of telecommunications law to be highly informative.

Professor Howell has much experience and expertise in the areas of intellectual property, telecommunications, and Internet-related law. He has an extensive publication record, and has been involved in organizing several conferences and seminars on these topics. This work of Professor Howell will be of great value to all who have an interest in these subjects, and I commend him for the contribution that *Canadian Telecommunications Law* will make to our understanding in this area of the law, and for the time and effort that he obviously spent in creating this work.

Justice Marshall Rothstein
Ottawa
October, 2010

CHAPTER 1

HISTORICAL AND CONSTITUTIONAL FRAMEWORK

A. THE SCOPE OF TELECOMMUNICATIONS LAW

Historically, telecommunications law in Canada was exclusively within administrative law. A body of rulings from the Canadian Radio-television and Telecommunications Commission (CRTC), accompanied by judicial determinations by way of appeal, review, or enforcement, provided the applicable jurisprudence. It built on a substantial history of a regulated industry. The 1980s, however, brought the beginning of political and economic change. By the 1990s, these changes were a flood, swollen beyond anything imaginable by the technological revolution of digitization and the medium of the Internet in particular. The theme of media convergence that had initially focused on the operational and business convergence of telephone systems with formerly telegraph and cable television communication expanded through digitization and the Internet to one of a multimedia visual and aural expression, converted to electronic "bits" and communicated as such.

A medium so international, decentralized, and almost universally accessible as the Internet is, practically speaking, beyond the scope of effective regulation, at least as traditionally contemplated. Indeed, cyberspace, the so-called world of Internet communications,[1] was initially characterized as a separate and distinct (virtual) locale beyond

---

1   William Gibson, *Neuromancer* (London: Gollancz, 1985).

the scope of regulation.[2] Yet cyberspace is a creation of, and is used and inhabited by, humankind in real societies and is, therefore, subject to the legal and governmental structures applicable in those societies. While certainly extraterritorial, cyberspace is not extraterrestrial. The extent of its pervasiveness is such that all areas of law are potentially applicable to its application if real society is to participate in the medium while also being protected from adverse consequences that would otherwise disrupt society.[3]

Despite theoretical and practical difficulties in application, legal concepts and principles have effectively adapted to new situations in many contexts and will undoubtedly move to encompass current and future technology and media of communication appropriately. This may be by way of direct application of existing law and policy or by creation of new infrastructure such as the dispute resolution mechanism for Internet domain names.

Further difficulties may be posed for the jurist. Is there still, or should there be, a subject area identified as telecommunications law? If so, what might it comprise? Should issues of telecommunications be simply subcategorized and allocated to existing substantive topics in the legal curriculum? At this point in a rapidly changing industry, sufficient core areas of law and policy relevant to telecommunications in itself still exist that justify a separately designated area of law. This core is represented by the statutory and regulatory framework of point-to-mass, broadcasting, and point-to-point communications, reflected in a legislative ordering as recent as 1991 and 1993. This framework will continue for the immediate future, notwithstanding that even at the time of enactment, the legislation presented a structure challenged by the Internet and other technological innovation encompassing both individual and mass communication. A new legislative and administrative framework may be needed to reflect the significant and ongoing changes that the industry now reflects. This is contemplated, but divergent political perspectives, well demonstrated in 2003 in reports from respective standing committees of the House of Commons concerning

---

2   See, for example, the series of essays on this theme in B. Kahin & C. Nesson, ed., *Borders in Cyberspace*, Harvard Information Infrastructure Project (Cambridge, MA: MIT Press, 1997). Note also Public Notice CRTC 1999-197, Ottawa, 17 December 1999, in which even the Canadian Radio-television and Telecommunications Commission (CRTC) withheld, for the time being, any attempt to regulate Internet-related communications.

3   Michel Racicot *et al.*, *The Cyberspace Is Not a 'No Law Land': A Study of the Issues of Liability for Content Circulating on the Internet* (Ottawa: Industry Canada, 1997), online: archive.ifla.org/documents/infopol/canada/icrls.pdf.

telecommunications[4] and broadcasting[5] suggest that the exercise will be contentious, despite the gathering momentum for change as detailed in the introduction to Chapter 2.

In the meantime, the categorization of broadcasting and non-broadcasting remains as a functional foundation but is weathered not only by the process of deregulation but also by the inclusion within telecommunications law of other areas not formerly contemplated as central or even relevant to the topic. These include elements of competition law, intellectual property law, privacy law, and private international law. They are crucial inclusions to any holistic treatment of "telecommunications law" in today's environment.

A refocusing on aspects of constitutional law is also necessary. While constitutional jurisdiction was relatively clear with respect to the traditional media of telephone, television, cable, and satellite distributions, the constitutional dimensions applicable to the Internet and related areas are much less certain. The communications revolution from 1930s through the 1970s of radio, television, and cable provided the technological framework for both the constitutional determinations and the governmental and regulatory measures that have served the industry to the present. Ironically, the political dimensions of this period reflect the same political polarity that is demonstrated in the two parliamentary reports in 2003 and that will shape the future political debate over the restructuring of the constitutional and legal infrastructure to take account of the current revolution flowing from digital technology in a global environment. This, indeed, is the one constant dimension.

---

4   House of Commons, Standing Committee on Industry, Science and Technology, *Opening Canadian Communications to the World* (April 2003), online: Parliamentary Internet Parlementaire http://cmte.parl.gc.ca/Content/HOC/committee/372/inst/reports/rpl032302/instrp03/instrp03-e.pdf. See also Minister of Industry, *Government Responds to Industry Committee's Recommendations on Foreign Investment Restrictions in Telecommunications* (25 September 2003), online: www.ic.gc.ca/eic/site/ic1.nsf/eng/02475.html.

5   House of Commons, Standing Committee on Canadian Heritage, *Our Cultural Sovereignty: The Second Century of Canadian Broadcasting* (June 2003), online: www2.parl.gc.ca/HousePublications/Publication.aspx?DocId=1032284&Language=E&Mode=1&Parl=37&Ses=2&File=5. See also Minister of Canadian Heritage, *The Government of Canada's Response to the Report of the Standing Committee on Canadian Heritage, Our Cultural Sovereignty: The Second Century of Canadian Broadcasting* (2003), online: www2.parl.gc.ca/Content/HOC/Committee/381/CHPC/GovResponse/RP1726418/CHPC_Rpt02_GvtRsp/GvtRsp_Part1-e.pdf.

B. THE REGULATORY HISTORY

Not surprisingly, the regulation of telecommunications in Canada presents the two broad categories of the traditional telecommunications media. First are point-to-point communications, comprising historically fixed wired links between two specific points, the telegraph and the telephone. Second are point-to-mass, historically comprising wireless microwave (Hertzian) or radio communications that derive from a specific source and are available, without control by the sender, to any person possessed of the appropriate receiving equipment within the range of the signal. The description "telecommunications" was given to the former and "broadcasting" to the latter. This division is currently reflected in the *Telecommunications Act* (1993)[6] and the *Broadcasting Act* (1991).[7]

Despite the technical convergence of media by digitization and satellite communications, a point-to-point and point-to-mass distinction reflects a distinct policy difference that remains of significance today in Canada. The broadcast, point-to-mass traditional media of television and radio exert as much, if not more, political, social, and economic influence on society today as they have in the past. Regulation of broadcasting therefore remains a significant feature of federal government policy, distinguishable from the regulation of traditional point-to-point media such as the telephone. This difference is further illustrated by the now almost complete deregulation of telephone services in Canada. It is also of some international significance in international trade in services under the World Trade Organization (WTO), presenting moves toward international deregulation of the telecommunications industry in various contexts, but not with respect to broadcasting, over which national jurisdictions still seek to retain control. Perhaps, therefore, a distinction between point-to-point and point-to-mass communications might be usefully retained at least as an initial vehicle of description, analysis, and evaluation.

1) Point-to-Point Media

The first point-to-point telecommunications medium was the telegraph. It was linked, in Canada, with the construction of railways in the late nineteenth and early twentieth centuries. Telegraph lines paralleled railway tracks and afforded wired communications between cities and

---

6   *Telecommunications Act*, S.C. 1993, c. 38.
7   *Broadcasting Act*, S.C. 1991, c. 11.

towns. Within most cities and towns a locally focused telephone service developed. These local services were gradually interconnected to
establish regional systems.[8]

These beginnings were the roots of a dual telecommunications infrastructure in Canada, which after 1979 formed the basis for regulated
competition in long-distance telephone services. Telegraphic facilities
were between centres but without connection to individual businesses
and homes. Telephone services had such connections, however, affording
national and international links between homes and businesses. The
telegraph, albeit modernized technologically, was therefore in business
decline by the 1970s.[9] The modern, technically efficient infrastructure
that it presented did, however, allow for the creation of competition
without the need to resort to foreign service providers. The thrust of
"regulated competition" from 1979 was the forced interconnection of
operators using the modernized telegraph system with local telephone
providers, to gain competing direct access to users. Additionally, there
was a linkage and convergence of the telegraph infrastructure with that
of cable television, facilitating an additional direct connection to businesses and homes. More recently, wireless telecommunications and Internet convergence have, of course, diminished the need for physical
connections, but physical interconnection is still the predominant sector of the industry.

Both telegraph and telephone were regulated by a single authority
from 1908. Amendment of the *Railway Act*[10] extended the jurisdiction
of the Board of Railway Commissioners to all telegraph and telephone
service providers. Essentially, regulation consisted of setting rates and
determining disputed compensation for the interconnection of telephone services.[11] The board was renamed as the Board of Transport
Commissioners of Canada in 1938.[12] From 1968, jurisdiction was vested in the Canadian Transport Commission (exercised by the Railway
Transport Committee from 1968 to 1972), reporting with respect to
telecommunication matters to the federal Minister of Transport.[13] From

---

8   For a description of the telegraph system and its development see R.E. Babe,
    Telecommunication in Canada: Technology, Industry, and Government (Toronto:
    University of Toronto Press, 1993) Part 2, cc. 3–5.
9   See *ibid.* at 62, noting that by 1976 the telegraph market constituted only 4.4
    percent of total Canadian communications.
10 *Railway Amendment Act*, S.C. 1908, c. 61.
11 *Ibid.*, s. 4.
12 *Transport Act*, S.C. 1938, c. 53, s. 3(1).
13 *National Transportation Act*, S.C. 1966–67, c. 69, ss. 6(1), 14, and 94. See Can-
    adian Transport Commission, *The Second Annual Report of the Canadian Trans-
    port Commission, 1968* (Ottawa: Queen's Printer, 1969) at 11.

1972, the Telecommunications Committee replaced the Railway Transport Committee in telecommunications matters.[14]

Regulatory convergence between point-to-point telecommunications and point-to-mass broadcasting was effected in 1976, when jurisdiction for telecommunications was given to the (renamed) Canadian Radio-television and Telecommunications Commission (CRTC),[15] which had been established in 1968 as the Canadian Radio Television Commission to regulate broadcasting.[16] Within three years of gaining jurisdiction for telecommunications, the CRTC set in motion a process to deregulate the telephone industry.

The telecommunications industry by 1979 reflected the dominance of telephone providers, with rates set by the CRTC. Worldwide a move to deregulate and demonopolize telephone service providers was underway. This signalled a general economic environment tending toward revitalization of private enterprise, competition, and capitalism.[17] The CRTC promoted objectives that included maintaining Canadian ownership of telecommunications, providing competition for the incumbent telephone providers, and utilizing the existing high-quality ex-telegraph telecommunications infrastructure.[18]

The telecommunications telephone sector is now so significantly deregulated and competitive that regulatory jurisdiction over the sector has required formal guidelines to reconcile the role of the CRTC with that of the Competition Bureau in a context that is continuing to develop.[19] The latter has jurisdiction under the federal *Competition Act*[20] to preserve competition within industries that constitutionally fall within federal legislative jurisdiction. Being a statute of general application, the *Competition Act* applies to all relevant industries, including those subject to specific regulation by another regulator. However,

---

14　Canadian Transport Commission, *The Sixth Annual Report of the Canadian Transport Commission, 1972* (Ottawa: Queen's Printer, 1973) at 23.

15　*Canadian Radio-television and Telecommunications Commission Act*, S.C. 1974-75-76, c. 49, s. 14(2). The word "Telecommunications" was added to the title of the Commission to reflect this additional jurisdiction.

16　See text accompanying note 66, below in this chapter.

17　This move was typified by the election of the Thatcher government from 1979 in the United Kingdom and President Ronald Reagan for two terms in the United States from 1981.

18　See *CNCP Telecommunications: Interconnection with Bell Canada* (17 May 1979), Telecom Decision CRTC 1979-11, 5 C.R.T. 177 [Telecom Decision CRTC 79-11].

19　See, *CRTC/Competition Bureau Interface*, online: www.crtc.gc.ca/eng/publications/reports/crtc_com.htm. See Chapter 2, text accompanying notes 17–19 and 97–114.

20　*Competition Act*, R.S.C. 1985, c. C-34.

judicial interpretation has recognized a "Regulated Conduct Defence" for activities performed under a valid regulatory scheme.[21] Considerable uncertainty exists as to the scope of this defence in the telecommunications industry.[22]

The procedure followed by the CRTC to implement deregulation involved exercising the statutory power to "forbear" from regulating, wholly or partially, conditionally or unconditionally, any telecommunications service or class of services of a Canadian carrier,[23] or to "exempt" any class of Canadian carriers from the requirements of the *Telecommunications Act*.[24] In both contexts, the CRTC must conclude that the exercise of the particular procedure is consistent with Canadian telecommunications policy.[25] The latter has been interpreted and developed by the CRTC to include the policies of deregulation involving the need to determine if a sufficient level of competition exists. For this purpose, the CRTC applies criteria[26] substantially similar to those applied by the Competition Bureau when exercising its authority under the *Competition Act*.

The deregulation process extended over twenty years. The initial move in 1979 was tentative and cautious but has been described as "perhaps the single most important case that has ever come before a regulatory board dealing with telecommunications in Canada."[27] It was limited in scope to data and "private live voice" transmissions,[28] and prescribed monitoring and "just and expedient compensation" for Bell Canada.[29] The second step, in 1992, was the interconnection of public

---

21 *Garland v. Consumers' Gas Co.*, [2004] 1 S.C.R. 629.

22 Competition Bureau, *Consultations on the Information Bulletin on the Regulated Conduct Defence* (29 October 2004), online: www.competitionbureau.gc.ca/eic/site/cb-bc.nsf/eng/00340.html.

23 *Telecommunications Act*, above note 6, s. 34, but see 34(2): "competition sufficient to protect interest of users."

24 *Ibid.*, s. 9.

25 The statutory criteria establishing Canadian telecommunications policy are set out in *ibid.*, s. 7.

26 See *Review of Regulatory Framework* (16 September 1994), Telecom Decision CRTC 1994-19, online: CRTC www.crtc.gc.ca/eng/archive/1994/DT94-19.HTM, Part 2 "General Framework" and Part 3 "Forbearance" [Telecom Decision CRTC 94-19].

27 Telecom Decision CRTC 79-11, above note 18 at Part 9, para. 1.

28 Private line voice service concerned voice communications within a subscriber's organization. Public long-distance service was not included.

29 The requirement of "just and expedient compensation" did not include the value of any business loss to Bell Canada, or other incumbent, from the interconnection, nor any loss on the basis of "expropriation of a proprietary right."

long-distance voice services,[30] with a sharing of contribution costs favourable to the startup interconnector in the public interest of promoting competition and recognizing the historically dominant position of telephone service providers.[31] The third step was a recognition that long-distance service rates should not be held at levels that included subsidization of local service rates. Accordingly, "local rate rebalancing" was effected from 1995 through 1998,[32] severing the historical regulatory linkage of long-distance tolls with local service.

As a result, long-distance telephone rates could, from 1 January 1998, be regulated on a "price," rather than an "earnings," basis. Maximum rates, or "caps," were set, enabling service providers to offer rates below the cap as market competition permitted.[33] Similarly, local rate rebalancing and unbundling of service components facilitated competition in local pay telephone service by giving competitive local exchange carriers wired or wireless access to the incumbent local exchange carrier's networks at filed tariffs.[34]

This situation is essentially the modern position and is described fully in Chapter 2 in the context of the *Telecommunications Act*. It is sufficient to note here that deregulation and unbundling of services has facilitated considerable competition, going well beyond the competitive framework created by the historical infrastructure of two terrestrial telecommunications systems, as earlier described. A consequence of this framework was an almost singular competitive divide between the principal established telephone service providers or carriers, allied within an organization known as Stentor Resource Centre Inc. (Stentor),[35] on the one hand, and the newly created alternative carriers,

---

The level set by the CRTC was determined simply as a matter of public interest. See Telecom Decision CRTC 79-11, above note 18 at Part 9, para. 4.

30   *Competition in the provision of public long distance voice telephone services and related resale and sharing issues* (12 June 1997), Telecom Decision CRTC 1992-12, online: www.crtc.gc.ca/eng/archive/1992/DT92-12.htm.

31   *Bell Canada v. Unitel* (1992), [1993] 1 F.C. 669, 99 D.L.R. (4th) 533 (C.A.).

32   Telecom Decision CRTC 94-19, above note 26 at Part 2(B).

33   *Price cap regulations and related issues* (1 May 1997), Telecom Decision CRTC 1997-8 and 1997-9 at Part 3, online: www.crtc.gc.ca/eng/archive/1997/DT97-8. HTM.

34   *Ibid.*

35   Stentor Resource Centre Inc. comprised and was an alliance of the following established telephone companies: AGT, BC Tel, Bell, Island Tel, MT&T, MTS, NB Tel, Newfoundland Telephone, NorthwesTel, Québec Téléphone, and Sask. Tel. See online: www.thecanadianencyclopedia.com/index.cfm?PgNm=TCE&Params=A1ARTA0008092.

on the other.[36] This structural divide collapsed in 1998, and competition was engaged between all industry players.

2) Point-to-Mass Media

Guglielmo Marconi's receipt of the first transatlantic wireless transmission from Cornwall, England, to St. John's, Newfoundland, on 12 December 1901 released long-distance telecommunications from fixed points and wired facilities.[37] It enabled wireless or microwave radio communication and subsequently mass telecommunication or broadcasting. The first mass broadcast did not occur until 1919,[38] but regulation in Canada was in place from 1905, utilizing criminal law sanctions to ensure the licensing of wireless marine communications.[39] From 1913, "land radiotelegraph stations" were included.[40]

By the mid- to late 1920s, the modern purposes of wireless regulation were established as control of radio or microwave frequencies from an operating perspective[41] and control over content of public broadcasts.[42] With respect to radio broadcasting, the broad debates were first, the need for accessibility throughout all of Canada and the choice between public or private control, and second, the need or otherwise of public ownership or regulation to ensure the presence of Canadian content in broadcast programming, given the transborder reception in Canada of broadcast radio signals from United States.[43] These two fea-

---

36   The principal initial alternative carrier was Unitel Communications Inc. (formerly the telegraph entity CNCP Telecommunications), which became AT&T Canada from September 1995. Prior to 1995, a portion of Unitel Communications was owned by the television cable operator Rogers Communications Inc. See online: www.your.rogers.com/aboutrogers/historyofrogers/overview.asp?shopperID=5DQRBPMNF9R18MWWJWBHVR7QRNW9EGB9.

37   Memorial Dedication, Signal Hill, St. John's, NL, reproduced pictorially by Marconi Club of Newfoundland, online: www.ucs.mun.ca/~jcraig/marconi.html. Marconi had earlier succeeded in wireless communications over shorter distances, including the English Channel in 1899. See *Funk & Wagnalls New Encyclopedia*, vol. 16 (1996) at 438.

38   *Babe*, above note 8 at 202.

39   *Wireless Telegraphy Act*, S.C. 1905, c. 49.

40   *Radiotelegraph Act*, S.C. 1913, c. 43.

41   *Ibid.*, noted by F.W. Peers, *The Politics of Canadian Broadcasting 1920–1951* (Toronto: University of Toronto Press, 1969) at 29 as leaving radio stations "with full discretion in what was broadcast."

42   *Ibid.* at 29ff. traces the move toward government influence over content.

43   *Ibid.* at 34–36. These debates led to the appointment in 1928 of a royal commission chaired by Sir John Aird. See Canada, Royal Commission on Radio Broadcasting, *Report* (Ottawa: King's Printer, 1929) (Chair: John Aird) [Aird Report].

tures were, of course, related. The medium of broadcast creates and influences public ideas and opinions and was (and still is) seen as facilitating a national identity and spirit from the perspective of both Canadian content and accessibility. These objectives were considered more readily attainable through a public broadcast system.[44] A model closer to that of the British Broadcasting Corporation (BBC) was considered preferable for Canada, rather than the private sector ownership of the American model. [45]

The decision of the Privy Council in 1931, finding federal legislative jurisdiction for radio communications,[46] enabled the passage of the *Canadian Radio Broadcasting Act* in 1932.[47] The Canadian Radio Broadcasting Commission (CRBC) was created and authorized "to regulate and control broadcasting in Canada," including broadcasting carried on by federal and provincial governments.[48] The Act authorized the Commission to regulate content between "national" and "local" programs with the aim of using the medium to foster a Canadian national identity;[49] control the extent of advertising (the source of revenue for private broadcasting stations);[50] and prohibit the creation of a privately owned network system.[51] The primary objective was the creation of a national public network, funded by licence fees for possession of reception equipment, and by purchasing existing privately owned stations.[52]

These directions were continued in 1935 with the establishment of the Canadian Broadcasting Corporation (CBC) under the *Canadian Broadcasting Act* (1936).[53] This structure remained until 1958, when a further restructuring occurred. From 1936 to 1958, the CBC consisted of a board that reflected regional interests and inherited the regulatory

---

44   Peers, *ibid.* at 47–55, discussing the conclusion of the Aird Commission in favour of a publicly owned system rather than to utilize private ownership and competition.

45   *Ibid.* at 53, noting that private facilities would over time become dependent on United States sources for revenue. In effect, only public facilities were thought to have sufficient revenue and positioning to achieve the objectives of Canadian content and accessibility.

46   See below note 78.

47   *Canadian Radio Broadcasting Act*, S.C. 1932, c. 51.

48   *Ibid.*, s. 8.

49   *Ibid.*, s. 8(b).

50   *Ibid.*

51   *Ibid.*, s. 8(f).

52   *Ibid.*, s. 9. In effect, the recommendations of the Aird Commission that "[a] national company . . . own and operate all radio broadcasting stations," (Aird Report, above note 43 at 7) were being pursued.

53   *Canadian Broadcasting Act*, S.C. 1936, c. 24.

powers of the CRBC for the whole broadcasting industry. Regulatory jurisdiction included existing privately owned operators as well as the CBC itself, which the Board directed through a general manager.[54] The Board was therefore both the source of direction for the publicly funded and operated CBC service and the regulator for all Canadian broadcasting. This duality reflected a system designed as a single national broadcasting system, emphasizing the public character of broadcasting directly through the predominance of the CBC and indirectly through its control over private broadcasters.[55]

Many private broadcasters formed an association known as the Canadian Association of Broadcasters (CAB) to protect their interests within the so-called single system. In reality, members of CAB saw themselves in competition with the CBC and from this stance considered the merging of the competitor and regulator in the CBC Board of Governors to be anomalous.[56] Additionally, the Act expressly precluded private operators from forming a network.[57]

The 1957 Report of the Royal Commission on Broadcasting (the Fowler Commission) summarized the many stresses that were then apparent in Canadian broadcasting.[58] The context was accentuated by the development of mass television broadcasting, especially with respect to the considerable transborder reception of US broadcasting in Canada,[59] and an apparent inability to establish similar growth in Canada within the existing infrastructure.[60]

Principal changes were effected in the *Broadcasting Act* (1958).[61] First, a new regulator was established, the Board of Broadcast Govern-

---

54   *Ibid.*, s. 6.
55   *Ibid.*, ss. 8 (objects of the CBC) and 22 (regulation of private broadcasters). Such an approach was only slightly broader than the recommendation of the Aird Commission for one "national company": Aird Report, above note 43 at 7. See also above note 52.
56   Of course, the anomaly essentially reflected the divergent political opinion as to whether the whole system should be coordinated as one or be seen to involve competition between the government-funded CBC and the privately funded CAB broadcasters. See F.W. Peers, *The Public Eye: Television and The Politics of Canadian Broadcasting 1952–1968* (Toronto: University of Toronto Press, 1979) at 67ff.
57   *Canadian Broadcasting Act*, above note 53, s. 21.
58   Canada, Royal Commission on Broadcasting, *Report* (Ottawa: Queen's Printer, 1957) at 1–13 (Chair: R.M. Fowler). The Commission was appointed in 1954.
59   *Ibid.* at 8–9.
60   *Ibid.* at 11 noting that advertising revenue in Canada was not sufficient itself to pay for a Canadian broadcasting system.
61   *Broadcasting Act*, S.C. 1958, c. 22, enacted by a Parliament led by a Progressive Conservative Party government.

ors (BBG), independent of the CBC, with the regulatory powers formerly exercised by the Board of Governors of the CBC.[62] Second, the creation of privately owned networks was authorized.[63] As a result, in 1961 the BBG licensed the creation of the Canadian Television Network (CTV),.enabling national competition with the CBC. Third, the broadcasting service (both CBC and privately owned) was to be "basically Canadian in content and character."[64]

A decade later, the *Broadcasting Act* (1968)[65] preserved the basic regulatory and operational structure established in 1958, but effected important changes that reflect the current regulatory structure. The BBG was replaced by the Canadian Radio-television Commission (CRTC) as the regulating authority.[66] The publicly owned CBC and privately owned systems would continue to compete, but all broadcasting undertakings, public or private, were legislatively declared to be "a single system," dispelling any trend that might have followed from the changes in 1958 to view broadcasting in Canada as a dual system of private and public networks with competition between them.[67] This "single system" was part of a new "Broadcasting Policy for Canada," enacted in significant detail[68] and, importantly, recognizing the public role of the CBC to provide "the national broadcast service" with specifically stipulated objectives.[69] Any conflict between the CBC's national broadcast service and "private elements" in the broadcasting system was directed to be resolved "in the public interest but [with] paramount consideration to the objectives of the national broadcast service."[70]

The key definition in both regulatory processes and judicial enforcement in the years following 1968 was that of "broadcasting undertaking."[71] This is retained in the *Broadcasting Act* (1991).[72] A li-

---

62 *Ibid.*, s. 3. For a description of the constitution, functions, and performance of the BBG, see A. Stewart & W. Hull, *Canadian Television Policy and the Board of Broadcast Governors 1958–1968* (Edmonton: University of Alberta Press, 1994) at 9–25. The authors describe the years 1958–68 as "watershed years" in Canadian broadcasting (*ibid.* at 3).

63 *Broadcasting Act*, above note 61, s. 13(5).

64 *Ibid.*, s. 10.

65 *Broadcasting Act*, S.C. 1967–68, c. 25, enacted by a Parliament led by a Liberal Party government.

66 *Ibid.*, ss. 5(1) and 15.

67 *Ibid.*, s. 2(a).

68 *Ibid.*, s. 2.

69 *Ibid.*, s. 39.

70 *Ibid.*, s. 2(h).

71 *Ibid.*, s. 3(d).

72 *Broadcasting Act*, above note 7.

cence is required to operate a "broadcasting undertaking."[73] Persons engaging in activities that fall within this definition but who do not hold a licence from the CRTC are infringing. From 1968, the definition included a "broadcasting transmitting undertaking" ("programming undertaking" from 1991), a "broadcasting receiving undertaking" ("distribution undertaking" from 1991), and a "network." This reflected the then developing technology of cable television (CATV) consisting of the receipt by antennae of broadcast signals and their retransmission (rediffusion) by cable to subscribers who may or may not have been able to receive the initial wireless broadcast signal. Cable retransmitters were "broadcast receiving undertakings" (or from 1991 "distribution undertakings") and were brought within the regulatory framework.

Much litigation ensued through to current times over an appropriate application of the definitions in various circumstances of receipt and retransmission of broadcast signals. These are discussed in Chapter 2, explaining the current regulatory position. Later technologies of direct-to-home (DTH) satellite television and Internet broadcasting are included.

C. CONSTITUTIONAL DIMENSIONS

As noted earlier, a consistent theme in the regulatory process in Canadian broadcasting and telecommunications has been that transmission, receipt, and retransmission of signals occur within a single system and that the elements or features of operations or infrastructure are not categorized as separate from the whole. This has enabled a comprehensive regulatory scheme focused on the overall objective of a system, rather than on any component parts or sectors. A similar policy and conceptualization have prevailed in a constitutional context with respect to legislative competence between federal and provincial sources. The federal jurisdiction has prevailed, frequently on the basis of the indivisibility of technical function and overall objective.

The contest between federal and provincial jurisdictions with respect to broadcast and non-broadcast electronic communications has been vigorously engaged from the advent of widespread radio communication in the 1920s. Majority decisions of the Supreme Court of Canada have, nevertheless, consistently recognized federal jurisdiction, and today there is no longer any doubt that constitutionally broadcast media of radio and television, cable and satellite modes of transmission, and

---

73   *Ibid.*, s. 32(1).

non-broadcast media of telephone, including wireless devices[74] of inter-provincial or international range, are within federal jurisdiction with respect to their regulation.

Such certainty is, however, weakened, even within the traditional media, in the following contexts:

1) The existence of circumstances that might enable some provincial jurisdiction to be established with respect to regulation of these media. This reflects that while judicial determinations have consistently preferred federal jurisdiction, the potential of appropriate circumstances that might support a measure of provincial jurisdiction has neither been considered nor precluded and, on occasion, the potential has been acknowledged.

2) The scope of federal jurisdiction concerning the content of broadcast programs.

In addition, the medium of the Internet has presented new dimensions. The breadth of its use and capacity applies so pervasively in activities traditionally of provincial jurisdiction (for example, the sale of goods and the ability to apply a retail sales tax) that a major redistribution favouring exclusive federal jurisdiction would occur if the Internet were to be jurisdictionally evaluated in the same manner as has occurred with respect to the traditional media of telecommunications.

1) The Traditional Approach

The 1920s saw the first constitutional litigation in the contexts of aviation and radio transmission by Hertzian wave.[75] Both activities broke the nexus with a fixed pathway. The railway and the telegraph comprised physical linkages. Section 92(10)(a), *Constitution Act, 1867*[76]

---

74   These devices include radio-telephone, cell telephone and satellite telephone systems, described fully in Chapter 2, text accompanying notes 159–90 ("Wireless Communications").

75   Radio transmissions, whether satellite communications or straight line ("line of sight") terrestrial, are described as "Hertzian waves" or "microwaves" and are electromagnetic waves measured by vibrations (cycles) per second. They are abbreviated "Hz" and one Hz equals one cycle per second. The expression "Hertzian" is derived from Heinrich Rudolf Hertz (1857–94), the German physicist who first detected the waves. See Alan Freedman, *Computer Desktop Encyclopedia*, 2d ed. (New York: American Management Association, 1999), s.v. "Hertz," "microwave," and "radio." See also, online: www.ideafinder.com/history/inventors/hertz.htm.

76   *Constitution Act, 1867* (U.K.), 30 & 31 Vict., c. 3, reprinted in R.S.C. 1985, App. II, No. 5.

expressly provided for railways and telegraphs to be a federal juris-diction, if in the nature of works and undertakings extending beyond provincial boundaries.[77] Being expressed as an exception to section 92 provincial jurisdictions, each in this extended context became a head of exclusively federal jurisdiction as if it were an enumerated head under section 91 federal jurisdictions.[78]

The Privy Council decided *Re Aerial Navigation, A.G. Canada v. A.G. Ontario* on 21 October 1931[79] and *Re Regulation and Control of Radio Communication* on 9 February 1932.[80] Although the primary basis of finding an exclusive federal jurisdiction for aviation was section 132, *Constitution Act, 1867*, concerning the implementation in Canada of treaties between the British Empire and other countries,[81] reference was also made to the broader grounds of the residual federal jurisdiction in section 91 "Peace, Order, and good Government of Canada" (POGG), given that aviation was not expressly enumerated under either section 91 or section 92, and the fact that aerial navigation had then reached dimensions that affected the whole of Canada.[82] An express analogy was drawn by the Privy Council between the *Aviation* and the *Radio Reference* proceedings.[83]

The latter proceedings also involved an international convention,[84] but not one between the British Empire and other countries. Section 132, *Constitution Act, 1867*[85] was therefore inapplicable. Nevertheless, the Board considered the existence and need for implementation of an international obligation to be a relevant factor in at least the first of the

---

77   The key expression is "connecting the Province with any other or others of the provinces, or extending beyond the Limits of the Province" (s. 92(10)(a)).

78   *Re Regulation and Control of Radio Communication*, [1932] A.C. 304, [1932] 2 D.L.R. 81 (P.C.) [*Radio Reference*].

79   *Re Aerial Navigation, Attorney General Canada v. Attorney General Ontario*, [1932] 1 D.L.R. 58 (P.C.) [*Aviation Reference*].

80   *Radio Reference*, above note 78.

81   *Aviation Reference*, above note 79 at 67–68 and 70, concerning the *Convention Relating to the Regulation of Aerial Navigation*, dated 13 October 1919 during the sittings of the Peace Conference at Paris after World War I, signed by Canada and in effect throughout the British Empire and certain other jurisdictions from 1 June 1922.

82   *Ibid.* at 70.

83   *Radio Reference*, above note 78 at 82–83 (D.L.R.).

84   The *International Radiotelegraph Convention, 1927* concerned the regulation of wireless or Hertzian wave radio communications, especially the need for the allocation of and non-interference with frequencies. Canada signed the Convention in Washington, DC on 25 November 1927 and ratified it on 12 July 1928. See *ibid.* at 84.

85   *Constitution Act, 1867*, above note 76.

following two grounds of its decision in favour of an exclusive federal jurisdiction for radio communications:

1) Federal jurisdiction was residual in section 91 "Peace, Order, and good Government of Canada," given that radio communications is not mentioned explicitly in either section 91 or section 92[86] and that the whole subject of radio communication is sufficiently covered by the international arrangements applicable to, and binding upon, Canada as a whole.[87] In effect, the Board concluded that the international dimensions of radio communications were such that a national or federal jurisdiction was warranted.

2) Broadcasting by radiocommunications fell within the matters exempted from provincial jurisdiction under section 92(10)(a), being excluded first by the expression "telegraphs," and second by the general exclusion for "Works and Undertakings connecting the Province with any other or others of the Provinces, or extending beyond the Limits of the Province."[88] Two important secondary determinations were included within this finding. First, the expression "telegraph" was defined as "[a]n apparatus for transmitting messages to a distance, usually by signs of some kind,"[89] thereby freeing this expression from any one technological mode and presenting a more general situation of transmission of information or intelligence. Second, the expression "undertaking" need not refer to an entity or an organization, but may be an activity or phenomenon such as "broadcasting," and it need not be physical.[90] This may, today, be of considerable significance in considering an application of this exclusion to a system of communication lacking organizational focus, as is the position with the Internet.

---

86 *Radio Reference,* above note 78 at 83–84 (D.L.R). The opening words of s. 91, *Constitution Act, 1867,* enabling federal laws for "the Peace, Order, and good Government of Canada" (the POGG power) have been analyzed on both a "general theory" (whereby the enumerated categories in s. 91 are merely examples of the POGG power) and a "residual theory" (whereby the POGG power is what is left after the subtraction of the enumerated powers in ss. 91, federal, and 92, provincial). The latter today appears to be the preferred view. See P.W. Hogg, *Constitutional Law of Canada,* looseleaf vol. 1 (Scarborough, ON: Carswell, 2006, updated to 2009) at para. 17(1).

87 *Radio Reference, ibid.* at 84. The Board made a direct analogy between aeronautics and aviation on the one hand and radio communications on the other.

88 *Ibid.* at 85.

89 *Ibid.* at 87.

90 *Ibid.* at 86.

Importantly, in both ground (1) and (2) above, the Privy Council rejected an approach of dividing or deconstructing an activity into separate or constituent parts (such as sending and receiving of a message) and assessing constitutional jurisdiction according to the nature of each component part.[91] Instead, the constitutional assessment under section 92(10)(a) is to be focused upon an undertaking as a whole. This requirement has been consistently reaffirmed.[92] The dissenting minority in the Supreme Court of Canada in the *Radio Reference* had urged that the assessment be based on a deconstructed model. Once separated, aspects could more readily be seen as being within sections 92(13) ("Property and Civil Rights in the Province") and 92(10) ("Local Works and Undertakings").[93]

Although the majority in the Supreme Court of Canada in the *Radio Reference* had decided similarly to the Privy Council on the basis of both section 91 (POGG) and section 92(10)(a) (interprovincial undertaking),[94] a distinction must be drawn between these two constitutional options. A jurisdiction based on section 91 (POGG) presents an exclusively federal jurisdiction for the particular activity. Provincial jurisdiction may be found only by redescribing the subject area. For example, a closed circuit television security surveillance system may be defined and distinguished from the subject of "telecommunications" to establish a provincial jurisdiction for such systems. This reflects that a federal jurisdiction based on section 92(10)(a) is predicated upon the activity extending beyond provincial limits. The example of a closed circuit television security surveillance system should not invoke the exception, as it would ordinarily be confined to a particular location within a province. Similarly, an organization's intranet[95] system of interlinked computers encrypted against access and interference from outside of the organization may present a telecommunications system that can be said to be contained wholly within a province.

---

91   *Ibid.* at 85–88.
92   See, for example, *A.-G. Ontario v. Winner*, [1954] 4 D.L.R. 657 (P.C.); *Alberta Government Telephones v. Canada (Canadian Radio-television and Telecommunications Commission)*, [1989] 2 S.C.R. 225, 61 D.L.R. (4th) 193, aff'g [1985] 2 F.C. 472 (T.D.) [*Alberta Government Telephones*]; and text accompanying note 116 below.
93   *Re Regulation and Control of Radio Communication*, [1931] S.C.R. 541, [1931] 4 D.L.R. 865 at 874–80, Rinfret J dissenting.
94   *Ibid.* at 867, 874, and 893.
95   "An inhouse Web site that serves the employees of an enterprise. Although intranet pages may link to the Internet, an intranet is not a site accessed by the general public" (Freedman, *Computer Desktop Encyclopedia*, above note 75, s.v. "intranet").

The section 91 (POGG) jurisdiction described in the *Aviation Reference* and the *Radio Reference*, emphasizing the nature of an activity as the concern of Canada as a whole, was reaffirmed in *A.-G. Ontario v. Canada Temperance Federation*[96] and now may be seen as falling within the "national concern" branch of the residual section 91 jurisdiction. General jurisprudence concerning this jurisdiction is analyzed by Hogg.[97] For present purposes, it is sufficient to acknowledge that despite an earlier period of restrictive interpretation,[98] recent authorities establish the "national concern" branch of section 91 (POGG) federal jurisdiction.[99] This may be of substantial significance in the context of today's globalized marketplace through the medium of the Internet. Global digitized communications, international treaties, and international harmonization of laws and policies in many areas, including commerce, privacy, data protection, intellectual property, and jurisdiction, will require Canada to respond on a national basis to these matters because they affect the country as a whole in a manner identical to aviation and radio communications in the 1920s. Indeed, the globalism in markets and communications of today can be seen as a macrocosm of the earlier changes.

Section 91 was not, however, significantly utilized in post–*Radio Reference* proceedings concerning the traditional modes of telecommunications. While acknowledging this power, courts reiterated the federal jurisdiction by reliance on section 92(10)(a). These proceedings concerned broadcast television signals received by antennae and redistributed by cable television distributors to subscribers. The courts continued to reject a deconstruction of the overall operation that would involve distinguishing the process of reception from that of retransmis-

---

96   *A.-G. Ontario v. Canada Temperance Federation*, [1946] A.C. 193 at 205–6, [1946] 2 D.L.R. 1 (P.C.) [*Canada Temperance Federation*].

97   Hogg, above note 86 at para. 17(3).

98   This period was circa 1911–46, during which time the s. 91 (POGG) jurisdiction was generally narrowed to situations of not only "national concern" but also "national emergency." This restriction was repudiated in 1946 with the Privy Council's decision in *Canada Temperance Federation*, above note 96.

99   Hogg, above note 86 at para. 17(3)(a). The position is well illustrated by subsequent developments in aviation. In 1947, a replacement international convention in aviation was acceded to by Canada. However, the situation by this time reflected Canada as an entirely self-governing country independent of any notion of the "British Empire." This rendered s. 132 of the *Constitution Act, 1867* inapplicable. A "national concern" test under s. 91 (POGG) was recognized to ensure continued exclusive federal jurisdiction for aviation. See *Johannesson v. West St. Paul*, [1952] 1 S.C.R. 292. Hogg, *ibid.* at para. 17(3)(a), n. 45, provides a succinct analysis of this development.

sion.[100] Provincial attempts to assert some measure of regulation were therefore denied.

Non-broadcast (telephone) telecommunications were also recently evaluated under section 92(10)(a) by the Supreme Court of Canada in *Alberta Government Telephones v. Canada (Canadian Radio-television and Telecommunications Commission).*[101] The development of non-broadcast telecommunications (telegraph and telephone) in Canada is set out earlier.[102] Telephone services in eastern Canada, primarily the Bell Telephone Company network, and in British Columbia, provided by a United States-based entity that came to be known as BCTel,[103] had been regulated federally from the 1920s.[104] Likewise, telegraph services were provided by Canadian Pacific and Canadian National railways and were, therefore, federally regulated. However, telephone services in the western Canadian provinces of Alberta, Saskatchewan, and Manitoba had evolved to be provided by provincial Crown entities.[105] Two principal issues were thus involved in the *Alberta Government Telephones* proceeding. First, was Alberta Government Telephones (AGT) subject to federal regulation through the Canadian Radio-television and Telecommunications Commission (CRTC)? Second, was AGT, being a provincial Crown agent, entitled to Crown immunity against federal regulation? The Court found both a federal regulatory jurisdiction and a provincial Crown immunity.[106] A regulatory vacuum ensued until Parliament removed the immunity in 1993.[107] Under section 92(10)(a), the Court found AGT to be engaged in a federal work or undertaking and thereby to fall within the exception in that provision to provincial jurisdiction, rendering AGT's work and undertaking to be exclusively federal. The Court decided that submissions concerning section 91

---

100 See, for example, *Capital Cities Communications Inc. v. Canadian Radio-Television Commission* (1977), [1978] 2 S.C.R. 141, 81 D.L.R. (3d) 609, 36 C.P.R. (2d) 1. [*Capital Cities*].

101 *Alberta Government Telephones*, above note 92.

102 See text accompanying notes 8–9, above in this chapter.

103 See Babe, above note 8 at 111–13.

104 See text accompanying notes 10–11, above in this chapter.

105 See Babe, above note 8 at 102–11.

106 These conclusions had also been reached by Reed J at trial in *Alberta Government Telephones*, above note 101. The Federal Court of Appeal concurred with respect to Alberta Government Telephones (AGT) being subject to federal regulation, but reversed on the issue of provincial Crown immunity: [1986] 2 F.C. 179. In the Supreme Court of Canada, Wilson J dissented on the issue of provincial Crown immunity. See *Alberta Government Telephones*, above note 92 at 301–7 (S.C.R.).

107 *Telecommunications Act,* above note 6, s. 3.

(POGG) jurisdiction were unnecessary to deal with after the finding under section 92(10)(a).[108]

Unlike the *Radio Reference* proceeding, the Court was not considering whether an activity or phenomenon such as "broadcasting" was interprovincial, but whether AGT as an entity or enterprise was itself an interprovincial work or undertaking.[109] No consideration was given to whether a telephone service could be considered as falling within the expression "telegraph" in section 92(10)(a), as earlier interpreted by the Privy Council.[110]

No single comprehensive test or formulation is applicable to a determination concerning section 92(10)(a). An inquiry must proceed simply on the facts of each case, but with some analogy being found from decided cases,[111] and is a matter of substance, rather than any apparent form, especially of corporate organization.[112] From both a technical perspective of physical and non-physical system linkages and a business perspective, AGT was found to be operating an interprovincial undertaking and to be within the exception afforded by section 92(10(a). This applied directly to AGT's own system operations, including its active participation in a national organization that cooperated, integrated, and interconnected telephone service across Canada and internationally.[113] The Court rejected AGT's argument emphasizing that as all physical plant was located within Alberta, the appropriate jurisdiction was provincial.[114] This submission did not envisage a div-

---

108 *Alberta Government Telephones,* above note 92 at 268 (S.C.R.). Likewise, s. 91 (POGG) jurisdiction is not reported as dealt with by Reed J at trial nor by the Federal Court of Appeal.

109 *Alberta Government Telephones, ibid.* at 242–54 (review of the facts as to the nature of AGT's enterprise) and 257ff.

110 See text accompanying note 88, above in this chapter. Perhaps the transmission of voice could not be included within a transmission of a "sign."

111 *Alberta Government Telephones,* above note 92 at 258 (S.C.R.) following the summary provided by the Supreme Court of Canada in the earlier case (involving labour relations) *Northern Telecom Ltd. v. Communications Workers of Canada,* [1980] 1 S.C.R. 115 at 132, referring to "the normal or habitual activities of the business as those of a going concern, without regard for exceptional or casual factors."

112 *Alberta Government Telephones, ibid.* at 263–64 and 267.

113 *Ibid.* AGT had argued that Reed J at trial had focused too much on "its relationship with the national 'association'" (known then as "Telecom Canada"), which had existed since 1931 (formerly known as "Trans Canada Telephone System," TCTS, and later as "Stentor") almost to the extent that she had focused on whether this association, not itself a legal entity, was the relevant interprovincial undertaking (*ibid.* at 262–63). The court rejected this submission.

114 *Ibid.* at 258–59.

ided jurisdiction between federal and provincial authorities. The Court acknowledged the intention of all parties as "all or nothing" between either exclusively federal or exclusively provincial jurisdiction.[115] However, the Court was asked to distinguish between physical and non-physical aspects of AGT's business and operations.[116] Its refusal to make such a distinction and instead to consider the overall business operation is consistent with the reasoning in *Radio Reference*.

The same equipment and networks were used by AGT for local, national, and international communications.[117] However, Reed J at trial found AGT to have engaged in a "significant degree of continuous and regular interprovincial activity."[118] The Supreme Court of Canada emphasized the expression "significant" with respect to this conclusion[119] and later referred to the need to find a "*sufficient* organization interconnection."[120] Furthermore, a factor of trivial interprovincial connection was disregarded.[121] This confirms that the interprovincial activities must meet a threshold of substantiality to cause the exception in section 92(10)(a) to be engaged. Naturally, a precise level is not stipulated, but in making an overall assessment of the nature of the business in its operations, a merely incidental level of interprovincial activity will be insufficient.

Additionally, a measure of uncertainty exists in contexts arising from an earlier proceeding in *Fulton v. Energy Resources Conservation Board* before the Supreme Court of Canada.[122] This case involved the construction of an electrical transmission line *near to* the border between the provinces of Alberta and British Columbia, where it would ultimately connect with a transmission line being constructed from British Columbia. The entity in Alberta was found to be a local work or undertaking. The following two situations present some doubt:

1) Situations of an undertaking merely *proposing* or *planning* to act in a manner that would, upon completion, cause the undertaking, or the

---

115 *Ibid.* at 256–57.

116 AGT developed this submission by claiming that the *physical* interprovincial connections were insufficient to constitute AGT an interprovincial undertaking (*ibid.* at 260).

117 *Ibid.*

118 See *Alberta Government Telephones*, above note 106 at 532–33 (F.C.A.).

119 *Alberta Government Telephones*, above note 92 at 254 (S.C.R.).

120 *Ibid.* at 255 [emphasis added].

121 *Ibid.* at 244 and 258 concerning the provision of telephone service to residents of Lloydminster, a border town between Alberta and Saskatchewan.

122 *Fulton v. Energy Resources Conservation Board*, [1981] 1 S.C.R. 153, 118 D.L.R. (3d) 577, [1981] 4 W.W.R. 236 [*Fulton*].

activity being performed, to be interprovincial. The Court in *Fulton* had interpreted earlier authorities[123] as recognizing an intention (at least when all necessary planning had been done) to operate interprovincially as sufficient to establish federal jurisdiction under section 92(10)(a) if the entity concerned was in a position to itself effect the interprovincial connection and thereby potentially to be described as "a single promoter" in this respect.[124] Subsequently, in *Alberta Government Telephones*, AGT argued that it could not *by itself* effect the interprovincial telephone connections and therefore could not be an interprovincial undertaking.[125] This was rejected, the Court distinguishing *Fulton* on the basis that the construction in that case had not occurred at the time of the proceeding.[126] The current issue, therefore, is how a proposal or planned development should be considered in a section 92(10)(a) context. A solution is to treat any proposed activity as simply a factor to be weighed in an overall inquiry into the nature of the undertaking or activity. The relative importance of a proposal to the overall operation of the undertaking, together with the level of completion of the proposal, should be considered. It is suggested that this approach is likely to be more effective and afford a more accurate result than to attempt to demarcate conceptually between current and proposed activities.

2) Situations in which a federal regulatory jurisdiction exists but is not currently exercised may allow scope for an exercise of provincial jurisdiction. The basis for this proposition is not entirely clear. It is reflected in a passage by Laskin CJ for the Court in *Fulton* and quoted in *Alberta Government Telephones* as: "Unexercised federal authority may give leeway to the exercise of provincial authority *in relation to local works and undertakings*, and that is how I assess the situation in [*Fulton*]"[127] [emphasis added].

This is a difficult passage. If an undertaking is found to be interprovincial, then the federal jurisdiction through section 92(10)(a) (as an exception to provincial jurisdiction) would result in an *exclusive* federal

---

123 *Ibid.* at 166 referring in particular to *Attorney-General for Ontario v. Winner*, [1954] A.C. 541, 4 D.L.R. 657 (P.C.); and *City of Toronto v. Bell Telephone Co. of Canada*, [1905] A.C. 52 (P.C.).

124 See *Fulton, ibid.*, noted in *Alberta Government Telephones*, above note 92 at 266 (S.C.R.).

125 See *Alberta Government Telephones, ibid.* at 266.

126 *Ibid.* at 266–67.

127 See *Fulton*, above note 122 at 162 (S.C.R.), cited in *Alberta Government Telephones, ibid.* at 267.

jurisdiction.[128] Ordinarily, this would leave no basis for any provincial regulation. Such could occur only if the subject matter was one of *concurrent* federal and provincial jurisdiction, as discussed below, or if an inquiry under section 92(10)(a) were found to include a factor concerning the likelihood of actual or prospective federal regulation. The latter possibility, giving rise to provincial jurisdiction, appears to be contemplated in *Alberta Government Telephones* from the interpretation of the passage in *Fulton*. The Court in *Alberta Government Telephones* referred to *Fulton* and noted "there is a sense that had the federal government wished to assert jurisdiction over the interconnection of the electrical transmission lines. . . . it could have done so." The fact that it had not asserted jurisdiction and appeared unlikely to do so encouraged the finding of a local undertaking in that case.[129]

2) The Regulation of Content

The scope of federal jurisdiction to regulate the *content* of telecommunications has been queried,[130] given the focus of the *Radio Reference* on the technical and operational aspects of the medium (especially the non-interference with radio wave frequencies).[131] However, considerable scope for federal jurisdiction over content has been recognized. In particular, the promotion of Canadian policies and identity interests in broadcast programming, commonly referred to as the "Canadian content" requirements, as a primary feature of broadcast policy is stipulated in detailed objectives in the *Broadcasting Act* (1991).[132] The constitutionality of these provisions is generally unchallenged,[133] allowing significant federal jurisdiction concerning content. Conversely,

---

128 See above note 78 and accompanying text.
129 *Alberta Government Telephones,* above note 92 at 267 (S.C.R.).
130 Hogg, above note 86 at para. 22(12)(c); and Ronald I. Cohen, *Advertising to Children: The Constitutional Validity of Quebec's Regulation* (1974) 12 C.P.R. (2d) 173.
131 See above note 85.
132 *Broadcasting Act,* above note 7, s. 3(1).
133 No direct constitutional challenge has been mounted against the concept of a national, federally directed policy of "Canadian content." See J. Russell, "Demystifying Canadian Content: Challenging the Television Broadcast Regulator to 'Say What It Means and Mean What It Says'" (1993) 2 Media and Communications Law Review 171 at 185ff.; and G. Henley, "Preferences about Preferences: A Positive Justification for Canadian Content Regulation" (1993) 3 Media and Communications Law Review 127 at 151ff., concerning the relationship of "Canadian content" regulation and "freedom of expression" protection under s. 2(3) of the *Canadian Charter of Rights and Freedoms,* Part 1 of the *Constitution Act, 1982,* being Schedule B to the *Canada Act 1982* (U.K.), 1982, c. 11.

the *Telecommunications Act* (1993), dealing with non-programming or point-to-point communications, stipulates that carriers cannot interfere with content of communications.[134]

The advent of cable television retransmission provided a further opportunity to apply a holistic approach. The majority of the Supreme Court of Canada in *Capital Cities Communications Inc. v. Canadian Radio-Television Commission*[135] upheld the jurisdiction of Parliament to enable the federal regulator, the Canadian Radio-television Telecommunications Commission (CRTC), to determine content by authorizing Canadian cable television redistributors to delete and substitute commercial advertising in television signals received from the United States and redistributed by cable to Canadian subscribers. The policy objective was described by the CRTC as "to restore the logic of the local licence and strengthen Canadian Television service." The cable television redistributor would be obliged to contract with local Canadian television stations for replacement commercial messages or advertising.[136] In effect, the issue concerned proceeds from advertising, the source of revenue for local television stations but not for cable television redistributors, which gain their revenue from subscriber fees. The cable transmission of signals received from US television stations would cause Canadian or local advertisers to redirect their advertising (and therefore revenue) away from Canadian local television stations to those in the United States. The process of deletion and substitution was designed to forestall this consequence.

This rationale was thus closely related to the operation of the television broadcast and redistribution system, albeit from a financial perspective. It is obviously broader than the technical or system perspective presented in the *Radio Reference*, but it is much closer to this than to a purely content regulation *per se*. Nevertheless, with little analysis, the majority in *Capital Cities* made a broad determination that content regulation could not be distinguished from system regulation and drew the following analogy: "[I]t would be as if an interprovincial or international carrier of goods could be licensed for such carriage but without federal control of what may be carried or of the conditions of carriage"[137] It was essentially an "all or nothing" conclusion. The dis-

---

134 *Telecommunications Act*, above note 6, s. 36.
135 *Capital Cities*, above note 100.
136 At the time of the proceedings, the CRTC had authorized only public service announcements to be substituted for deleted commercial advertising as the cable television companies had not at that time arranged commercial substitution with the local Canadian television stations. *Ibid.* at 148–49.
137 *Ibid.* at 160–61.

senting judgment of Pigeon J[138] focused on the economic impact on the television stations in the United States and considered the action of the CRTC to be "economic aggression,"[139] by the usurping of the economic value of a station's business, describing the benefit to Canadian television stations as "protectionism."[140] Pigeon J considered this sufficient to reject the procedures that the CRTC was adopting.

The dissent also sought to utilize the 1937 Radiocommunications Convention between Canada and the United States, which prohibited a retransmission or rebroadcast of programs taken from a broadcasting station in either jurisdiction or "interference" with the services of the other country,[141] to conclude that the programming of television stations in the United States should be treated in the same manner as programs of television stations in Canada. In this latter respect, both the majority[142] and the dissent[143] appear to have accepted that the substitution of commercial messages could not occur with the programs of local Canadian television stations, as to do so would violate the rights given to those stations in the broadcast licence issued to them by the CRTC.[144] This might suggest some jurisdictional limitation. Arguably, a licence and the value attaching to it may be seen as a proprietary item to be protected by tort law, perhaps as "Property and Civil Rights in the Province"[145] but, of course, the CRTC could have limited the licence in the first place or could subsequently amend it.[146]

The majority appeared to strengthen the finding of federal jurisdiction over content by also noting, with approval, the submission for the federal Crown relying on section 91(2) (regulation of trade and commerce), with reference to the "importation" of television programs re-

138 Beetz and de Grandpre JJ joined the reasons given in dissent by Pigeon J.
139 *Capital Cities*, above note 100 at 182 (S.C.R.).
140 *Ibid.*
141 *Ibid.* at 183–84 re the *Inter-American Radiocommunications Convention* of 13 December 1937, art. 11 (no interference) and art. 21 (no rebroadcast). The majority rejected these propositions, finding "interference" to relate to technical interference with the Hertzian waves rather than the content of any signal and a rebroadcast to refer only to radio wave transmission, not cable. See *ibid.* at 174–76. In any event, these provisions of the Convention were found not to have been legislatively implemented into Canadian law, which would be necessary before any enforcement in domestic law could occur. See *ibid.* at 173.
142 *Ibid.* at 171. Laskin CJ found that the Commission could base its decision on a policy statement. The Commission's July 1971 Policy Statement permitted removal of commercials of stations *not* licensed in Canada.
143 *Ibid.* at 182.
144 *Ibid.* at 180–81.
145 *Constitution Act, 1867*, above note 76, s. 92(13).
146 *Broadcasting Act*, above note 7, s. 9.

ceived through Hertzian waves. Counsel analogized such intangible electronic receipt with the importation of physical products over which the federal Crown can regulate subsequent transactions.[147]

Federal jurisdiction over the content of broadcasts has been recognized by other courts, including the Ontario Court of Appeal[148] in upholding in 1973 a then provision of the *Broadcasting Act* restricting political party messages and programs on the day preceding a federal, provincial, or local election.[149] The basis again was the indivisibility of telecommunications into technical or organizational dimensions on the one hand and content on the other.[150]

There are significant reasons, however, why this conclusion should cause some residue of uncertainty. First, there is today the substantial pervasiveness of the Internet as a telecommunications system or medium. It encompasses nearly all features of society. Any regulation of this medium *as a communications system* is almost certainly a federal jurisdiction.[151] However, if the simple conclusion of indivisibility of system and content is to prevail with respect to regulation of content on the Internet, then many provincial constitutional jurisdictions will become federal. Politically and jurisprudentially this is unlikely, as is further discussed later in this chapter. Second, even within the traditional media of radio and telecommunications, the relationship between system and content has never received detailed or thorough judicial analysis. The response has always been more intuitive — that separation is impossible or, at least, not practical. Third, the factual context of *Capital Cities*, the principal proceeding in which the Supreme Court of Canada considered content, was a closely divided decision[152] and has been demonstrated to have more accurately involved the *system* of cable retransmission than content *per se*.[153]

An example illustrates the potential difficulties. A defamatory publication (libel or slander) is made in a televised interview. The medium itself cannot be relied upon to provide a general federal jurisdiction for defamation. The proceeding is at common law tort or civil code delict.

---

147 *Capital Cities*, above note 100 at 162–63 (S.C.R.).
148 *CFRB v. Canada (Attorney-General)* (1973), 38 D.L.R. (3d) 335, [1973] 3 O.R. 819 (C.A.).
149 *Broadcasting Act*, R.S.C. 1970, c. B-11, s. 28.
150 *CFRB v. Canada (Attorney-General)*, above note 148 at 824 (O.R.).
151 The Internet is the ultimate international/interprovincial medium of communication. It cannot be contained even within national, let alone provincial, boundaries. See above note 77 concerning *Constitution Act, 1867*, s. 92(10)(a).
152 See *Capital Cities*, above note 100.
153 See *Attorney General (Que.) v. Kellogg's Co.*, [1978] 2 S.C.R. 211 at 221, 83 D.L.R. (3d) 314 [*Kellogg's*].

If Parliament were to attempt to provide legislatively for a statutory tort for defamation that occurs on telecommunications media, such would be likely to be held invalid or be severely limited. This has been expressly considered and found in part unconstitutional in a different but related context.[154] However, if Parliament were to provide (directly or by CRTC regulation) for broadcasters to have systems and safeguards to prevent or limit the likelihood of defamation occurring in broadcast programs, or to deny a renewal of a broadcast licence on the grounds that the holder had persistently allowed defamatory broadcasts, then such jurisdiction would probably be upheld. A reported example in this context, albeit not a constitutional law proceeding, concerns the protection of privacy and the broadcasting of an interview without the interviewee's consent.[155]

Demarcations of this nature inherently distinguish issues of content that are closely linked with the telecommunications system itself from those that primarily invoke general or other law pertaining to content itself. From a constitutional perspective, this involves the application of a "pith and substance" principle that determines the constitutional category (and therefore the relevant jurisdiction) applicable to that activity or circumstance. This principle, however, must be distinguished from the related, but different, situations of those described historically as "interjurisdictional immunity," involving a law valid in one constitutional jurisdiction (say, provincial) being sought to apply to an undertaking or activity regulated by the other constitutional jurisdiction (federal). In this context, the inquiry is not one of categorization but of the extent to which the law will apply outside of its jurisdiction;[156] and the "double aspect" or "double matter" principle, whereby a subject includes aspects that amount to a roughly equal division between categories of federal and provincial jurisdictions.[157] Both jurisdictions may regulate the subject area, and in the event of an actual conflict the federal law prevails as a matter of "paramountcy."[158] There may also be subjects such as "the environment" that are so pervasive as to be incapable of allocation to one or the other constitutional jurisdic-

---

154 See *MacDonald v. Vapor Canada Ltd.*, [1977] 2 S.C.R. 134, concerning the constitutionality of parts of the *Trade-marks Act*, R.S.C. 1985, c. T-13, s. 7, which provides federal legislative grounds of "unfair competition" in the nature of codification of various common law tort or contract or civil code *delict* or obligation.

155 *R. v. CKOY Ltd.* (1978), [1979] 1 S.C.R. 2, 90 D.L.R. (3d) 1.

156 Hogg, above note 86 at para. 15(8)(a).

157 See *Canadian Western Bank v. Alberta*, 2007 SCC 22, [2007] 1 S.C.R. 624 at para. 30 [*Canadian Western Bank*].

158 *Ibid.* at para. 32.

tion exclusively but subject to regulation by both.[159] Such a description and constitutional approach may well be appropriate to the subject of "cyberspace" and the Internet.

3) Constitutional Categorization

Categorization as a "pith and substance" analysis can be illustrated with respect to the proceeding for defamation, as discussed earlier,[160] establishing an exclusive jurisdiction according to an assessment of the *nature* of the subject matter. Characterized as a civil proceeding for defamation under tort or delict, the situation is exclusively within provincial jurisdiction, but any stipulation of safeguards or checks within telecommunications media to prevent or lessen the occurrence of defamatory comment in the media concerned would be characterized as telecommunications regulation and thus exclusively federal jurisdiction. Activities that are relatively distinct can be readily characterized in this manner. More closely related contexts require greater analytical refinement.

The principles of paramountcy and interjurisdictional immunity allow for such refinement. However, since 2007, situations that may have been seen as interjurisdictional immunities must be seen contextually, with determinations that de-emphasize the perspective of immunity of one jurisdiction from the other, in preference for legislation of both levels continuing in their ordinary operation for the purposes within the constitutional authority of each level.[161] If the dominant features of the respective measures overlap and conflict, then federal supremacy is to prevail.[162] An absence of relevant federal legislative measures would,

---

159 See *Friends of Oldman River Society v. Canada*, [1992] 1 S.C.R. 3, 88 D.L.R. (4th) 1, [1992] 2 W.W.R. 193; and Hogg, above note 86 at para. 29(7).

160 See text accompanying notes 154 & 155, above in this chapter. The approach to "pith and substance" is reiterated by the S.C.C. in *Chatterjee v. Ontario (Attorney General)*, 2009 SCC 19, [2009] 1 S.C.R. 624, 304 D.L.R. (4th) 513 at para. 16 [*Chatterjee*], as involving two distinct tests. First, the purpose of the enacting body and the legal effect of the enactment must be determined. Second, these are then examined and allocated under the head(s) of constitutional legislative competence.

161 See *ibid.* (provincial forfeiture *in rem* of the proceeds of unlawful activity being in no operational conflict with the federal criminal power), and *Canadian Western Bank*, above note 157 (federally chartered banks being authorized by federal legislation to engage in insurance-related activities being subject to provincial insurance legislation with respect to those activities).

162 See *Chatterjee*, above note 160 at para. 36; and *British Columbia (Attorney General) v. Lafarge Canada Inc.*, 2007 SCC 23, [2007] 2 S.C.R. 86, 281 D.L.R. (4th) 54 [*Lafarge*] applying federal supremacy for development work on waterfront

however, deny any paramountcy and allow any provincial measures to take effect in preference to leaving a regulatory vacuum that would follow from the application of an immunity theory.[163]

The consequences of this approach, described as cooperative federalism,[164] discourage characterization of broad subject areas as exclusively one or the other constitutional jurisdiction and refocus on identifying the *vital* or *dominant* features of the legislative measures in order to determine whether there is an operational conflict that would lead to federal paramountcy in these respects.[165] While this approach avoids the creation of areas, or "enclaves," of jurisdictional immunity[166] and is likely to enhance a provincial perspective when not in operational conflict with any vital or dominant features of a federal measure, an application of paramountcy in situations of vital or dominant federal measures has been challenged when the impact of the provincial activity, though in operational conflict with a vital or dominant federal measure, *is not of significant* impact upon that measure, leading to a continuing assertion of the interjurisdictional immunity principle in this situation.[167]

Likewise, while the avoidance of a regulatory vacuum in favour of cooperative federalism is a new and developing principle that will be of significance for telecommunications, and for the Internet in particular, the identification of vital or dominant features is not far removed from an application of the interjurisdictional immunity principle that has been utilized historically in a telecommunications context. Both approaches are considered and compared.

Historically, there are three stages in the analysis of interjurisdictional immunity:[168]

1) Pre-1966 jurisprudence applied a test to determine whether a provincial law, when applied to a federally regulated undertaking, would

---

land owned by the Vancouver Port Authority, a federal undertaking, subject to federal land use planning (*ibid.* at para. 68) rather than provincial measures to this effect).

163 *Lafarge, ibid.* at para. 73.

164 *Canadian Western Bank,* above note 157 at para. 24.

165 See *Chatterjee,* above note 160; and *Lafarge,* above note 162.

166 *Chatterjee, ibid.* at para. 2.

167 See *PHS Community Services Society v. Canada (Attorney General),* 2010 BCCA 15 at para. 55ff., leave to appeal and cross-appeal to the S.C.C. granted, [2010] S.C.C.A. No. 49, tentative hearing date 12 November 2010 [*PHS Community Services*].

168 Hogg, above note 86 at para. 15(8)(c).

"sterilize" the operations of the federally regulated undertaking or activity.[169]

2) The period 1966 to 1989 saw some de-emphasis of the sterilization test in favour of a broader test asking whether a "vital part" of the federally regulated undertaking was affected. This would, naturally, include any "sterilization" of the undertaking but would also go considerably beyond such a position. The "vital part" test was established in proceedings involving the Bell Telephone Company and the issue of provincial minimum wage standards. Immunity was granted.[170] Proceedings in 1988 again involved Bell Telephone, this time concerning the application to Bell of Quebec provincial occupational health and safety laws. The Supreme Court of Canada reaffirmed the test and granted immunity to Bell.[171] Substantial debate, from a general constitutional law perspective, has ensued over the breadth or scope of application of this "vital part" test.[172]

3) The year 1989 brought a modification by the Supreme Court of Canada of the "vital part" test, despite the test having been affirmed just the year before[173] and perhaps purposely to ameliorate the overinclusiveness of that test.[174] The modification in *Irwin Toy v. Quebec*[175] involved a telecommunications context and must be closely analyzed.

Irwin Toy involved two features. First, the subject matter was advertising, specifically the prohibition by provincial statute of commer-

---

169 See *City of Toronto v. Bell Telephone Co.*, [1905] A.C. 52 (P.C.) giving a federally regulated telephone company immunity from municipal requirements as to the erection of communications infrastructure.

170 *Commission du Salaire Minimum v. Bell Telephone Co.*, [1966] S.C.R. 767 at 774.

171 *Bell Canada v. Quebec*, [1988] 1 S.C.R. 749, 51 D.L.R. (4th) 161, [1988] 21 C.C.E.L. 1.

172 See Hogg, above note 86 at para. 15(8)(c), and especially his notes 121 and 129, giving references to other commentators and noting positions and trends in the debate, including with reference to his own commentary.

173 In addition to *Bell Canada v. Quebec*, above note 171, the S.C.C. delivered judgment that day in other cases, outside of telecommunications but affirming the "vital part" test. See Hogg, *ibid.* at his note 124 and accompanying text.

174 Hogg, *ibid.* in his note 134, citing Gibson (1990) 69 Can. Bar Rev. 339, agrees to this effect.

175 *Irwin Toy ltd. v. Quebec*, [1989] 1 S.C.R. 927, 58 D.L.R. (4th) 577, [1989] 39 C.R.R. 193 [*Irwin Toy*]. The court initially comprised seven members, but Estey and LeDain JJ took no part in the decision. The remaining five members were unanimous on the interjurisdictional issue. The proceeding the previous year, in *Bell Canada v. Quebec*, above note 171, upholding the "vital part" test was also initially a seven-member court but Chouinard J did not continue in the proceeding.

cial advertising directed at persons under thirteen years of age,[176] and whether this prohibition could be enforced in the federally regulated television medium. The significance of this is that the very same context — the application to television of a provincial restriction of advertising to children — had been found to be valid by the Supreme Court of Canada in *Attorney General (Que.) v. Kellogg's Co.* in 1978.[177] This case was applied and followed in *Irwin Toy.*[178] Second, the legal test to determine interjurisdictional immunity was modified to provide that:

1) the "vital parts" or "essential and vital elements" of a federal undertaking, including its management, are exclusively federal under sections 91(29) and 92(1), *Constitution Act, 1867,*[179] and they constitute the "basic, minimum and unassailable context" of that exclusively federal power;[180]
2) these "vital parts" or "elements" cannot be assailed by provincial legislation that purports to apply to the federal undertakings concerned, but even these "vital parts" can "normally" be affected incidentally by the effect of the legislation without the provincial legislation being found to be invalid as *ultra vires* the constitutional jurisdiction of the province;[181] and
3) the distinction between provincial legislation that "purports to apply" to the "vital parts" of a federal undertaking and affects that undertaking only "incidentally" is referred to by the descriptions "direct" and "indirect";[182] but
4) whether *direct* (thereby invalidated under the "vital parts" test as set out above) or *indirect* (not invalidated under the "vital parts" test), if the effect of the legislation "sterilizes" or "impairs" the operation, including the management, of the federal undertaking then the provincial legislation is invalid as *ultra vires* the constitutional jurisdiction of the province.[183]

To summarize, the principle of interjurisdictional immunity enables provincial legislation, within a valid head of provincial jurisdiction, to (1) regulate directly or indirectly non-vital parts of a federal undertaking, short of "sterilization" or "impairment" of its operations, including

---

176 *Consumer Protection Act,* R.S.Q. 1983, c. P-40.1, ss. 248–49.
177 *Kellogg's,* above note 153.
178 *Irwin Toy,* above note 175 at 953 (S.C.R.).
179 *Constitution Act, 1867,* above note 76.
180 *Irwin Toy,* above note 175 at 955 (S.C.R.).
181 *Ibid.*
182 *Ibid.* at 957.
183 *Ibid.*

its management; and (2) affect indirectly or incidentally vital parts of a federal undertaking, again short of sterilization or impairment of its operations. In both *Kellogg's* and *Irwin Toy*, the Quebec provincial legislation regulated advertising for children on a *general* basis, not being specifically directed to the medium of television,[184] nor to the providers of any telecommunications service.[185] Therefore, while advertising was considered to be a "vital part" of television broadcasting operations,[186] the affect was *indirect* in the sense of being insignificant. No operational sterilization or impairment was found in either *Kellogg's* or *Irwin Toy*. Only some incidental loss of advertising revenue was involved.[187]

The recent trend to de-emphasize interjurisdictional immunity in favour of cooperative federalism will not change this result. The Quebec legislative regulation of advertising in neither *Kellogg's* nor *Irwin Toy* could be said to be in *operational conflict* with the federal jurisdiction over broadcasting undertakings. Both levels of government can, therefore, regulate within their respective jurisdictions. There would be no paramountcy in the absence of operational conflict.[188] However, in *Kellogg's* the Supreme Court appears to accept, contrary to its finding in *Irwin Toy*, that advertising is not a "vital part" of the operations of a broadcast undertaking.[189] This may produce a significant difference under cooperative federalism. If advertising is a vital or dominant feature of federal regulation of a broadcasting undertaking, a federal paramountcy would apply to any conflicting federal advertising measures,[190] even, perhaps, if the impact on federal jurisdiction is not significant.[191] If, however, advertising is not a vital or dominant federal measure, provincial regulation would apply, despite any apparent operational conflict. As noted earlier, the apparent absence of any measures of significance, or indirectness, in the *impact* on vital or dominant federal measures, has led to some continuing emphasis on interjurisdictional immunity.[192]

---

184 See *Kellogg's*, above note 153 at 225 (S.C.R.); and *Irwin Toy, ibid.* at 950–51 (noting the position in *Kellogg's*) and 953.
185 *Irwin Toy, ibid.*
186 *Ibid.* at 957.
187 *Ibid.* at 958.
188 See text accompanying notes 160–63, above in this chapter.
189 *Kellogg's*, above note 153 at 225 (S.C.R.).
190 See text accompanying note 162, above in this chapter.
191 See text accompanying note 167, above in this chapter.
192 See *PHS Community Services*, above note 167 and accompanying text.

4) The Internet

Today, the Internet is pervasive of both federal and provincial constitutional jurisdictions and some measure of judicial innovation may be necessary to establish the scope of the division of powers with respect to this medium. Certainly all of the principles of constitutional demarcation between federal and provincial jurisdiction discussed above in the context of the traditional media (radio, television and cable, and satellite communications) will be relevant to the Internet. The holistic, one-system approach under section 91 (POGG) or section 92(10)(a) will enjoy a weight of precedent. Notwithstanding the absence of an Internet "entity" or "organization," its activities as a phenomenon, which need not be physical, are within the expression "undertaking" in section 92(10)(a).[193] As a system of telecommunication it is utterly global and can present features of traditional broadcasting (point-to-mass) and traditional telecommunications (point-to-point).[194] All of these features are exclusively federal jurisdiction. Additionally, the Internet is at the centre of interprovincial and international electronic trade and commerce. Other exclusively federal powers with respect to copyright, patents, and registered trademarks are also of central dimension on the Internet and present Canada's continued commitments to and implementation of international treaties with respect to the digitized and electronic media.[195] A federal footprint on the Internet is, therefore, both inevitable and desirable to meet these subject matters in their national and international dimensions.

A footprint, however, does not cover an entire garden and the Internet presents a substantial and pervasive garden. There is room to preserve federal exclusivity in the important media or system-related contexts without losing the conceptual and policy sophistication of identifying appropriate provincial exclusivity or shared jurisdiction. If an exclusively federal jurisdiction were to be applied to the Internet as categorically as has been done with the traditional media, a substantial and questionable expansion of federal jurisdiction would be the outcome. This would be entirely inconsistent with the recent emphasis

---

193 See above note 90. See also E.F. Judge, "Communications: Distribution of Powers in the Internet Age" in Joseph E. Magnet, ed. *Constitutional Law of Canada* (Edmonton: Juriliber, 2001) at 716–19; and Karen Ng, "Spam Legislation in Canada: Federalism, Freedom of Expression and the Regulation of the Internet" (2005) 2 U.O.L.T.J. 447 at 469ff.

194 See Chapter 2, Section A.

195 See, for example, the 1996 World Intellectual Property Organization (WIPO) treaties specifically focused upon digitized and electronic media, discussed in Chapter 3, text accompanying notes XX–XX.

on cooperative federalism.[196] Even in the context of traditional media, the "one-system" approach has been questioned in light of the diverse opportunities presented by technology today.[197] The Internet is an even more compelling context for a more diverse conceptualization of constitutional demarcation.

A shared federal and provincial jurisdiction, with some exclusively federal or provincial jurisdiction applying the principles of "pith and substance," will be a likely outcome.[198] McTaggart,[199] writing in a context of regulation, has usefully characterized the Internet as having four aspects, or "layers," described (in reverse order) as physical, operational, application, and content. The physical is the system or network; the operational is the mechanisms that make the system or network operational, namely standards, protocols, and Internet service provider (ISP) activities. Applying a constitutional analysis, these two layers would readily meet the traditional jurisdictional analysis of sections 91 (POGG) and 92(10)(a) for interprovincial and international communications systems. The applications layer, described by McTaggert as software applications to make content available and enable transactions,[200] could be seen as exclusively federal within the "one-system," or nonsegregated, approach to a communications system,[201] even if the software must be installed on user equipment. However, consider the position if a software application is downloaded and is defective. Is the resulting fitness of the product, or merchantable quality, or other sale of goods or consumer protection issue, encompassed within the federal jurisdiction? Such matters are provincial jurisdiction,[202] providing an opening that is widened considerably in the content layer. Indeed, Internet-related electronic consumer transactions have been reinforced

---

196 See text accompanying notes 160–63, above in this chapter.

197 See Katherine Swinton, "Federalism and Telecommunications: Boon or Barrier to Competition" (1991) 18 Can. Bus. L.J. 188 at 189–92.

198 See Hudson N. Janisch & Richard Schultz, "Federalism's Turn: Telecommunications and Canadian Global Competitiveness" (1991) 18 Can. Bus. L.J. 161.

199 Craig McTaggart, "A Layered Approach to Internet Legal Analysis" (2003) 48 McGill L.J. 571 at 625, para. 1.

200 *Ibid.*

201 See text accompanying notes 90–92, above in this chapter.

202 The division between a "good" and a "service" may be uncertain with respect to some computer products (discussed in Barry B. Sookman, *Computer, Internet and Electronic Commerce Law*, looseleaf (Toronto: Thomson/Carswell, 1989, updated to 2010) at para. 2(17)), but sale of goods as a topic is well established as a provincial jurisdiction. See generally *Monk Corp v. Island Fertilizers Ltd.*, [1991] 1 S.C.R. 779, 80 D.L.R. (4th) 58. See also below note 264 noting implementation by provincial legislation of the *United Nations Convention on Contracts for the International Sale of Goods.*

as provincial jurisdiction with the enacting by almost every provincial and territorial jurisdiction of a *Canadian Uniform Electronic Commerce Act* pursuant to the Uniform Law Conference process, to bring consistency in provincial regulation of a matter of essentially national and international dimension.[203] This process has long been utilized in commercial matters[204] and application in the electronic context has occurred without controversy or questioning of the traditional categorization of matters as provincial powers.

Overall, the pervasiveness of the Internet, touching upon all aspects of society, will attract constitutional comparison with similarly broad areas. These include the environment, health care, and consumer protection. Trends and decisions in areas of broad context provide a clear recognition of the complexity and pervasiveness that deny any holistic, topical exclusivity to federal or provincial spheres, but invoke a blended texture of federal and provincial control. Consumer-related measures in other contexts afford a mixed dimension. Features may be brought within federal regulation, as with restrictions and requirements for the advertising of tobacco products, utilizing the federal criminal law power[205] while remaining provincial for other purposes.[206] Indeed, in a specifically Internet context, Manitoba has enacted consumer protection measures.[207]

In an environmental context, the leading authority is *R. v. Hydro-Québec* (a 5:4 majority decision).[208] Hydro-Québec had been charged under the *Canadian Environmental Protection Act* for the emission of a toxic substance into Canadian waters.[209] The federal legislation listed various toxic substances but also provided for a system of "Interim Orders" that might be made by the federal Minister of the Environ-

---

203 See Uniform Law Conference of Canada, *Status of Uniform Acts Recommended by the Commercial Law Strategy*, updated to 2007, online: www.ulcc.ca/en/cls/CLS_Status_Acts_En.pdf.

204 *Ibid.* listing uniform legislation in many commercial contexts.

205 See *RJR-MacDonald v. Canada*, [1995] 3 S.C.R. 199, 127 D.L.R. (4th) 1 [*RJR-MacDonald*]; and *Constitution Act, 1867*, above note 76, s. 91(27).

206 See, above notes 153 and 175 concerning *Kellogg's* and *Irwin Toy* and commercial advertising to children, even through the medium of television.

207 *Consumer Protection Act*, S.M. 1992, c. 32, s. 36, C.C.S.M. c. 200, Part XVI, ss. 127–35.

208 *R. v. Hydro-Québec*, [1997] 3 S.C.R. 213, 151 D.L.R. (4th) 32, rev'g [1995] R.J.Q. 398 (C.A.), aff'g [1992] R.J.Q. 2159 (S.C.), aff'g [1991] R.J.Q. 2736 (C.Q.) [*R. v. Hydro-Québec*].

209 *Canadian Environmental Protection Act*, R.S.C. 1985 (4th Supp.), c. 16, s. 113(i)(o) and ss. 34–35, adopting and enforcing the *Chlorobiphenyls Interim Order*, P.C. 1989-296 restricting the emission of chlorobiphenyls ("OPCBs") into Canadian waters to 1 gram per day.

ment. An order is in effect for only fourteen days unless approved by the Governor in Council after the federal Ministers of the Environment and Health have offered to confer with the governments of any affected provinces. An approved order remains in effect for two years. However, after a federal–provincial advisory committee established under the Act has given its advice, the Governor in Council may add a substance to the list of toxic substances. The arrangement therefore presents an assertion of federal jurisdiction, but with mechanisms of federal–provincial consultation.

The minority in the Supreme Court of Canada and the decisions of the courts in Quebec denied federal jurisdiction, finding the process to be *ultra vires* the Parliament of Canada. Lamar CJ and Iacobucci J gave the minority reasons,[210] following a traditional procedure of (1) determining the "pith and substance" of the legislation; then (2) determining whether that subject matter fell within a head of federal jurisdiction. The pith and substance was held to be "protecting the environment and human life and health from any and all harmful substances by regulating these substances."[211] The federal categories of (1) the criminal law power, (2) Peace, Order, and good Government (POGG), and the trade and commerce power were considered but denied.[212] These reasons were also reflected in the determinations of the Quebec courts.[213]

La Forest J,[214] for the majority, found a federal jurisdiction under the criminal law power,[215] but importantly contemplated "the environ-

---

210 The minority comprised Lamer CJ, and Sopinka, Iacobucci, and Major JJ.

211 *R. v. Hydro-Québec*, above note 208 at 244 (S.C.R.).

212 The criminal law power (*Constitution Act, 1867*, above note 76, s. 91(27)) was denied because the legislative objective did not fall into the recognized public purpose of "health" as the scope was seen to extend beyond human health into the realm of "general ecological protection" (*R. v. Hydro-Québec, ibid.* at 247) and did not intend criminalization of prohibitions, but rather regulation (*ibid.* at 254–55). The POGG jurisdiction was denied for failing to meet "the characteristics of singleness, distinctiveness and indivisibility" under POGG (*ibid.* at 264) rather it "encroach[ed] widely" on provincial heads of jurisdiction (*ibid.* at 263). The trade and commerce jurisdiction was denied as the pith and substance did not concern trade and commerce, despite any incidental effect on the organization making the emissions (*ibid.* at 265).

213 The judicial history before the courts in Quebec is summarized by Lamer CJ and Iacobucci J, *ibid.* at 233–35 and by La Forest J (giving the reasons of the majority) at 269–72.

214 The majority comprised La Forest, L'Heureux-Dubé, Gonthier, Cory, and McLachlin JJ.

215 *Constitution Act, 1867*, above note 76, s. 91(27). The court found only one limitation on the exercise of the criminal law power, that "it cannot be employed colourably" in the sense of invading areas of exclusive provincial jurisdiction

ment" as involving many areas of constitutional responsibility[216] and found that both levels of government could be engaged to protect it completely.[217] The role of the court is to balance between these levels given that the Constitution must respond to "emerging realities" of the subject matter.[218] This approach of a shared subject area was supported by reference to *RJR-MacDonald Inc. v. Canada*[219] in the further joint area of health. Significantly, La Forest J distinguished, and did not consider, any application of the national dimensions doctrine (POGG) that would give full federal power to regulate.[220] In *R. v. Crown Zellerbach Canada Ltd.*, a 4:3 majority upheld federal power under this doctrine to prevent the dumping of any substance at sea, except as allowed by permit. The majority allowed this power to apply to the dumping of wood waste in a cove connected to the sea.[221] La Forest J gave the minority reasons,[222] which included a warning against conceptualizing broad topics as new heads of power and constitutionally assigning them to the federal jurisdiction through the national dimensions doctrine (POGG) with a consequent removal of a provincial dimension.[223] The reasons of La Forest J for the minority in *Crown Zellerbach* and for the Court in *R. v. Hydro-Québec* are therefore consistent and illustrate a perspective of a shared jurisdiction for broadly conceptualized and pervasive fields.

---

under s. 92 (*R. v. Hydro-Québec, ibid.* at 291). This was further explained by noting the criminal law power not to regulate but "by discrete prohibitions to prevent evils falling within a broad purpose" (*ibid.* at 297). Compare, above notes 210–13 for the formulation in this respect by the minority.

216 *Ibid.* at 286.

217 *Ibid.* at 288.

218 *Ibid.* at 267.

219 *RJR-Macdonald Inc.*, above note 205. The minority also supported this case, finding it to present a sufficiently "legitimate public purpose" for the exercise of the criminal law power. See *R. v. Hydro-Québec, ibid.* at 297–99 (S.C.R.) and 244–45 (minority); and *Schneider v. R.*, [1982] 2 S.C.R. 112, rejecting a conclusion at trial that had relied on the aviation and telecommunications cases to find the exclusive federal power to control narcotic drugs to exclude a provincial initiative to provide treatment for heroin addiction.

220 *R. v. Hydro-Québec, ibid.* at 297.

221 *R. v. Crown Zellerbach Canada Ltd.*, [1988] 1 S.C.R. 401, 49 D.L.R. (4th) 161, [1988] 3 W.W.R. 385 [*Crown Zellerbach*], concerning the *Ocean Dumping Control Act*, R.S.C. 1985, c. O-2. The minority in *R. v. Hydro-Québec* distinguished this case on the basis that the legislation was properly limited to pollution of salt as opposed to fresh water. See *ibid.* at 263.

222 The minority were Beetz, Lamer, and La Forest JJ with the reasons being given by La Forest J.

223 *Crown Zellerbach*, above note 221 at para. 68.

5) Privacy and *PIPEDA*

Earlier, two mechanisms that might be used to encompass federal and provincial interests in matters requiring a more or less uniform national response were noted. The first is the Uniform Law Conference process, providing through interprovincial consultation model laws for implementation, with or without changes, by provincial legislatures in matters recognized as within provincial jurisdiction but nevertheless requiring some interprovincial uniformity.[224] The second is federal–provincial consultation.[225] The *Personal Information Protection and Electronic Documents Act* (*PIPEDA*)[226] presents a third mechanism in a context of privacy of personal information.

Enacted in 1999, *PIPEDA* is to provide privacy protection for "personal information" collected from individuals by organizations in the private sector. The protection of personal information and privacy is of crucial significance to modern telecommunications through the medium of the Internet and is discussed in Chapter 4. The constitutional dimensions that are presented are, however, relevant to the current analysis. Although *PIPEDA* is neither limited to nor focused specifically upon electronic collections of information, it is expressed to encompass every organization "in respect of personal information that . . . the organization collects, uses or discloses in the course of commercial activities."[227] Today, this presents substantially electronic media. *PIPEDA* includes an assertion of federal jurisdiction over provincially regulated entities with respect to privacy of personal information through a mechanism that preserves a provincial legislative response within a province so long as the enactment is equivalent or superior to *PIPEDA*. As such, it may be an incursion upon section 92(13) (property and civil rights in the province). This jurisdiction, however, is like that of s. 92(10)(a) and limited to activities *within* the province. Any extraprovincial affect of an exercise of section 92(13) must be strictly included.[228]

Privacy as both a legal conception and a qualitative feature fundamental to our society, is well established as inclusive of both federal

---

224 See text accompanying note 203, above in this chapter.

225 See text accompanying notes 209ff., above in this chapter, concerning toxic substances emitted into Canadian waters.

226 *Personal Information Protection and Electronic Documents Act*, S.C. 2000, c. 5 in force 1 January 2001 [*PIPEDA*].

227 *Ibid.*, s. 4(1)(a).

228 *Reference re Upper Churchill Water Rights Reversion Act*, [1984] 1 S.C.R. 297, 8 D.L.R. (4th) 1.

and provincial jurisdictions.[229] In a manner similar to areas such as environment, health, and consumer protections, privacy is a broadly conceptualized and pervasive field that cannot appropriately be assigned exclusively to either constitutional jurisdiction. Instead, it should be contextualized to determine the relevant constitutional allocation in a particular instance.

Section 30(1) declares *PIPEDA* to be inapplicable to any organization in respect of its collection, use, or disclosure of personal information "within a province whose legislature has the power to regulate the collection, use or disclosure of the information" unless done in a "federal work, undertaking or business"[230] or disclosed extraprovincially.[231] This period of exclusion ended three years after section 30 came into force.[232] Accordingly, from 1 January 2004,[233] *PIPEDA* became applicable to all organizations, including provincially regulated works, undertakings, or businesses. However, sections 25 and 26(2) (b) provide a further mechanism requiring the federal Privacy Commissioner to report to Parliament after the end of each calendar year as to provincially enacted legislation that is "substantially similar" to *PIPEDA* and for the Governor in Council to consider exempting from *PIPEDA* any organization, class of organizations, activity, or class of activities that meet this criterion.

Industry Canada and the federal Minister of Industry, in preparing recommendations to the Governor in Council for an exemption, follow a procedure set out in the *Canada Gazette*.[234] The objectives include obtaining benefits from interprovincial harmonization and minimizing instances of dual regulatory regimes while still allowing provinces to regulate with flexibility to adapt and tailor according to specific needs but within the intent and key principles of the federal provisions. *PI-*

---

229 See Chapter 4, text accompanying notes 26–34.
230 This description is defined in *PIPEDA*, above note 226, s. 2.
231 *Ibid.*, s. 30(1).
232 *Ibid.*, s. 30(2).
233 Section 30 came into effect on 1 January 2001. See S.I./2000-29 (26 April, 2000), P.C. 2000/584 (14 April, 2000), C. Gaz. 2000.II.914, *Order Fixing the Dates of the Coming into Force of Certain Parts of the Act*, Personal Information Protection and Electronic Documents Act. See also Industry Canada, "Privacy and the Digital Economy," online: www.ic.gc.ca/epic/site/ecic-ceac.nsf/en/h_gv00045e.html.
234 C. Gaz. 2002.I.2385, Government Notices: Dept. of Industry: *Process for the Determination of "Substantially Similar" Provincial Legislation by the Governor in Council*, Personal Information Protection and Electronic Documents Act.

PEDA is stated as providing a threshold or minimum requirement. Provincial initiatives must be equal or superior.[235]

While Quebec has been found to have substantially similar legislation,[236] the province has filed a reference to the Court of Appeal of Quebec for a determination with respect to the constitutionality of *PIPEDA*, but to date this action has not proceeded.[237] The essential issue is whether there is a federal jurisdiction to set a nationwide *minimum standard* for the collection, use, and disclosure of personal information by the private sector. Given that *PIPEDA* itself envisages a shared jurisdiction, an exclusive federal jurisdiction is not contemplated. A shared jurisdiction in this broadly conceptualized topic is consistent with trends to this effect in similarly broad areas,[238] and has been presented as facilitating federal and provincial regulation in their respective spheres.[239] It is, however, beyond a contextual division of "one level of government [legislating] in relation to one aspect of a matter [and] the other level to control another."[240] The subject of the legislation is identical between federal and provincial jurisdictions. Scope for provincial jurisdiction is limited to simply enacting more stringent privacy protection or to particularizing the key principles of *PIPEDA* to local circumstances.[241] The mechanism of federal inclusion of provincially regulated entities, in the absence of equivalent or more stringent provincial requirements, is unique to *PIPEDA* in federal and provincial constitutional relations. It may well achieve a nationwide minimum standard, which may be crucial in meeting international expectations, yet it is uncertain in constitutional validity. First, more stringent protections in particular provinces may be as disruptive to commerce as would less stringent provisions. Both would digress from efforts toward harmonization and the minimizing of dual or multiple regulatory regimes.[242] Second, there is some incongruity in an approval process

---

235 *Ibid.* at 2387; and Privacy Commissioner of Canada, *Report to Parliament Concerning Substantially Similar Provincial Legislation*, Cat. No. IP34-11/2002 (June 2003), online: www.priv.gc.ca/legislation/leg-rp_030611_e.pdf at 2.

236 Privacy Commissioner, *ibid.* at 9ff.

237 The author gratefully acknowledges the assistance in this context of Me Bertrand Gervais, Coordinator of the Research Service of the Court of Appeal of Quebec, in providing information about this filing and the current position.

238 See text accompanying notes 196–211, above in this chapter.

239 See Mahmud Jamal, "Is *PIPEDA* Constitutional?" (2006) 43 Can. Bus. L.J. 434 at 442–54.

240 *Reference re Employment Insurance Act (Can.)*, 2005 SCC 56, [2005] 2 S.C.R. 669, 258 D.L.R. (4th) 243 at para. 8.

241 See text accompanying note 234, above in this chapter.

242 *Ibid.*

that requires a provincial Crown in its legislative capacity to submit its enactment to the federal Crown in its executive capacity.

However, from a practical perspective the minimum standard approach of *PIPEDA* represents a substantial federal occupation of a field (privacy of personal information) and, significantly, any provincial legislation of recognized equivalency is enabled to apply only to operations *within* the province by non-federally regulated undertakings. The federal *PIPEDA* continues to apply to federal undertakings (including telecommunications undertakings) operating within the province as well as to a general use or disclosure of personal information outside the province.[243] The general branch of the trade and commerce power[244] has been identified by the federal government as the appropriate federal jurisdiction.[245] This power was considered in 2005 by the Supreme Court in *Kirkbi AG v. Ritvik Holdings Inc.*[246] with respect to section 7(b) of the federal *Trade-Marks Act*,[247] and in 1989 in *General Motors of Canada Ltd. v. City National Leasing*[248] concerning (what is now) the federal *Competition Act*.[249] To meet this jurisdiction there must be a regulatory scheme and agency; regulation must be of trade in general, as opposed to a particular industry; there must be a potential for jeopardizing the operational success of the scheme by a failure to involve all provinces; and there must be constitutional incapacity for provincial regulation.[250] The focus in the latter respect is whether the federal scheme would be adversely affected in its application without the inclusion in the scheme of intraprovincial operations, rather than whether the provinces could jointly enact a suitable law.[251]

PIPEDA certainly concerns national rather than local issues, but if those concerns are characterized as simply the privacy of personal in-

---

243 This is expressly stipulated in the *Gazette* notice of the equivalency approval. See, for example, the notice of the equivalency approval for Alberta, S.O.R./2004-219 (12 October, 2004), P.C. 2004-1163 (12 October, 2004), C. Gaz. 2004.II.1636, *Organizations in the Province of Alberta Exemption Order*, Personal Information Protection and Electronic Documents Act.

244 *Constitution Act, 1867*, above note 76, s. 91(2).

245 See *Province of Quebec Exemption Order*, S.O.R./2003-374.

246 *Kirkbi AG v. Ritvik Holdings Inc.*, 2005 SCC 65, [2005] 3 S.C.R. 302 [*Kirkbi*].

247 *Trade-marks Act*, above note 154.

248 *General Motors of Canada Ltd. v. City National Leasing*, [1989] 1 S.C.R. 641 [*General Motors*].

249 *Competition Act*, above note 20.

250 See *General Motors*, above note 248 at para. 56.

251 See *ibid.* at para. 60; and *Kirkbi*, above note 246 at para. 29. See also Jamal, above note 239 at 448–51, citing Patrick J. Monahan, *Constitutional Law*, 2d ed. (Toronto: Irwin Law, 2002) at 680.

formation, then the linkage to federal legislation is insufficient.[252] There must be commercial or economic factors that necessitate the inclusion within the federal enactment of intraprovincial features necessary for attaining national uniformity. To the extent that *PIPEDA* may encourage commerce, particularly if electronically based, it may present a linkage similar to that found in competition or trademark law,[253] but it is likely to be more problematic. While Part I of *PIPEDA* is primarily applicable to organizations that collect, use, or disclose personal information during commercial activities,[254] the overall purpose is expressed simply as the protection of privacy of personal information. Employment-related personal information is included,[255] as is that of associations and trade unions.[256] Similarly, while "personal health information" is excluded,[257] health-related private sector organizations are included with respect to personal information, subject to provincial equivalency.[258] On the other hand, domestic purposes[259] and journalistic, artistic, or literary purposes[260] are excluded, reinforcing the primarily commercial focus of the legislation.

PIPEDA is applicable to cross-border or international activities involving the transfer of personal information by included organizations,[261] and these dimensions may have been influential upon federal enactment of a minimum standard. Dealing with or accessing the information sources of a foreign entity may be denied or restricted

---

252 See Edward Belobaba, "Quebec Is Right to Challenge the Constitutionality of *PIPEDA*" *Law Times* (13 September 2004) at 7; and Colin H.H. McNairn & Alexander K Scott, *A Guide to the Personal Information and Protection of Electronic Documents Act* (Markham, ON: Butterworths Canada, 2006) at 9–13.

253 See Jamal, above note 239 at 447–48.

254 *PIPEDA*, above note 226, s. 4(1)(a). The term "commercial activities" is defined in s. 2.

255 *Ibid.*, s. 4(1)(b).

256 *Ibid.*, s. 2 (definition of "organization").

257 *Ibid.*, s. 30(1.1).

258 See, for example, the determination of equivalency of Ontario's *Personal Health Information Protection Act*, S.O. 2004, c. 3 in S.O.R./2005-399 (28 November 2005), P.C. 2005-2224 (28 November 2005), C. Gaz. 2005.II.3001, *Health Information Custodians in the Province of Ontario Exemption Order*, Personal Information Protection and Electronic Documents Act.

259 *PIPEDA*, above note 226, s. 4(2)(b).

260 *Ibid.*, s. 4(2)(c).

261 Office of the Privacy Commissioner of Canada, "Your Privacy Responsibilities: A Guide to Canada's Personal Information Protection and Electronic Documents Act" (September 2006) at 7, online: www.privcom.gc.ca/information/guide_e.pdf, discussed by Adam N. Atlas, *Canada: The Impact of PIPEDA on Cross-Border Business* (June 2004), online: www.adamatlas.com/publications/WDPR-Atlas.doc.

in the absence of equivalency between the jurisdictions. The European Directive on Personal Information Privacy stipulates that EU member states must provide for a denial of transfer of personal information to a third country unless that country "ensures an adequate level of protection."[262] The determination of the Commission of the European Communities as to whether Canada meets this standard described and emphasized the process of federal minimum provisions with the mechanism of exemption in respect of provincial laws that are substantially similar to *PIPEDA*.[263]

The actions and responses of foreign jurisdictions are not in themselves determinative in a constitutional division of powers issue in Canada,[264] but such responses do provide the contextual flavour of national and international dimensions that will assist in meeting the tests to establish a general trade and commerce federal jurisdiction. Crucial international recognition may be denied by a failure to involve transactions in all provinces, including intraprovincial transactions, and to ensure that federal *PIPEDA* covers use and disclosure of personal information outside of the province and activities of federal undertakings operating within a province that is recognized as having provincial legislative equivalency.[265]

The remaining requirement of a scheme and agency that regulates trade in general, rather than a particular industry, is met so long as *PIPEDA* is seen to be sufficiently focused on commerce.

On balance, it is suggested that a sufficiently federal jurisdiction has been established for *PIPEDA*, providing a further example of a significant constitutional dimension in a context crucial to ensuring effective national and international telecommunications.

---

262 EC, *Commision Directive 1995/95/46 of the European Parliament and of the Council (24 October 1995) on the protection of individuals with regard to the processing of personal data and on the free movement of such data*, [1995] O.J. L 281/31 at 25(1).

263 EC, *Commission Decision 2002/02/2 of the European Communities (20 December 2001) on the adequate protection of personal data provided by the Canadian Personal Information Protection and Electronic Document Act*, [2002] O.J. L2/13.

264 International treaties involving provincial jurisdiction have been effectively implemented by provincial legislation. In British Columbia, see, for example, the *International Sale of Goods Act*, R.S.B.C. 1996, c. 236 implementing the *United Nations Convention on Contracts for the International Sale of Goods*, noted in s. 1 and set out in the Schedule to the Act.

265 See above note 243.

D. SCOPE OF PROVINCIAL JURISDICTION IN TELECOMMUNICATIONS

The analysis overall in this chapter presents a conclusion weighted heavily toward federal jurisdiction, exclusive or shared as the case may be. A useful conclusion might therefore focus distinctly on the limited scope of any potential provincial authority, first with respect to telecommunications as a system or process, and second with respect to issues of content, use, or application of telecommunications media.

1) The System or Process of Telecommunications

First, under section 92(10)(a), an entity or activity that is entirely within the province in its operation and is without features, connections, or consequences of national or international dimension will be within exclusively provincial jurisdiction as a local work or undertaking. Such situations will be extremely limited but might include a closed circuit television or radio system without external connection, a telephone or data system limited exclusively to a singularly provincial entity and internal communications only, a similarly constrained computer or intranet system, or even a wireless communication system that cannot receive or transmit outside a local calling area.

Second, if the interprovincial links and connections are trivial, they may be disregarded. An example is a substantially local intranet system with only a limited and well-defined external access or accessibility, perhaps through specifically dedicated links to identified and specific internal and external sources.

Third, the potential in relation to works or undertakings in the context of unexercised federal jurisdiction is unclear. This potential opening for a province may be easier to establish in a context of concurrent or shared federal and provincial jurisdiction. However, as described earlier, there is some contemplation of provincial authority in the light of an unexercised (and unlikely or not intended to be exercised), federal jurisdiction as it pertains to works and undertakings.[266] An instance may be the intranet example noted above, where additionally the federal authorities do not intend to, or are unlikely to, exercise federal authority. However, it is suggested that the relevant federal link that would ordinarily establish federal jurisdiction may need also to be relatively incidental for this ground to succeed.

---

266 See text accompanying note 127ff., above in this chapter.

The limited scope of these examples reflect an entity, system or process of telecommunication as a whole that cannot be seen as a local undertaking within section 92(10)(a) and which does not permit separate sub-categorization of component features.

2) Content, Use, or Application

Despite the very significant inclusion of content-related issues within federal jurisdiction in the context of the traditional media,[267] greater scope will exist for provincial jurisdiction when the conceptual focus moves away from the system or the mode of communication itself and toward issues of content or use or application. Greater opportunity should exist in this context when applied to the medium of the Internet, where the pervasiveness is such that all areas of law, federal and provincial, may potentially present issues within the scope of the medium. This should facilitate recognition of matters of exclusive provincial jurisdiction, upon an application of the "pith and substance" test. The sale of goods, tritely within provincial jurisdiction,[268] may be an example. Internet-related sale and purchase of goods is likely to be seen as an instance of simple use of a medium to achieve the core feature of marketing products within a province even if they originate elsewhere, as has always been the position. This potential is amply supported by the analysis of the Supreme Court of Canada in both *Kellogg's* and *Irwin Toy* with respect to the pith and substance between a provincial jurisdiction to regulate advertising to children and the protection of children, and the medium of federally regulated television transmissions, a traditional medium that contained the particular advertising.[269]

Beyond this, if a subject area is neither exclusively federal under a section 92(10)(a) analysis nor provincial under a pith and substance analysis, the Internet in its pervasiveness may, like the protection of the environment, attract a characterization as a *shared* category, with the court balancing between the two levels of government. Here some uncertainty follows upon both the recent trend to de-emphasize the traditional principle of interjurisdictional immunity in favour of a principle of cooperative federalism;[270] and the novel formulation in the federal

---

267 See text accompanying note 130ff., above in this chapter.
268 Sale of Goods legislation is enacted provincially. See, for example, *Sale of Goods Act*, R.S.B.C. 1996, c. 410, including legislation to implement international treaty matters. See also, for example, *International Sale of Goods Act*, above note 264.
269 See text accompanying note 175ff., above in this chapter.
270 See text accompanying note 163ff.

PIPEDA legislation that gives effect to federal privacy legislation with respect to provincially controlled entities in the absence of an approved provincial legislative response consistent with the policies and objectives of the federal legislation. Whether such a mechanism meets constitutional muster has not received judicial consideration, but it may yet be subject to test in this respect.[271] A provincial challenge to such a mechanism would be axiomatic if the mechanism were to be regularly utilized in federal legislation.

---

271 See text accompanying note 237, above in this chapter.

REGULATORY STRUCTURE AND FEATURES

A. INDUSTRIES AND SECTORS IN FLUX

The *Broadcasting Act* (1991)[1] and the *Telecommunications Act* (1993)[2] were designed to consolidate and modernize the telecommunications legislative structure in Canada. The division between point-to-mass broadcasting and point-to-point telecommunications is the essence of this structure. In addition, the *Radiocommunication Act*[3] provides regulation of technical features in broadcasting, including the allocation of radio frequencies. However, rapid technological, political, and social changes, mooted even as the 1991 and 1993 legislation were being enacted, challenged the broadcasting/telecommunications demarcation and by 2003, a new and integrated legislative structure between all three enactments was being contemplated.[4]

---

1 *Broadcasting Act*, S.C. 1991, c. 11.
2 *Telecommunications Act*, S.C. 1993, c. 38.
3 *Radiocommunication Act*, R.S.C. 1985, c. R-2, as am. by S.C. 1989, c. 17.
4 House of Commons, Standing Committee on Canadian Heritage, *Our Cultural Sovereignty: The Second Century of Canadian Broadcasting*, (June 2003) at 17 and 62, online: www2.parl.gc.ca/HousePublications/Publication.aspx?DocId=1 032284&Language=E&Mode=1&Parl=37&Ses=2 [Canadian Heritage Report]. See also Canadian Radio-television and Telecommunications Commission (CRTC), *2008–2009 Estimates*, Part 3, Report on Plans and Priorities, Section I, Chairman's Message, online: CRTC www.crtc.gc.ca/eng/publications/reports/ rpps/2008_09.htm. Unless accompanied by a url, all CRTC documents refer to print versions.

Organizational integration is reflective of system convergence. Technological change, particularly that of digitization, has provided the capacity for convergence between these two systems and industries of communications, and over 2007–8 the topic received attention in the study by the Canadian Radio-television and Telecommunications Commission (CRTC) in its New Media Project Initiative.[5] Yet significant differences of concept and policy remain between broadcasting and non-broadcasting. This is illustrated aptly by openly conflicting policies with respect to Canadian ownership in both broadcast and non-broadcast sectors by two standing committees of the House of Commons. Reporting almost simultaneously in 2003, the industry-focused non-broadcast standing committee favoured removal of all ownership restrictions in both sectors. The cultural- and heritage-focused standing committee viewed any amelioration of Canadian ownership requirements as a matter of concern.[6]

To have contemplated in 1991–93 giving legislative guidance to any sense of contextual integration between the two systems would have been quite premature. The inability and impracticality of affording advance legislative direction with respect to technological change was recognized as early as 1979 by the CRTC,[7] just three years after the 1976 integration of regulatory jurisdiction in the CRTC.[8] At that time, there was little inkling of the position pertaining today, and the merging of regulatory control over both systems seems to have reflected convenience more than logic. In hindsight, however, it was a fortuitous change that has provided the CRTC, through its respective divisions, with a working experience and expertise in both sectors. This feature of a common regulator administering integrated legislation will certainly bring efficiencies in areas of convergence, but otherwise the legislation

---

5   See text accompanying note 39, below in this chapter, and CRTC, *Perspectives on Canadian Broadcasting in New Media: A Compilation of Research and Stakeholder Views* (May 2008), online: CRTC www.crtc.gc.ca/Eng/media/rp080515.pdf. See also comments by the CRTC Chairman: "We are seeing more and more evidence that the new technologies are not only driving innovation, but also a convergence between the two industries" in *CRTC 2008–2009 Estimates, ibid.*

6   See text accompanying notes 76–77, below in this chapter.

7   See *CNCP Telecommunications: Interconnection with Bell Canada* (17 May 1979), Telecom Decision CRTC 79-11, 5 C.R.T. 117 at Part 9, s. 1 [Telecom Decision CRTC 79-11], noting: "It may be that a point has been reached where, with the rapidity of technological developments, it is impossible to anticipate all such changes and to develop a comprehensive policy prior to the consideration of specific cases."

8   See Chapter 1, text accompanying notes 15–16.

and the administration in both qualification and decision making will necessarily present composites within the whole.

The overall political objective, both historical and current, is identical for broadcast and non-broadcast communications in the promotion of a national Canadian interest, presented in the context of *programming* for broadcasting and *ownership* for non-broadcasting. Even this, however, is today more difficult to attain. Social and political perspectives, nationally and internationally, have imposed new dimensions. In particular, the global political resurgence from the 1980s of capitalism, private enterprise, and competition was led by key Asian economies.[9] In the West, Thatcherism and Reagonomics challenged regulation, state ownership, and high taxation.[10] Although initially uncertain, the trend was consolidated with the collapse of the Communist bloc in 1989, ending the Cold War and enshrining capitalism, competition, and freer trade principles in regional and global trading arrangements from the late 1980s to mid-1990s.[11] Global telecommunications infrastructure and computer technology, freed from the all-consuming demands of Cold War strategic defence requirements, became available for development as civilian commodities.[12]

Convergence of broadcast and non-broadcast services in Canada was seen initially as between telephone and television cable transmissions utilizing the dual infrastructure of the telephone and former telegraph services, along with satellite industries. In effect, it presented a Canadian-owned competition model.[13] Actively promoted by government,[14] it has reasonably succeeded. Former exclusively cable providers are active in the provision of non-broadcast services, and

---

9   See David Reynolds, *One World Divisible: A Global History Since 1945* (New York: W.W. Norton, 2000) c. 12 at 403ff.

10   *Ibid.* at 453.

11   See, for example, *North American Free Trade Agreement Between the Government of Canada, the Government of Mexico and the Government of the United States,* 17 December 1992, Can. T.S. 1994 No. 2, 32 I.L.M. 289 (entered into force 1 January 1994) [*NAFTA*], online: Foreign Affairs and International Trade Canada www.international.gc.ca/trade-agreements-accords-commerciaux/agr-acc/nafta-alena/texte/index.aspx); and the *Marrakesh Agreement Establishing the World Trade Organization,* 15 April 1994, (entered into force 1 January 1995), online: www.wto.org/english/docs_e/legal_e/04-wto_e.htm.

12   Reynolds, above note 9 at 494–538, is essential reading in these respects.

13   See *Telecommunications Service in Canada: An Industry Overview,* s. 6.2 "Convergence Policy," online: www.ic.gc.ca/epic/site/smt-gst.nsf/en/sf06287e.html.

14   See Minister of Canadian Heritage (S. Copps) & Minister of Industry (J. Manley), News Release, "Competition and Culture Set to Gain in Convergence Policy Framework" (6 August 1996), online: www.ic.gc.ca/epic/site/smt-gst.nsf/en/sf05266e.html.

broadcast services flow from former exclusively telephone providers.[15] Wireless, direct-to-home (DTH) satellite and, significantly, the Internet have, however, pushed convergence well beyond this initial idea. Internet-accessible video rental services provide sufficient public accessibility to be equivalent to broadcasting, but with an individualized choice and communication mechanism reflective of non-broadcast point-to-point. Likewise, the Internet medium YouTube, individualized and decentralized as it is, is nevertheless entirely accessible to the public and is intended to be. It is in the nature of broadcasting. These signals may additionally be received and responded to on cell telephone technology territorially or extraterritorially, creating both convergence dimensions and potential well beyond Canadian or any national regulation.

Despite a measure of disappointment expressed in 2007 that greater convergence had not occurred and an opinion that convergence in its full sense would ultimately depend on the dominance of Internet Protocol Networks, seen to be the next generation networks (NGNs),[16] it is suggested that the convergence experienced to date is significant and a substantial fulfillment of technical and economic projections, though of course with much more to follow.

Point-to-point telecommunications has essentially ceased to be a regulated industry. The CRTC itself engaged in reshaping the industry by regulating deregulation incrementally, from a key policy change first mooted in 1979. Competition had to be crafted in a service sector that had for decades enjoyed legislatively sanctioned monopoly protection and strict regulation. Rate setting had to be changed from a cost recovery calculation to a market-based assessment. New entrants had to receive regulated protection from the incumbent providers, including regulated access to incumbent-owned infrastructure. Consumers, encouraged by falling rates, had to develop trust and goodwill with new entrants, overcoming an inertia that initially favoured incumbents. Composite services had to be separated or "unbundled" to encourage

---

15   Compare the 2003 revenue profiles of Bell Canada Enterprises Inc. (BCE), with nearly 88 percent wired, wireless, and Internet telecommunication, 7.2 percent media broadcasting (CTV network), 1.7 percent financial services, and 3.6 percent other ventures, and Rogers Communications Inc., with 47 percent wireless telecommunications, 36 percent television and Internet cable services, and 17 percent media/radio, television station, and channels. See, online: www.ic.gc.ca/epic/site/smt-gst.nsf/en/sf06204e.html.

16   See Leonard Waverman, "Benefiting from Convergence: Access, Mobility and Ubiquity," a discussion paper prepared for the Canada Roundtable on the Future of the Internet Economy, Industry Canada (Ottawa: 2 October 2007), online: www.ic.gc.ca/epic.site/ecic-ceac.nsf/cn/gv00416e.html.

new entrants and competition in the particular parts and to prevent monopolistic practices in linking services together.

The mechanism that has been utilized by the CRTC is the "exemption" and "forbearance" provisions of the *Telecommunications Act* (1993).[17] Each application to the CRTC has been presumptively "regulated," but measures are not imposed if sufficient market competition within recognized competition theory is present. So successful has the CRTC been in prescribing market and competition theories in this manner that a role for the CRTC in this context is no longer clear. The Competition Bureau may have a greater claim on bringing the telecommunications sector within the mainstream of competition theory. On the other hand, a sector-specific regulator in an area of dynamic change does bring an expertise and a promptness of response that is not enjoyed by the Competition Bureau or other, more general regulator. Whatever the future structure may be, the CRTC, as sector regulator, is pursuing competition theory consistent with that pursued by the Competition Bureau itself. Negotiations from 2003 between these two agencies produced a framework governing their immediate relationship in the telecommunications sector, but from 2006 a new structure has been envisaged.

Any such sector-specific development should be made with an awareness of the broader study ordered in 2007 to consider Canada's competition and investment policies, with the objective of encouraging greater foreign investment.[18] The final report of this Competition Policy Review Panel, submitted to the Minister of Industry in June 2008, includes consideration of the telecommunications and broadcasting sectors and recommends increased foreign direct investment in the telecommunications sector and a review of broadcasting and cultural policies toward a similar liberalization in the broadcasting sector.[19]

At an international level, a cautious measure of deregulation flowed from national commitments in the *Annex on Telecommunications* to the *General Agreement on Trade in Services (GATS)*, ratified in 1994 on the

---

17   *Telecommunications Act*, above note 2. See also text accompanying notes 90–96, below in this chapter.

18   See Competition Policy Review Panel, *Sharpening Canada's Competitive Edge* (Consultation Paper) (Ottawa: 2007), online: www.ic.gc.ca/eic/site/cprp-gepmc.nsf/eng/h_00009.html [*Canada's Competitive Edge*]. Appendix 2 refers to sectoral restrictions on foreign direct investment, including telecommunications, broadcasting, and cultural industries.

19   See Competition Policy Review Panel, *Compete to Win* (Final Report) (Ottawa: 2008) at 45–49) recommendation 11, online: www.ic.gc.ca/epic/site/cprp-gepmc.nsf/en/h_00040e.html [CPRP Final Report].

creation of the World Trade Organization (WTO).[20] Canadian icons Telesat and Teleglobe entered into private structures and reorganizations, but beyond this little change has flowed from formal international trade arrangements that, in effect, peaked in 1994. Since then, global trade negotiations have in general found consensus to be elusive.

Despite this, the relentless progression of technology ensures international as well as national competition. The mobile telephone challenges the existence of land lines. Mobile devices may also be acquired extraterritorially. Service may originate from a Canadian carrier or from a foreign carrier. User fees are by electronic transfer. A device acquired in Europe from a European carrier, for example, can be legally used in Canada for international, and national and local calls. The Internet technology of Voice over Internet Protocol (VoIP) presents a similar consequence. The downloading to a computer terminal of the European service provider Skype (owned by eBay) provides Canadians with an inexpensive, high-quality aural and visual communication option internationally, nationally, and locally through desktop or laptop modems as well as access to land line and cellphone service. Indeed, hand-held mobile devices with digitized data text (electronic mail), Internet browsing, financial transactional systems, and personal or business data storage challenge characterization as one or another category of service. Perhaps the most exotic is the Iridium satellite telephone system, which operates from and to any point on the planet, including the north and south poles, by a direct link between handsets and a constellation of satellites.

Future directions in Canadian non-broadcasting telecommunications policy and law were considered in 2003 by the House of Commons Standing Committee on Industry, Science and Technology. The Committee's wide-ranging recommendations included a reorganization of both telecommunications and broadcasting entities as "carriage" and "content" organizations, given the prevailing convergence, industry, and market factors.[21] Likewise, an expert Telecommunications Policy Review Panel (TPRP) appointed in 2005 by a federal Liberal Party minor-

---

20 *GATS, Annex on Telecommunications, Final Act Embodying the Results of the Uruguay Round of Multilateral Trade Negotiations*: Annex 1B, General Agreement on Trade in Services, Annex on Telecommunications 15 April 1994, 33 I.L.M. 1167, s. 2(b), online: WTO www.wto.org/english/docs_e/legal_e/26-gats.pdf [*GATS, Annex on Telecommunications*].

21 House of Commons, Standing Committee on Industry, Science and Technology, *Opening Canadian Communications to the World* (April 2003) at 41–43, online: http://cmte.parl.gc.ca/Content/HOC/committee/372/inst/reports/rp1032302/instrp03/instrp03-e.pdf [Report of the Standing Committee].

ity government but reporting in March 2006 to the Minister of Industry in a federal Conservative Party minority government,[22] in compliance with its mandate, addresses primarily non-broadcast telecommunications but does include reference to Canadian broadcasting policy given the linkage between these sectors. TPRP's many recommendations include integrated measures in the convergence found in the allocation of spectrum frequencies in wireless communications, to bring greater consistency and transparency. Currently, broadcast frequencies are allocated by the CRTC and non-broadcast frequencies by Industry Canada. The CRTC is recommended to undertake both allocations.[23]

From an economic perspective, TPRP recommended as the next step in Canadian deregulation that market forces prevail as the presumptive norm, unfettered by regulation unless telecommunications policy cannot be achieved within an appropriate time frame in the market.[24] This presents a subtle repositioning in emphasis from the deregulation process used before the direction in 2006 involving a presumptive need for regulation subject to the CRTC exempting or forbearing to regulate in the interest of market forces. Additionally, the social focus of TPRP is on access, particularly for rural residents and for persons with disabilities.[25] An organizational refocusing recommends the creation of a Telecommunications Competition Tribunal (TCT) as a transitional measure for a period of five years to expedite deregulation and complete the adoption of competition and market policies. TCT is recommended as a joint entity of the CRTC and Competition Bureau. It is projected to have all the powers of both tribunals and will utilize the organizational infrastructure and resources of each.[26] The objective is to bring efficiency and coordination between the agencies — maintaining the expertise in telecommunications and the ability of prompt response found in the CRTC, but including the broader competition-related expertise and experience of the Competition Bureau — and thereby to hasten further deregulation in favour of market forces.

In the longer term, an enhancement of telecommunications expertise for CRTC commissioners and specialist staff is recommended, with

---

22   Industry Canada, Multimedia and Editorial Services Section, *Telecommunications Policy Review Panel 2006 Final Report*, online: www.telecomreview.ca/eic/site/tprp-gecrt.nsf/vwapj/report_e.pdf/$FILE/report_e.pdf [TPRP Report].

23   *Ibid.*, c. 5, Recommendations 5(9) & 5(10) (discussed at 5-21 to 5-27, PDF at 165–71).

24   *Ibid.*, c. 4, Recommendations 4(1)–4(17) (discussed at 4-17 to 4-28, PDF at 133–44).

25   *Ibid.*, c. 6, Recommendation 6(1) (discussed at 6-6 to 6-7, PDF at 178–79).

26   *Ibid.*, c. 4, Recommendations 4(1) & 4(2) (discussed at 4–17, PDF at 133).

a core of just five commissioners to determine both telecommunications and broadcasting matters and the prospect of additional commissioners being added for broadcasting determinations.

The economic regulatory recommendation of TPRP was implemented by direction of the Governor in Council to the CRTC in December 2006.[27] Currently, however, recommended legislative amendments
to the *Telecommunications Act* (1993) in implementation of the TPRP
report have been reserved for consideration by government.[28]

Different policy dimensions exist for point-to-mass broadcasting,
for which the traditional media of radio, television, cable, and DTH
satellite systems still constitute the primary media and are sufficiently
centralized to continue to be subject to effective national regulation.
The political and cultural dimensions of mass communication have
discouraged deregulation both nationally and internationally. No international trade or other economic protocol, such as *GATS*, encompasses
broadcasting. National broadcasting objectives and regulatory policies
reinforce national control over these services. Broadcasting and its content arouse a significant political and policy division between interests
in cultural sovereignty and those of a more economic and industrial
dimension. The House of Commons Standing Committee on Canadian
Heritage, reporting just two months after the Standing Committee on
Industry, Science and Technology,[29] advocated continued regulation, no
amelioration in Canadian ownership requirements, and the enhancement of Canadian cultural elements through strengthened Canadian
content requirements.[30]

Although currently maintaining listenership and viewership, with
enhanced prospects in this respect from qualitative features stemming
from digitization of traditional media, broadcasting cannot escape the
consequence of technology and the difficulty it brings to effective regulation. New media, particularly that of the decentralized, universally
available and user-controlled Internet, are providing Canadians with a
means of bypassing the regulated, traditional broadcasting system and

27 *Order under Section 8, Telecommunications Act Issuing a Direction to the CRTC on
    Implementing the Canadian Telecommunications Policy Objectives*, S.O.R./06-355,
    s. 2(202), online: www.gazette.gc.ca/archives/p2/2006/2006-12-27/pdf/g214026.
    pdf [*Order under Section 8*]. See also *Regulatory Impact Analysis Statement*,
    S.O.R./06-355, s. 1, online: www.gazette.gc.ca/archives/p1/2006/2006-06-17/pdf/
    g1-14024.pdf.(setting out and explaining the proposed order and seeking public
    comment).
28 *Regulatory Impact Analysis Statement*, *ibid.*, under the heading "Alternatives."
29 See Canadian Heritage Report, above note 4, and Report of the Standing Com-
    mittee, above note 21.
30 Canadian Heritage Report, *ibid.* at 13.

have been acknowledged in this respect by the CRTC.[31] In this medium, political or territorial borders are of little significance in the transmission of and access to unregulated information by individual residents of almost every country. Only a determined exercise of national policing policy can bring success in restricting access to, or transmissions by, the Internet, at least while it is dependent on local or national servers and communications infrastructures.[32] Developed democracies, however, do not ordinarily attempt blunt measures to deny general access to Internet communications. Hence the Internet, being entirely decentralized and entirely globalized, is largely beyond traditional regulatory measures developed for the traditional media.

In Canada, the CRTC in 1999 determined the Internet to be substantially alphanumeric and refrained at that stage from any attempt to regulate the medium.[33] This characterization is not necessarily the position today, and in 2006 the Governor in Council formally requested the CRTC to undertake a factually focused study of the future environment facing the broadcasting system from the challenge of new media in an audiovisual context and the need to keep Canada relevant in the new media within the broadcasting objectives.[34] The CRTC reported in 2006[35] and is monitoring the position with updates provided in 2008 and 2009.[36] The chairman noted the primary objective as the establishing of "measures that would support the continued achievement of the *Broadcasting Act*'s objectives" in the new media, particularly the Internet,[37] being today firmly multimedia with broadcast and non-

---

31   See text accompanying notes 37–39, below in this chapter.

32   Reporters without Borders lists 15 countries that attempt to limit or preclude access by residents to the Internet. See *The Internet's Black Holes,* online: Reporters without Borders http://adsoftheworld.com/media/print/reporters_without_borders_the_internets_black_holes?size=_original.

33   *Exemption Order for New Media Broadcasting Undertakings* (17 December 1999), Public Notice CRTC 1999-197, online: CRTC www.crtc.gc.ca/eng/archive/1999/PB99-197.htm.

34   *Order issuing a direction to the CRTC to examine the future environment facing the broadcasting system*, P.C. 2006-519, C. Gaz.2006.I.1577, online: http://canadagazette.gc.ca/archives/p1/2006/2006-06-17/pdf/g1-14024.pdf.

35   *The Future Environment Facing the Canadian Broadcasting System* (14 December 2006) CRTC BC92-60/2006, online: CRTC www.crtc.gc.ca/Eng/publications/reports/broadcast/rep061214.htm.

36   *Communications Monitoring Report* (31 July 2008), online: CRTC www.crtc.gc.ca/eng/publications/reports/PolicyMonitoring/2008/cmr2008.htm and Broadcasting Order CRTC 2009-660 (22 October 2009).

37   CRTC, News Release, "CRTC Launches Consultation on Broadcasting in New Media for Future Hearing" (15 May 2008), online: CRTC www.crtc.gc.ca/eng/NEWS/RELEASES/2008/r080515.htm.

broadcast capacities. The December 2006 report provided the foundation for the CRTC's New Media Project Initiative,[38] established in 2007
and reported upon in May 2008, with respect to new media broadcasting activity, particularly public Internet and mobile platforms.[39]

These extraordinary dimensions and contexts most certainly
present a world turned upside down in every sense of this phrase for
any regulating authority. The many reports and policy determinations
point in a direction ahead, but in a significantly unpredictable environment in terms of technological change, policy and objectives divergence,
and, very likely, differences in the political perspectives of the parliamentary parties in a manner similar to that reflected in the historical
development of the telecommunications industry.[40] Governmental and
organizational change, however, ultimately requires legislative amendment and reformulation. Until this is effected, the existing legislative
framework provides the parameters of law and related policies.

The primary juristic entity under the *Broadcasting Act* (1991) is a
"broadcasting undertaking."[41] The corresponding focus under the *Telecommunications Act* (1993) is a "Canadian carrier" as a "telecommunications common carrier."[42] The *Telecommunications Act* is inapplicable "in
respect of broadcasting by a broadcasting undertaking."[43] The *Broadcasting Act* is inapplicable to a "telecommunications common carrier"
when that carrier is "acting solely in that capacity."[44] If acting beyond
this capacity, the carrier may be subject to the *Broadcasting Act* if the
activities in which it is engaged constitute the carrier as a "broadcasting undertaking." Likewise, a "broadcasting undertaking" engaging in
non-broadcast communications may be subject to the *Telecommunications Act*.

In addition, the *Radiocommunication Act*[45] provides regulation of
the technical features of radio and television communication, including allocation of radio frequencies, provisions for non-interference with
signals, and inspection and approval of broadcast apparatus. It is to be
interpreted as a component in the broadcast system "in tandem" with

---

38   See CRTC, Media Release, "New Media Project Initiative" (4 June 2009), online:
       CRTC www.crtc.gc.ca/ENG/media/media3.htm.
39   CRTC, *Perspectives on Canadian Broadcasting in New Media – A Compilation of
       Research and Stakeholder Views* (19 June 2008), online: CRTC www.crtc.gc.ca/
       Eng/media/rp080515.pdf.
40   See Chapter 1, Section B, particularly text accompanying note 42ff.
41   *Broadcasting Act*, above note 1, s. 2(1).
42   *Telecommunications Act*, above note 2, s. 2(1).
43   *Ibid.*, s. 4.
44   *Broadcasting Act*, above note 1, s. 4(4).
45   *Radiocommunication Act*, above note 3.

the *Broadcasting Act* (1991) and sharing the broadcasting policy and objectives of that Act.[46]

The regulatory framework of non-broadcast telecommunications is considered in Section B of this chapter, followed by that of broadcasting in Section C.

B. NON-BROADCAST TELECOMMUNICATIONS

This sector has traditionally focused on the connection of point-to-point parties and the *carriage* of communications, not the content of the communications. A "Canadian carrier" as a "telecommunications common carrier" is legislatively forbidden to "control the content or influence the meaning or purpose of" a communication it carries for the public.[47] A Canadian carrier may, however, transmit broadcast programs.[48]

1) Rates, Conditions, and Preferences

Canadian carriers are not required to hold an operating licence in the manner required for broadcasting undertakings. Instead, statutory and regulatory controls exercised (since 1976) by the CRTC concern the setting of rate tariffs and conditions of operation. The Act prohibits a Canadian carrier from providing a telecommunications service other than under a tariff that has been filed with and approved by the Commission. The tariff must be "just and reasonable" and be applied by the carrier without unjust discrimination or "undue or unreasonable preference" to any person, including to itself, or with "undue or unreasonable disadvantage" to any person.[49] If these requirements are not

---

46 See *Bell ExpressVu v. R.*, [2002] 2 S.C.R. 559 at paras. 44–47. The description "in tandem" is used by the Court in para. 46. See also *Shuswap Cable Ltd. v. The Queen* (1986), 31 D.L.R. (4th) 349 at 360 (F.C.) [*Shuswap*], with respect to the intertwining of the *Broadcasting Act* and the *Radiocommunication Act* in the process of licensing broadcasting undertakings.

47 *Telecommunications Act*, above note 2, s. 36.

48 *Ibid.*, s. 28.

49 *Ibid.*, ss. 24–27. If a Canadian carrier is transmitting "programs," as defined in the *Broadcasting Act*, above note 1, s. 2, and any issue of unjust discrimination, preference, or disadvantage is raised before the Commission, regard must be had by the Commission to the broadcasting policy for Canada as outlined in *Broadcasting Act*, ibid., s. 3. See *Telecommunications Act*, above note 2, s. 28(1).

being met in any "service or class of services" operated by an "affiliate" of a Canadian carrier, the Commission may order the Canadian carrier to itself take over the service or class of services.[50] The expression "affiliate" is defined for this purpose as a person who either controls or is controlled directly or indirectly by the carrier.[51] The Commission may also order a Canadian carrier to discontinue a service or class of services if the degree of competition is sufficient to ensure just and reasonable rates without undue or unreasonable preference and if the discontinuance would further these purposes.[52]

2) Canadian Ownership

Although this feature is shared with broadcasting undertakings, unlike the position under the *Broadcasting Act* (1991), which simply provides that the broadcasting system "shall be effectively owned and controlled by Canadians,"[53] the *Telecommunications Act* (1993) stipulates precise and detailed requirements for Canadian ownership. Two categories of Canadian carrier are recognised: the first comprises carriers that meet the specified formula for Canadian ownership,[54] the second, those that do not but that were "grandfathered" in the system with effect from 22 July 1987 and have continued to meet the regulatory criteria controlling any subsequent increase in foreign ownership or control.[55]

Canadian ownership is applicable to the entity that qualifies as a "Canadian carrier," being the entity that owns or operates transmission facilities as illustrated below. This necessarily excludes from these requirements "re-sellers" or wholesalers of transmission services operating in infrastructural space leased by the Canadian carrier to the wholesalers or re-sellers established as competing operators in the telephone deregulation process.[56]

---

50   *Telecommunications Act, ibid.,* s. 35(1).

51   *Ibid.,* s. 35(3).

52   *Ibid.,* s. 35(2).

53   *Broadcasting Act,* above note 1, s. 3(1). See text accompanying notes 364–74, below in this chapter.

54   *Telecommunications Act,* above note 2, ss. 7(d), 16(1), and 16(3). See also *Canadian Telecommunications Common Carrier Ownership and Control Regulations,* S.O.R./94-667, online: CRTC www.crtc.gc.ca/eng/LEGAL/OWNER.htm and Can LII www.canlii.org/ca/regu/sor94-667/sec5.html.

55   *Telecommunications Act, ibid.,* s. 16(2); *Canadian Telecommunications Common Carrier Ownership and Control Regulations, ibid.,* s. 17.

56   See text accompanying note 62, below in this chapter.

Figure 1, Canadian Carrier

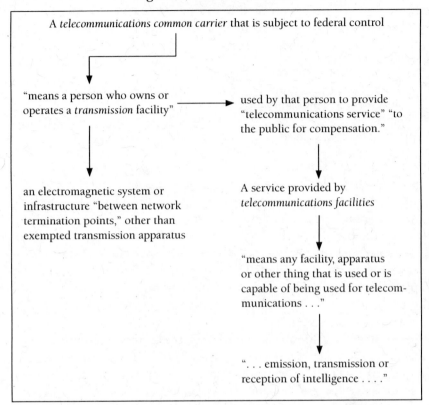

A *telecommunications common carrier* that is subject to federal control

"means a person who owns or operates a *transmission* facility" → used by that person to provide "telecommunications service" "to the public for compensation."

an electromagnetic system or infrastructure "between network termination points," other than exempted transmission apparatus

A service provided by *telecommunications facilities*

"means any facility, apparatus or other thing that is used or is capable of being used for telecommunications . . ."

". . . emission, transmission or reception of intelligence . . . ."

The qualifying criteria for Canadian ownership are prescribed both in the *Telecommunications Act* (1993) and regulations under the Act. Section 16 of the Act stipulates three criteria: first, not less than 80 percent of members of the corporation's board of directors must be individual Canadians;[57] second, Canadians must beneficially own not less than 80 percent of the corporation's voting shares issued and outstanding;[58] and third, the corporation may not in fact be otherwise subject to foreign control.[59] These statutory provisions are, however, to be interpreted by

---

57   *Telecommunications Act*, above note 2, s. 16(3)(a).
58   *Ibid.*, s. 16(3)(b). The beneficial ownership may be held "directly or indirectly," but may not be by way of only security holdings.
59   *Ibid.*, s. 16(3)(c). The expression "control" is defined in s. 2 as meaning "in any manner that results in control in fact, whether directly through the ownership of securities or indirectly through a trust, agreement or arrangement, the ownership of any body corporate or otherwise."

application of regulations promulgated in 1994.[60] The consequence is an expansion of foreign ownership in a practical sense.

The increase in foreign ownership is effected as follows:

1) Under section 16 itself non-Canadians may own 20 percent of the Canadian carrier's voting shares.

2) Under the Regulations non-Canadians may own up to 33⅓ percent of the voting shares of a Canadian carrier's parent or holding corporation, partnership, or trust. Canadians must own only 66⅔ percent of any such parent organization.[61]

Non-voting shares are not subject to any restriction. Additionally, the non-Canadian holders of 20 percent of the Canadian carrier and 33⅓ percent of the carrier's parent organization may engage in a leasing scheme by combining their holdings into a separate entity that leases the Canadian carrier's facilities so as to operate as a "re-seller" of leased telecommunication services.[62] There is no requirement of Canadian ownership for re-sellers that contract with Canadian carriers for capacity. Any regulatory restrictions imposed on a Canadian carrier for the particular service must necessarily be passed on by the Canadian carrier to re-sellers of that service.

The overall position was reviewed by the Commission in the 2009 Globalive licence application proceeding.[63] A need to establish both *de jure* (legal) control and control *de facto* (in fact) was reiterated by the Commission.[64] In this instance, the Commission found only *de jure*, not *de facto*, Canadian control to be established.[65] The determination was controversial. The Governor in Council reversed by variation[66] to

---

60   *Canadian Telecommunications Common Carrier Ownership and Control Regulations*, above note 54.

61   *Ibid.* at paras. 5, 20, & 21.

62   See Barbara Miller, "Foreign Ownership in Canadian Telecommunications: Can an Explosion Be Regulated?" *Breaking the Mould: Reconceiving Telecommunications Regulation* (17–18 February 2000) at 4–8, online: www.fasken.com/Publications/Detail.aspx?publication=2579.

63   *Review of Globalive Wireless Management Corp. under the Canadian ownership and control regime* (29 October 2009), Telecom Decision CRTC 2009-678, online: www.crtc.gc.ca/eng/archive/2009/2009-678.htm [Telecom Decision CRTC 2009-678].

64   *Ibid.* at para. 24.

65   *Ibid.* at paras. 33 and 119.

66   The *Telecommunications Act*, above note 2, s. 12(1) enables the Governor in Council under stipulated circumstances to "vary or rescind" or "refer back for reconsideration" any decision under the Act by the CRTC. See below text accompanying notes 82–84 concerning the powers of the Governor in Council under the Act.

the effect that Globalive was not subject to *de facto* non-Canadian control.[67] The Governor in Council and the Commission both cited[68] as the source for determining *de facto* control the National Transport Agency decision in *Canadian Airlines International Ltd.* involving "the ongoing power or ability, whether exercised or not, to determine or decide the strategic decision-making activities of an enterprise."[69] Multiple factors were considered. The Commission in this instance focused on the scope of debt financing by a non-Canadian source.[70] The Governor in Council noted the *Telecommunications Act* (1993) as not imposing limits on foreign investment[71] and interpreted the Act to emphasize an absence of control by non-Canadians rather than to establish positively Canadian control.[72]

Canada's ownership restrictions are reported as near the restrictive end on a spectrum of comparison with other developed or member countries of the Organisation for Economic Co-operation and Development (OECD).[73] The TPRP panel recommended that the *Telecommunications Act* (1993) be amended to give the Governor in Council authority to waive the foreign ownership and control restrictions on Canadian carriers, pending an overall review of foreign ownership and investment in not only telecommunications but generally in Canada.[74] This has been considered and endorsed by the Competition Policy Review Panel,[75] and is consistent with the House of Commons Standing Committee on

---

67   *Governor in Council*, Order P.C. 2009–2008 (10 December 2009), a variation of Telecom Decision CRTC 2009-678, amended by Telecom Decision CRTC 2009-678-1. A PDF of the order is attached to Canada News Centre, "Government of Canada Varies CRTC Decision on Globalive" (11 December 2009), online: http://news.gc.ca/web/article-eng.do?m=/index&nid=501719#order.

68   *Governor in Council, ibid.* at 3; Telecom Decision CRTC 2009-678, above note 63 at para. 34.

69   This key passage is cited by the CRTC in Telecom Decision CRTC 2009-678, *ibid.* at para. 34. See also *Re CanWest MediaWorks Inc.* (20 December 2007), Broadcasting Decision CRTC 2007-429, online: CRTC www.crtc.gc.ca/eng/archive/2007/db2007-429.htm at para. 24, applying, with respect to Canadian ownership under the *Broadcasting Act*, above note 1, the decision of the National Transport Agency, *Canadian Airlines International Ltd.*, No. 297-A-1993 (27 May 1993) regarding substantial Canadian ownership and control of Canadian airlines. See now Canadian Transport Agency, Agency Rulings, Decision No. 297-A-1993, online: www.otc-cta.bc.ca/decision-ruling/drv.php?id=3040&1ang=eng.

70   Telecom Decision CRTC 2009-678, *ibid.* at para. 106.

71   *Governor in Council*, above note 67 at 2.

72   *Governor in Council, ibid.* at 3.

73   See *Canada's Competitive Edge*, above note 18, App. 2 – Telecommunications.

74   See TPRP Report, above note 22.

75   See CPRP Final Report, above note 19 at 337.

Industry, Science and Technology, reporting in 2003, recommending the removal of all restrictions on ownership and control of Canadian carriers.[76] The formal response from the then Government of Canada to the Standing Committee was, however, more restrained. It pointed out the divergence of this opinion from that presented just two months later, in June 2003, by the Standing Committee on Canadian Heritage, expressing concern at the prospect of the Canadian ownership requirements in both broadcasting and non-broadcasting being ameliorated.[77] The decision of the Governor in Council with respect to Globalive in 2009 moved toward a broader participation by a more liberal interpretation of *de facto* control within Canadian communications policy by enhancing competition in the wireless telephone service[78] after the applicant had succeeded in gaining wireless spectrum in the 2007–08 Advanced Wireless Spectrum auction,[79] a process implemented by government with the objective of enhancing competition.

3) Canadian Telecommunications Policy

In addition to promoting ownership and control by Canadians, Canadian telecommunications policy recognizes that telecommunication services are essential to Canada's identity and sovereignty and focuses upon the following issues:

- *Provision of Services.* An "orderly development" of "high quality" and "affordable" telecommunications services to ensure universality of accessibility and service throughout Canada without distinction between regions or between urban or rural areas; and to "safeguard, enrich and strengthen the social and economic fabric of Canada and its regions."

---

76   See Report of the Standing Committee, above note 21 at 37. Other options were discussed at 22–37. They included removal of the *control* element but not *ownership* or the reduction to a 51:49 percent ratio with a maximum of 49 percent foreign ownership.

77   See Minister of Industry, News Release, "Government Respon[se] to Industry Committee's Recommendations on Foreign Investment Restrictions in Telecommunications" (25 September 2003), online: www.ic.gc.ca/eic/site/ic1.nsf/eng/02475.html.

78   *Governor in Council*, Order P.C. 2009-2008 (10 December 2009), above note 67 at 2 and 4.

79   See below note 179 describing the success of Globalive and Quebecor in the spectrum auction. The accompanying text describes wireless spectrum and the auction process.

- *Competition and Market Forces.* Recognition of an "increased reliance" on economic efficiency and market forces assisted "where required [by] efficient and effective" regulation as the political and ideological framework for telecommunications services.
- *Research, Development, and Innovation.* The stimulation of research and development in Canada with respect to the telecommunications industry and "innovation" in providing telecommunications services.
- *Promotion of Use.* Promotion of use of Canadian facilities, nationally and internationally, responding to the "economic and social requirements of users."
- *Privacy.* A recognition of the privacy interests of users.[80]

The objective of competition and market forces supported and enabled the process of deregulation from 1979 with the introduction of competitive market theory through controlled regulatory oversight by the CRTC. Likewise, this objective supports the direction given in December 2006 by the Governor in Council to the CRTC in implementation of the TPRP Report, prescribing market forces to be the presumptive norm unless telecommunications policy cannot be achieved without regulatory intervention.[81] Competitive market forces are, therefore, the primary means of achieving Canadian telecommunications policy, apart from that of Canadian ownership requirements for Canadian carriers.

Directions from the Governor in Council to the CRTC are enabled in sections 8 to 11.[82] Directions must be general in application and of broad policy concerning the telecommunications objectives. The process is recognition in itself of the political dimensions inherent in telecommunications policy and objectives. A government of the day is accordingly enabled to implement a redirection in attaining the objectives while still preserving the benefit of an independent regulator with respect to particular applications or decisions. Additionally, section 12 provides a further jurisdiction to the Governor in Council, acting within one year after a decision by the Commission, to vary or rescind the decision or require the Commission to reconsider all or part of the decision. The process is prescribed in sections 12 to 15.[83] The legislatively prescribed objectives in themselves cannot be changed by such a direction. Nor can the legislative structure of the forbearance procedure be changed by a direction from the Governor in Council. Accordingly,

---

80 *Telecommunications Act*, above note 2, s. 7.
81 See text accompanying notes 24–25, above in this chapter.
82 *Telecommunications Act*, above note 2, ss. 8–11.
83 *Ibid.*, ss. 12–15.

the TPRP has recommended legislative amendment to the forbearance process to reflect the policy redirection.[84]

The direction in December 2006 ordered the CRTC to "rely on market forces to the maximum extent feasible" with any regulation being "to the minimum extent necessary" as well as being "efficient and proportionate."[85] In addition to prescribing related "operational practices" for the CRTC,[86] the direction requires that regulatory measures specify the particular telecommunications policy objective sought to be advanced by the regulatory measure; demonstrate compliance with the direction; if advancing a non-economic objective, do so in a "symmetrical and competitively neutral manner" between the parties involved; and "be technologically and competitively neutral . . . to enable competition from new technologies and not to *artificially favour either Canadian carriers or resellers.*"[87]

It is a strong direction for market forces. Given that this has been a significant policy of the CRTC for some time, however, and that the TPRP itself contemplated a reasonable measure of continuing regulation, especially a context of social regulatory measures (e.g., access),[88] the aim of the direction is more one of greater emphasis, presumption, degree, and mindset. Regulation is to be more of an exception than it has been. It is not regulation with a broad measure of forbearance, but broad forbearance with minimal regulation if exceptionally required to meet telecommunication objectives. The CRTC has confirmed in its three-year work plan from 2008 that this refocusing has been implemented.[89]

The concepts of exemption and forbearance are the legislative vehicles through which regulatory measures are avoided in favour of competition and market forces. The *Telecommunications Act* encompasses a variety of situations, providing to the CRTC the power to:

---

84   TPRP Report, above note 22, c. 3, Recommendations 3-3 and 3-4. The expression "Governor in Council" "means the Governor General of Canada acting by and with the advice of, or by and with the consent of, or in conjunction with the Queen's Privy Council for Canada." See *Interpretation Act*, R.S.C. 1985, c. I-21, s. 35(1).

85   *Order under Section 8*, above note 27 at para. 1(a).

86   *Ibid.* at para. 1(c).

87   *Ibid.* at para. 1(b) [emphasis added]. The portion emphasized is suggestive of a potential for foreign competition, at least through re-sellers.

88   See TPRP Report, above note 22 at 175.

89   *CRTC 3-Year Work Plan, 2008–2011*, Chairman's Message, online: CRTC www.crtc.gc.ca/eng/BACKGRND/plan2008.htm [*CRTC 3-Year Work Plan*], referring to "a more focused regulatory approach.".

1) *Exempt* from application of the Act "any class of Canadian carriers," subject to the imposition of conditions. The Commission must hold a public hearing and must be satisfied that any exemption would be consistent with the objectives of the Canadian telecommunications policy;[90] and

2) *Forbear*[91] or refrain from exercising its powers under five specific provisions, as follows:

- section 24, the imposition of conditions in any tariff approved by the Commission;
- section 25, the prohibition against a Canadian carrier carrying on business otherwise than under an approved tariff;
- section 27, requiring just and reasonable rates and no discrimination or undue or unreasonable preferences;
- section 29, the prevention, without the prior approval of the Commission, of Canadian carriers from giving effect to specified types of agreements or arrangements concerning interchange or management of telecommunications facilities, or apportionment of rates or revenues; and
- section 31, preventing, without the authority of the Commission, a Canadian carrier from limiting its liability concerning a telecommunications service.

The Act provides that any forbearance be subject to conditions and may be exercised only if it is "consistent with the Canadian telecommunications policy objectives."[92] The Act requires that the Commission forbear if it determines that the particular service is or will be subject to a sufficient level of competition protecting users. If, to the contrary, the Commission concludes on the facts that to forbear will "impair unduly" a competitive market, then it must not forbear.[93] These provisions are conceptually consistent with the enhanced emphasis on competition ordered in the direction of the Governor in Council in December 2006.[94]

Significantly, the power to forbear cannot extend beyond the five specified sections concerning, broadly, rates, preferences, and operational situations. It can have no application to the *eligibility* of a carrier to operate as a telecommunications common carrier in Canada. This is

---

90 *Telecommunications Act*, above note 2, s. 9(1).
91 *Ibid.*, s. 34(1).
92 *Ibid.*
93 *Ibid.*, ss. 34(1)–(3).
94 See above note 27.

determined under the Canadian ownership provisions in section 16.[95] However, the *exemption* power can be exercised by the Commission with respect to "the application of [the] Act," enabling it to exempt "any class of Canadian carriers" from even the Canadian ownership require- ments.[96] Neither the TPRP Report, nor the direction by the Governor in Council refer, at least directly, to this provision.

While the path to deregulation can be traced to 1979 with the fledgling policy of opening the long-distance telephone market to competition within Canada,[97] it is Telecom Decision CRTC 94-19 that established the criteria the Commission would apply when contem- plating an exercise of its forbearance power.[98] It also draws an accurate comparison between these criteria and themes found in competition law and policy.[99] By the mid 1990s, this situation had presented a per- spective of conflict between the CRTC and the Competition Bureau that would ultimately question whether industry activities should continue to reside with the CRTC or whether the supervision of the Competi- tion Bureau and Tribunal under the general *Competition Act*[100] would be more appropriate. A globalized marketplace and technological innova- tion had increased this potential. More technically, this issue was fo- cused on an application of the "regulated conduct defence," which may provide a shield against general competition regulation as a result of a prior determination by the CRTC to regulate or to exempt or forbear in the particular instance.[101]

The regulated conduct defence was reviewed in 2004 by the Su- preme Court of Canada in a context not related to telecommunications, but nevertheless involving a regulated utility collecting consumer pay-

---

95 *Telecommunications Act*, above note 2, s. 16(4) contains the prohibition against Canadian carriers operating without eligibility under s. 16.

96 *Ibid.*, s. 9(1).

97 Chapter 1, text accompanying notes 27–32.

98 *Review of Regulatory Framework* (16 September 1994), Telecom Decision CRTC 94-19, online: CRTC www.crtc.gc.ca/eng/archive/1994/DT94-19.HTM [Telecom Decision CRTC 94-19].

99 *Ibid.* at 33.

100 *Competition Act*, R.S.C. 1985, c. C-34.

101 See Don Mercer, Deputy Director of Investigation and Research (Criminal Mat- ters), Bureau of Competition Policy, "The Regulated Conduct Defence and the Telecommunications Industry" (28 September 1995) at ss. 6 & 7 in particular, online: www.competitionbureau.gc.ca/eic/site/cb-bc.nsf/eng/00986.html. More recently, see David Teal, Mergers Branch, Competition Bureau of Canada, "Tele- com Regulation and Competition Law in Canada" (27 June 2007), online: www. competitionbureau.gc.ca/eic/site/cb-bc.nsf/eng/02395.html.

ments under a regulator's authorizing determinations.[102] The collections were found to be an infringement of the *Criminal Code*.[103] Consumer refunds were ordered under equitable unjust enrichment analysis[104] for the period subsequent to the utility being on notice of possible *Criminal Code* violation notwithstanding compliance with the regulator's rate-setting determinations.[105] Collections made prior to notice of this possibility were protected.[106] The influence, if any, of this case upon "regulated conduct" as a defence in a telecommunications context has not been determined.[107] From a regulatory perspective this issue is likely to be subsumed within the administrative guidelines discussed below and the recommendations of the TPRP concerning the creation of a joint CRTC/Competition Bureau Telecommunications Competition Tribunal (TCT) for a transitional period of five years and a smaller but more streamlined CRTC with enhanced telecommunications expertise.[108] However, the relevance to telecommunications of the "regulated conduct defence" could still be tested in judicial proceedings.

---

102 *Garland v. Consumers' Gas Co.*, [2004] 1 S.C.R. 629 [*Garland*], concerning regulatory determinations of the Ontario Energy Board (OEB) sanctioning the collection of a "late payment penalty" on utility bill payments from customers. See also *A.G. of Canada v. Law Society of British Columbia*, [1982] 2 S.C.R. 307 at 347ff. for an earlier review of this defence by the S.C.C.

103 *Criminal Code*, R.S.C. 1985, c. C-46, s. 347, concerning "entering into an agreement or arrangement to receive interest at a criminal rate."

104 The test for unjust enrichment was established in Canada in *Pettkus v. Becker*, [1980] 2 S.C.R. 834 at 848, with the criteria of (1) an enrichment of the defendant; (2) a corresponding deprivation of the plaintiff; and (3) an absence of juristic reason for the enrichment. In *Garland*, above note 102, it was the third limit that received consideration on the basis of compliance with the rate setting of the regulator, the OEB. Precedent had established "disposition of law" as a juristic reason that could permit an enrichment. *Garland, ibid.* at 844, para. 49ff.

105 The orders of the OEB, being a provincial regulating authority, were found to be "inoperative" against the *Criminal Code* on the basis of constitutional paramountcy: *Garland, ibid.* at 655, para. 53.

106 Although the determination of the OEB was "inoperative" *ab initio* as *ultra vires* the province, compliance with OEB determinations provided a "reasonable expectation" of the parties that compliance was lawful. See *Garland, ibid.* at para. 55.

107 The influence may be limited by the absence of any constitutional paramountcy. Both the CRTC and the Competition Bureau/Tribunal are within federal jurisdiction.

108 See text accompanying note 26, above in this chapter.

Guidelines agreed to in 1999 and updated through 2007[109] between the CRTC and the Competition Bureau currently address the relationship of these tribunals. They provide an allocation of jurisdiction in various contexts, including exclusive jurisdiction to each tribunal. The CRTC determines exclusively issues of interconnection and access utilizing the specialized technical and economic expertise and the timely mechanism for dispute resolution provided by the Commission. Similarly, the Competition Bureau has exclusive jurisdiction in broader matters of its relative expertise: conspiracies to fix prices or lessen competition, bid rigging, and price maintenance.[110] Areas of shared jurisdiction or more complex mergers (of industry providers) are noted as invoking the jurisdiction of the Competition Bureau on competition issues inherent in any merger within industry and the CRTC with issues of Canadian ownership. Various market practices such as false or misleading advertising could also bring a shared jurisdiction. Exclusive dealing, tied selling, and other trade restraints may be exclusively for the Competition Bureau.[111] In the present context of exclusion or forbearance under the *Telecommunications Act* (1993), the guidelines provide that any unconditional exemption or forbearance in whole and unconditionally by the CRTC will invoke the jurisdiction of the Competition Bureau over the activities concerned until such time as the CRTC reviews, rescinds, or varies the exemption of forbearance.[112] Additionally, the Competition Bureau claims jurisdiction over activities partially exempted or conditionally forborne by the CRTC.[113] The CRTC has agreed to identify in its determinations the powers and duties it will no longer exercise.[114]

Implementation of the direction of the Governor in Council to the CRTC in December 2006 to "rely on market forces to the maximum extent feasible,"[115] has been acknowledged by the CRTC[116] but at the time of writing the Commission had not published any indication of its procedures to this effect. However, until the relevant legislative amendments have been made to the *Telecommunications Act*, as recommended by the TPRP,[117] especially to the forbearance procedure, the perimeters

---

109 CRTC, *CRTC/Competition Bureau Interface* (Report) (1999) online: CRTC www.crtc.gc.ca/eng/publications/reports/crtc_com.htm.
110 *Ibid.*, Parts 3 & 4.
111 *Ibid.*, Part 2.
112 *Ibid.*, Part 1.
113 *Ibid.*, second point.
114 *Ibid.*, third point.
115 See text accompanying notes 27 and 85–86, above in this chapter.
116 See *CRTC 3-Year Work Plan*, above note 89.
117 See text accompanying note 84, above in this chapter.

of existing legislation will continue to set the limits of any policy re-direction under the process for directions in section 8.

Telecom Decision CRTC 94-19, made prior to the 2006 direction, stipulates the exercise of regulatory principles between incumbent telephone companies and new entrants in the long-distance voice market. The Commission provided a detailed synopsis of its approach to the utilization of the forbearance procedure. The Commission accepted that its role in this context presented themes established in competition policy. A framework includes the following criteria:

1) If a market is or becomes workably competitive the Commission must forbear.[118]
2) The relevant market must be identified and defined. The Commission relied on the phrase "a service or a class of services" in the Act[119] to enable it to define a relevant market as "the smallest group of products and geographic area in which a firm with market power can profitably impose a sustainable price increase."[120]
3) A market (as identified and defined) is not workably competitive if a dominant firm possesses substantial market power by reason of market share, demand conditions, or supply conditions.

The Commission was led to defining "market power" and chose to reject using a fixed percentage of market control (35 percent is specified in the Competition Bureau's *Merger Enforcement Guidelines*,[121] which were serving as a comparison). The Commission chose instead to consider not only market share but also demand and supply conditions. These conditions concern the impact in the marketplace of a dominant supplier unilaterally imposing a permanent price increase. Demand conditions consider the presence of other suppliers and the economic feasibility of customers switching to those supplies, the ability of customers to reduce consumption of the product, and whether the product is essential to a customer's process. Supply conditions refer to the ability of rival firms to increase supply of the product and to accommodate "a substantial number" of new customers.[122] Factors such as significant innovation and technological change, strong marketing activities,

---

118 Telecom Decision CRTC 94-19, above note 98 at 64.
119 *Telecommunications Act*, above note 2, s. 34.
120 Telecom Decision CRTC 94-19, above note 98 at 66.
121 Competition Bureau Canada, *Merger Enforcement Guidelines* (September 2004), online: www.cb-bc.gc.ca/eic/site/cb-bc.nsf/eng/01245.html.
122 Telecom Decision CRTC 94-19, above note 98 at 68.

and an expanding scope of competitors' activities were recognized as diminishing any market dominance.[123]

The procedures noted reflect the independence of the Commission in developing the Canadian telecommunications policy. Indeed, the very first move toward deregulation of the telecommunication industry was made in 1979, notwithstanding a submission by incumbent carriers that a decision of such magnitude should be left to government.[124] However, the Act does enable the Governor in Council to give the Commission policy directions of general application,[125] and the Governor in Council may also make regulations concerning a Canadian carrier's eligibility under the Act or require that the CRTC reconsider an issue.[126] The Minister of Industry has a role with respect to technical standards. The Minister must be satisfied that any order in this context will advance the policy objectives under the Act and to this end must consult the Commission.[127]

Important powers of the Commission in achieving a competitive market for telecommunications services under the Canadian telecommunications policy are:

1) An order of interconnection of facilities between a Canadian carrier and other telecommunications facilities. The Act makes clear that while the Commission may order such compensation as it considers "just and expedient," it need not order that compensation be paid. This issue was of some controversy, as discussed earlier.[128]

2) An order requiring a Canadian carrier to adopt a specified method of identifying costs and of financial accounting for the purposes of the Act.[129]

3) An order requiring a Canadian carrier to provide, periodically or otherwise, information necessary for the purposes of the Act.[130] The Commission may likewise order such information from any other person, but not if the information "is a confidence of the executive council of a province."[131] The Act enables parties submit-

---

123 *Ibid.* at 69.
124 Telecom Decision CRTC 79-11, above note 7 at Part 9, s. 1 (General Conclusions).
125 *Telecommunications Act*, above note 2, ss. 8 and 10–14.
126 *Ibid.*, s. 22. See, for example, *Order Varying Telecom Decision* (28 December 1994) CRTC 94-19, S.I./94-143 concerning rate rebalancing between distance and local calls: increasing local call rates and reducing distance rates.
127 *Telecommunications Act*, above note 2, s. 15.
128 *Ibid.*, s. 40.
129 *Ibid.*, s. 37(1)(a).
130 *Ibid.*, s. 37(1)(b).
131 *Ibid.*, s. 37(2).

ting information to designate the information as confidential,[132] but the Commission may release so designated information if it considers that disclosure is in the public interest.[133] Unfettered, this presents an extraordinary degree of power with respect to information provided to the Commission by third parties or non-Canadian carriers. However, an appeal on a question of law[134] lies to the Federal Court of Appeal, with leave of the court,[135] or a review may be sought from the Governor in Council on the merits.[136] Apart from the determination by the Commission to disclose information in the public interest, the confidentiality of information, if so designated by the supplier when initially presented to the Commission, is maintained. It is generally even inadmissible in judicial proceedings. One exception is proceedings for failing to submit the information, which in itself provides an initial procedure for judicial review of any order to supply made by the Commission.[137]

The current regulatory framework for the establishment of competitive telecommunication services from Telecom Decision CRTC 94-19[138] included rate assessment reform. Focusing on the long-distance market rate assessment by *price* was adopted over the historical monopolistic emphasis on *earnings*. The latter simply enabled a service provider to determine the extent of earnings that it considered it needed and to set rates that achieved that target. The move to price regulation facilitated competition by establishing a rate "price cap" with the encouragement to price services below the cap in competition between incumbents and new entrants to the market.[139]

The intention to include local exchange service is implicit, but first local rates had to increase over a transition period to bring them closer to local costs, compensating for the lost subsidy of local service from long-distance service that had been the historical position. This "rate

---

132 *Ibid.*, s. 39(1). The purposes allowed, for a designation under this section, include trade secret, financial, competitive, commercial, or scientific secrets.

133 *Ibid.*, ss. 39(4) & 39(5).

134 A matter such as whether information constitutes a trade secret and whether a public interest in disclosure outweighs the private commercial interest in non-disclosure, would constitute a question of law.

135 *Telecommunications Act*, above note 2, s. 64.

136 *Ibid.*, s. 12. See text accompanying notes 220–25, below in this chapter, concerning use of s. 12 in the context of Internet voice communications.

137 *Ibid.*, ss. 39(2), 39(3), and 39(6). Other specified exceptions are proceedings for "forgery, perjury or false declaration in relation to submission of the information."

138 Telecom Decision CRTC 94-19, above note 98.

139 *Ibid.* at Part 2.

rebalancing" occurred from 1996 to 1998. It provided a basis for Telecom Decision 97-8[140] to enhance local exchange competition with measures including interconnection by incumbent local exchange carriers (ILECs) of competitive local exchange carriers (CLECs) by wireline or wireless service providers (WSPs); the provision of industry standard network interfaces; unbundling or separation of component services or features of local networks; and a universal application of public interest features, including 911 emergency service, message relay service (MRS) for hearing impaired, and privacy or security features for customers. ILECs were also subject to rate setting by price cap.[141]

In 2005, the CRTC expressed concern that CLECs had gained little market share in local exchange telephone since 1997 and called for public comment on how the forbearance mechanism might be modified from the overall principles prescribed in Telecom Decision CRTC 94-19[142] to enhance local exchange competition.[143] In this context, attention has focused on theories invoking either "facilities-based" or "service-based" competition. The latter involves the new entrant or CLEC using by purchase, lease, or other arrangement the facilities infrastructure of the ILEC. Facility-based competition is seen as more competitive as the entrant must provide its own facilities, resulting in opportunities for technological and economic efficiencies from innovation.[144] Responding to submissions received, the CRTC stipulated criteria for local telephone forbearance of regulation of ILECs.[145] These criteria were modified by the Governor in Council.[146]

---

140 *Local competition* (1 May 1997), Telecom Decision CRTC 97-8, online: CRTC www.crtc.gc.ca/eng/archive/1997/DT97-8.htm [Telecom Decision CRTC 97-8].

141 See also *Local Pay Telephone Competition* (30 June 1998), Telecom Decision CRTC 98-8, online: CRTC www.crtc.gc.ca/eng/archive/1998/DT98-8.htm.

142 See text accompanying note 98, above in this chapter.

143 *Forbearance from Regulation of Local Exchange Services* (28 April 2005), Telecom Public Notice CRTC 2005-2, online: CRTC www.crtc.gc.ca/eng/archive/2005/pt2005-2.htm [Telecom Public Notice CRTC 2005-2].

144 See Lemay-Yates Associates Inc., "The Implications of Facilities-based Competition in Telecom" (Report presented to AT &T Canada Inc., August 2002), online: www.lya.com/en/PDF/ATTC%20Report%20FINAL2.pdf; Marc Bourreau & Pinar Dogan, "Service-based vs. Facility-based Competition in Local Access Networks" (2004) 16 Information Economics and Policy 287, online: www.ses.telecom-paristech.fr/bourreau/Recherche/policyLL.pdf.

145 *Forbearance from the Regulation of Retail Local Exchange Services* (6 April 2006), Telecom Decision CRTC 2006-15, online: CRTC www.crtc.gc.ca/eng/archive/2006/dt2006-15.htm [Telecom Decision CRTC 2006-15].

146 *Order Varying Telecom Decision CRTC 2006-15*, S.O.R./2007-71 (4 April 2007), P.C. 2007-532 (4 April 2007), C. Gaz. 2007.II.408–14 [P.C. 2007-532]. See also

Overall, there are three alternative tests, any one being sufficient to allow forbearance. A "competitive principles" test originates in the Competition Bureau submission to the CRTC[147] and allows forbearance when:

(1) At least two independent facilities-based service providers must exist, the ILEC and a facilities-based entrant, capable of offering local service that has been determined to fall within the relevant product market for ILEC local service;

(2) The entrant [is] able to obtain and retain a customer base;

(3) The entrant's variable costs of providing local service are similar to or lower than the ILEC's variable costs of providing local service;

(4) Neither the ILEC nor the entrant [is] capacity-constrained;

(5) There [is] evidence of vigorous rivalry between the ILEC and the entrant in the provision of local service; and

(6) Industry characteristics are such that the ILECs are unlikely to engage in anti-competitive behaviour.[148]

Meeting these criteria is taken as demonstrating that an ILEC does not have "market power," the factual criterion that will preclude forbearance.[149] Addressing this issue, the Commissioner of Competition considered the Bureau's proposal as sufficient to avoid the time and complexity of factually establishing market power, while also avoiding an analysis of simply "market share," itself seen as insufficient to assess the competitive measure of a market accurately.[150]

---

the accompanying Regulatory Policy Statement (*ibid.* at 414–21) setting out and explaining the order.

147 Commissioner of Competition, "Telecom Public Notice CRTC 2005-2 – Forbearance from Regulation of Local Exchange Services" (Paper presented to the CRTC 27 September 2005), online: Competition Bureau www.competitionbureau.gc.ca/eic/site/cb-bc.nsf/en/01950e.html.

148 Telecom Decision CRTC 2006-15, above note 145 at para. 213, modified by para. 242(a)(i) of P.C. 2007-532, above note 146 at para. 2.

149 *Ibid.* at para. 214.

150 See *ibid.* at para. 237 (not subject to modification by the Governor in Council), adopting from Telecom Decision CRTC 94-19 (the general forbearance CRTC decision), above note 98, that "market power" can be assessed by three factors: first, market share; second, the ability to make price changes that affect customer response; and third, the ability to impose supply conditions that affect the ability of competitors to respond to a price change. Compare Commissioner of Competition, above note 147, drawing a comparison with the concept of "market power" in the *Merger Enforcement Guidelines 2004*, Part 2, online: www.cb-bc.gc.ca/eic/site/cb-bc.nsf/vwapj/2004%20MEGs.Final.pdf/$file/2004%20MEGs.Final.pdf.

A "competitive facilities" test concerns *residential* service and allows forbearance if, in addition to the ILEC, there are "at least two independent facilities-based telecommunications service providers," including mobile wireless services. The additional two providers must each be capable of serving at least 75 percent of the residential lines capable of being served by the ILEC. One of these two additional providers must also be a fixed-line provider, in addition to the fixed-line service of the ILEC.[151]

A "competitive facilities" test concerns *business* service and allows forbearance if, in addition to the ILEC, there is at least another independent facilities-based fixed-line telecommunications provider capable of serving at least 75 percent of the business lines capable of being served by the ILEC.[152]

The criterion constituting an "independent" provider refers to being neither owned nor affiliated with other providers referred to in the respective assessment.[153] In addition, "facilities-based" for the purpose of these requirements may include a combination of facilities owned and facilities leased from other providers.[154] A prerequisite for forbearance is the demonstration by an ILEC that for six of the eight months prior to seeking forbearance it has, on average, consistently met the quality criteria for services it has provided to competitors.[155]

The key modification of the Governor in Council was the removal of requirements that limited ILECs in offering promotions or "win back" advantages to customers returning to ILECs from new entrant competitors.[156] In December 2007, the CRTC called for submissions as to criteria to be applied to determine the eligibility of promotional offerings for forbearance purposes.[157] In May 2008, the CRTC determined that promotions should have a combined enrolment and benefit period of not more than twelve months with a cooling-off period of at least half of this combined period. There must also be no other current, or recently lapsed, promotions involving the same services and geographic area.[158]

---

151 Telecom Decision CRTC 2006-15, above note 145 at para. 242(a)(ii).
152 *Ibid.* at para. 242(a)(iii).
153 *Ibid.* at para. 243.
154 *Ibid.*
155 *Ibid.* at para. 519.
156 *Ibid.* at paras. 483–88 deleted and substituted by new para. 483 by Order of Governor in Council at para. 3.
157 *Regulatory framework for local wireline service promotions of incumbent local exchange service* (19 December 2007), Telecom Public Notice CRTC 2007-21, online: CRTC www.crtc.gc.ca/eng/archive/2007/pt2007-21.htm.
158 *Forbearance from the regulation of promotions for retail residential and business local wireline services* (22 May 2008), Telecom Decision CRTC 2008-41, online:

4) Wireless Communications

The enhanced competition available in long-distance and local ex-change services pales in comparison to that resulting from wireless communication devices. Indeed, mobile cellular telephone service may well supplant wireline telephone service as the primary voice telephone system in the society of tomorrow, if not of today. In 2004, Industry Canada reported an average annual revenue growth rate of 14 percent in the wireless sector since 1998. The wireline segment had been "rela-tively stagnant" over the period.[159] In addition, there is a convergence of mobile voice communications systems with alphanumeric communi-cations services such as the RIM Blackberry[160] or similarly operating devices,[161] voice over Internet service,[162] and wireless Internet connect-ors such as WiFi and Bluetooth.[163]

The primary basis of wireless technology is radio (micro/Hertzian wave) frequencies, the spectrum for which is finite and is controlled by governments in availability and allocation.[164] Point-to-point societal radio communications was focused primarily on walkie-talkies and

---

CRTC www.crtc.gc.ca/eng/archive/2008/dt2008-41.htm.

159 See Industry Canada, *Telecommunications Service in Canada: An Industry Over-view*, Market Segments, s. 22, (Canadian Service Market, 2007), online: www.ic.gc.ca/epic/site/smt-gst.nsf/en/sf06019e.html.

160 The Blackberry combines cell telephone (GSM standard, see text accompany-ing note 167, below in this chapter) with e-mail and Internet technology. The manufacturer, Research in Motion (RIM), reports 3.65 million subscribers from 1999 to 2005. See Tracy V. Wilson, "How a Blackberry Works," online: communication.howstuffworks.com/blackberry.htm; and McGill University-Network and Communications Services, "How Does the Blackberry Work?" online: http://knowledgebase.mcgill.ca/display/2n/articleDirect/index.asp?aid=2484&r=0.3787958.

161 See J.A. Martin, "Mobile Computing: Blackberry Alternatives," *PC World* (19 January 2006), online: www.pcworld.com/article/124082/mobile_computing_blackberry_alternatives.html.

162 See text accompanying notes 203–25, below in this chapter.

163 These systems provide a short range (usually within buildings), inexpensive wireless connection for Internet and e-mail access. A wireless adapter in, say, a laptop converts data to a radio signal and transmits it to a router via antennae. The router makes a wired connection to the Internet system. See "How WiFi Works," online: computer.howstuffworks.com/wireless-network.htm; and "How Bluetooth Works," online: www.howstuffworks.com/bluetooth.htm.

164 The limited spectrum resource is described succinctly in *Cognitive Radio, Spectrum and Radio Resource Management*, Wireless World Research Forum, Working Group 6, White Paper at 16 noting: "*Apparent Spectrum Scarcity*: The current method of allotting spectrum provides each new service with its own fixed block of spectrum. Since the amount of usable spectrum is finite, as more services are added, there will come a time at which spectrum is no longer

Citizens' Band (CB) radio. These devices are characterized by high-power transmitters but limited channels, limited range, and limited capacity because the sender and the receiver utilize the same frequency and only one can talk at a time. In the latter respect, they are known as "half-duplex" devices.[165] Limitations on capacity and range have been ameliorated first by cell technology and then by digital conversion and compression technology. Cell technology is the division of an urban area into "cells," or sub-areas.[166] Signals are received by low-power transmitters in each cell, then passed to others, with ultimate connection to the national telephone or cable transmission system, which may include satellite systems. Additionally, utilizing dual frequencies sufficiently separated from each other gives the capacity for simultaneous switching of sending and receiving, known as "full duplex" capacity.

From a North American perspective (Canada and the United States) there is a technical limitation to global usage of a cellphone if a service provider utilizes the historically common frequency standard known as Code Division Multiple Access (CDMA). The rest of the world utilizes the Global System for Mobile Communications (GSM) standard. Cellphone transmissions cannot "roam" (i.e., search for connectivity when outside their geographic origin or home network) between CDMA and GSM frequency standards. However, some cellphone service providers in North America do operate on the GSM standard, and therefore have global calling capacity. In Canada, these are historically linked with providers utilizing the cable infrastructure system (principally Fido and Rogers).[167] The Apple iPhone, released in the United States in June 2007 and in Canada in July 2008, is GSM standard and combines cell telephone with e-mail, messaging, Internet browsing, photography, and personal music selections.[168] An overview of the service providers

---

available for allotment," online: www.wireless-world-research.org/fileadmin/.../ WG6_WP4.pdf. See also Chapter 1, note 84.

165 A walkie-talkie is described as having a range of 1.6 km (1 mile) with a typical 0.25 watt transmitter and one channel. A CB radio device brings a range of 8 km (5 miles) with a typical 5 watt transmitter and approximately 40 channels. See Julia Layton, Marshall Brian, & Jeff Tyson, *How Cell Phones Work*, online: www. howstuffworks.com/cell-phone.htm.

166 *Ibid.* Additionally there is "time division multiplexing," whereby signals are separated on the same frequency by different time allocations.

167 See Layton, Marshall, and Tyson, above note 165. Principal Canadian service providers, Telus and Bell, switched as recently as 2010 from CDMA to GSM frequency standard for their mobility services. See online: www.electronista.com/ articles/08/10/10/bell-and-telus.pick.4g/.

168 See Tracy V. Wilson, *How the iPhone Works*, online: http://electronics.howstuffworks.com/iphone.htm.

in the Canadian mobile voice and data communications system is provided by Industry Canada.[169]

Operating outside the cellphone system, wholly satellite-based systems involving voice or data transmission need no terrestrial antennae. Each handset is itself a terminal that transmits and receives directly to and from a satellite. However, communications to non-satellite connections are transmitted to whichever satellite is located above an appropriate terrestrial gateway through which signals are downlinked to the global telephone or Internet infrastructure. Satellite system service providers may provide global or regional coverage. The Iridium system comprises sixty-six satellites orbiting at an altitude of 780 kilometres and allocated evenly in six orbital planes. Each satellite orbits the earth in 100 minutes with ease of transfer of voice and data between satellites. Communication is possible from and to any place on earth, including the poles. This contrasts with cell telephone, on which calls can be made only from places within range of an antenna.[170]

In October 1993, the CRTC found the provision of wireless telecommunications to constitute a "telecommunications service" within the *Telecommunications Act* (1993) and if provided by a Canadian carrier[171] under the Act to be subject to regulation by the Commission.[172] However, forbearance was exercised by the CRTC with respect to cell telephone services and public cordless telephone service, including when offered by affiliates of the telephone companies but not if provided by the telephone companies themselves. Various safeguards, including that of confidentiality of subscribers and prevention of financial cross-subsidizations, were retained with respect to these affiliates, the

---

169 See Industry Canada, above note 159, s. 4(2)(8), Wireless Satellite Internet and Mobile Internet (2007), online: www.ic.gc.ca/epic/site/smt-gst.nsf/en/sf07005e. html.

170 See Iridium Communications, "About Iridium" and "How It Works," online: www.iridium.com/about/howitworks.php. In Canada see *Infosat Communications*, online: www.infosat.com/prod_serv/voice/mobile/iridium/default.aspx. Other providers of beyond regional coverage include Inmarsat (www.mackay-satellite.com/satellite-equipment/inmarsat/isatphone) and Globestar (www. globestar.com).

171 See Figure 1 in text following note 56, above in this chapter, illustrating the meaning of "Canadian carrier" within the *Telecommunications Act*, above note 2, s. 2(1) definitions.

172 *Regulation of Wireless Services* (12 August 1994), Telecom Decision CRTC 94-15 at para. 4 (Conclusions), online: CRTC http://crtc.gc.ca/eng/ archive/1994%5CDT94-15.htm [Telecom Decision CRTC 94-15].

primary consideration being the independence of the mobile service from the telephone companies primary or land-line service.[173]

Forbearance was confirmed in December 1996 after the CRTC had sought public comment[174] and considered the position afresh.[175] In the intervening period, there had been doubts as to the categorization of cell telephone and public cordless telephone services as constituting a market distinct from other types of mobile wireless telecommunications services. Such a categorization had, in turn, recognized that these services[176] competed (by product substitution) with each other, thereby operating within the same market. The CRTC determined the division of mobile services to be between mobile voice wireless services connected to public switched (land-line) services on the one hand and all remaining wireless services on the other.[177]

In May 2008, Industry Canada opened the Internet-based bidding process in an auction of 105 megahertz (MHz) of Advance Wireless Service (AWS) radio frequency spectrum. Of this, 40 MHz was reserved for new entrants. These entrants could also bid for the remaining frequencies. The objective was the enhancement of competition in wireless cell telephone services,[178] and it succeeded. At the conclusion on 27 July 2008, two new entrants were reported to have acquired enough spectrum to build a national wireless company.[179] Regional suppliers were also strengthened.[180]

Cell telephone technology, being radio technology, must be allocated a frequency band in the overall spectrum of frequencies that include

---

173 *Ibid.* An exemption was also provided for "other wireless services" (mobile radio and paging) by non-telephone companies.

174 *Regulation of Mobile Wireless Services* (10 January 1996), Telecom Public Notice CRTC 96-2, online: CRTC www.crtc.gc.ca/eng/archive/1996/PT96-2.htm.

175 *Regulation of Wireless Communications Services* (23 December 1996) Conclusions, Telecom Decision CRTC 96-14, online: CRTC www.crtc.gc.ca/eng/archive/1996/DT96-14.htm.

176 In addition, "enhanced specialized mobile radio" (ESMR) was included, *ibid.*

177 *Ibid.*, Conclusions. In the result, forbearance was exercised with respect to both categories. The latter category had been "exempted" in Telecom Decision 94-15, above note 172. The exemption was revoked.

178 Industry Canada, "Government of Canada Opens Up Wireless Industry to More Competition" (27 May 2008), online: www.ic.gc.ca/eic/site/ic1.nsf/eng/04212.html.

179 Simon Avery, "Wireless License Sale Sets Stage for Cheaper Services" *The Globe and Mail* (21 July 2008) (re "Globalive" and "Quebecor"), online: www.reportonbusiness.com/servlet/story/RTGAM.20080721.wwireless0721/BNStory/Business/home.

180 Alberta (Shaw), Quebec (Quebecor), and Atlantic Canada (Bragg), Simon Avery, *ibid.*

broadcasting services, governmental and industry communications, and even remotely controlled apparatus or devices.[181] A frequency, in itself, is a measure of the oscillation of radio electromagnetic wavelengths. The spectrum extends from extremely low to extremely high, with many intermediate bands[182] at which various transmissions operate. As noted earlier, the availability of these pathways through the air are intangible but finite.[183] The Minister of Industry has a statutory obligation for Canada's radio frequency spectrum.[184] International arrangements are set by treaty[185] and overseen by the International Telecommunication Union (ITU).[186] The intangible, extraterritorial nature of frequency was, it will be recalled, influential in determining radio communications to be within constitutionally federal jurisdiction.[187]

Since 1992, Industry Canada has issued three editions of a Spectrum Policy Framework for Canada (SPFC): first in 1992, then 2002, and most recently 2007.[188] From 2007, a distinction has been drawn between the one overall policy objective stipulated in the SPFC and the guidelines to be followed to this end. The objective is to utilize the frequency spectrum resource for the social and economic benefits of Canadians. The primary source of the objective is the *Radiocommunication Act*, but relevant objectives under the *Telecommunications Act* are included and the overall formulation is seen as encompassing those of both enactments.[189] Given the generality of the one objective, the guidelines are the essential point of focus. They emphasize market forces; minimally intrusive, efficient, and effective regulation only when re-

---

181 This spectrum is conveniently illustrated in a colour-coded chart provided by Industry Canada. See online: www.ic.gc.ca/eic/site/smt-gst.nsf/vwapj/spectallocation-08.pdf/$FILE/spectallocation-08.pdf.

182 For example, ELF (extremely low frequency), ULF (ultra low frequency), MF (medium frequency), and UHF (ultra high frequency).

183 See note 164, above in this chapter.

184 *Department of Industry Act*, S.C. 1995, c. 1. s. 4(1)(k)(ii).

185 A classic example is Industry Canada, *Treaty Series 1962 No. 15: Operation of Certain Radio Equipment or Station* (24 October 1962), online: www.ic.gc.ca/eic/site/smt-gst.nsf/vwapj/1962-15E.PDF/$FILE/1962-15E.PDF. Now the International Telecommunication Union publishes a collection of radio regulations every four years. See online: www.itu.int/ITU-R/information/docs/rr-res646-en.pdf.

186 International Telecommunication Union, *ibid*.

187 Chapter 1, Section C(1).

188 Industry Canada, "SPFC – Spectrum Policy Framework for Canada," Notice DGTP.001-07 (2007), online: www.ic.gc.ca/epic/site/smt-gst.nsf/en/sf08776e.html [Spectrum Policy Framework].

189 *Ibid*. at para. 43; *Radiocommunication Act*, above note 3; *Telecommunications Act*, above note 2.

quired; transparent and reasoned regulation with public consultation; flexible use of spectrum, including its reallocation where appropriate; clearly defined obligations and privileges in any allocation; and international harmonization, but with protection of Canada's sovereignty, security, and public safety.[190]

5) Construction and Expropriation Powers

In exercising jurisdiction under the Act, the CRTC may exercise extensive powers concerning the provision of telecommunications facilities; their construction, operation, and maintenance; the acquisition of any property; and the imposition of any "system or method to be adopted."[191]

An order may apply to "any person interested in or affected by the order" and may be made subject to conditions, including the payment of compensation[192] and who shall bear the costs of the work ordered.[193] Any land (or interest in land) can be acquired through the procedures in the federal *Expropriation Act*[194] upon the Canadian carrier obtaining the approval of the Commission and advising the appropriate Minister of the Crown, who then exercises discretion as to an expropriation involving payment of compensation.[195]

Both a Canadian carrier and a "distribution undertaking" (i.e., a cable television or radio distributor as defined in the *Broadcasting Act* (1991)) are authorized to "break up" any highway or other public place for the purpose of laying transmission lines and cables, so long as there is no undue interference with public use of the area.[196] Consent of the relevant municipality or other local authority is required, but if it is not given, the Commission may grant approval. In effect, the Commission acts as an adjudicator between the Canadian carrier or distribution undertaking and the local authority.[197] The activities would need in pith and substance to constitute "telecommunications" in order to avoid issues of constitutional jurisdiction.[198]

---

190 Spectrum Policy Framework, above note 188 at para. 4(4).
191 *Telecommunications Act*, above note 2, s. 42(1).
192 *Ibid.*
193 *Ibid.*, s. 42(2).
194 *Expropriation Act*, R.S.C. 1985, c. E-21.
195 *Telecommunications Act*, above note 2, s. 46.
196 *Ibid.*, s. 43(1).
197 *Ibid.*, ss. 43(3)–45.
198 See Chapter 1, Section C(3).

6) Unsolicited Telecommunications

The Commission is empowered to prohibit or regulate use of facilities for unsolicited telecommunications. A balance with freedom of expression must be struck.[199] An example of an exercise of this jurisdiction is the "Do Not Call" registry concerning telemarketing.[200]

7) Canadian Carrier and the Internet

The essential juristic entity for application of the *Telecommunications Act* (1993) has been noted as the "Canadian carrier." The definition of this entity is interwoven with many other expressions defined in the Act, and has been illustrated earlier.[201] The key features constituting a "Canadian carrier" as a "telecommunications common carrier" is the ownership or operation of a system or infrastructure "between network termination points"[202] that provides services to the public for compensation by transmissions of intelligence. The Internet is a medium capable of broadcast and non-broadcast telecommunications. The latter includes Internet voice telecommunications, a developing vehicle that has attracted determinations by the CRTC despite being Internet based. Additionally, there may be broader dimensions of applying the status "Canadian carrier" to Internet communications and in particular to Internet service providers (ISPs).

a) Internet Voice Communications
In 1999, the CRTC determined that for the time being it would not attempt to regulate the Internet, at least from the perspective of broadcasting.[203] Voice communication services using Internet Protocol (IP) are different. In 2004, the CRTC provided its preliminary views on the regulatory framework for such services.[204] The Internet enables media

---

199 *Telecommunications Act*, above note 2, s. 41. Compare the striking of a balance between freedom of expression and the provisions of the *Broadcasting Act*, above note 1, s. 2(3) and (regarding the CBC) s. 46(5). See text accompanying notes 362–63, below in this chapter.

200 See Chapter 3, text accompanying note 236. See also Chapter 3, Section D(2) concerning spam.

201 *Telecommunications Act*, above note 2, s. 2. See text following note 56, above in this chapter.

202 *Ibid.*, s. 2: definition of "transmission facility," linked through the definition "telecommunications common carrier" to "Canadian carrier."

203 See text accompanying note 33, above in this chapter.

204 See *Regulatory framework for voice communication services using Internet Protocol* (7 April 2004), Telecom Public Notice CRTC 2004-2, online: CRTC www.crtc. gc.ca/eng/archive/2004/pt2004-2.htm [Telecom Public Notice CRTC 2004-2].

of voice, pictures, video, and data to be expressed in bytes and communicated through an IP. By 2004, high-quality voice communications could efficiently use IP through broadband high-speed access.

Referred to as VoIP, the communications had developed beyond the regular peer-to-peer (P2P) computer connections using software common to both sender and receiver, such as with file swapping of musical or video subject matter. VoIP now utilizes regular telephone numbers with universal access through regular telephone switching networks.[205] In effect it presents an alternative telephone system, leading the CRTC, applying the principle of technological neutrality, to determine that VoIP ought to be subject to the regulatory framework, including forbearance, applicable to Canadian carriers.[206]

Stages can be identified in the regulatory response to VoIP. The preliminary position of the CRTC was that in 2004, when public opinion was sought,[207] VoIP was determined to be treated as a local exchange service with respect to the ability to make and receive calls exclusively within a local calling area.[208] This would bring VoIP within the regulatory framework for local competition established by the Commission in 1997.[209] VoIP service provided by ILECs (the established telephone company in an area) would need to comply with existing tariffs, or new tariffs for which approval might be sought by the carrier. This would not be applicable to VoIP service provided by non-incumbents, such as incumbent telephone companies from outside of the area or new CLECs.[210]

Additionally, the Commission addressed the relationship of VoIP with key ancillary features ordinarily required to be met by local exchange providers: emergency 911 regular and 911 enhanced[211] provisions, MRS for hearing impaired, and technical features to protect privacy.[212] The Commission contemplated that as soon as practicable these requirements should be met by VoIP as a condition of providing service. In the meantime, VoIP subscribers were to be informed of

---

205 The telephone numbers are those on the North American Numbering Plan, giving access through the Public Switched Telephone Network (PSTN). See Telecom Public Notice CRTC 2004-2, *ibid.* at paras. 1–7.
206 *Ibid.* at paras. 18 and 23.
207 *Ibid.* at para. 30.
208 *Ibid.* at para. 25.
209 Telecom Decision CRTC 97-8, above note 140. See text accompanying notes 140–41, above in this chapter.
210 Telecom Public Notice CRTC 2004-2, above note 204 at para. 24.
211 Essentially, Automatic Location Identification (ALI) of a 911 caller involving the passing to emergency services of the location of the caller.
212 Call tracing and call blocking were specifically noted.

the unavailability of such services.[213] Access to VoIP by persons with disabilities was identified to be considered[214] and non-re-seller VoIP service providers were determined to be within the contribution requirements to the central fund for subsidization of local residential services in rural and remote areas.[215]

The second stage was the CRTC's principal determinations in May 2005.[216] The Commission confirmed point-to-point computer connections not connecting to the Public Switched Telephone Network (PSTN)[217] would not be subject to the regulation.[218] However, connections to the PSTN would be subject to regulation and ILECs would have to meet all the requirements imposed on local telephone companies noted in its preliminary determination.[219] The Commission declined to forbear from such regulation, finding VoIP to operate in the same market as local telephone exchange services.

The third stage brought the Commission into conflict with the government. Utilizing section 12 of the Act,[220] the ILECs petitioned the Governor in Council and succeeded in gaining an order that the Commission reconsider its determination.[221] The Commission invited further public comments[222] but confirmed its earlier decision.[223] The Governor in Council responded with a formal variation ordering the CRTC to forbear. VoIP was seen as a distinct class of local telephone

---

213 Telecom Public Notice CRTC 2004-2, above note 204 at paras. 26 & 27.

214 *Ibid.* at para. 27.

215 *Ibid.* at para. 28.

216 *Regulatory framework for voice communication services using Internet Protocol* (12 May 2005), Telecom Decision CRTC 2005-28, online: CRTC www.crtc. gc.ca/eng/archive/2005/dt2005-28.htm [Telecom Decision CRTC 2005-28]; and *Regulatory framework for voice communication services using Internet Protocol* (30 June 2005), Telecom Decision 2005-28-1, online: CRTC www.crtc.gc.ca/eng/ archive/2005/dt2005-28-1.htm.

217 See above note 205.

218 Telecom Decision CRTC 2005-28, above note 216 at paras. 16 & 17.

219 See text accompanying notes 211–15, above in this chapter.

220 *Telecommunications Act,* above note 2, s. 12. See text accompanying notes 82–84, above in this chapter, describing the nature of orders by the Governor in Council.

221 *Reconsideration of Regulatory framework for voice communication services using Internet Protocol* (10 May 2006), Telecom Decision CRTC 2005-28, P.C. 2006-1314, online: CRTC www.crtc.gc.ca/eng/archive/2006/pt2006-6.htm.

222 *Telecom Public Notice – Reconsideration of Regulatory framework for voice communication services using Internet Protocol* (1 September 2006), Telecom Decision CRTC 2006-53, online: CRTC www.crtc.gc.ca/eng/archive/2006/dt2006-53.htm.

223 *Reconsideration of Regulatory framework for voice communication services using Internet Protocol* (1 September 2006), Telecom Decision CRTC 2006-53, online: CRTC www.crtc.gc.ca/eng/archive/2006/dt2006-53.htm.

service, involving no provision of network facilities and presenting new and rapidly evolving technology. Forbearing for ILECs (area incumbents) was seen as promoting competition, given that CLECs (competing carriers) were not subject to regulation.[224] The CRTC implemented the variation.[225]

b) Are Internet Service Providers Canadian Carriers?

A useful test of the scope of this entity "Canadian carrier" is to analyze whether it can apply to an ISP or an operator of an website. The requirement of emitting, transmitting, or receiving intelligence is met. Whether it is a service to the public for compensation will depend on the context but would ordinarily be met. The requirement of ownership or operation of a system or infrastructure "between network termination points" is more difficult. It is suggested that a system need not be physical, so that an ISP would be likely to qualify by providing a digital electronic connection to the Internet.[226] Similarly, a website operator would be likely to qualify, as signals are emitted and received upon a connection or access by a user. Would such communications occur, however, "between network termination points"? Every Internet connection has termination points, but are they "network" termination points? The expression "network" is not defined in the *Telecommunications Act* (1993) and the definition of such in the *Broadcasting Act* (1991) is focused on programs and cannot, therefore, assist. An Internet-related definition of "network" is "[a] group of two or more computer systems linked together."[227] This, it is suggested, would be sufficient to bring an ISP or a website operator within the *Telecommunications Act* (1993).

This may be significant, quite apart from any regulatory potential, which the Commission has rejected at the present time. First, if an ISP or website operator qualifies as a Canadian carrier, then the statutory

---

224 *Order Varying Telecom Decision CRTC 2005-28*, P.C. 2006-1314, C. Gaz.2006. II.1941.

225 *Access-independent VoIP Services Pursuant to Order in Council P.C. 2006-1314* (16 November 2006), Telecom Circular CRTC 2006-10, online: www.crtc.gc.ca/eng/archive/2006/ct2006-10.htm.

226 In 2004, the Supreme Court of Canada found the provision of an Internet connection by an ISP to be within the phrase "providing the means of telecommunications" in the *Copyright Act*, R.S.C. 1985, c. C-42, s. 2.4(1)(b), and thereby exempt from liability for "communicating a work to the public by telecommunication" under s. 3(1)(f) of the *Copyright Act*. See *Society of Composers, Authors and Music Publishers of Canada v. Canadian Association of Internet Providers*, [2004] 2 S.C.R. 427 at para. 54ff. [*Tariff 22*].

227 See *Webster's Computer and Internet Dictionary*, 3d ed., s.v. "network."

prohibition against control over content[228] may preclude any potential ISP liability for content on its server.[229] Second, the *Telecommunications Act* (1993) expressly provides a civil remedy for anyone sustaining injury from an act or omission contrary to the Act. If an ISP is a Canadian carrier and fails to meet the terms of the Act (for example, by unjustly discriminating with respect to access to its server or engaging in an undue or unreasonable preference concerning the provision of a telecommunications service),[230] a civil proceeding may be available.

8) International Dimensions

a) Cables and Satellites

Cable and satellite communications have blended together in the communications infrastructure. Television broadcasts have switched significantly to satellite delivery, particularly with respect to reception by cable companies for retransmission, network distribution to affiliates, pay television, and specialty services networks. While early satellites merely reflected a radio signal back to earth, later generations amplified and retransmitted the earthbound signal, presenting three broad stages of communication satellites from the 1960s, '70s, and '80s.[231] The greater reach (footprint) of satellite-to-earth signals presents for Canadian regulations a macrocosm of the traditional cross-border receipt of microwave radio and television signals. Prevention of receipt of unauthorized signals is difficult, necessitating government and regulatory bodies to accept that any countering of cultural influence would have to follow through positive promotion of Canadian culture through Canadian radio, television, and cable industries. Canada, of course, wishes to utilize technology and to be at the forefront of technological development, even though it is the same technology that itself diminishes Canada's ability to maintain its cultural policies.[232]

From the 1980s into the '90s, the industry saw growth in the direct broadcast satellite (DBS) system, which enabled recipients to receive sat-

---

228 *Telecommunications Act*, above note 2, s. 36 ("[e]xcept where the Commission approves otherwise").

229 See also Chapter 5, text accompanying notes 266–84.

230 *Telecommunications Act*, above note 2, s. 72. A two-year limitation period from the day on which the act or omission occurred is imposed.

231 John Strick, "Socio-Economic Influences of Satellite Communications Technology" in Rowland M. Lorimer & Donald C. Wilson, eds., *Communication Canada: Issues in Broadcasting and New Technologies* (Toronto: Kagan & Woo, 1988) 263 at 266–67.

232 See Jean McNulty, "Technology and Nation-Building in Canadian Broadcasting" in *Communication Canada*, *ibid.* at 176 and 180–81.

ellite transmissions in much the same way as cable companies receive terrestrial signals but by means of increasingly smaller satellite signal receiving dishes. These DTH satellite systems operate with geostationary satellites[233] that present a hemispheric footprint encompassing all of the North America.[234] Short of controlling the physical possession of receiving dishes,[235] the CRTC can only authorize or license a Canadian provider to receive broadcast signals from the United States for retransmission (with Canadian programs[236]) to Canadian subscribers and enable authorized or licensed DTH providers to bring proceedings against any activity by an unlicensed operator.[237] The Commission not only licensed Canadian DTH satellite distribution undertakings[238] but facilitated competition by authorizing certain satellite relay distribution undertakings (SRDUs) in Canada[239] to distribute DTH television and radio links in addition to cable distributions.[240]

For several years, there was uncertainty whether an owner of a television satellite signal receiving dish would violate any law by using that equipment. There appears to be no infringement of the *Broadcasting Act* (1991) by receiving DTH signals for personal use.[241] However, in 2002

---

233 See note 330, below in this chapter, describing geostationary satellites.

234 See Strick, above note 231 at 278.

235 This is an unattractive policy option. A licensing system is more viable. The policy position has now been encompassed within similar issues arising with respect to the Internet.

236 See text accompanying notes 403–4, below in this chapter, with respect to Canadian content and DTH satellite programs.

237 See, for example, *ExpressVu Inc. v. NII Norsat International Inc.*, [1998] 1 F.C. 245, [1997] F.C.J. No. 1004 (T.D.), aff'd (1997), 81 C.P.R. (3d) 345 at para. 5 (C.A.) [*Norsat*].

238 In Canada, the two DTH providers are Bell ExpressVu, owned by BCE Inc., and Star Choice, owned by Shaw Communications Inc.

239 The original purpose of the SRDUs was to extend Canadian radio and television services to remote and underserved communities. See Decision CRTC 81-252 (14 April 1981), licensing Canadian Satellite Communications Inc. (CANCOM) and thus combining satellite and conventional broadcasting.

240 See *A Policy Framework for the Introduction of Competition to the Satellite Relay Distribution Industry* (23 June 1998), Public Notice CRTC 1998-60, online: CRTC http://crtc.gc.ca/eng/archive/1998%5CPB98-60.htm; *Licence renewal for the national satellite relay distribution undertaking carried on by Cancom* (23 June 1998), Decision CRTC 98-171, online: CRTC www.crtc.gc.ca/eng/archive/1998/DB98-171.htm; and *New national satellite relay distribution undertaking* (23 June 1998), Decision CRTC 98-172, online: CRTC www.crtc.gc.ca/eng/archive/1998/DB98-172.htm [Decision CRTC 98-172], granting a licence to Star Choice to distribute services both DTH and to terrestrial BDUs (i.e., cable television distributors).

241 See text accompanying note 331, below in this chapter.

the Supreme Court of Canada[242] determined that use in Canada of equipment to decrypt programming signals is prohibited under the *Radiocommunication Act*.[243] The decision settled a judicial divergence as to whether the prohibition against decoding applied to *all* encrypted programming capable of receipt in Canada, essentially programming signals from distributors in the United States not licensed by the CRTC to broadcast in Canada,[244] or simply the decoding of encrypted signals of DTH broadcasters licensed by the CRTC to broadcast in Canada.[245] The prohibition was determined to encompass all encrypted programming.[246] The act of unauthorized decoding constitutes the offence.[247] Mere possession of decoding equipment is not an offence[248] but possession that gives rise to a reasonable inference of (or intended) contravening use is an offence.[249] Owners of such equipment would have defences, including lawful excuse and due diligence to prevent the commission of an offence. Furthermore, to constitute the offence there would have to be a reasonable inference of a circumventing use being made of the equipment.[250] Ultimately, of course, it is the distributors of dishes or de-encryption devices in Canada for US-based DTH services that will be the primary target of proceedings for potentially aiding and abetting others to infringe.[251] In February 2004, Bill C-2 was introduced in the House of Commons and was referred to committee on 17 February 2004.[252] It lapsed when Parliament was prorogued for the 28 June 2004 election. This Bill provided a statu-

---

242 *Bell ExpressVu v. R.*, above note 46.
243 *Radiocommunication Act*, above note 3.
244 This position had been taken by the Federal Court of Appeal in *Norsat*, above note 237 (C.P.R.), and in various provincial proceedings noted in *Bell ExpressVu v. R.*, above note 46 at paras. 12–24.
245 This position was taken by the Court of Appeal of British Columbia in *Bell ExpressVu v. R.* under appeal and by courts in other provinces, including the Court of Appeal of Ontario, noted in *Bell ExpressVu v. R.*, *ibid.* at para. 23.
246 *Ibid.* at para. 55.
247 *Ibid.* at para. 33.
248 Apparently, Canada Customs still allows the importation of satellite receiving dishes *per se*. See *Radiocommunication Act*, above note 3, s. 4(1)(b). However, see text accompanying note 252, below in this chapter, re Bill C-2 (lapsed).
249 *Radiocommunication Act*, *ibid.*, s. 10(1)(b).
250 These limitations were expressly noted, but also expressly neither interpreted nor explained, by the Supreme Court in *Bell ExpressVu v. R.*, above note 46 at para. 54.
251 See *DIRECTV Inc. v. Gray* (2003), 19 B.C.L.R. (4th) 382 (S.C.).
252 Bill C-2, *An Act to Amend the Radiocommunication Act*, 3d Sess., 37th Parl., 2004. The background explanation accompanying the Bill provides a useful description of the "black market" and "grey market" between directly stolen signals and those of subscribers to US systems [Bill C-2, Background].

tory infrastructure for supervision and administration of DTH television signals. It would have prohibited the importation of de-encryption devices without an import certificate[253] and provided for a system of statutory damages upon infringement.[254] The Bill was described as dealing primarily with sellers and importers of de-encryption devices for commercial gain, rather than with individual persons who simply receive unauthorized signals.[255]

In 2004, the CRTC conducted a major review of the operations of the DTH industry, essentially examining the operational record of the two Canadian providers, Bell ExpressVu and Star Choice.[256] Both had commenced operation in 1997. By 2004, they were the primary competitors of the cable broadcasting distribution undertakings. By 2002, they had two million subscribers, half of whom were new subscribers as opposed to subscriptions switched from cable systems.[257] Yet because of high capital costs, neither DTH distributor was profitable.[258]

The decisions by the CRTC present a prime example of regulated competition. The regulatory objective from the commencement of DTH transmissions has been the creation of "a competitive balance among new and existing distribution undertakings" presenting sufficient flexibility to support the DTH medium.[259] Existing requirements to carry the English- and French-language networks of the Canadian Broadcasting Corporation (CBC) and one affiliate of the CTV network, as the other national television network, as well as all English- and French-language pay and specialty services channels, were noted.[260] However, the CRTC would not extend requirements set in 2003 to distribute some signals of small Canadian stations and to provide equitable distribution of television signals of large broadcast groups.[261] The CRTC

---

253 *Ibid.* at para. 2. The proposal would have amended the *Radiocommunication Act,* above note 3, s. 4(3).

254 *Ibid.* at para. 10. The expression "statutory damages" refers to an award of damages without the need to prove loss.

255 See Library of Parliament, Legislative Summaries, Bill C-2, Part D1, L.S.-473E, online: www2.parl.gc.ca/Content/LOP/LegislativeSummaries/37/3/c2-e.pdf.

256 *Introductory statement to Broadcasting Decisions CRTC 2004-129 and 2004-130, which renew the licences of the ExpressVu and Star Choice direct-to-home satellite distribution undertakings* (31 March 2004), Broadcasting Public Notice CRTC 2004-19, online: CRTC www.crtc.gc.ca/eng/archive/2004/pb2004-19.htm.

257 *Ibid.* at para. 5.

258 *Ibid.* at para. 7.

259 *Ibid.* at para. 9.

260 *Ibid.* at para. 10.

261 *Ibid.* at para. 27 concerning Decisions CRTC 2003-257 & CRTC 2003-258. Other Canadian television broadcasters had sought the requirement of a min-

acknowledged the difficulty of scarce satellite capacity in a context in which this is likely to increase fivefold with the introduction of high-definition services. In such a situation, a reduction in carriage of conventional signals would be likely.[262]

All in all, the CRTC appears satisfied for the time being with the services provided and programming structure of the two DTH providers.

Satellite telecommunications are not, however, limited to broadcast signal transmissions. The telephone industry, data flow, teleconferencing, mobile telephone, and radio[263] and, most recently, Internet communications utilize satellite linkages. The rapid advance of satellite technology has led to predictions of satellite superiority and industry dominance. However, the development of fibre optic cable has brought the cable or terrestrial systems into strong competition with satellite systems, especially for non-broadcast signals that do not involve a dispersion of signals to receivers across a wide geographical area.[264] Fibre optic cable comprises threads of glass or plastic that utilize a wave of light, instead of an electrical current, to transmit signals. The light is reflected or bounced along one of the many glass threads that make up the cable. The capacity is infinitely greater than that of copper wire or even coaxial cable,[265] but most significantly, fibre optic cable enables data to be transmitted digitally, rather than analogically[266] and facilitates the merging of computer and communications technologies.[267]

b) Teleglobe, Telesat, and the *General Agreement on Trade in Services*

Satellite communications are essential in both broadcast and non-broadcast sectors for servicing remote areas not connected by fibre optic

---

imum number of signals from each large broadcast group or a "carry one, carry all" policy for broadcast signals to individual markets (*ibid.* at paras. 33 and 38).

262 *Ibid.* at para. 26.

263 See Strick, above note 231 at 268–69 noting the strategic benefit of satellite telephone and data links for economic service access to remote geographic regions and for mobile services, particularly the cellular telephone system.

264 See *ibid.* at 272–73, noting that "[s]atellites excel in multi-point delivery and are distance insensitve."

265 See *ibid.*; see also V. Mosco, *Transforming Telecommunications in Canada* (Ottawa: Canadian Centre for Policy Alternatives, 1990) at 31.

266 See *Webster's Computer and Internet Dictionary*, 3d ed., s.v. "fiber optics." Disadvantages of fibre optics are that it is expensive to install, fragile when handled, and "difficult to split" in installation.

267 See L. Edwards, "Telematics in Canada: The Vanishing Opportunity" in *Communication Canada*, above note 231 at 250. The expression "telematic" refers to this merging.

cable and for international communications. The historical Canadian entities Telesat Canada[268] and Teleglobe Canada[269] (undersea cable) for many years provided successful monopoly service to the Canadian telecommunications industry. Both are now privatized and have undergone corporate mergers, acquisitions, and restructuring. The historical monopoly enjoyed by both entities was removed to meet obligations agreed to by Canada with respect to international trade in services under the World Trade Organization (WTO). In October 2007, Telesat Canada was acquired by Canada's Public Sector Pension Investment Board and merged with Loral Space & Communications Inc. to form a

---

268 Telesat Canada was created in 1969 by the *Telesat Canada Act*, S.C. 1969, c. 51 and owned by the federal government (50 percent) and the principal telephone carriers (50 percent). Its task was to manage Canada's satellites and, in effect, act as the satellite carrier for the telephone carriers represented through Telecommunications Canada (this organization later evolved to Stentor). See Chapter 1, note 35. Telesat Canada was privatized in 1992 by the *Telesat Canada Reorganization and Divestiture Act*, S.C. 1991, c. 52, which also extended Telesat's monopoly over satellite communications. BCE fully acquired Telesat in 1998, and Telesat's ten-year monopoly over satellite communications ended 1 March 2000.

269 In 1950, the government of Canada created the Canadian Overseas Telecommunications Corporation (COTC) with the merging of the Canadian Marconi Company and Cable and Wireless Ltd. The COTC was renamed Teleglobe Canada Inc. in 1975. It focused on submarine cable communications outside of North America, with its first trans-Atlantic coaxial cable (TAT-1) established in 1956. In 1998, Teleglobe Canada Inc. was privatized. Canadian ownership requirements were removed along with the monopoly over overseas cable telecommunications (terminated 1 October 1998). See *An Act to Amend the Telecommunications Act and the Teleglobe Canada Reorganization and Divestiture Act*, S.C. 1998, c. 8, meeting Canada's obligations under the World Trade Organization (WTO) *General Agreement on Trade in Services* (*GATS*). With private-sector affiliations (Excel Telecommunications Inc.), Teleglobe expanded into the broadband Internet hosting service, merging with Bell Canada Enterprises (BCE Inc.) from 1 November 2000. However, the bursting telecommunications bubble, with resulting severe cash flow and excess capacity problems, led in 2002 to the limitation of funds from BCE Inc. to Teleglobe, which sought creditor protection in both Canada and the United States. Emerging from protection in May 2003, Teleglobe returned to its core voice and data assets as a private company with Cerberus Capital Management. On 1 June 2004, Teleglobe acquired ITXC and became a public company registered on the NASDAQ. It is focused on Internet voice communications, drawing on its global physical infrastructure from its days as Teleglobe Canada, as well as on satellite communication. In 2006, Teleglobe was acquired into the India-owned Tata Communication Group. See Tata Communications, *Teleglobe Overview*, online: www.tatacommunications.com/about/overview.asp.

new company, Telesat, with a fleet of twelve satellites with three more under construction.[270]

The conclusion of the Uruguay Round of the *General Agreement on Tariffs and Trade (GATT)* negotiations in 1994, leading to the creation of the WTO with effect from 1 January 1995, included two significant side agreements to the primary agreement on trade in goods: the *Agreement on Trade-Related Aspects of Intellectual Property (TRIPs Agreement)*[271] and the *General Agreement on Trade in Services (GATS)*. *GATS* was intended to provide a framework of the same stature as *GATT* so that international trading arrangements would reflect the duality of "goods and services."[272] This, in turn, reflects the importance of services, especially to developed and newly developed countries whose economies are primarily and increasingly informational and service based.

The *GATS* consists of the following:

- *General Obligations and Disciplines* (GODs) are set out in Part II (Articles II to XV). These provisions bind member states, unless excluded by a particular state.
- *Annexes* elaborate on the application of the GODs in the context of specific services, including the *Annex on Telecommunications* and the *Annex on Negotiations on Basic Telecommunications*.
- *Specific Commitments* of member states are made within the context of Part III (Articles XVI to XVIII). These commitments concern market access, national treatment and, importantly, additional commitments. The latter is prescribed in Article XVIII in the following terms: "Members may negotiate commitments with respect to measures affecting trade in services not subject to scheduling under Articles XVI or XVII, including those regarding qualifications, standards or licensing matters. Such commitments shall be inscribed in a member's schedule."
- *Commitment to Progressive Liberation* is made in Part IV (Articles XIX to XXI) by member states agreeing to these provisions. Their essence is that participating member states shall continue negotiations toward "achieving a progressively higher level of liberalization" with the objective of providing "effective market access"

---

270 See announcement, Telesat, Press Release, "Telesat Canada and Loral Skynet Close Merger" (31 October 2007), online: Telesat www.telesat.ca/en/Press_Releases/TELESAT_CANADA_AND_LORAL_SKYNET_CLOSE_MERGER.

271 The *TRIPs Agreement* acknowledges the importance of intellectual property recognition and enforcement in ensuring international trade. It stipulates minimum standards for the categories of intellectual property.

272 See E. McGovern, *International Trade Regulation*, looseleaf (Globefield, Exeter: Globefield Press, 1995) at 31(11-1).

(Article XIX). Each member set out in a schedule the commitments it made under Part III and the schedules of such commitments were annexed to *GATS* (Article XX).

• *Institutional Provisions* deal with the organizational and procedural matters of *GATS*.[273]

The *Annex on Telecommunications* notes the objectives with respect to telecommunications as twofold: first, telecommunications is recognized as a "distinct sector of economic activity" in its own right; and second, telecommunications is acknowledged as providing the means of communication vital to trade in goods and other services and as such requires some agreed "measures affecting access to and use of" facilities that are available to the public.[274] The *Annex* does not apply to programming broadcast by radio and television.[275] The principal focus is utilization of telecommunication infrastructure of networks and services that are available to and for use by the public in a member country,[276] for transmission of customer-supplied information between points or among network points without any change in content or form.[277] In effect, this refers to the point-to-point communications that would fall under the *Telecommunications Act* (1993). The *Annex* lists as examples "telegraph, telephone, telex, and data transmission." These modes are not, however, exhaustive. In an Internet context, a service provider for e-mail communications appears to be within the definition. Similarly, operation of a website with predominantly alphanumeric services (electronic commerce) would probably be included. Possibly, even the provision of Internet-related non-alphanumeric services would be included, as the *Annex* excludes only "radio or television programming."[278]

The *Annex* presents four aspects of utilization of telecommunications service and infrastructure:

1) transparency
2) access
3) technical cooperation
4) international standards and compatibility.[279]

---

273 *GATS, Annex on Telecommunications*, above note 20.
274 *Ibid.*, s. 1 ("Objectives").
275 *Ibid.*, s. 2(b).
276 *Ibid.*, s. 2(a).
277 The key definitions to this effect are "Public telecommunications transport service" and "public telecommunications transport network" in *ibid.*, ss. 3(b) & 3(c).
278 *Ibid.*, s. 2(b).
279 *Ibid.*, ss. 4–7.

Transparency requires member states to make available to the public information concerning conditions of access and use, tariffs, specifications of interfaces, conditions of interconnection, registration and licensing requirements, if any, and information about the entities or bodies responsible for standards that might affect access and use. Access and use, including transborder, must essentially be non-discriminatory, and member countries must grant this to service suppliers of other member countries on reasonable and non-discriminatory terms, certainly upon a principle of national treatment.[280] Several specifically enumerated circumstances are included.[281]

Some amelioration is provided for developing country members under reasonable conditions, reflecting the level of development that enables the particular country to gain access to and use of systems to strengthen its domestic infrastructure and service and to facilitate international participation and trade in telecommunications.[282] No member country, whether developed or developing, is obligated to authorize a service provider from another member country to establish telecommunications services or networks within its borders. In other words, national ownership requirements may be maintained unless otherwise agreed by a member country.[283]

Technical cooperation is aimed at removing barriers to the smooth flow of telecommunications services between member countries, including the use of uniform standards in infrastructure and equipment. This was recognized to be of particular importance in relation to ensuring the inclusion of developing countries. Members endorsed and encouraged their participation with international and regional development programs and organizations, including the United Nations Development Program, the International Bank for Reconstruction and Development and, importantly for technical equipment and infrastructure standards, the International Telecommunication Union (ITU).[284]

---

280 See McGovern, above note 272 at 27(33), n. 15, concerning the terms of the *GATS, Annex on Telecommunications*, above note 20.

281 *GATS, Annex on Telecommunications*, ibid., s. 5.

282 *Ibid.*, s. 5(g).

283 *Ibid.*, s. 2(c)(i).

284 *Ibid.*, ss. 5 & 6. The ITU is an international organization, today within the United Nations structure, that continues to establish standardization within the telecommunications industry. The Telecommunications Standardization Sector of the ITU was created on 1 March 1993 but is a modern replacement for an earlier consultative committee on telegraph and telephone extending back to 1865. See *The International Telecommunication Union: An Experiment in International Cooperation* (New York: Arno Press, NY Times Company, 1972), online: www. itu.int/ITU-T/Index.html.

The terms of the *Annex on Telecommunications* address principally the issues of access and usage. The acknowledgement in the *Annex* that telecommunications presents a trade commodity in itself[285] is not elaborated upon. In essence, the *GATS* as completed in 1994 provided only for "access" to and "use" of telecommunications facilities, not for telecommunications as a sector of economic activity in itself. However, from 1994 to 1997, the Council of Trade in Services and many member countries addressed this broader perspective in schedules of "Commitments on Telecommunications" setting out how far each country would proceed in liberalizing trade in telecommunications services. The commitments focused on "basic" services and "value added" features, and these further negotiations were within the framework of Article XVII of *GATS*, the *Annex on Negotiations on Basic Telecommunications*.[286]

A Ministerial Decision on Negotiations on Basic Telecommunications taken at the signing of *GATS* (1994) established a Negotiating Group on Basic Telecommunications to conduct the negotiations and report no later than 30 April 1996. A report was duly provided[287] and was adopted by the Council of Trade in Services on 30 April 1996, reflecting two years of deliberations. Key features of the report were first, effective competition, with the incumbent carriers being prevented from anti-competitive practices; second, interconnection for new entrants to the market; and third, non-discrimination in a transparently administered system with regulatory bodies being independent entities, separate from other providers.

Accepting the Negotiating Group's report, the Council made the *Decision on Commitments in Basic Telecommunications*,[288] and adopted

---

285 *GATS, Annex on Telecommunications*, above note 20, s. 1.

286 The expressions "basic telecommunications" and "value added telecommunications services" are described in detail, with examples, by the WTO, online: WTO www.wto.org/english/tratop_e/serv_e/telecom_e/telecom_coverage_e. htm. Value added services involve a supplier "adding value" to the basic customer information by enhancing form, content, storage, or retrieval. Examples are given as "on line data processing," "on line data base storage and retrieval," "electronic data interchange," "e-mail," and "voicemail." WTO *Annex 1B, General Agreement in Trade in Services*, WTO Doc. Annex 1, Part 4, art. 29, online: www.wto.org/english/docs_e/legal_e/26-gats_02_e.htm.

287 WTO, *Report of the Negotiating Group on Basic Telecommunications*, WTO Doc. S/ NGBT/18 (30 April 1996), Document number 96-1837, online: http://docsonline. wto.org.

288 WTO, *Decision on Commitments in Basic Telecommunications adopted by the Council for Trade in Services on 30 April 1996*, WTO Doc. S/L/19 (1996), online: WTO http://docsonline.wto.org.

the *Fourth Protocol* to *GATS*[289] with schedules of commitments of members in agreement attached. However, recognizing that further negotiations could be fruitful, the Council of *GATS* established a further Group on Basic Telecommunications (GBT) to resolve outstanding issues. Subsequently, agreement was reached on 15 February 1997[290] and the report made to the Council of *GATS* and subsequent reference paper contained schedules of commitments of participating countries toward liberalizing trade in telecommunications services. The Protocol and annexed documents, including the reference raper, came into effect on 5 February 1998.[291]

Canada's commitment[292] included:

1) Removing, with effect from March 2000, Telesat's exclusive right to provide satellite services and earth stations for Canadian services within Canada and the United States. This introduced competition in the satellite communications industry.

2) Removing, with effect from October 1998, Teleglobe's exclusive right to carry (by undersea cable) Canadian telecommunications to foreign, non-US, jurisdictions.

This presented a significant opening of the Canadian international telecommunications market to foreign competition. The *Annex on Telecommunications*, the *Fourth Protocol*, and the February 1997 GBT report and reference paper are together commonly described as the World Trade Organization (WTO) Telecommunication Pact and have been referred to as a beginning to ensure global competition with respect to the provision of telecommunications services. The direction of *GATS* and the WTO Telecommunication Pact are entirely consistent with the thrust of deregulation from 1979 of the telecommunications industry in Canada.

Article XIX of *GATS* commits member governments to continue to liberalize trade in services, including telecommunications. A new round of negotiations commenced in 2000 and continues currently.[293]

---

289 WTO, *Fourth Protocol to the General Agreement on Trade in Services*, WTO Doc. S/L/20 (1996), online: WTO http://docsonline.wto.org.

290 WTO, *Report of the Group on Basic Telecommunications*, WTO Doc. S/GBT/4 (1997) at para. 9, online: WTO www.wto.org/english/news_e/news00_e/4.doc.

291 WTO, *History of the Telecommunication Negotiations*, "The Fourth Protocol" (1994), online: WTO www.wto.org/english/tratop_e/serv_e/telecom_e/telecom_history_e.htm.

292 WTO, *Group on Basic Telecommunications — Communication from Canada — Schedule of Specific Commitments on Basic Telecommunications — Revision*, WTO Doc. S/GBT/W/1/Add.6/Rev.2 (1997), online: WTO http://docsonline.wto.org.

293 For the current negotiations on telecommunications services, see online: www.wto.org/english/tratop_e/serv_e/telecom_e/telecom_e.htm. As of August 2010,

c) Telecommunications and NAFTA

The *North American Free Trade Agreement* (NAFTA)[294] includes limited provisions concerning telecommunications. In substance, the position is similar to that under the WTO/GATS. NAFTA, Chapter 13, Articles 1301 to 1310, provides for three broad features: first, access to and use of public telecommunications by persons of another party to *NAFTA*; second, the provision of "enhanced or value added services"; and third, measures concerning equipment standards.

Each party is to provide access and use to persons of another party on reasonable and nondiscriminatory terms to public telecommunications facilities. This includes technical and business access by interconnection, switching, signalling, and processing.[295] There is an open market between the parties with respect to "enhanced or value added services." These are telecommunications services that employ computer-processing applications that enhance that customer-transmitted information by restructuring or providing different dimensions or involve customer interaction with the information.[296] Standards-related measures concern a technical conformity or compatibility to allow interconnection and facilitate efficient operations between operators from the various parties.[297]

C. BROADCASTING AND BROADCASTING UNDERTAKINGS

Regulatory control over broadcasting is provided by the requirement of a licence to operate as a "broadcasting undertaking." This essential category is established from a number of interconnected definitions in the *Broadcasting Act*.[298] It is illustrated in Figure 2.

The categories of "network," "programming undertaking," and "distribution undertaking" reflect a structure similar to that under the

---

108 governments have made efforts to improve their existing commitments or to commit for the first time in the telecommunications sector.

294 implemented by the *North American Free Trade Agreement Implementation Act*, S.C. 1993, c. 44.

295 *NAFTA*, above note 11, art. 1302.

296 See *ibid.*, art. 1310 for a precise definition of "enhanced or value added services." Compare the WTO/GATS definitions, above note 286.

297 See *NAFTA*, above note 11, art. 1304 for detailed provisions in this respect.

298 *Broadcasting Act*, above note 1, s. 2(1).

Figure 2, Broadcasting

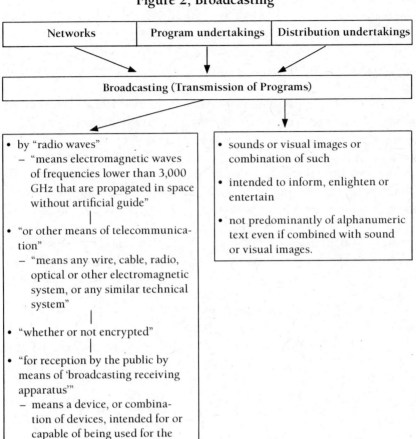

earlier *Broadcasting Act* (1968).[299] A network is defined non-exclusively to include the delegation of control over programs and schedules of a broadcasting undertaking to another undertaking or person. A programming undertaking is an originator of program transmission (such as a television station) directly or through a distribution undertaking "for reception by the public by means of broadcasting receiving apparatus."[300] A distribution undertaking receives broadcast signals

---

299 *Broadcasting Act*, R.S.C. 1985, c. B-9, provided for "broadcasting undertaking" to include: "a broadcasting transmitting undertaking, a broadcasting receiving undertaking and a network operation. . . ."

300 The expression "broadcasting receiving apparatus" is defined in Figure 2.

and retransmits them through the air or otherwise "to more than one permanent or temporary residence or dwelling unit or to another [distribution] undertaking" (essentially a cable television or cable radio operator). These categories reflect the media of radio, television, and cable distribution — historically, the ambit of broadcasting for all practical purposes.[301]

Today, certain new media may also be within these definitions. By way of example, consider the Internet-based undertaking YouTube, headquartered in California and from 2005 universally available as a user-generated, video-focused broadcast medium.[302] Music, motion picture, and television video clips, user original video clips, and alphanumeric text became available to all Internet users for viewing or transmitting of content. In effect, YouTube is a centralized operational infrastructure providing for decentralized user blogs.[303] Almost immediately, YouTube was accepted as a mainstream medium. Examples of usage are the Royal Channel, which hosts the blog of the British monarchy,[304] the House of Lords and other features of the United Kingdom's Parliament,[305] and significant use in political campaigning[306] and in aid of Canadian policing efforts.[307] Indeed, a Canadian site for YouTube[308] was launched in November 2007 and, importantly for Canadian broadcasting, has been described by YouTube officials as designed to

---

301 It is difficult to envisage a transmission of programs that would not fall into one of the subcategories of network, programming undertaking, or distribution undertaking and yet also meet the definition of "broadcasting," given that a "broadcast" must be "for reception by the public."

302 See YouTube, "Company History," online: www.youtube.com/t/about.

303 The expression "blog" is a truncation of "web-log," or a website that displays postings by one or more persons. It can include video clips and may then be known as a "video blog" or "vblog." See, online: www.Answers.com.

304 The Royal Channel, online: YouTube www.youtube.com/theroyalchannel.

305 UK Parliament, online: YouTube www.youtube.com/user/UKParliament.

306 See Midsouthblack, *YouTube Is the New Home of Political Campaigns (Senator Barack Obama Presidential Campaign)*, online: midsouthblack.wordpress.com/category/youtube-is-the-new-home-of-political-campaigns/.

307 See, for example, Hamilton police posting security footage on YouTube to track a suspect: The Utube Blog, *Crime and YouTube: Canadian Police Use YouTube*, online: http://theutubeblog.com/2006/12/21/crime-and-youtube-canadian-police-use-youtube/. Likewise, note Toronto police using YouTube in an attempt to find a missing teenager via CTV, *Police use YouTube to search for missing teen* (31 January 2007), online: CTV http://toronto.ctv.ca/servlet/an/local/CTVNews/20070131/youtube_police_search_070131/20070131?hub=TorontoHome.

308 Online: YouTube youtube.com/.

promote Canadian-generated context.[309] YouTube has also entered into numerous arrangements with or has been used by television networks and other content providers, including the CBC[310] and CTV.[311]

If the definition "broadcasting undertaking" were to be considered with respect to YouTube, there would need to be a consideration of whether the activity is broadcasting, whether programs are being transmitted, and whether YouTube is a network, a programming undertaking, or a distribution undertaking. First, the transmissions are broadcasts. If not radiowaves, they are "other means of telecommunication" as defined.[312] The transmissions are for the public (YouTube can be accessed freely by any user). The accessor's computer or other reception device qualifies as a broadcast receiving apparatus, as it is either intended for or capable of being used for the reception of broadcasting. The transmission is not solely for performance or display in a public place. Second, the transmissions are programs. They are sounds and images, intended to inform, enlighten, or entertain. They are not predominantly alphanumeric text, as YouTube is primarily a video medium. Finally, is YouTube a network, programming undertaking, or distribution undertaking? A distribution undertaking has to receive *broadcast signals* for retransmission. This would require that a blogger's postings be classified as such. It is suggested that a blog would, literally, meet the definition of broadcast and of program so as to be a broadcast signal transmitted to YouTube for distribution, rendering YouTube a distribution undertaking. It is not a programming undertaking as the program transmission originates with the blogger, not YouTube. It may, however, be a network within the residual or express scope of that non-exclusively defined category.[313]

Regulation of YouTube or similar media is not necessarily suggested. The purpose here is to demonstrate the potential application

---

309 Matt Hartley, "YouTube Launches in Canada," *The Globe and Mail* (7 November 2007), online: http://v1.theglobeandmail.com/servlet/story/RTGAM.20071106. wyoutube1106/BNStory/Technology/home.

310 CBC YouTube Channel, online: YouTube www.youtube.com/cbc, and CBC Official Blog, "Inside the CBC.Com," online: CBC www.insidethecbc.com/youtubecbc.

311 CTV Channel Television, "Unused 1989 ITV Generic Idents", online: YouTube www.youtube.com/watch?v=9m004d3rrNc&watch_response.

312 *Broadcasting Act*, above note 1, s. 2(1). At the very least, the transmissions are by an electromagnetic system.

313 To qualify within the included express meaning of network, the blogger would have to constitute a programming undertaking. This could literally be the position, as the blogger is the originator of the program transmission for reception by the public.

to new media of the definitions relevant to broadcasting undertakings. Indeed, apart from the Canadian YouTube, this may be impossible in any practical manner given the extraterritorial status of its headquarters. Yet as a medium, it is a glimpse at the future of a significant and growing component of broadcasting in Canada. The 1999 determination of the CRTC to withhold any attempt to regulate the Internet was predicated on a number of assumptions, the principal two being that Internet transmissions comprised predominantly alphanumeric text and that they were essentially customized or tailored by an individual user rather than being directed to the public.[314] YouTube, or any other video-streaming display service, is not predominantly alphanumeric. It is video. Nor is it a transmission that is customized by a viewer or limited for viewing by a particularized individual or group. It is available to the public. Internet blogging services intended for more restricted or controlled distribution, such as to individuals or within groups, should be distinguished on this basis and will often be customized by interactive personal exchanges between users.[315] However, the mere imposition of access codes in themselves, in a manner similar to those for pay television services, should not limit the public nature of any service.[316]

The 2006 Governor in Council requested under section 15 of the *Broadcasting Act*,[317] that the CRTC consider audiovisual programming and provide a factual report about the future of the broadcasting system in the light of new media, particularly the Internet, and to ensure a strong Canadian presence in this media. The CRTC engaged in public hearings and has responded in an ongoing manner.[318]

Returning to more traditional media, the 1991 enactment confirmed that a non-profit enterprise may still constitute a "broadcasting undertaking."[319] This followed from the Federal Court of Appeal finding

---

314 CRTC, News Release, "CRTC Won't Regulate the Internet" (17 May 1999), online: The Toronto Star www.thestar.com/news/canada/article/645653; *Exemption order for new media broadcasting undertakings*, Public Notice CRTC 1999-97 (17 December 1999).

315 For example, services such as Facebook or MySpace involving membership and access codes with an intent for more limited distribution.

316 For example, programs of streaming video open to the public by simply obtaining an access code, as in the case of wildlife viewing that is effectively transmission to the public. See "Live Wildlife Cams Streaming Video Live Broadcast Webcam," online: Wavelit www.wavelit.com/.

317 *Broadcasting Act*, above note 1, s. 15.

318 See text accompanying note 34ff., above in this chapter, and accompanying note 436ff., below in this chapter.

319 *Broadcasting Act*, above note 1, s. 4(3) stipulates: "For greater certainty, this Act applies in respect of broadcasting undertakings whether or not they are carried

that in order to qualify as an "undertaking," the broadcasting installation had to be in direct commercial use. A receipt of satellite broadcasts and a retransmission of the signals throughout a hotel was not a "broadcasting undertaking" when no fee was charged to occupiers of the hotel rooms for receipt of the signal.[320] The Saskatchewan Court of Appeal subsequently took the opposite position[321] and the Supreme Court of Canada affirmed.[322]

Other issues have been clarified. First, the meaning of "broadcasting" omits the phrase (from the 1968 Act) requiring that "the transmissions [be] intended for direct reception by the general public."[323] This phrase would have enabled a cable television operator to intercept a signal sent from a broadcaster to an affiliate station and to claim that the signal was not a broadcast signal as it was not intended by the broadcaster to be received *directly* by the general public.[324] The current definition requires that the transmission be simply "for reception by the public."[325] Second, the phrase "or other means of telecommunication,"[326] used with the narrower expression "radio waves" in the definitions of "broadcasting" and "distribution undertaking" avoids any dispute over the technical means of transmission (or retransmission) in order to constitute a broadcasting undertaking.[327]

---

on for profit or as part of, or in connection with, any other undertaking or activity."

320 *Lount Corp. v. Canada (Attorney General)*, [1985] 2 F.C. 185 (C.A.) [*Lount*].

321 *R. v. Nipawin & District Satellite T.V. Inc.* (1988), 65 Sask. R. 151 (C.A.).

322 *R. v. Nipawin & District Satellite T.V. Inc.*, [1991] 1 S.C.R. 64 at para. 2 [*Nipawin*].

323 *Broadcasting Act*, above note 299, s. 2.

324 See *R. v. Shellbird Cable Ltd.* (1982), 67 C.P.R. (2d) 148 (Nfld. C.A.), leave to appeal to S.C.C. refused (1983), 46 N.R. 623 (decided on other grounds against the cable operator).

325 *Broadcasting Act*, above note 1, s. 2.

326 *Ibid.*, s. 2(1) (the definitions of "broadcasting" and "distribution undertaking") and s. 2(2), stipulating: "For the purposes of this Act, 'other means of telecommunication' means any wire, cable, radio, optical or other electromagnetic system, or other similar technical system."

327 See, for example, *Shuswap*, above note 46 considering the phrase "propagated in space without artificial guide," currently a limitation upon the meaning of "radio waves" as defined in *Broadcasting Act*, above note 1, s. 2, and thereby qualifying the receipt or transmission of "broadcasting" at paras. 359–60. The court decided that a retransmission to earth from a satellite in geostationary orbit constituted a transmission "without artificial guide" so as to constitute a receipt and retransmission of "broadcasting" by a cable operator. The particular operator had contended that an earthbound or "down" link was artificially created to conform to a "footprint" or reception area and therefore was "artificially guided" not amounting to a broadcast signal. See also *R. v. Maahs and Teleprompter Cable Communications Corp.* (1974), 6 O.R. (2d) 774 (Dist. Ct.), where a cable television

Operators of DTH satellite systems will constitute a broadcasting undertaking even though these communication signals are encrypted,[328] being received by way of subscription. Operators of these systems are termed DTH satellite distribution undertakings[329] and utilize satellites in geostationary orbit.[330] Recipients who merely receive signals will not be included as such. However, if any retransmission occurs to condominiums, apartments, or other dwelling units it will constitute a broadcast undertaking,[331] so long as the entity is an undertaking for the reception and retransmission of broadcasting,[332] even when done in connection with another undertaking or activity or without profit.[333] Decryption by a recipient of DTH signals will, however, constitute an infringement and, possibly, an offence under the *Radiocommunication Act.*[334]

---

distributor received the transmission from a physical cable crossing over a bridge between the United States and Canada. Arguably, the receipt in Canada was neither by "radiocommunication" nor by "radio waves." However, after 1991, a "distribution undertaking" need simply *receive* broadcast signals (without reference to technical means), then retransmit the signals. See definition of "redistribution undertaking" (*Broadcasting Act, ibid.,* s. 2).

328 *Ibid.* The definition of "broadcasting" refers to "any transmission of programs, whether or not encrypted."

329 *Directions to the CRTC (Direct-to-Home (DTH) Satellite Distribution Undertakings) Order,* S.O.R./95-319 (6 July 1995), P.C. 1995-1105 (6 July 1995), C. Gaz. 1995. II.1924–27.

330 A geostationary orbit is an orbit that has a rotational period geosynchronized (or equal with) the rotational period of the planet so that the satellite appears to be stationary in its positioning. See T.S. Kelso, "Basics of the Geostationary Orbit" *Satellite Times* (May 1998), online: Satellite Times http://celestrak.com/columns/v04n07/.

331 See definition of "distribution undertaking" in the *Broadcasting Act,* above note 1, s. 2(1). The retransmission need not only be by radio waves but by cable as some "other means of telecommunication" inserted in the definition in 1991. See also *Terra Communications Ltd. v. Communicomp Data Ltd.* (1973), 1 O.R. (2d) 682 at 692 (H.C.) [*Terra*] reaching this conclusion even without the 1991 statutory phrase. This would also have been the result in *Nipawin,* above note 322, but it was decided in another context.

332 See *Broadcasting Act, ibid.,* s. 2(1) definition of "distribution undertaking."

333 *Ibid.,* s. 4(3). Contrast pre-1991, *Lount,* above note 320.

334 See text accompanying notes 247 and generally notes 241–50, above in this chapter.

1) Broadcasting Policy and Oversight

The Canadian national interest with respect to broadcasting is reflected primarily through a "broadcasting policy for Canada,"[335] supported by statutory "object and powers"[336] of the CRTC, which is afforded oversight of the industry by the powers of regulation[337] and licensing.[338] The Act is explicit and reflective of the historical position that "the Canadian broadcasting system constitutes a single system and that the objectives of the broadcasting policy . . . can best be achieved by providing for the regulation and supervision of the Canadian broadcasting system by a single independent public authority"[339]

Enforcement is provided by summary offences[340] for carrying on a broadcasting undertaking without a licence; contravening or failing to comply with any regulation or order made under Part II of the *Broadcasting Act* (1991); and contravening or failing to comply with any condition of any licence issued under the Act.

In addition, civil proceedings may be brought by the holder of a valid licence for injunction[341] or, possibly, compensatory[342] relief against an infringer. However, unlike the *Telecommunications Act* and the *Radiocommunication Act*, which expressly address civil proceedings in context,[343] the *Broadcasting Act* is silent in this matter.

The licensing jurisdiction of the CRTC may be exercised by the issuance of policy statements in the nature of guidelines concerning the procedure and may include policies upon which the Commission may act in considering individual licence applications.[344] Terms and

---

335 *Broadcasting Act*, above note 1, s. 3.

336 *Ibid.*, ss. 5 and 9.

337 *Ibid.*, s. 10.

338 *Ibid.*, s. 9(1).

339 *Ibid.*, s. 3(2).

340 *Ibid.*, s. 32.

341 See, for example, *Terra*, above note 331 at 696.

342 See *Whistler Cable Television Ltd. v. IPEC Canada Inc.* (1992), 75 B.C.L.R. (2d) 48 (S.C.). The basis for any such proceeding is uncertain. It might be the general tort of "Unlawful Interference with Trade or Business," whereby the illegality or unlawful means is the defendant's infringement of the Act at paras. 10–12 and 30–31. Alternatively, it might be a proceeding for the tort of "Breach of Statute" by intentional, as opposed to accidental, conduct at paras. 16–17, 24, and 27–30. The court found that the breach of statute tort was the more appropriate choice.

343 *Telecommunications Act*, above note 2, s. 72; *Radiocommunication Act*, above note 3, s. 18.

344 *Broadcasting Act*, above note 1, ss. 5(3) and (6), discussed in *Capital Cities Communications v. Canadian Radio-Television and Telecommunications Commission*, [1978] 2 S.C.R. 141 at 170–71 [*Capital Cities*]. At the time the Court was

conditions reflecting the broadcasting policy and regulatory objects may be imposed by the Commission on individual licence holders at the time of grant or renewal of a licence.[345] Such terms and conditions, as well as any policy statement of the Commission, cannot, however, be contrary to any regulations that are in force,[346] and must be "related to the circumstances of the licensee,"[347] in the sense that there is some nexus to the particular licensee.[348]

The Commission is also empowered to "exempt" broadcasting undertakings from obtaining a licence and otherwise complying with Part II of the Act if compliance would not materially contribute to the implementation of the broadcasting policy.[349]

It is apparent that the jurisdiction and powers of the Commission are substantial, as is intended from its status as an independent regulator interpreting and applying the broadcasting policy legislated by Parliament. However, political control can be applied by the Governor in Council[350] issuing to the Commission "directions of general application on broad policy matters" concerning the broadcasting policy and the objectives of the regulatory policy. The Act specifies a stringent procedure that must be followed[351] and cannot be applied in respect of a particular applicant for a licence, nor of the amendment (or renewal,

using the *Broadcasting Act*, R.S.C. 1970, c. B-11, ss. 15–17, while these sections changed (with some wording differences) to ss. 5(3) and 6 in the *Broadcasting Act* (1991), the issues raised are essentially the same.

345 See *Canadian Radio-Television and Telecommunications Commission v. CTV Television Network Ltd.*, [1982] 1 S.C.R. 530 at 545 [*CTV Television Network*].

346 See *Capital Cities*, above note 344 at 170. See also *CTV Television Network*, *ibid.* at 545 to the same effect. In *CTV Television Network*, *ibid.* at 546, a more stringent position was argued: that the subject matter should be "outside of the regulation-making power" before being eligible subject matter for policy statements.

347 *Radiocommunication Act*, above note 3, s. 9(1)(b). See also *CTV Television Network*, *ibid.* at 543.

348 In *CTV Television Network*, *ibid.* at 545, the condition (a requirement to present "26 hours of original new Canadian drama") did have a particular linkage with the licensee who had a history in this respect known to both the licensee and the CRTC as being unsatisfactory.

349 *Broadcasting Act*, above note 1, s. 9(4).

350 Recall, this expression "means the Governor General of Canada acting by and with the advice of, or by and with the advice and consent of, or in conjunction with the Queen's Privy Council for Canada." See *Interpretation Act*, above note 84, s. 35(1). Noted with respect to telecommunications, above note 84.

351 *Broadcasting Act*, above note 1, ss. 7 & 8. The procedure includes the laying of the order before each House of Parliament (s. 7(5)), the requirement that the Minister of Industry, who administers the Act, consult the Commission before the Governor in Council makes the order (ss. 7(6) and 8(4)), and that notice

suspension, or revocation) of a licence in a particular instance.[352] However, with respect to these licensing matters, the Governor in Council is given discretion to review a decision of the Commission,[353] either on petition by any person or on the Governor in Council's own motion. This provides a mechanism to reconsider decisions on their merits. Other general powers are given to the Governor in Council allowing for directions to be given to the Commission with respect to specified situations.[354]

This overall jurisdictional structure is completed first, by an appeal to the Federal Court of Appeal "on a question of law or a question of jurisdiction," but leave to appeal must first be obtained from the court;[355] and second, from a technical perspective, a broadcasting undertaking in seeking a broadcast licence from the Commission must also obtain a technical construction and operating certificate from the Minister of Industry, acting under the *Radiocommunication Act*.[356] The issuance of this certificate by the Minister and the broadcasting licence by the Commission are intertwined,[357] with the primary decision being that of the Commission.[358]

The broadcasting policy for Canada and related regulatory objects and powers are set out in considerable detail in the *Broadcasting Act*.[359] Building upon the key structural criterion of "a single system [regu-

---

be published in the *Canada Gazette* inviting the submission of representations from "interested persons" (s. 8).

352 *Ibid.*, s. 7(2).

353 *Ibid.*, ss. 28–29.

354 *Ibid.*, ss. 26–27. These powers may be exercised with respect to the maximum number of channels or frequencies for which licences may be issued within a geographical area (s. 26(1)(a)), the reservation of channels for the use of the CBC or for any other special purpose (s. 26(1)(b)), the classes of applicants to whom licences, amendments, or renewals may not be granted (s. 26(1)(c)), the circumstances in which the CRTC may issue licences to agents of provinces that would be otherwise ineligible (s. 26(1)(d)), and the broadcast of any program "to be of urgent importance to Canadians generally or to persons resident in any area of Canada" (s. 26(2)). Section 27 gives the Governor in Council power to issue interpretation and/or application directions regarding para. 3 of the *Canada–United States Free Trade Agreement Implementation Act*, S.C. 1988, c. 65.

355 *Ibid.*, s. 31(2).

356 *Radiocommunication Act*, above note 3, s. 5(1)(a)(iv).

357 *Broadcasting Act*, above note 1, ss. 22(1)(b) and 22(3). See text accompanying note 46, above in this chapter, with respect to the relationship between the two enactments.

358 See *Shuswap*, above note 46 at 346.

359 *Broadcasting Act*, above note 1, s. 3 (broadcasting policy) and ss. 5, 9, & 10 (regulatory and licensing objects and powers of the CRTC).

lated and supervised] by a single independent public authority,"[360] the essential features emphasize:

- effective Canadian ownership and control of the broadcasting system;
- public ownership of radio frequencies;
- "public, private and community elements" within the one single system operating primarily in both official languages;
- programming as the vehicle to provide "a public service essential to the maintenance and enhancement of national identity and cultural sovereignty";
- strengthening "the cultural, political, social and economic fabric of Canada" including "employment opportunities";
- encouraging "Canadian expression" across a broad range of opinion and creativity and through programming to reflect:
  - gender and children equality
  - linguistic duality
  - multiculturalism and multiracialism, including the "special place" of aboriginal peoples;
- a "high standard" of programming originating from broadcasting undertakings;
- an ability in the system to adapt to "scientific and technological change"; and
- a requirement that each element of the system contribute to Canadian programming, but that the Canadian Broadcasting Corporation ("CBC"), as "the national public broadcaster," is subject to particular requirements that enhance the objectives of the broadcasting policy.[361]

Freedom of expression and journalistic creation and independence are expressed to be preserved.[362] The containment of these features within the overall attainment of a national broadcast policy is achieved by treating them as elements of interpretation or construction of the Act itself.[363]

---

360 *Ibid.*, s. 3(2).
361 *Ibid.*, ss. 3(1)(d), (i), (l), (m), and Part 3 (dealing with administrative matters concerning the CBC). Section 46 of Part 3 details objects and powers of the CBC with respect to the specific programming requirements that ss. 3(1)(l) & (m) require of the corporation.
362 *Ibid.*, s. 2(3) and (regarding the CBC) s. 46(5).
363 *Ibid.*, s. 2(3) stipulates that the construction and application of the Act shall reflect the features of "freedom of expression and journalistic creative and pro-

The statutory objective of effective Canadian ownership and control applies to the broadcasting system as a whole,[364]rather than to individual undertakings or components within the system.[365] This is to be contrasted with the eligibility requirement of Canadian ownership of Canadian carriers under the *Telecommunications Act*, where such requirements are statutorily focused on the entities themselves.[366] From a practical perspective, effective Canadian ownership in a broadcasting context is focused by Direction of the Governor in Council to the CRTC.[367] No broadcasting licence, amendment, or renewal may be granted by the CRTC to a non-Canadian applicant.[368] The Direction sets out eligibility as Canadian, including "a qualified corporation" and "a qualified successor."

A qualified corporation requires the chief executive officer (or equivalent) and 80 percent of the directors to be Canadian. If the corporation has share capital, Canadians must beneficially own and control, directly or indirectly and not by way of security, at least 80 percent of all issued and outstanding voting shares and at least 80 percent of the votes.[369] If the entity is a subsidiary of a Canadian parent corporation, the Canadian ownership requirement includes two-thirds (66⅔%) of the issued and outstanding voting shares and votes of the parent. Neither the parent corporation nor its directors can exercise "control

---

gramming independence." The principle of the enhancement of Canadian programming has not in itself been seen as restrictive of free expression. See *CTV Television Network*, above note 345 at 540 where the Supreme Court of Canada rejected that a requirement of "26 hours of original new Canadian drama" infringed a guarantee of freedom of expression under the *Broadcasting Act*, above note 299, s. 3(c). The court found that *within* the stipulated new Canadian programming there were no freedom of expression restrictions. Prior to 1991, the *Broadcasting Act*, s. 3(c) provided: "but the right to freedom of expression and the right of persons to receive programs, subject only to generally applicable statutes and regulations, is unquestioned."

364 See *Broadcasting Act*, above note 1, s. 3(1)(a) stipulating that "the Canadian Broadcasting *system* shall be effectively owned and controlled by Canadians" [emphasis added].

365 *Rogers Communications Inc. v. Canada (Attorney General)*, [1998] F.C.J. No. 368 (T.D.).

366 See text accompanying notes 53ff., above in this chapter.

367 *Direction to the CRTC (Ineligibility of Non-Canadians)*, S.O.R. 97-192 (8 April 1997), P.C. 1997–486 (8 April 1997), C. Gaz. 1997.II.1222–28.

368 *Ibid.*, part 2.

369 *Ibid.*, part 1 definition of "qualified corporation."

or influence"[370] over programming decisions of the broadcasting undertaking.

The convergence policy announced in August 1996 by Industry Canada and Canadian Heritage on behalf of the federal government[371] brought some changes. The objective of the policy was to encourage competition between Canadian broadcasting undertakings and Canadian carriers of telecommunications in each other's core business. The difficulty was that not all Canadian carriers qualified under the Canadian ownership requirements for a broadcasting undertaking licence. Two principal responses followed.

First, the Governor in Council by Direction to the CRTC established "a qualified successor" as a "class of applicant" for a broadcasting licence. This relates directly to the category of Canadian carriers that do not meet the requirements of Canadian ownership even for Canadian carriers but were "grandfathered" in the telecommunications system with effect from 22 July 1987.[372] The broadcasting class of "qualified successor" enables these entities to participate equally in broadcasting by being eligible to qualify, from an ownership perspective, for a broadcasting licence.[373] Although challenged, the Federal Court upheld this approach as enabled by the broad formulation in the *Broadcasting Act* (1991) of *effective* Canadian ownership focused on the system as a whole, rather than component undertakings.[374]

Second, the prohibition against issuing a broadcasting licence to Canadian carriers owned by a province or by an agency of a province (Crown corporations), as stipulated by Governor in Council Direction to the CRTC in 1985,[375] had to be reviewed if they were to be eligible to compete in any convergence. The prohibition was removed for provincial Crown corporations in 1997.[376] A similar though not total prohibi-

---

370 The expression "influence" is not defined, but "control" means "control in fact" directly or indirectly through securities, trusts, agreements or otherwise. *Ibid.*

371 See Minister of Canadian Heritage, note 14 and accompanying text, above in this chapter.

372 Refer to text accompanying note 55, above in this chapter.

373 See *Direction to the CRTC*, above note 367, definition of "qualified successor" in Part 2.

374 See text accompanying notes 364–65, above in this chapter.

375 See *Direction to the CRTC (Ineligibility to Hold Broadcasting Licences)*, S.O.R./85-627 (27 June 1985), P.C. 1985-2108 (27 June 1985), C. Gaz. 1985. II.3058–60.

376 *Order Amending the Direction to the CRTC (Ineligibility to Hold Broadcasting Licences)*, S.O.R./97-231 (22 April 1997), P.C. 1997-629 (22 April 1997), C. Gaz. 1997.II.1388–91. See also a discussion of this 1997 process in *Government Notices*, Department of Canadian Heritage, Broadcasting Act (25 June 2005),

tion concerning municipally owned Canadian carriers[377] was removed in 2007.[378]

DTH satellite distribution undertakings, as broadcasting undertakings,[379] are required to meet the Canadian ownership requirements. Currently, two Canadian operators have been licensed by the CRTC: Star Choice and Bell ExpressVu.[380] Providers of "pay-per-view" specialty programming channels or services through DTH undertakings must also meet these ownership requirements.

The expansion of DTH distribution, including pay-per-view services,[381] has been seen as enhancing distribution options for Canadians in a manner favourable to competition policy by providing a competitive environment between all participants, including DTH and cable distribution undertakings and specialty programming services (pay-per-view) through both DTH and cable facilities,[382] with no participatory distinction between established Canadian broadcast distributors and Canadian carriers of telecommunications.

2) Canadian Content

To many a bulwark against foreign cultural assimilation,[383] to others an unworkable impairment of free expression and free market principles,[384] the Canadian content requirements are a significant feature of Canadian

---

online: www.gazette.gc.ca/archives/p1/2005/2005-06-25/html/notice-avis-eng. html.

377 Municipally owned Canadian carriers could be issued with a broadcasting licence if the area was not served by another broadcasting undertaking.

378 *Order Amending the Direction to the CRTC (Ineligibility to Hold Broadcasting Licences)*, S.O.R./2007-73.

379 See text accompanying notes 233–37 and generally Figure 2, above in this chapter.

380 See Spectrum Management and Telecommunications, Direct-to-Home (DTH) Satellite Broadcasting, Backgrounder, online: http://strategis.ic.gc.ca/eic/site/ smt-gst.nsf/eng/h_sf05562.html.

381 *Direction to CRTC (Direct-to-home (DTH) Pay-per-view Television Programming Undertakings*, S.O.R./95-320 (6 July 1995), P.C. 1995-1106 (6 July 1995), C. Gaz. 1995.II.1928–31.

382 See, generally, Competition Bureau, *DTH and Pay-Per-View — Proposed Directions to the CRTC* by George N. Addy (Director to Standing Committee on Canadian Heritage, 1995) evaluating the (then) proposed (now implemented) government policy in these contexts, online: www.cb-bc.gc.ca/eic/site/cb-bc.nsf/ eng/00972.html.

383 See, for example, J. Michael Robinson, "The Information Revolution — Culture and Sovereignty — A Canadian Perspective" (1998) 24 Can.-U.S.L.J. 147.

384 See, for example, John A. Ragosta, "The Information Revolution — Culture and Sovereignty — A U.S. Perspective (1998) 24 Can.-U.S.L.J. 155.

broadcasting. The requirements are considered the primary means of meeting the broadcasting policy objective of enhancing a "national identity and cultural sovereignty."[385] Both the cultural and the economic elements of Canadian programming are emphasized in legislative stipulations. First, the Act stipulates, within the broadcasting system "each element . . . shall contribute" to creating Canadian programming. The manner of these contributions will depend on the nature of the particular broadcasting element;[386] and second, ordinarily, every broadcasting undertaking "shall make maximum use, and in no case less than predominant use" of Canadian resources in creating and presenting programs.[387]

From the beginning of radio broadcasting, a source of concern for Canadian authorities was the proximity of the United States.[388] Canada's much smaller and more thinly spread population, with anglophone Canadians sharing with Americans a common language and many common interests,[389] along with the more highly powered stations in the United States, were seen as early as the 1930s as placing Canada in danger of being ancillary to American broadcasting.[390]

With the dual (public and private) components of the single broadcasting system receiving formal recognition in 1958,[391] reliance simply on the public CBC network to provide suitable levels of Canadian programming was considered insufficient. The then regulator (the Board of Broadcast Governors) stipulated "Canadian content" television require-

---

385 *Broadcasting Act*, above note 1, s. 3(1)(b).

386 *Ibid.*, s. 3(1)(e).

387 *Ibid.*, s. 3(1)(f).

388 A. Weir, *The Struggle for National Broadcasting in Canada* (Toronto: McClelland & Stewart, 1965) at 293. See also above, Chapter 1, Section B, setting out the history and development of Canadian regulatory control over broadcasting with the objectives of Canadian control, Canadian content, and availability throughout Canada.

389 This situation was even more acute with respect to television broadcasts beginning in the 1950s. See D. Ellis, *Evolution of the Canadian Broadcasting System: Objectives and Realities, 1928–1968* (Ottawa: Supply and Services Canada, 1979) at 34.

390 Weir, above note 388 at 98 referring to the later 1920s and 1930s, notes the power capacity of American radio stations as being 50 kilowatts contrasting with Canadian stations of mainly 500 watts, with American networks beginning to "dominate the scene." Indeed, Weir later notes a contemporary belief that an American network had sought to acquire all Canadian stations and to incorporate them into a continental network (*ibid.* at 129).

391 See Chapter 1, text accompanying note 61.

ments with effect from 1 April 1961[392] and radio from November 1961.[393] These minimum levels of Canadian programming were required to be presented during peak audience periods.[394] The structure and approach is therefore substantially that of today and has a significant impact on programming on radio[395] and television.[396]

What will qualify as "Canadian content" is assessed according to formulae declared by the CRTC. With respect to musical selection for radio broadcasts, the MAPL ("music, artist, production, and lyrics") system requires that a qualifying musical selection meet at least two of following criteria: a Canadian composed the music, wrote the lyrics, or performed the music or lyrics, or a live performance was recorded wholly in Canada or performed wholly in and broadcast live in Canada.[397] An instrumental performance of a musical composition need have only the tune (or the lyrics) composed by a Canadian.[398]

Canadian content television policy was restructured in 1999[399] and was further reviewed in 2003 by the House of Commons Standing Committee on Canadian Heritage.[400] Key elements included (1) the creation of priority programming with respect to Canadian programs

---

392 *Radio (TV) Broadcasting Regulations*, S.O.R. 59/456, C. Gaz. 1959.II.456. See Regulation 6 ("Canadian Content"). See, generally, Andrew Stewart & William Hull, *Canadian Television Policy and the Board of Broadcast Governors 1958–1968*" (Edmonton: University of Alberta Press, 1994) c. 3 "Canadian Content."

393 See *Radio (A.M.) Broadcasting Regulations*, S.O.R./61-486, C. Gaz. 1961.II.486. See Regulation 12 ("Canadian content"). For a useful timeline with respect to "Canadian content," see Fraser Institute, "Highlights in the Evolution of Canadian Content Regulations," Appendix A of *Canadian Content Regulations Do Not Promote Canadian Culture* (1998), online: The Fraser Institute, online: http://oldfraser.lexi.net/publications/forum/1998/august/appendix1.html.

394 Weir, above note 388 at 372ff.

395 *Radio Regulations, 1986*, S.O.R./86-982, s. 2(2), as am. by *Commercial Radio Policy 1998*, Public Notice, CRTC 1998-41 at para. 11, online: CRTC http://crtc. gc.ca/eng/archive/1998%5CPB98-41.htm, increasing the level of Canadian content for popular music selections to 35 percent from 30 percent from 6:00 a.m. to 6:00 p.m.).

396 *Television Broadcasting Regulations, 1987*, S.O.R./87-49, s. 4, being 60 percent of the broadcast year during 60 percent of "the evening broadcast period," which is between 6:00 p.m. and midnight.

397 *Radio Regulations, 1986*, above note 395, s. 2.2(2). The terms "Canadian," "broadcast day," "broadcast week," and "musical selection" are defined in s. 2.

398 *Ibid.*, ss. 2.2(2)(b) & (c).

399 *Building on Success: A Framework for Canadian Television*, Public Notice CRTC 1999-97, online: CRTC www.crtc.gc.ca/eng/archive/1999/PB99-97.HTM.

400 *Canadian Heritage Report*, above note 4. See also Minister of Canadian Heritage, *The Government of Canada's Response to the Report of the Standing Committee on Canadian Heritage, Our Cultural Sovereignty: The Second Century of Canadian*

in drama, comedy, music, dance, variety, documentary, and entertainment, emphasizing regional production and the interests of local audiences; (2) the retention of delivery requirements that 60 percent of the broadcast year and at least 50 percent of the peak period (6:00 p.m. to midnight) be devoted to qualifying Canadian programming by private television broadcasters;[401] and (3) a measure of flexibility reflected in "time credits" awarded under specified circumstances toward required hours. Evidence before the Standing Committee in 2003 suggested that at least some of these changes were less than successful, and the Committee recommended that a review be undertaken of the priority programming mechanism in particular.[402]

Canadian programming criteria are also applicable to pay television and specialty services television[403] and to pay-per-view services.[404]

The significant difficulty lies in defining, or providing, a formula to determine just what is required to qualify a program as Canadian. The Standing Committee describes an historical shift in determining this, from an arbitrariness of subjective determination based on content to a perceived greater objectivity by reference to a point system whereby accumulation is achieved from meeting secondary criteria.[405] However, the Standing Committee then illustrates convincingly the ultimate arbitrariness of the points system, based on the inconsistent and illogical results it produces.[406]

The Standing Committee seeks in turn to avoid the difficulties inherent in both positions by recommending that nationality of the creators be the determining factor and that a production made by a Canadian be assumed to be a Canadian production.[407] This is also seen as simplifying a convoluted, multifaceted system of rewards[408] and in-

---

Broadcasting (2003), online: www2.parl.gc.ca/Content/HOC/Committee/381/
CHPC/GovResponse/RP1726418/CHPC_Rpt02_GvtRsp/GvtRsp_Part1-e.pdf.

401 The CBC is required to devote 75 percent of the broadcast day and 80 percent peak time (7:00 to 11:00 p.m.) to qualifying Canadian programming. See *Canadian Heritage Report*, above note 4 at 135, Fig. 5(2) "Canadian Content Airtime Requirements."

402 *Ibid.* at 148ff.

403 At least 15 percent of programming must be Canadian. See *Canadian Heritage Report*, above note 4 at 135, Fig. 5(2).

404 Ratios are 1:20 and 1:7 for Canadian and non-Canadian films and Canadian and non-Canadian events. *Ibid.*

405 *Ibid.* at 160.

406 *Ibid.* at 160–65.

407 *Ibid.* at 165 and Recommendation 5.2(b).

408 The rewards may be by grant, licence fee "top up," funding support, tax credit, provincial, or private support.

centives for creating Canadian programming. By looking simply to nationality, the recommendation presents a less structured application of the more detailed points system that allocates points according to the participation of Canadians in various occupational capacities.[409]

No attempt is made here to evaluate the merits of, or the need for, a policy of mandated Canadian content requirements in a world of technical and industry convergence with the capacity for unrestricted global communications and a global market environment. Nor is any opinion expressed in these respects. The current regime sustains a Canadian cultural and entertainment industry. However, the apparent economic dimensions of Canadian content, though fully envisaged in the broadcasting policy for Canada,[410] does encourage foreign interests to perceive the requirements as industrial rather than cultural.[411] The continuing assessment by government and the CRTC[412] of the evolving incidence of broadcasting policy for new media, decentralized in operation and universal in scope, suggests some likely innovation in these contexts. Certainly, regulation by stipulation of time and venue for programming in such media is idle. Canadian content in this media will necessarily be focused more on indirect *encouragement* and *incentive* than on direct demand and stipulation.

Radio, television, and cable distribution will, however, continue to be the primary media for the immediate future and the current regulatory process for Canadian content is likely to continue in these media. Internationally, traditional broadcast media are expressly excluded from the *GATS, Annex on Telecommunications*[413] and a "cultural exception" exists under the *North American Free Trade Agreement (NAFTA)*.[414] Nevertheless, the successful proceeding against Canada before the WTO in respect of the magazine industry in Canada (a "Canadian cultural industry") and import restrictions and tariff protection against for-

---

409 The CRTC uses what is described as the "CAVCO scale," the "Canadian Audio Visual Certification Office" point system established by the Department of Canadian Heritage for other Canadian content-related purposes. See *Canadian Heritage Report*, above note 4 at 134, Fig. 5(1) for occupations and point weightings. Points are gained from the participation of Canadians in various occupational capacities.

410 See, for example, *Broadcasting Act*, above note 1, ss. 3(1)(d)(i) ("economic fabric of Canada") and 3(1)(d)(iii) ("employment opportunities").

411 See Ragosta, above note 384 at 157.

412 See text accompanying note 318, above in this chapter.

413 *GATS, Annex on Telecommunications*, above note 20.

414 *NAFTA*, above note 11, art. 2106.

eign "split-run" periodicals[415] might be seen as a harbinger of changing global ideology with respect to measures that may act as a barrier to international trade, even if seen as "cultural" in Canada.

3) Content Diversity

Related to Canadian content requirements is the developing perspective of diversity in broadcasting content. It is described as a "diversity of voices" and reported by Broadcasting Public Notice CRTC 2008-4, setting out guidelines for the procedures of the Commission in this context.[416] It is focused primarily on the consolidation of ownership of broadcasting facilities, but also includes the diverse cultural dimensions of Canadian society. The broadest formulation is the provision of diverse viewpoints by way of ownership regulation or by programming obligation. To date, the notion "voice" is interpreted as editorial sources of news and information programming locally, nationally, and internationally. The Commission recognizes the value of drama and other programming genre in the social and cultural dimensions of Canadian society but is focused exclusively on editorial news commentary in this current report. Likewise, the scope of the report is limited to the traditional media involving professional journalists with professional standards, codes, and dispute resolution processes, on the basis that Canadians overall still view traditional media as "more trustworthy and credible," despite the growth of unregulated and often unprofessional commentary in the new media.[417]

A broader diversity dimension considers Aboriginal and other ethnic or minority issues and concludes that special measures need not be taken to enhance these perspectives through ownership or holding of broadcasting undertaking licences, as they continue to be addressed by current licencees under monitoring by the CRTC.[418]

The Commission did, however, prescribe detailed guidelines concerning the "diversity of voices" and consolidation of ownership, identifying three levels: diversity of elements, plurality of editorial voices, and

---

415 WTO, Appelate Body Report, *Canada — Certain Measures Concerning Periodicals* (Complaint by the United States), WTO Doc. WT/DS31/AB/R (1997), online: WTO http://docsonline.wto.org/.

416 *Regulatory Policy: Diversity of Voices* (15 January 2008), Broadcasting Public Notice CRTC 2008-4 at para. 6, online: CRTC www.crtc.gc.ca/eng/archive/2008/pb2008-4.htm.

417 *Ibid.* at paras. 9–10.

418 *Ibid.* at paras. 107–19. See also Canadian Association of Broadcasters, *Report on Diversity in Broadcasting* (2006–7), online: www.cab-acr.ca/english/research/07/sub_apr3007.htm.

diversity of programming. The elements reflect the statutory prescription of the broadcasting system: bilingualism in English and French; public, private, and community components; and the maintenance and enhancement of national identity and cultural sovereignty. The public, private, and community element was determined as the source of access to diversity, with a focus on plurality of ownership within the private component of this element[419] to best achieve the diversity of editorial programming with national, regional and local content, the latter being specifically emphasized.[420]

The common ownership policy for radio and terrestrial ("over-the-air" (OTA)) television was retained. In markets in which fewer than eight commercial radio stations are operating in the same language, a person may own or control up to three of those stations, but with only two in the same frequency (AM or FM) band. If the market has eight or more stations, a person may own or control a maximum of two in the AM frequency and two in the FM frequency.[421] OTA television is recognized as the primary source of news for many Canadians. Only one OTA television station in a market may be owned by any one person.[422]

Cross-media ownership policies were established for the first time in three contexts. First, an application to change the effective control of a broadcasting undertaking will not ordinarily be approved by the CRTC if the change will result in the same person controlling a local radio station, a local television station, and a local newspaper serving the same market.[423] Second, the potential cross-ownership of OTA television and discretionary pay and specialty television services has produced an overall policy that will ordinarily deny ownership by one person of more than 45 percent of the total television audience share, with a careful scrutiny of an application involving 35–45 percent.[424] Third, broadcasting distribution undertakings (BDUs), being cable and DTH television services, are subject to a cross-ownership limit that

---

419 Broadcasting Public Notice CRTC 2008-4, above note 416 at para. 16, notes that a future report will address the CBC public broadcaster.
420 Ibid. at paras. 11–21.
421 Ibid. at para. 39. In addition, a person can own one digital radio station for every analog radio station owned. Ibid. at para. 40.
422 Ibid. at paras. 46–50.
423 Ibid. at paras. 51–68. Para. 66 provides definitions of "market," "local newspaper," "local radio station," and "local television station." The Globe and Mail and The National Post are considered national newspapers (rather than local) in all markets. Ibid. at para. 66.
424 Ibid. at para. 87 and generally paras. 69–89.

would prevent one person from controlling *all* BDU services in a given market.[425]

Vertical ownership integration is considered in two contexts: first, the same ownership of programming undertakings and distribution undertakings; and second, programming undertakings and program production entities. The tension in this context reflects the desire of broadcasters to gain rights — essentially copyright — in the programs to more readily exploit the content in new media or digitized distributions. OTA broadcasters therefore urged the CRTC to ameliorate the requirement of 75 percent priority programming (six hours each week) originating with independent producers. Conversely, the independent producers saw the 75 percent requirement as essential, though still not sufficient. Vertically integrated ownership by the broadcaster of the production entity would considerably enhance the broadcaster in controlling rights in any production and facilitate exploitation. The Commission retained the 75 percent priority programming requirements.[426]

The CRTC currently has no policies concerning the cross-ownership of traditional broadcasting undertakings with new media undertakings. Addressing this in 2008, the Commission determined to leave the matter until it had completed planned studies of the impact of new media in Canadian broadcasting.[427] Similarly, the Commission is to undertake a review of community-based broadcasting by radio and television and channels in cable distribution. A satisfactory level of community and university campus–based radio in English and French was acknowledged, but community-based television was seen as deficient, and existing cable channels were found to be moving away from a local to a regional focus.[428]

Necessarily, the CRTC has implemented policies that seek to protect the integrity of the determinations and processes noted above from a change in ownership or effective control of a broadcasting undertaking during the term of the undertaking's first broadcasting licence or upon the sale of an undertaking shortly after the vendor has acquired or gained control over the undertaking. Each of such transactions is examined to prevent trafficking in publicly owned and controlled broadcasting licences that would, additionally, bring into question the

---

425 *Ibid.* at para. 105 and generally paras. 90–106.
426 Broadcasting Public Notice CRTC 2008-4, above note 416 at paras. 147–48.
427 *Ibid.* at para. 159. As to the planned studies of new media, see text accompanying notes 33–39, above in this chapter.
428 *Ibid.* at paras. 160–73.

integrity of the original licensing process.[429] This process must reconcile the accepted policy that the transfer of licences should be determined by market factors. This has been achieved by the application, from 1989 to 1996 on transfer transactions of all broadcasting undertakings, of a "benefits policy" that recognizes a public interest by allocating in the market transaction a percentage of its value (10 percent for television and 6 percent for radio) for incremental spending for the benefit of the audience in the particular market as well as the overall broadcasting system. The Commission considers the application for transfer as a whole, including this benefit factor. From 1996, distribution undertakings were excluded from the benefits policy, by reason of adequate competition in this sector. The benefits policy remains for programming undertakings and networks. This was reaffirmed in 2008 given the significant contribution made by this policy to Canadian programming.[430] Distributions undertakings do, however, contribute 3 percent of gross annual revenues to Canadian programming.[431]

4) New Media Analysis

The social, political, and economic implications of new media with all their uncertainties and unknowns press heavily on government and regulators alike. Never before has a phenomenon of technology been of such a dimension as to challenge the very sovereignty of territorial government. In June 2006, the Governor in Council issued under section 15 of the *Broadcasting Act*, a direction to the CRTC to hold hearings and provide a factual report on the future environment for broadcasting in the light of new media.[432] The Commission reported extensively in June 2006 with the benefit of industry and public consultation.[433] A consensus of stakeholders accepted the current legislative framework. Any change advocated was seen to invoke existing regulatory and administrative processes.[434] The Commission distinguished the objectives in broadcasting policy in section 3(1) of the *Broadcasting Act*, describing them as cultural

---

429 *Ibid.* at paras. 151–56.
430 *Ibid.* at paras. 120–36.
431 *Ibid.* at para. 125.
432 *Order issuing a direction to the CRTC to examine the future environment facing the broadcasting system*, P.C. 2006-519 (8 June 2006), online: www.gazette.gc.ca/ archives/p1/2006/2006-06-17/html/order-decret-eng.html.
433 CRTC, *The Future Environment Facing the Canadian Broadcasting System*, Report prepared pursuant to section 15 of the *Broadcasting Act* (14 December 2006), online: CRTC www.crtc.gc.ca/Eng/publications/reports/broadcast/rep061214. htm [CRTC Report].
434 *Ibid.* at paras. 332–37.

in nature, from the objectives of regulatory policy in section 5(2), establishing the process of achieving the objectives with flexibility in technology, consumer choice, and administrative burdens.[435]

Some comfort was taken from evidence that traditional media undertakings in Canada were still the prime source for most audiovisual information provided to Canadians in the unregulated new media,[436] yet the Commission acknowledged that the new media enabled Canadians to bypass the regulated system for both news and entertainment, adversely affecting the broadcasting objectives in both business and culture.[437] A broad policy divergence emerged between broadcasters and distributors, emphasizing the abundance of Canadian content on the new media[438] and of user choice, and cultural groups, urging regulation of the new distribution sources.[439]

The Commission identified three categories of audiovisual content in the new media: user-generated (including YouTube) content; relatively inexpensive, commercial content; and high-quality, relatively expensive drama and documentary programs. Regulation was considered unnecessary in the first two categories. User-generated content was described as outside the intended scope of the *Broadcasting Act*, and relatively inexpensive commercial content was seen to involve sufficient Canadian competition. The third category — high-quality, relatively expensive drama and documentary programming — was seen as insufficient or simply fledgling in Canadian content in the new media.[440] Here the political divergence between proponents of consumer choice and those of Canadian content was seen as stark and significant.[441]

The Commission resolved to monitor the sector through 2007 and 2008,[442] with review being triggered on either of adverse economic impact of new media on traditional media undertakings (being seen as inevitable at some stage)[443] or insufficient or decreasing Canadian presence in new media.[444] As in the Direction from the Governor in Council, the CRTC emphasized the need for Canada to "remain relevant" in

435 *Ibid.* at para. 347.
436 *Ibid.* at paras. 338 and 361–62. See also text accompanying note 417, above in this chapter.
437 CRTC Report, *ibid.* at paras. 339–41.
438 Canadian websites were said to dominate in the news and information category, *ibid.* at para. 354.
439 *Ibid.* at paras. 343–45.
440 *Ibid.* at paras. 352–54.
441 *Ibid.* at paras. 348 and 355.
442 *Ibid.* at paras. 435–40.
443 *Ibid.* at para. 366.
444 *Ibid.* at para. 439.

the global digital media,[445] and accepted that existing forms of regulation may need modification to provide an incentive basis, given the nature of the new media, and that this may require approaches beyond its jurisdiction.[446]

In 2009, after considering the submissions from stakeholders and the public, the CRTC determined to continue the 1999 exemption[447] from broadcasting regulation of "new media broadcasting undertakings," including "all Internet-based and public mobile point to point broadcasting services."[448] New media broadcasting undertakings are, nevertheless, subject to: first, a reporting requirement to enable the CRTC to continue to monitor the development of new media broadcasting,[449] and, second, a requirement of avoiding the giving of undue preference to any person, including the undertaking itself. The burden of proof in any proceeding lies with the undertaking in demonstrating compliance with this requirement.[450]

5) Digital Technology in Traditional Media

Considerable technological change is also occurring in traditional broadcasting media. The CRTC describes it as the migration of broadcast signals from historically analog to digital, then ultimately to high-definition digital signals. Digital transmissions are acknowledged to allow significantly more flexibility in the provision and accessing of a broadcast service, with greater opportunities of consumer choice and control over their viewing. This will facilitate a more market-focused approach to broadcasting services. The compression of digital signals will also allow greater capacity in distribution systems that will facilitate the creation of new services. The principal new service is qualita-

---

445 *Ibid.* at para. 440. See above note 432 for the Direction of the Governor in Council.

446 *Ibid.* at paras. 398 and 435.

447 See text accompanying note 314ff. in this chapter.

448 *Amendments to the Exemption Order for new media broadcasting undertakings (Appendix A to Public Notice CRTC 1999-197); Revocation of the Exemption Order for Mobile television broadcasting undertakings*, Broadcasting Order CRTC 2009-660 (22 October 2009) at paras. 1 and 4–10 defining "new media broadcasting undertakings." The reference to the revocation of the exemption order for mobile television broadcasting undertakings refers to measures that had been made for these media in 2007, now incorporated within the current order.

449 Broadcasting Order CRTC 2009-660, *ibid.* at paras. 19–26. See Broadcasting Notice of Consultation CRTC 2010-97 (18 February 2010) seeking comments from interested parties with respect to this requirement.

450 Broadcasting Order CRTC 2009-660, *ibid.* at paras. 11–18.

tive — the availability of high-definition digital television (HDTV). The difference lies in the detail, or the resolution, of the image that is transmitted and received by viewers. Higher resolution brings greater detail and precision. These factors overall will significantly enhance the value of the media and assist in maintaining the competitive position of traditional media against new media.[451]

The current regulatory position concerning digital transmissions by cable distribution systems is set out by the CRTC in consolidating Broadcasting Notices 2006-23 and 2006-74.[452] The Commission's efforts concerning digitization began in 2000 with the creation of a Digital Migration Working Group to establish a consensus throughout the industry, including both programming and distribution entities and also with regard to the views of consumers. Industry-wide consensus could not be reached, however, and the Working Group was adjourned *sine die* in 2003. From 2005, the Commission narrowed its focus to a migration in only pay and specialty service television, considering first a framework for these broadcasts by cable distribution.[453] A framework for similar programming in high-definition DTH satellite distributions was reserved for later determination.[454] It was subsequently included within public hearings from January through May 2008, reviewing the framework for broadcasting distribution undertakings and discretionary programming.[455]

The determinations concerning cable pay and specialty service emphasize digital television, especially HDTV, as essentially a *replacement* of analog so that the existing licencees should be the holders of the new HDTV licences, transitional licenses, or simply amended analog licences.[456] However, new entrants will be considered if the existing analog licence holder fails to apply for an HDTV distribution transitional licence within a reasonable time.[457] The determinations general-

---

451 See text accompanying note 443, above in this chapter.
452 *Digital Migration Framework* (27 February 2006), Broadcasting Public Notice CRTC 2006-23, online: CRTC www.crtc.gc.ca/eng/archive/2006/pb2006-23. htm; and *Regulatory Framework for the Licensing and Distribution of High Definition Pay and Specialty Services* (15 June 2006), Broadcasting Public Notice CRTC 2006-74, online: CRTC www.crtc.gc.ca/eng/archive/2006/pb2006-74.htm.
453 Broadcasting Public Notice CRTC 2006-23, *ibid.* at paras. 7–9.
454 Broadcasting Public Notice CRTC 2006-74, above note 452 at para. 3
455 *Review of the regulatory frameworks for broadcasting distribution undertakings and discretionary programming services* (5 July 2007), Broadcasting Notice of Public Hearing CRTC 2007-10 at para. 13, online: CRTC www.crtc.gc.ca/eng/archive/2007/n2007-10.htm.
456 Broadcasting Public Notice CRTC 2006-74, above note 452 at para. 57.
457 *Ibid.* at paras. 47 and 79.

ly include detailed Canadian content requirements for digital services, consistent with the broadcasting objectives.

OTA (non-cable, non-DTH satellite) television service in the migration to digital transmission has been slow. Only in 2007 was a digital conversion deadline mandated. With effect from 31 August 2011, licences for broadcasting OTA will be issued only for digital signals.[458] Analog broadcasts will terminate at that time, subject to a narrow exception for continued analog transmissions to northern and remote communities if no digital service is to be provided.[459] Viewers will need either to acquire a television receiver equipped with a digital tuner or to acquire a device (set-top converter box) that will convert OTA standard definitional television (SDTV) digital signals to a format capable of being received by analog receivers. Cable or DTH subscribers will receive SDTV digital signals through an analog receiver. A corresponding conversion to digital television transmissions in the United States was effected on 12 June 2009, and the position described above applies to Canadian reception of US television transmissions. While even cable and DTH subscribers will need a conversion device to view OTA HDTV, many will be satisfied with basic SDTV digital signals (640 pixels, 480 lines), which produce an image quality similar to analog.[460]

The delay in Canada resulted from some lack of consensus,[461] but more so from the determination in 2002 that transition to digital broadcasting should be left to market influences.[462] Digital conversion in the United States was contemplated as providing the Canadian market with an incentive to convert. Additionally, the program production communities in Canada did not embrace HD technology in productions until 2006–7, when still only 5 to 7 percent of all Canadian productions were in HDTV format.[463] A study has compared Canada's progress in the digital migration with that in a number of other jurisdictions.[464]

---

458 *Determinations regarding certain aspects of the regulatory framework for over-the-air television* (17 May 2007), Broadcasting Public Notice CRTC 2007-53, online: CRTC www.crtc.gc.ca/Eng/archive/2007/pb2007-53.htm, especially para. 61.

459 *Ibid.* at paras. 55–65, especially paras. 55 and 65.

460 See Office of Consumer Affairs, Industry Canada, *Analog-to-Digital Television Transmission in Canada,* online: www.ic.gc.ca/epic/site/oca-bc.nsf/en/ca02336e. html.

461 See text accompanying note 453, above in this chapter.

462 See Broadcasting Public Notice CRTC 2007-53, above note 458 at para. 50.

463 Michael McEwen, "A Report to the CRTC on Digital Transition Strategies in a Number of Different Countries" (1 September 2006), online: CRTC www.crtc. gc.ca/Eng/publications/reports/radio/mcewen.htm.

464 *Ibid.*

6) Commercial Radio

Commercial radio was the first broadcast technology. It is still important today, being the principal source of local news, events, and entertainment and a focus of local business advertising. In December 2006, the CRTC issued simultaneously three major reviews of commercial radio concerning the Commission's general commercial radio policy,[465] the procedures for radio licence and small market applications,[466] and digital radio policy.[467]

Commercial radio signals are still substantially analog sound signals carried by electromagnetic microwave transmission on either an AM (amplitude modulation) or an FM (frequency modulation). AM transmissions are lower in the spectrum (approximately 535 to 1,705 kHz) than FM transmissions (approximately 88 to 108 MHz).[468] AM transmissions have very limited range as a "ground wave" (a radio wave staying at ground level), but proceed great distances by refracting (hitting and bouncing off) the atmospheric layer known as the ionosphere so that they can circle the globe in triangular style, in lines between earth and the ionosphere. FM transmissions proceed along sight lines ultimately passing through the ionosphere and into space. They must be intercepted on the way, usually by tall antennae placed on high ground. However, FM is substantially less affected by external interference and has a greater (high to low) sound frequency range, enhancing the quality of sounds (such as music) with greater range extremes than the human voice.[469]

---

465 *Commercial Radio Policy 2006* (15 December 2006), Broadcasting Public Notice CRTC 2006-158, online: CRTC www.crtc.gc.ca/eng/archive/2006/pb2006-158.htm.

466 *Revised policy concerning the issuance of calls for radio applications and a new process for applications to serve small markets* (15 December 2006), Broadcasting Public Notice CRTC 2006-159, online: CRTC www.crtc.gc.ca/eng/archive/2006/pb2006-159.htm.

467 *Digital Radio Policy* (15 December 2006), Broadcasting Public Notice CRTC 2006-160, online: CRTC www.crtc.gc.ca/eng/archive/2006/pb2006-160.htm.

468 Kilohertz refers to the number of cycles per second in a measure of thousands. Megahertz presents a measure of millions. The expression "modulation" refers to how the sound is carried on a magnetic radio wave. Either the rate of oscillation or the height (high or low) of the waves is modified. AM sound modifies the height (amplitude) of the wave. As a result, AM signals are susceptible to "interference" by other radio transmissions or electrical currents. The height of FM transmissions are not affected in this manner and can transmit sounds of more extreme (higher or lower) frequencies. See, "AM, FM Waves and Sound," online: www.cybercollege.com/frtv/frtv017.htm.

469 *Ibid.*

As with other media, digitization revolutionizes transmission, reception, and quality of the sounds received. In an analog signal the sound is included within the electromagnetic carrier signal. It is subject to all interferences with the signal, particularly so with AM transmissions. With digital technology the sound or content is converted to fragments coded numerically (digits) and transmitted many times in these fragments with the electromagnetic signals. A receiving device collects the digitized fragments as they flow through the air and reassembles or decodes the numbering to produce the content. The duplication in the fragmenting of the transmission increases the chances of successful reception of sufficient packages of fragments to reassemble a high-quality content or sound product. In addition, interference is avoided by compression of digital signals into smaller packages, enabling many signals to travel on a "broadband" frequency, described as 1,500 times wider than that in analog radio.[470]

From 1995, the Commission has considered digital radio broadcasting (DRB) to be a replacement for AM and FM analog services. Despite a promising start, digital conversion was found by the Commission in 2006 to have "stalled."[471] Principal reasons were identified. First, the cost of DRB receivers is high because the market is limited. This reflects the absence of a universal technical format for DRB, with Canada having chosen L-Band (in the 1,452 MHz to 1,492 MHz frequency block) while the United States has chosen another[472] and much of the rest of the world yet another.[473] The cost of each receiver in Canada is therefore correspondingly greater. Displays on the DRB receivers must also accommodate both French and English languages, narrowing the market further to an essentially Canadian context.[474] Second, the DRB services approved from 1995 to the present are spot centred in urban markets with signals that do not extend to traffic corridors between centres, thereby negating DRB as a medium for reception in vehicles.[475] Third, new technologies and distribution formats have incorporated radio and have to some extent eclipsed DRB in the traditional radio

---

470 See "Digital Radio" (updated to June 2007), online: www.explainthatstuff.com/digitalradio.html.

471 Broadcasting Public Notice CRTC 2006-160, above note 467 at para. 4.

472 In the United States, DRB uses a technology known as "In-Band-On-Channel" (IBOC). See *ibid.* at para. 5.

473 *Ibid.*, referring to the frequency block "Band III," a very high frequency (VHF) band. See, for example, the United Kingdom using Band III (217.5–230 MHz), in Digital Radio Now, online: www.getdigitalradio.com/about-digital-radio.

474 Broadcasting Public Notice CRTC 2006-160, above note 467.

475 *Ibid.* at para. 6.

medium. New technologies include satellite radio services,[476] Internet delivery of streaming radio,[477] and other audio-related technologies such as file sharing and podcasting.[478]

The Commission noted its relationship with Industry Canada with respect to frequency spectrum. Allocation and authorization of new technical standards lies with the Department, not the Commission, which licenses the broadcasting system in order to attain the broadcasting objectives within the relevant technical framework approved by the Department.[479] Given this limitation, the Commission, within its jurisdiction, removed restrictions on the type of broadcast services that can be developed in the Canadian L-Band DRB frequency. This recognized that only the introduction of "innovative services" can stimulate sufficient consumer interest in L-Band DRB.[480] As for programming, DRB L-Band operators would be subject to the requirements applicable to FM analog services, with considerable opportunity to seek further exemptions to enhance innovation.[481] Use of the US standard In-Band-On-Channel (IBOC) technology was considered, and the Commission indicated that it would provide an expedited process for applicants that

---

476 Satellite radio signals are always digital, producing near-CD quality music that rivals the quality of an FM analog signal but over a greater distance and without static, from satellites in geostationary orbit approximately 35,000 km above Earth. The signal is received and decoded directly from the satellite by a listener's radio receiver. The footprint of the signal is such that distance from a source, especially when a listener is mobile, is irrelevant. However, line of sight is still essential and in urban areas buildings can obstruct the signal. To avoid this, terrestrial repeater transmitters are sometimes used. See Kevin Bonsor, "How Satellite Radio Works" (26 September 2001), online: www.howstuffworks. com/satellite-radio.htm. The CRTC licensed three Canadian providers in 2005. See CRTC, News Release, "The CRTC Authorizes Canada's First Three Subscription Radio Services" (16 June 2005). Provisions were stipulated to ensure Canadian content and to benefit established and new Canadian artists. Two of these licensees have subsequently merged. See "Sirius completes acquisition of XM Satellite" *Reuters* (29 July 2008), online: www.reuters.com/article/ idUSN2926292520080730?sp=true.

477 See Debra Beller, "How Internet Radio Works" (27 March 2001), online: electronics.howstuffworks.com/internet-radio.htm. The Internet allows receipt of high-quality radio broadcasts from anywhere in the world. Broadcasters simply upload their signals to the Internet. They may be delivered to an accessor either by downloads or by streaming audio. The former is stored by the accessor on the accessing computer. The latter is not; it is simply continuous in a manner similar to regular radio.

478 *Ibid.* at para. 8.

479 *Ibid.* at para. 33.

480 *Ibid.* at paras. 36–38.

481 *Ibid.* at para. 41.

might use this technology if such is approved by Industry Canada. Essentially, IBOC technology provides for the carriage of both analog and digital, the latter being carried on top of the former. Analog receivers can receive the analog signal and digital receivers the digital signal, or both signals with a choice to the listener.[482]

In effect, in 2006, the Commission set out to ameliorate the regulatory provisions within its jurisdiction to try to make DRB an attractive option and thereby facilitate conversion from analog. Significantly, unlike OTA television, there is no deadline for conversion in radio from analog to digital, and analog is expected to remain as a viable option for many years. In the meantime, in May 2007, Industry Canada announced a public consultation to reassess L-Band, noting that this standard may no longer assist in moving radio to DRB.[483] The future seems to lie with the US IBOC format.

Beyond DRB issues, the Commission reviewed commercial radio and found the industry to be financially healthy, especially FM broadcasters, but with some uncertainty due to future competition from the new media. Applicants for licences and renewals are therefore to be questioned with respect to plans for employing new distribution platforms.[484] This seems to be designed to ensure participation and relevance of Canadian radio in the new media.[485] Reflecting this uncertainty and the finding that youth listeners, in particular, are more inclined to utilize the unregulated new technologies and media,[486] the amount of Canadian content in air play was not increased overall.[487] The ceiling of financial contributions to organizations developing Canadian content and Canadian artists was increased[488] and a commitment to cultural diversity within Canadian content was reaffirmed.[489]

---

482 *Ibid.* at paras. 51–57.

483 Industry Canada, *SAB-001-07 Spectrum Planning Activities and Review of the 1995 Transitional Digital Radio Policy* (28 May 2007), online: www.ic.gc.ca/epic/site/smt-gst.nsf/en/sf08772e.html.

484 Broadcasting Public Notice CRTC 2006-158, above note 465 at para. 31.

485 See text accompanying note 39, above in this chapter.

486 Broadcasting Public Notice CRTC 2006-158, above note 465 at para. 82.

487 *Ibid.* at paras. 81–94. Small increases in concert music and "jazz and blues" were made, *ibid.* at para. 94.

488 *Ibid.* at paras. 97–124.

489 *Ibid.* at paras. 129–54.

D. SUMMATION AND PROGNOSIS

This chapter commenced with a perspective that sought to highlight the dramatic and diverse developments and restructuring occurring in the telecommunications industry and the laws and policies that provide the juristic and policy framework. The intervening discussion followed the legislative focus of telecommunications (point-to-point) and broadcasting (point-to-mass) from the *Telecommunications Act* (1993) and the *Broadcasting Act* (1991), respectively. Calls to combine these provisions into one enactment are supported by the convergence of the two sectors within the technologies of new media and new delivery platforms and, perhaps, by the participation of industry providers in both sectors. A legislative integration may therefore assist in meeting these situations and will also bring a measure of presentational logic and convenience. However, across the industry as a whole, some elements of each sector will continue to present distinctions from the others, despite convergence in other areas.

Non-broadcast telecommunication is essentially an intangible market commodity of a sector that has been substantially deregulated and is operating under rules and policies designed to promote competitive operations in the public interest of lowering costs and prices. In consequence, the role of the Competition Bureau has been enhanced against that of the CRTC and the sector has been seen as key to developing greater competitiveness in general within the Canadian economy. It is also included within the international framework of the *General Agreement on Trade in Services (GATS)* through the *Annex on Telecommunications* within the World Trade Organization (WTO). Canadian ownership requirements may be seen as protecting a national interest in assets of strategic, economic, and social importance, but removal or at least some amelioration in this requirement is now contemplated in the interest of global investment strategies and the maintaining of competition.

Broadcasting, however, is linked inexorably with the political dimensions of creating a national and cultural identity for Canada. It is a sector focused on *content*. While certainly of economic importance, broadcasting is not simply an economic commodity. Broadcasts provide an overall public service in the distribution of news and commentary of global, national, regional, and local significance and entertainment. Content informs and shapes public opinion and encourages policies of social equality, diversity, and inclusion. Broadcasting remains a heavily regulated sector and any attempt to deregulate or to remove Canadian ownership requirements is likely to produce political embroilment to an extent that cannot similarly be expected over point-to-point tele-communications.

The spectrum of political diversity in this respect is amply illustrated by the conflicting reports of the two House of Commons standing committees presented in 2003. The Standing Committee on Canadian Heritage laid bare an apprehension of foreign ownership and, with an objective of preserving cultural identity, urged government to keep broadcasting off the table in future international trade negotiations and to seek exemptions of culture or cultural industries from any future trade commodification.[490] The Standing Committee on Industry, Science and Technology, on the other hand, was more focused on industry and foreign investment in Canada. While containing two dissenting positions,[491] the majority recommended a recategorization of telecommunications as "carriage" organizations and "content" organizations. Carriage organizations would include telecommunications common carriers (principally telephone companies) and broadcasting distribution undertakings (principally broadcast cable companies). Content organizations would include programming undertakings, such as television and radio stations and DTH providers.[492]

Policy dimensions inherent in such recommendations are reflected elsewhere,[493] and are consistent with the reality of convergence and the direction of *GATS* encouraging progressive liberalization of national control over telecommunications as a sector of economic activity. The economic objectives are increased competition with access to foreign capital for investment, with lower costs through economies of scale. The Standing Committee reports[494] Canada to have the most restrictive provisions on foreign capital of any country in the Organisation for Economic Co-operation and Development (OECD). The Standing Committee's Report outlines further the position in other OECD countries of small or medium economies, such as New Zealand and Australia, where lesser or only partial national ownership measures are imposed. These can be lower percentage limits or limits imposed only on the primary national carrier, with the market open to entry by competing entities without foreign ownership restrictions.[495]

---

490 See Canadian Heritage Report, above note 4 at 525–33.
491 Report of the Standing Committee, above note 21. Dissenting opinions are given by the Bloc Québécois (79–82) and the New Democratic Party (83–88).
492 *Ibid.* at 41–43.
493 See above notes 74–77.
494 Report of the Standing Committee, above note 21 at 7.
495 *Ibid.*, Appendix 4 at 69–71.

A likely outcome in Canada will be an amelioration, but not abolition, of Canadian ownership requirements of primarily *carrier* entities,
including broadcast distribution undertakings, which essentially compete with telecommunication common carriers. However, primarily
content providers (radio and television broadcasters and DTH television
services) are likely to retain Canadian ownership requirements in the
immediate future.

The features of broadcast regulation will nevertheless change.
Internet-related technologies have provided vehicles for Canadians to
bypass entirely the traditional media and delivery platforms of both
broadcast and non-broadcast telecommunications. Meeting broadcasting objectives will depend, in this new media, on *incentive* and *encouragement* to ensure participatory presence and on Canadian content of
a type and of a quality that will encourage access by users both in
Canada and abroad. Indeed, the CRTC has acknowledged that broader
involvement, beyond the jurisdiction of the CRTC, may be required
from government and industry.

The CRTC itself may be the subject of reorganization. The 2005–6
Telecommunications Policy Review Panel (TPRP) recommended the
creation of a transitional Telecommunications Competition Tribunal
(TCT) jointly between the CRTC and the Competition Bureau, and in
the longer term to enhance the telecommunications expertise of the
CRTC Commissioners and staff to form a core of five commissioners to
determine telecommunications matters. This is a sound approach. The
TPRP also recommended that this core be joined by additional commissioners, presumably with greater expertise in broadcasting when
issues of this sector are before the Commission. This latter aspect requires greater consideration. The TPRP was mandated to report on the
telecommunications sector, and the recommendation with respect to
institutional reform in that context is reflective of the relational position of the CRTC and the Competition Bureau and the overwhelming
significance of competition theory in that sector. Expertise in competition theory and practice might not, however, be sufficient or even
relevant in the broadcasting sector, at least beyond the incidence of
convergence. Accordingly, it is suggested that if a structural reform of
the nature proposed by the TPRP be made, decisions concerning the
broadcasting sector should proceed with a majority of commissioners
who have expertise in this sector, where to date the traditional media
(radio, television, and cable) is maintaining its customer base with new
media that is still essentially supplemental to, rather than substitu-
tive of, the traditional media. This situation will be reinforced in the
medium term at least by the higher quality that digitization, especially

HDTV, will bring to the traditional media. Other features that might re-inforce traditional media can be found in the recommendations of the Standing Committee on Canadian Heritage, which reported in 2003. These included (1) an enhancement of the ability of the CBC to fulfill its role as the national public broadcaster;[496] and, (2) that the CRTC per-mit Canadian broadcasting distribution undertakings to offer a wider range of international programming, albeit respectful of Canadian con-tent requirements, to provide a disincentive to viewers obtaining de-encryption devices for DTH television from US sources.[497]

---

496 Canadian Heritage Report, above note 4 at 177ff.
497 *Ibid.* at 522ff.

TRADEMARKS, DOMAIN NAMES, AND INTERFERENCES

A. INTRODUCTION

Trademarks are infringed routinely in the telecommunications media. A prime context is in advertisements on radio and television. However, this chapter is not concerned with trademark law in general, nor with infringements that simply happen to occur in telecommunications media. Rather, it is concerned with trademark issues that have specific application to telecommunications media. Invariably, these occur in the medium of the Internet, including domain name exclusivity in comparison with trademark protection.

Furthermore, trademark and, to some extent, copyright law, are sometimes used in an attempt to accord relief for what is essentially an interference with a website or digital electronic system. For example, in *Pro-C Ltd. v. Computer City Inc.* trademark infringement was found but was reversed on appeal, when a US entity with a trademark in the United States substantially common with a trademark in Canada embarked on a marketing drive that caused the Canadian entity to be overwhelmed with electronic inquiries to an extent that its system failed.[1] Certainly, there was some user or customer confusion in a general sense, or the Canadian business would not have been accessed, but this confusion

---

1   *Pro-C Ltd. v. Computer City Inc.* (2000), 7 C.P.R. (4th) 193, [2000] O.J .No. 2823 (S.C.J.), rev'd (2001), 14 C.P.R. (4th) 441 (Ont. C.A.), leave to appeal to S.C.C. refused, [2002] S.C.C.A. No. 5 [*Pro-C Ltd.*].

was not of the nature applicable in trademark or passing off to draw customers from one entity to the other. In effect the situation reflected a general tortious context of either intentional or negligent conduct by the defendant that caused loss to the plaintiff. In this instance, the conduct was not intentionally directed at the plaintiff's business,[2] so any relief would ordinarily be of the tort of negligence if the requisite duty and breach of the standard of care could be established, subject to limitations of remoteness of damage.[3]

The attempt in *Pro-C Ltd.* to cast relief as trademark infringement demonstrates the paucity of available legal responses for interference with communications media. If the defendant's conduct had been to damage the plaintiff's website and business intentionally it might have been characterized as a "denial of service" (DoS) activity. Might this then have invoked relief for tortious activities? Could this be argued equally with respect to other disruptions such as spamming or proliferation by "pop-up" notices that disrupt use? The intentional infliction of a virus to a system would certainly seem to demand a response. Could any or all of these situations constitute trespass? A related context is the intentional placement of "worms" that might not only destroy media and data but also surreptitiously usurp the use of an infected computer for the purposes of the usurper (for example, to transmit spam or engage in a denial of service with respect to a third party). Might this be both trespass and conversion? Might deposited sequences that track or monitor (for example, "cookies") or take information (for example, spyware) constitute trespass and privacy infringement?

Perhaps these issues call for comprehensive *sui generis* legislative measures, providing for both criminal and civil responsibilities, in these contexts. Or ought relief be left to be crafted judicially through a caselaw mechanism with reliance on civil code, common law, and equitable principles? This is far from a seemingly straight forward choice. It raises directly issues of constitutional legislative competence, as discussed in Chapter 1, and (in the absence of international treaty arrangements) challenges for the extraterritorial dimensions that must arise in a telecommunications context and will invoke an application of private international law (conflict of laws), discussed in Chapter 6.

---

2   *Ibid.* at 193, para. 148 (S.C.J., cited to C.P.R.).
3   Possibly proceedings in nuisance might be contemplated on the basis of *Motherwell v. Motherwell* (1976), 73 D.L.R. (3d) 62 (Alta. S.C. (A.D.)) [*Motherwell*], involving multitudinous daily telephone calls to an occupier of land causing harassment that amounted to an unlawful interference with the enjoyment of land.

This chapter will consider these matters primarily from a common law perspective, drawing upon fledgling developments in the United States. However, before visiting these nebulous topics, Internet-related features of trademark and passing off infringement, along with issues of domain name identifications, are considered.

B. INFRINGEMENT

In 2005, the Supreme Court in *Kirkbi AG v. Ritvik Holdings Inc.* emphasized that Canadian trademark law is a single system,[4] being a composite of federal statutory trademark law and provincial common law proceedings such as the torts of passing off and the equivalent proceedings under the *Civil Code of Québec*.[5] Section 7, *Trade-marks Act*[6] provides federal statutory relief in situations that mirror proceedings at common or civil law. Historically, this has compromised the scope of relief under section 7 with issues of constitutional validity.[7] The Supreme Court in *Kirkbi* removed doubts from section 7(b), which recognizes a federal proceeding in the nature of passing off.[8] The benefit of this is the ability to seek an order throughout all Canada from the Federal Court.

Sections 19 and 20, *Trade-marks Act*[9] provide for infringement of registered trademarks. Section 19 gives the owner of a registered trademark the "exclusive right to the use throughout Canada of the trademark" in respect of the wares and services for which it is registered. This section relates to use of the *actual* mark with the *actual* wares and services for which the mark is registered. A mere use of the mark as a trademark with the relevant wares and services may constitute an

---

4   *Kirkbi AG v. Ritvik Holdings Inc.*, 2005 SCC 65 at para. 31 [*Kirkbi*].
5   Art. 1457 C.C.Q. (formerly art. 1053 C.C.L.C.) is interpreted as providing relief in circumstances similar to the common law torts.
6   *Trade-marks Act*, R.S.C. 1985, c. T-13, s. 7.
7   For the historical difficulties concerning the constitutional validity of all or parts of this section, see *MacDonald v. Vapor Canada Ltd.*, [1977] 2 S.C.R. 134 [*MacDonald*]; *Asbjorn Horgard A/S v. Gibbs/Nortac Industries Ltd.*, [1987] 3 F.C. 544 (C.A.); *Dumont Vins & Spiritueux Ind. v. Celliers du Monde Inc.*, [1992] 2 F.C. 634 (C.A.); and *Smith & Nephew Inc. v. Glen Oak Inc.*, [1996] 3 F.C. 565 at 574–79 (C.A.), leave to appeal to S.C.C. refused, [1997] S.C.C.A. No. 433 [*Smith & Nephew*].
8   *Kirkbi*, above note 4 at para. 36.
9   *Trade-marks Act*, above note 6, ss. 19 & 20.

infringement without any need for confusion.[10] Use as a trademark presents an indication of origin[11] but this may be only evidentiary.[12] The Federal Court of Appeal, relying on the definition of "trade-mark," has emphasized this primary purpose so that a use that is not deceptive or confusing in this respect, might not violate section 19.[13] Section 20, however, precludes the use of trademarks or trade names that are "confusing" with respect to the registered mark. It is not limited to situations of the same class of wares or services but must still confuse as to origin.[14] The expression "confusing" is defined in sections 2 and 6.

In an Internet context, a trademark might be infringed by advertising and selling products or services from a website that displays the trademark of another supplier or a mark that is confusing with the trademark of that supplier. To constitute a "use" with respect to *services*, section 4(2), *Trade-marks Act* would enable a "use" to be made merely by advertising the services,[15] which would include a website display. The position is more restricted with respect to *wares*. The mark must "at the time of the transfer of the property in or possession of the wares, in the normal course of trade" be exhibited on the wares themselves or on the packaging in which they are distributed, or otherwise be associated with the wares so as to give notice of the association to the transferee of the property in, or possession of, the wares. As for *exports*, a mark on the wares or packages when exported from Canada is deemed to be "used" in Canada.[16]

---

10 From a literal perspective "the exclusive right to use" a registered mark is free of any requirement of confusion so long as the exact mark is used with the exact wares or services. See *Mr. Submarine Ltd.* v. *Amandista Investments Ltd.* (1987), 19 C.P.R. (3d) 3 at 9 (F.C.A.) "assuming, without deciding" to this effect.

11 See *Clairol International Corp.* v. *Thomas Supply & Equipment Co. Ltd.*, [1968] 2 Ex. C.R. 552 at 566 [*Clairol*]. This limitation flows from the meaning of the expression "trade-mark," as defined in s. 2 and developed in s. 4, requiring the mark to be affixed to wares (or their packaging) so as to be "associated with the wares" (s. 4(1)) and thereby distinguishing these wares or services from the wares or services of others, being the meaning of "trade-mark" in s. 2.

12 See H.G. Fox, *The Canadian Law of Trade Marks and Unfair Competition*, 3d ed. (Toronto: Carswell, 1972) at 335 discussing this aspect from an historical perspective, and more recently, Sheldon Burshtein, "Trade-Mark Use in Canada: The Who, What, Where, When, Why and How (Part II)" (1997) 12 I.P.J. 75 at 85, 107, & 108.

13 See *Smith & Nephew*, above note 7 at 571–73 (C.A.).

14 See Burshtein, above note 12 at 106 & 107.

15 *Trade-marks Act*, above note 6, s. 4(2) provides for a trademark to be "used or displayed in the performance or advertising of . . . services."

16 See *ibid.*, s. 4.

Display of a mark on a website selling wares will ordinarily give notice to the transferee of the property in, or possession of, the wares, of an association of the mark with the wares. This will enable a "use" to be established. The alternative, that the mark be on the wares or packaging "at the time of transfer of property in or possession of the wares" must necessarily occur subsequent to the website transaction, except in the case of digitized products (software programs and visual or sound products) transferred immediately from the website.[17]

Two remedial provisions in the *Trade-marks Act* present particular considerations. First, relief under section 22 does not involve any element of confusion as to origin of wares or services applicable to any mark. It provides for the diminution of the goodwill attaching to a registered trademark. In 2006, the Supreme Court confirmed unequivocally that relief by way of dilution was afforded to registered trademarks by section 22,[18] drawing "useful elucidation of relevant concepts" from dilution theory in the United States.[19] The essence of dilution and other categories of depreciation (for example, inaccurate comparative advertising) is damage by diminution of value without implication for the confusion of origin that would ordinarily follow from the meaning of trademark[20] or of that of "use" in section 4.[21] In some other contexts, however, section 22 requires the full meaning of use (i.e., including an element of confusion) under section 4 to be met.[22] The Court has acknowledged that depreciation under section 22 will include a non-confusing use that has caused a loss of distinctiveness of the mark (known as "blurring") or by associating the mark with an inferior or adverse source (known as "tarnishment").[23]

---

17   Michel Racicot *et al.*, "The Cyberspace Is Not a 'No Law Land': A Study of the Issues of Liability for Content Circulating on the Internet" (1998) 14 Computer L. & Sec. R. 96, s. 3.

18   *Veuve Clicquot Ponsardin v. Boutiques Cliquot Ltée*, [2006] 1 S.C.R. 824 at paras. 48–49 [*Veuve Clicquot*]. See Robert G. Howell, "A Watershed Year for Well Known or Famous Marks" in Ysolde Gendreau, ed., *An Emerging Intellectual Property Paradigm: Perspectives from Canada* (Cheltenham: Edward Elgar, 2008); Robert G. Howell: "Depreciation of Goodwill: A 'Green Light' for Dilution from the Supreme Court of Canada in An Accommodating Infrastructure" (2008) 17 Transnat'l L. & Contemp. Probs. 689 at 691.

19   *Veuve Clicquot, ibid.* at para. 126.

20   See text accompanying notes 12–14, above in this chapter.

21   See *Clairol*, above note 11 at 196 and 202 (followed in later cases).

22   *Clairol, ibid.*; *Veuve Clicquot*, above note 18 at paras. 46–48.

23   See *Veuve Clicquot, ibid.* at paras. 63 & 64 (re "blurring") and paras. 63 and 66 (re "tarnishment"). Justice Binnie used the expression "disparage, belittle, underrate."

Second, proceedings in the nature of statutory passing off under section 7(b), *Trade-marks Act* avoid reference to "use" and, therefore, the strictness of the meaning of "use" in the Act. Section 7(b) provides that "No person shall . . . (b) direct public attention to his wares, services or business in such a way as to cause or likely to cause confusion in Canada, at the time he commenced to direct attention to them, between his wares, services or business and the wares, services or business of another."[24] The requisite of "direct[ing] public attention" can be readily achieved by website presentation or through other telecommunications media.[25]

1) Passing Off/Unfair Competition

The expression "unfair competition" is not a legal term of art in Canada or the Commonwealth. It describes a marketplace activity that violates specifically recognized torts or civil wrongs[26] or, in Quebec, the equivalent violation of the *Civil Code*.[27] The principal common law proceeding is the tort of passing off, focused on a misrepresentation that causes public confusion that the product or business of the defendant is the product or business of the plaintiff or is linked or associated with the plaintiff's business.[28] The object of protection is the goodwill[29] of the plaintiff's business. The misrepresentation is usually made by the defendant using a trademark, name or other indicia of the plaintiff. These indicia need not be registered. Being proceedings at common law or under the *Civil Code of Québec*, the jurisdiction is provincial. This means that proceedings must be brought in provincial courts.

Despite this limitation, the scope of proceedings under the tort of passing off is broader and less technical than registered trademark

---

24 *Trade-marks Act*, above note 6, s. 7(b).

25 Likewise, s. 7(a), which has been earlier applied (without discussion of constitutional validity) by the Supreme Court in *S & S Industries Inc. v. Rowell*, [1966] S.C.R. 419 at 420, refers simply to "mak[ing] a false or misleading statement tending to discredit the business, wares or services of a competitor."

26 See Robert G. Howell, Linda Vincent, & Michael D. Manson, *Intellectual Property Law, Cases and Materials* (Toronto: Emond Montgomery, 1999) at 439–41.

27 See above note 5.

28 See *Consumers Distributing Co. v. Seiko Time Canada Ltd.*, [1984] 1 S.C.R. 583 at 608–9, 1 C.P.R. (3d) 1 at 21 (adopting a five-point test for passing off) [*Consumers Distributing*]; *Ciba-Geigy Canada Ltd. v. Apotex Inc.*, [1992] 3 S.C.R. 120 at 132, 44 C.P.R. (3d) 289 at 297 [*Ciba-Geigy*] (adopting a three-point test). See Howell, Vincent, & Manson, above note 26 at 445–47.

29 See *A.G. Spalding & Bros. v. A.W. Gamage Ltd.* (1915), 32 R.P.C. 273 at 284 (H.L.), resolving in English law that the object of proprietary protection in passing off is the business *goodwill*, not the particular *indicia* of the goodwill.

proceedings. In particular, the confining meaning of a "use" that will constitute an infringement under the *Trade-marks Act*, as described earlier,[30] is avoided. Similarly, the nature of indicia that can cause a misrepresentation is not specifically defined. Any indicia that identify a product or business will be sufficient. Indeed, the tort can encompass organizations that are not "trading" or business entities, such as clubs and associations,[31] but possibly not political organizations[32] or purely personal interests.[33]

Naturally there is considerable scope for the passing off proceeding in telecommunications media by presenting trademarks, logos, or symbols that the public might identify with products or business of another so that confusion is caused. Traditional media of radio, television, and cable have been instrumental in the development of passing off to encompass protection in Canada of pure reputation from businesses conducted extraterritorially, especially in the United States. This "reputation spillover" is considerable and has involved a broadening of the elements and scope of the passing off proceeding by redefining "goodwill" to constitute simply reputation without any business presence in the jurisdiction.[34] Increasing attention is also being given to the intent of the usurper of the mark or other indicia.[35] The global dimen-

---

30   See text accompanying note 9ff., above in this chapter.
31   See, for example, *Law Society of British Columbia v. Canada Domain Name Exchange Corp.* (2004), 34 C.P.R. (4th) 437 (B.C.S.C.), aff'd (2005), 43 C.P.R. (4th) 321 (B.C.C.A.) [*Law Society of British Columbia*]; *British Medical Association v. Marsh* (1931), 48 R.P.C. 565 (Ch.); *British Legion v. British Legion Club (Street) Ltd.* (1931), 48 R.P.C. 555 (Ch.); and *Canadian Board for Certification of Prosthetists and Orthotists v. Canadian Pharmaceutical Association* (1985), 5 C.P.R. (3d) 236 (Ont. H.C.).
32   See, for example, *Polsinelli v. Marzilli* (1987), 60 O.R. (2d) 713 (H.C.), aff'd (1987), 61 O.R. (2d) 799n (Div. Ct.). However, contrast *Devinder Shory Campaign v. Richard* (2008), 71 C.P.R. (4th) 89 (Alta. Q.B.) and see also text accompanying notes 89–91, below in this chapter, concerning use of passing off in an employer/employee (labour union) context.
33   See, for example, *Day v. Brownrigg* (1878), 10 Ch. D. 294 (C.A.) (name of residential house).
34   The leading Canadian cases are *Orkin Exterminating Co. v. Pestco Co. of Canada* (1985), 5 C.P.R. (3d) 433 (C.A.) [*Orkin*]; *Walt Disney Productions v. Triple Five Corp.* (1994), 113 D.L.R. (4th) 229, [1994] 6 W.W.R. 385 (Alta. C.A.), leave to appeal to S.C.C. refused, [1994] S.C.C.A. No. 204. Contrast *Walt Disney Productions v. Fantasyland Hotel Inc.* (1994), 56 C.P.R. (3d) 129 (Alta. Q.B.), aff'd (1996), 67 C.P.R. (3d) 444 (Alta. C.A.). See Robert G. Howell & Khaw Lake Tee, "Parallel Importation of Wares and Reputation Spillover: Examples of Transnationalization of Law" in D.M. Johnston & G. Ferguson, eds., *Asia-Pacific Legal Development* (Vancouver: UBC Press, 1998) at 106–8.
35   See *Orkin, ibid.* at 453.

sions of the Internet are likely to cause telecommunications to continue to expand the tort in this fashion.

Indeed, the element of misrepresentation in passing off is, today, very malleable. The tort has emerged in an "extended" format, especially with respect to the requisite content of the misrepresentation, or what it is that the public must be confused about. For example, a test as to whether the confusion is of some *association* between the parties is much broader than a test requiring confusion that the product or business is the *same* as between the parties.[36] In the latter case, the parties would ordinarily need to have some linkage or connection by business or product line.[37] In the former case, this need not be so,[38] diminishing the stringency of the element of confusion and positioning the passing off proceeding as closer to a remedy for simply the *misappropriation* of some business value.[39] A general misappropriation proceeding has not been accepted in Canada, but neither has it been rejected[40] as it has in some other Commonwealth jurisdictions.[41] In the United States, there

---

36 See, for example, *Visa International Service Association v. Visa Motel Corporation (c.o.b. Visa Leasing)* (1983), 1 C.P.R. (3d) 109 at 117–21, [1983] B.C.J. No. 1670 (Co. Ct.), aff'd (1984), 1 C.P.R. (3d) 121, [1984] B.C.J. No. 1746 (C.A.).

37 Rather than constituting a requirement or element in itself, a common field of activity may be seen as simply one factor to be considered in establishing the likelihood of public confusion. See Jeremy Phillips & Allison Coleman, "Passing Off and the 'Common Field of Activity'" (1985) 101 Law Q. Rev. 242.

38 See *National Hockey League v. Pepsi-Cola Canada Ltd.* (1992), 42 C.P.R. (3d) 390 at 401 (B.C.S.C.), aff'd (1995), 59 C.P.R. (3d) 216 (B.C.C.A.). Two categories of passing off were noted. The first involves parties who are competitors in a common field of activity. The second involves the defendant misrepresenting its product or business as "in some way approved, authorized or endorsed by the plaintiff or that there is some business connection [with the plaintiff]" (*ibid.* at 401 (S.C.)).

39 For a more detailed treatment of this trend, see Howell, "Depreciation of Goodwill," above note 18 at 694–99.

40 The potential for such a tort was not viewed with much enthusiasm but was left undecided by the British Columbia Court of Appeal in *Westfair Foods Ltd. v. Jim Pattison Industries Ltd.* (1990), 30 C.P.R. (3d) 174 at 182, 68 D.L.R. (4th) 481 at 488 (B.C.C.A.), aff'g (1989), 26 C.P.R. (3d) 28 at 48–49 (B.C.S.C.). In *MacDonald*, above note 6 at 156–57, Laskin CJC referred to such a tort as the type of proceeding sought to be remedial by the unconstitutional s. 7(e), *Trade-marks Act*, above note 6. Also see *Canada Safeway Ltd. v. Manitoba Food & Commercial Workers Local* 832 (1983), 25 C.C.L.T. 1 (Man. C.A.), criticized by Linda Vincent, "Everything You Want in a Tort — And a Little Bit More?" (1983) 25 C.C.L.T. 10.

41 In Australia, see *Victoria Park Racing and Recreation Grounds Company Limited v. Taylor* (1937), 58 C.L.R. 479 (H.C.A.); *Moorgate Tobacco Co. Ltd. v. Philip Morris Ltd.* (1984), 56 A.L.R. 193 (H.C.A.); and *Cadbury Schweppes Pty Ltd. v. Pub Squash Co. Pty Ltd.* (1980), [1981] 1 W.L.R. 193 (P.C.) on appeal from N.S.W.

is a misappropriation limb of unfair competition,[42] although significantly confined.[43]

Such developments may be of significance to media owners or operators utilizing indicia that broadly suggest some "association" with other businesses or, for example, suggest some endorsement of a product by a well-known figure or celebrity. Indeed, in the United States and (in a more fledgling sense) in Canada, the reputation attaching to celebrity figures is protected on a theory of misappropriation, without any requirement of a misrepresentation or the potential of public confusion.[44]

This expansion may not apply to section 7(b) proceedings. While proceedings under section 7(b) avoid meeting the definitional requirements of "use,"[45] the expression "confusion" in section 7(b) is likely to invoke the statutory definition of "confusing" in section 6. This section is expressed as applicable "[f]or the purposes of [the] Act"[46] and,

---

[*Cadbury Schweppes*]. In the United Kingdom, see *Harrods Limited v. Schwartz-Sackin & Co.* (1985), [1986] F.S.R. 490 (Ch.), rev'd on other grounds [1991] F.S.R. 209 (C.A.); and *Swedac Limited v. Magnet & Southerns* (1988), [1989] 1 F.S.R. 243 (Ch.). In South Africa, see *Lorimar Productions Inc. v. Stirling Clothing Manufacturers (Pty) Ltd.* (1981), [1982] R.P.C. 395 (S. Afr. S.C.). In Hong Kong, see *Shaw Brothers (Hong Kong) Ltd. v. Golden Harvest (H.K.) Ltd.* (1971), [1972] R.P.C. 559 (H.K. Full Ct.).

42   The classic authority is *International News Service v. Associated Press*, 248 U.S. 215 (1918). See Rudolff Callmann, "He Who Reaps Where He Has Not Sown: Unjust Enrichment in the Law of Unfair Competition" (1942) 55 Harv. L. Rev. 595.

43   See *National Basketball Association v. Motorola, Inc.*, 105 F.3d 841 at 852 (2d Cir. 1997); *Synercom Technology Inc. v. University Computing Co.*, 474 F. Supp. 37 at 39 (N.D. Tex. 1979). See also J. Thomas McCarthy, *McCarthy on Trademarks and Unfair Competition*, 4th ed. (Deerfield, IL: Clark Boardman Callaghan, 1996), s. 1(3)ff., and s. 10(51) (basic elements); *Restatement (Third) of Unfair Competition*, § 38 (St. Paul, MN: West, 1995–); and Douglas Baird, "Common Law Intellectual Property and the Legacy of *International News Service v. Associated Press*" (1983) 50 U. Chicago L. Rev. 411.

44   In the United States, see J.Thomas McCarthy, *The Rights of Publicity and Privacy*, looseleaf (New York: Clark Boardman, 1987). In Canada, see Robert G. Howell, "The Common Law Appropriation of Personality Tort" (1986) 2 I.P.J. 149; Robert G. Howell, "Publicity Rights in the Common Law Provinces of Canada" (1998) 18 Loyola of L.A. Ent. L.J. 487; Louise Potvin, "Protection against the Use of One's Likeness in Quebec Civil Law, Canadian Common Law and Constitutional Law" (1997) 11 I.P.J. 203 (Part 1) and 295 (Part 2); and David Vaver, "What Is Mine Is Not Yours: Commercial Appropriation of Personality under the Privacy Acts of British Columbia, Manitoba and Saskatchewan" (1981) 15 U.B.C. L. Rev. 241.

45   See text accompanying note 16ff., above in this chapter.

46   *Trade-marks Act*, above note 6, s. 6(1).

therefore, literally must encompass section 7(b). The Federal Court of Appeal has recently determined to this effect,[47] despite many instances of simply treating the proceeding as a statutory version of common law passing off,[48] as seems to have been contemplated but not discussed by the Supreme Court in *Kirkbi*.[49] While sections 6(2)–(4) are clear that confusion can occur across classes of wares or services, these provisions also stipulate that the confusion must be "in the same area,"[50] diminishing the ability to protect reputation of extraterritorial origin without an actual presence in the jurisdiction, a key factor with telecommunications media.[51] Second, the content of confusion is stipulated as wares or services being seen as "manufactured, sold, leased, hired or performed by the same person."[52] This is narrower than linkages by "connection" or "association" at common law. Section 6(5) concludes by requiring confusion to be determined by reference to "all the surrounding circumstances" including stipulated factors.[53]

2) Internet-Specific Infringement

The Internet has produced a number of trademark issues specific to the infrastructure of this medium.[54] These include significant issues of private international law, or conflict of laws, which are discussed in Chapter 6. The current analysis is focused on the substantive law

---

47   *Positive Attitude Safety System Inc. v. Albian Sands Energy Inc.* (2005), 43 C.P.R. (4th) 418 at paras. 30–32 (F.C.A.) [*Positive Attitude*]. Contrast *Pharmacommunications Holdings Inc. v. Avencia International Inc.* (2009), 79 C.P.R. (4th) 460, 2009 FCA 144 at para. 8 noting, without reference to *Positive Attitude*, *ibid.* s. 7(b) to be a codification of common law without any significant difference between common law and s. 7(b).

48   An electronic search reveals that prior to *Positive Attitude*, *ibid.*, there was only one instance of *Trade-marks Act*, above note 6, s. 6 being applied with s. 7(b).

49   *Kirkbi*, above note 4.

50   *Trade-marks Act*, above note 6, ss. 6(2)–(4). However, see *Remo Imports Ltd. v. Jaguar Cars Ltd.* (2006), 47 C.P.R. (4th) 1 at para. 310 (Fed Ct.) (interpreting "in the same area" as requiring simply that the parties be *entitled to sell* in the same place), rev'd on other grounds, 60 C.P.R. (4th) 130, [2007] FCA 258. This would be consistent with the common law approach of considering "goodwill areas." See text accompanying note 34, above in this chapter.

51   See text accompanying note 34, above in this chapter.

52   *Trade-marks Act*, above note 6, ss. 6(2)–(4).

53   *Ibid.*, s. 6(5).

54   For a comprehensive Canadian treatment of trademarks and the Internet, see Bradley J. Freedman & Robert Deane, "Trade-marks and the Internet: A Canadian Perspective" (2001) 34 U.B.C. L. Rev. 345 at 359ff. This is an excellent resource in this area.

of trademarks without consideration of cross-border or international dimensions. Some matters are specific consequences of trademark infringement within telecommunications media. Others arise from the interplay of trademark law with the system of Uniform Resource Identifiers (URIs) or domain names. In the first category, attention is given here to the practices of framing and unauthorized hypertext links, the unauthorized use of "metatags" to attract search engine links, and the principle developed in the United States of "initial interest confusion."

Framing concerns the division of a display on a computer screen into two or more windows or frames, each presenting a separate presentation and potentially causing a user to become confused over whether some connection or association exists between the sources of each presentation.[55] However, the mere presentation of windows on one screen does not in itself constitute confusion. In many situations, a distinction between the two or more presentations should be obvious. Ordinarily, confusion derives from a perception of integration of the windows into one presentation, even if as a composite.[56] Essentially, the matter in each instance is a question of fact.

Unauthorized hypertext linking is likely to breach copyright in the website to which linkage is made if the page from the second website is automatically displayed on the receiving website, rather than requiring the accessor to activate it by clicking on the link.[57] An automatic linkage might also breach trademark and result in passing off by causing confusion over some connection or association between the linked sites or the businesses represented by the trademarks displayed on the sites. Whether confusion might also arise from a non-automatic link, involving the need for the accessor to activate the link, will depend on the facts and context. The need to activate the link might reasonably dispel any confusion, but websites present internal as well as external links and some differentiation between the two might be useful to avoid confusion over source. Authority is sparse; there is none in Canada. *Ticketmaster Corp. v. Tickets.com, Inc.*[58] in the United States is the

---

55 See *IMAX Corp. v. Showmax Inc.* (2000), 5 C.P.R (4th) 81 (F.C.T.D.), presenting one frame displaying the plaintiff's "IMAX" trademark and another the defendant's "Showmax" trademark.

56 *Wells Fargo & Co. v. WhenU.com, Inc.*, 293 F. Supp. 2d 734 at paras. 93ff. (E.D. Mich. 2003) [*Wells Fargo*].

57 *Society of Composers, Authors and Music Publishers of Canada v. Canadian Association of Internet Providers*, [2004] 2 S.C.R. 427 at para. 25 [*Tariff 22*]. See Chapter 5, text accompanying notes 249–50.

58 *Ticketmaster Corp. v. Tickets.com, Inc.*, 2000 U.S. Dist. LEXIS 12987 (C.D. Cal. 2000), motion for preliminary injunction denied, aff'd 2001 U.S. App. LEXIS 1454 (9th Cir. 2001) [*Ticketmaster*]. For subsequent proceedings in trespass

leading case. Tickets were being advertised by the defendant, Tickets. com Inc., on its website. Linkage to the booking pages of the plaintiff, Ticketmaster Corp., was provided for bookings from Tickets.com, Inc. The court found the defendant to have sufficiently differentiated itself from the plaintiff to avoid user confusion.[59]

Unauthorized linking is, however, a topic of some broader difficulty in fact and law. From a factual perspective, confusion of association should be demonstrated. If it is not, then the linkage is simply an *intrusion* or unauthorized *usage* of the plaintiff's site. This is not passing off. It is, in effect, a misappropriation without a misrepresentation and as such is probably non-remedial in Canada.[60] An intrusion alone may invoke a notion of interference.[61] It is significant in a context of "deep linking," whereby the link is made to an internal page or location on the plaintiff's website. The earlier pages would ordinarily identify the second website as a source separate from the first, thereby avoiding any confusion, but these are bypassed.[62] Relief for deep linking *per se* was rejected in *Ticketmaster*,[63] notwithstanding that there may be an economic interference with the business of the plaintiff by bypassing advertising from third parties that the plaintiff may have in the entry pages to the site.

A defendant's use in its website of the meta-tags from the plaintiff's website is a more sophisticated method of providing a connection between the two websites. A primary method of an accessor in locating websites is through search engines or directories with which website owners register their sites. Search engines seek sites relevant to the accessor's search request by identifying information contained on the sites that are searched. Identifications are then ranked in the search results presented to the accessor. In seeking this information, search engines examine the meta-tags of sites registered with it. Meta-tags are not visible on the website screen. A website owner will ordinarily use in meta-tags identifying or key words that it is contemplated an accessor will also use in conducting a search. The closer the correlation between meta-tag information and an accessor's choice of search words,

---

to chattels, breach of contract, and copyright, see 2003 U.S. Dist. LEXIS 6483 (C.D. Cal. 2003). For anti-trust issues, see 2003 U.S. Dist. LEXIS 6484 (C.D. Cal. 2003), aff'd 2005 U.S. App. LEXIS 6227 (9th Cir. 2005).

59 *Ibid.*, both C.D. and 9th Cir. LEXIS 12987 and 6483.

60 See text accompanying notes 40–43, above in this chapter.

61 See text accompanying note 209ff., below in this chapter.

62 To be confusing there must be two sources for one to be seen as associated with the other.

63 *Ticketmaster*, above note 58.

the higher the ranking of the website in the results produced by the search engine.

Are meta-tags protected? From a trademark and passing off perspective, if the words are purely descriptive of the products or services offered by the website, they will lack the distinctiveness that is necessary to identify origin and will be non-remedial.[64] If the information used in the meta-tags contains trademarks or words depicting origin, however, there may be a greater prospect of relief, at least as passing off or a proceeding under section 7(b), *Trade-marks Act*.[65]

A registered trademark confusion or dilution proceeding is unlikely, even with a meta-tag use of a trademark as a depiction of origin. The requirement of establishing a "use" under section 4, *Trade-marks Act* would not be met. Even if the meta-tag is equivalent to the trademark that is exhibited on the wares or packaging, the usage at the time of the search by the search engine would be far removed from the point of transfer of property or possession of the product.[66] Likewise, it is difficult to conclude that use of the meta-tag in the search engine process is sufficient to give notice to the transferee that the product is associated with the wares. As for services, information in a meta-tag would not ordinarily be seen as being "used or displayed in the performance of advertising of those services."[67] In this latter respect, however, there is room to argue that the meta-tag information is an advertisement of the services of the website channelled indirectly to customers via the search engine. The searching and accessing through the search engine would be likely to be seen as a tool bringing options of potentially relevant supplies to the attention of a customer.

This analysis is equally applicable to passing off or an equivalent violation of the *Civil Code of Québec*. The meta-tag use must constitute a misrepresentation that causes confusion as to whether the product or business of the defendant is that of the plaintiff or is linked or associated with the plaintiff's business.[68] The misrepresentation and confusion must be focused on the actual consumer.[69] Meta-tags are presented to the search engine. They are not displayed. More significantly, however, it is difficult to determine the nature of any misrepresentation or confusion. A defendant's use of a plaintiff's meta-tags is usually simply to *divert* the searcher to the defendant's website. This can constitute a

---

64   See text accompanying note 11, above in this chapter.
65   *Trade-marks Act*, above note 6, s. 7(b).
66   *Ibid.*, s. 4(1). See text accompanying note 16, above in this chapter.
67   *Ibid.*, s. 4(2).
68   See text accompanying note 28ff., above in this chapter.
69   *Ciba-Geigy*, above note 28 at 140 (S.C.R.) and 303 (C.P.R.).

misrepresentation only if the accessor believes the defendant's website to be that of, or associated with, the plaintiff. If an accessor is simply looking for a product and is satisfied with that of the defendant, without connection or regard to the products or business of the plaintiff, it would be non-remedial as passing off, notwithstanding the utilization that has been made of the plaintiff's indicia.[70]

While the intention of the defendant is not a formal element in establishing passing off,[71] recent trends have accentuated the significance of an intent to confuse,[72] and this may encourage relief in cases of intentional usage of meta-tags. Intent has been utilized for this purpose in the United States. Mere use of a trademark in another's meta-tags is not proscribed if a legitimate use is intended.[73] The distinction has been posed between a use intended to confuse in a passing off sense[74] and one intended to fairly describe the content of the website without any objective of capitalizing on the goodwill of another.[75]

An analysis focused on intent may, however, be misplaced. Not itself an element of either trademark infringement or passing off, intent is relevant only as it assists in establishing confusion, on the theory that intended confusion is more likely to succeed than what might be a foreseeable consequence of unintentional activities.[76] Significantly, the presence of intent cannot in itself cause an activity to be a "use" of a mark as a trademark, as intent is not a criterion in section 4,[77] nor as

---

70   Compare the situation described as "reverse passing off," in which a defendant represents the product or business of the plaintiff to be that of his own. See, for example, *Bristol Conservatories Ltd. v. Conservatories Custom Built Ltd.*, [1989] R.P.C. 455 (C.A.).

71   See *Reckitt & Coleman Products Ltd. v. Borden Inc.*, [1990] 1 W.L.R. 491 at 499 (H.L.) referring to "a misrepresentation . . . (whether or not intentional)." The test for damage is "a reasonably foreseeable consequence," *Erven Warnink BV v. J. Townend & Sons (Hull) Ltd.*, [1979] 2 All E.R. 927 at 932–33 (H.L.). See also *Consumers Distributing*, above note 28 at 608 (S.C.R.). Or simply "actual or potential damage to the plaintiff," *Ciba-Geigy*, above note 28 at 132 (S.C.R.).

72   Ruth M. Corbin, "Intention to Deceive: The Role It Plays in Passing Off" (2004) 18 I.P.J. 97 at 101–4.

73   *Promatek Indus., Ltd. v. Equitrac Corp.*, 300 F.3d 808 at 814 (7th Cir. 2002) [*Promatek*].

74   For example, *Brookfield Communications v. West Coast Entertainment Corp.*, 174 F.3d 1036 at 1066 (9th Cir. 1999) [*Brookfield*] (concerning the terms "Movie Buff" and "MovieBuff"); *Brother Records v. Jardine*, 318 F.3d 900 at para. 907 (9th Cir. 2002); and *Promatek*, ibid.

75   *Wells Fargo*, above note 56 at 763.

76   This traditional significance of "intent" in passing off is noted by the Privy Council in *Cadbury Schweppes*, above note 41 at 203.

77   See text accompanying note 16, above in this chapter, for the requirements in the *Trade-marks Act*, above note 6, s. 4.

demonstrating origin[78] of a plaintiff's business, wares, or services in passing off. Reliance on the concept of "intent" to blur the distinction between *use* and *confusion* has been criticized in the United States,[79] although the scope of a "use" in this context in the United States (as a "use in commerce") is broader than that in Canada under section 4 but may be similar under passing off[80] if that tort is enabled in Canada to extend beyond business contexts.[81]

In an attempt to provide a remedial response in the Internet contexts of meta-tags and domain names that contain another's trademark or brand name, a further development in the United States utilizes the pre-Internet principle "initial interest confusion." Recognized by the Second Circuit in 1975,[82] the principle allows a trademark infringement even though the initial confusion is subsequently corrected before point of sale and without any apparent harm to the trademark holder. It is rationalized as avoiding a second user "free riding" on a first user with the possibility of a customer electing to stay with the second user, even after knowing of the initial confusion.[83] The application of this principle to the Internet is no surprise. The process of search engine identification and ranking of websites for investigation by an accessor is tailor made for this principle.[84] However, even if there is a sound basis for this principle within the concept of confusion, the separate

---

78   See text accompanying notes 11 and 64, above in this chapter, concerning origin.

79   See *Fragrancenet.com, Inc. v. Fragrancex.com, Inc.*, 493 F. Supp. 2d 545 (E.D.N.Y. 2007) (involving use of meta-tags in a website and in "sponsored links"). See also *1-800 Contacts, Inc. v. WhenU.com, Inc.*, 414 F.3d (2d Cir. 2005) (re defendant causing "pop-up" advertisements to appear on computer screens contemporaneously with the appearance of the plaintiff's website); and *Rescuecom Corporation v. Google, Inc.*, 456 F. Supp. 2d 393 (N.D.N.Y. 2006) (links to competitor's websites).

80   See *Lamparello v. Falwell*, 420 F.3d 309 (4th Cir. 2005), concerning websites that might have been (though were found not to be) confusing with respect to origin or affiliation in the context of a political and social debate concerning homosexuality and free speech.

81   See text accompanying notes 31–32, above in this chapter.

82   *Grotrian, Helfferich, Schulz, Th. Steinweg Nachf v. Steinway & Sons*, 523 F. 2d 1331 (2d Cir. 1975). See J. Thomas McCarthy, *Trademarks and Unfair Competition*, looseleaf, vol. 4 (Eagan MN: Thomson/West Group, 2009) s. 23(6), discussing "Initial Interest Confusion" with respect to meta-tags.

83   See M. Grynberg, "The Road Not Taken: Initial Interest Confusion, Consumer Search Costs, and the Challenge of the Internet" (2004) 28 Seattle U.L. Rev. 97 at 105–8.

84   *Ibid.* at 117–28, citing *Brookfield*, above note 74, involving the trademark "MovieBuff" being placed in the defendant's meta-tags.

requirement of use must still be met and, as noted above,[85] this is problematic in an Internet search engine context.[86]

Meta-tags were presented in Canada in *British Columbia Automobile Assn. (BCAA)*,[87] involving a labour, rather than a commercial, dispute. While the scope and application of passing off in a non-commercial context is not fully determined,[88] passing off was found in *BCAA* for one of the defendant union's websites, a version that contained so much of the plaintiff's website, including meta-tags, that there would be confusion of affiliation.[89] Other websites were not infringing. The non-commercial labour context, however, was found to ameliorate the likelihood of confusion of affiliation[90] and to enhance the defendant's right of free expression when balanced with the plaintiff's trademark rights.[91]

The Association's indicia were used by the defendant labour union to cause the origin of its website to be confused for that of the plaintiff Association. An infringement proceeding under the *Trade-marks Act* may have proved problematic in meeting the more stringent requirements for "use" under section 4,[92] but the establishing of origin in a common law context was met. *BCAA* also demonstrates use of meta-tags in a manner that leads to confusion of affiliation between the sites. While not discussing the merits or otherwise of the principle of "initial interest confusion," *BCAA* may additionally recognize as remedial an initial confusion, that would reasonably be quickly dispelled.[93] The defendant union certainly intended to confuse accessors to gain initial attention.[94] However, the very considerable amount reproduced from the plaintiff's website should lead this case toward that of simply regular passing off.

---

85 See text accompanying note 70, above in this chapter.
86 See Zachary J. Zweihorn, "Searching for Confusion: The Initial Interest Confusion Doctrine and Its Misapplication to Search Engine Sponsored Links" (2005–2006) 91 Cornell L. Rev. 1343; and, for an economic analysis, David W. Barnes, "Trademark Externalities" (2005) 10 Yale J.L. & Tech. 1 at 32ff.
87 *British Columbia Automobile Assn. v. O.P.E.I.U., Local 378* (2001), 10 C.P.R. (4th) 423 (B.C.S.C.) [*BCAA*].
88 See text accompanying notes 31–33, above in this chapter.
89 *BCAA*, above note 87 at paras. 208–12.
90 *Ibid.* at paras. 126 and 212.
91 *Ibid.* at para. 130.
92 *Trade-marks Act*, above note 6, s. 4. The defendant labour union was not using the plaintiff Association's indicia to advertise its services.
93 *BCAA*, above note 87 at para. 212. See also *Law Society of British Columbia*, above note 31 at paras. 21–33 (B.C.S.C.) where an Internet connection with an adult website should, perhaps, have been readily distinguishable from and therefore nonconfusing with the website of the Law Society of British Columbia, but nevertheless was held remedial in passing off.
94 *BCAA*, *ibid.* at para. 211.

Stipulating a new legal principle, such as initial interest confusion, within a broader framework of a factual assessment of confusion is questionable.[95] The essential inquiry is, ordinarily, confusion of a consumer at the completion of the transaction. An initial confusion with an actual desired product is ordinarily not sufficient. Consumers are expected to exercise a level of discernment appropriate to the nature and circumstances of the transaction. Purchases made in hurried or routine circumstances (such as from a supermarket shelf) that invoke an immediate confusion of brand may constitute passing off, not because the confusion was initial but because it was in circumstances effective in concluding the transaction.[96] This is conceptually different from an initial, but ultimately non-confusing, *diversion* of a customer to another product. Here the customer has knowingly chosen to remain with the diverter. While the indicia or marks of the first party have been utilized, it presents a situation more akin to misappropriation *simpliciter*, as, for instance, the taking of advantage of a first party's successful advertising campaign, without confusion by misrepresentation. A typical comparative example is the taking advantage of a competitor's thematic advertising. It establishes in consumers a connection between the parties, but one that is dispelled before completion of the transaction. In such an instance, the Privy Council noted the only potential relief to be that of misappropriation *simpliciter*, which it rejected.[97] The position concerning misappropriation relief in Canada is discussed earlier.[98] Such relief is unlikely to be recognized.

Overall, it is suggested that the element of confusion should remain factually and flexibly based without the intervention of a new legal principle. All factors should simply be weighed in an assessment of the likelihood of confusion. Arguably, a court might give weight to any deliberate intention to confuse, as has occurred in some other contexts,[99] but the test is still that of confusion. Too great an emphasis on intent

---

95   Compare the creation of the "common field of activity" rule in *McCulloch v. Lewis A. May (Produce Distributors) Ltd.* (1947), 65 R.P.C. 58 (Ch. D.) subsequently rejected as a rule in itself and described in England as simply reflecting a factor in the factual inquiry as to "confusion." See *Annabel's (Berkeley Square) Ltd. v. Schock*, [1972] F.S.R. 261 (C.A.). See above notes 37 & 38 and accompanying text.

96   See *Ciba-Geigy*, above note 28 at para. 52 (S.C.R.).

97   See *Cadbury Schweppes*, above note 41 dealing with an intentional and calculated "cashing in" on a competitor's advertising campaign but in circumstances in which the products were sufficiently differentiated at the store shelf.

98   See text accompanying notes 40–44, above in this chapter.

99   See above note 34, concerning protection of reputation from an extraterritorial source with no actual competition in the forum jurisdiction.

skews the analysis inappropriately toward pure misappropriation and blurs the tests of confusion and use of a trademark or source of origin.[100] Internet-related policy perspectives should, additionally, favour search efficiency and accessibility in the absence of true confusion. Comparative shopping through sponsored links would also produce positive benefits.[101]

3) Inducing or Procuring Infringement

The Internet presents a technology that encourages entrepreneurs to establish an electronic means of facilitating the exchange of commodities by client users in a manner similar to peer-to-peer file sharing of musical works.[102] Just as copyright holders have attempted to establish liability against facilitating intermediaries, trademark owners are likewise looking in this direction. The online auction source eBay has been a particular source. There is no cause of "authorizing" infringement of trademark or other rights in the manner that exists for copyright. Attention has therefore focused on principles of aiding, inducing, or procuring of infringement.

The infringement of intellectual property interests as well as other proceedings discussed in this chapter are remedial as civil wrongs or actions in tort. As such, combinations of tortfeasors may be contemplated. First, there is vicarious liability of a principal or employer in the course of agency or employment.[103] Second, the same tort or act of infringement may be committed by two or more persons as "joint tortfeasors" if they are acting in common design. All the joint tortfeasors cause one and the same act of infringement.[104] Third, two or more persons may cause the same *damage* to a plaintiff but commit separate acts of injury or infringement as "concurrent tortfeasors." The acts are several or independent. There is no common design.[105]

Joint and concurrent liability has given rise to so-called indirect or secondary infringement, which is variously described as "aiding and

---

100 See text accompanying notes 71–81, above in this chapter.

101 See Zweihorn, above note 86 at 1380.

102 The writer has benefited in the topic of this section from an unpublished paper by M.D. Manson & K.F. MacDonald, "Online Auction Houses: A Counterfeiter's Paradise?" (Vancouver: Smart & Biggar, 2005). The opinions and conclusions expressed herein, however, are those of the author.

103 Liability in these instances is an application of the tort doctrine *respondeat superior*. See Lewis N. Klar *et al.*, *Remedies in Tort*, looseleaf, vol. 4 (Toronto: Carswell, 2009) s. 62ff.

104 *Ibid.*, ss. 18–20(1).

105 *Ibid.*, s. 21.

abetting," "inducing and procuring," or "contributorily infringing" but is here referred to as "inducing and procuring." The authorization of infringement of copyright presents some comparison, but in copyright authorization in itself is a statutorily prescribed act of direct infringement.[106] The crucial feature in all such contexts is an infringement indirectly through the actions of another. It is a separate act of infringement to that of the immediate infringer. If there is a common design between the infringers, it will be "joint."[107] If not it will be "concurrent" in the sense of damage being factually caused by two or more persons. The essential inquiry in each instance involves identifying when facilitating conduct is sufficient to impose responsibility on the indirect tortfeasor.

Relief against inducing or procuring infringement has been established in Canadian intellectual property law in the context of patents, but more fledglingly for trademarks. However, the expression "contributory infringement," utilized and partially codified for patent infringement in the United States,[108] has been eschewed in Canada in the context of patent infringement[109] in favour of "knowingly and for his own ends induc[ing] or procur[ing] another to violate or infringe."[110] An indirect infringer must have knowledge of infringement by the immediate infringer.[111] It must be more than mere or incidental knowledge.[112] Indeed, there must be conduct by the alleged procurer that

---

106 See text accompanying notes 142 & 143, below in this chapter, and Chapter 5, text accompanying notes 226–38.

107 For example, see *Incandescent Gas Light Co. v. New Candescent Mantle Co.* (1898), 15 R.P.C. 81 (Q.B.) in which two separate but physically connected businesses each sold a separate component of a product with the design that a customer would combine them and in that combination infringe the patent.

108 35 U.S.C. § 271 (2003).

109 Codification and redefinition as "contributory infringement" in Canada was rejected by Canada, Royal Commission on Patents, Copyright and Industrial Design, *Report on Copyright* (Ottawa: Queen's Printer, 1959) at 107 & 108 (Chair: J.L. Isley).

110 *Copeland-Chatterson Co., Ltd. v. Hatton* (1906), 10 Ex. C.R. 224 at 247; *Slater Steel Industries Ltd. v. R. Payer Co. Ltd.* (1968), 55 C.P.R. 61 at 82 (Ex. Ct.) [*Slater Steel*]; and *Reading & Bates Construction Co. v. Baker Energy Resources Corp* (1986), 9 C.P.R. (3d) 158 at 183 (F.C.T.D.) [*Reading & Bates*].

111 See *Reading & Bates, ibid.* at 183 rejecting an interpretation of UK authority that would allow infringement from supply even without knowledge of infringement.

112 See *Slater Steel*, above note 110 involving the supply of equipment that could be used for no other than an infringing purpose if performed without consent. No indirect infringement was found. See also *Valmet Oy v. Beloit Canada Ltd.* (1988), 20 C.P.R. (3d) 1 at 14 (F.C.A.) [*Valmet Oy*].

actively encourages or invites infringement. This might be by supplying with the product instructions of a process or use that infringes,[113] or supplying all component parts with the purpose that the purchaser will assemble them and thereby infringe.[114] Ordinarily, procurer and infringer will be joined in the same proceeding.[115]

The test is therefore narrow, requiring (1) actual knowledge, (2) inducing or procuring, and (3) the possibility of some gain to the inducer. Developed in patent, it has been applied in a trademark context involving the violation of section 7(b), *Trade-marks Act*,[116] and in passing off.[117] It is to be distinguished from a separate and broader formulation that merely the supply or authorization of use of the means (i.e., a licence to use a mark or name) that allows a person to pass off a product can constitute passing off against a supplier.[118] Such a proposition is overly broad.

In the United States, contributory infringement of a registered trademark was recognized in *Inwood Laboratories, Inc. v. Ives Laboratories* by the United States Supreme Court in 1982. Within the context of that case, the court prescribed a narrow test of intentional inducement or continuing to supply a product with knowledge of continuing actual infringement by the receiver.[119] Described subsequently as one test with two prongs,[120] the second is the continuing to supply category, for which the test "knows or has reason to know" of the infringing activity is prescribed.[121] In *Inwood*,

---

113 See *Innes v. Short and Beal* (1898), 15 R.P.C. 449 (Ch.); and *Proctor & Gamble Co. v. Bristol-Myers Canada Ltd.* (1979), 39 C.P.R. (2d) 145 at 166 (F.C.T.D.), aff'd (1979), 42 C.P.R. (2d) 33 (F.C.A.), leave to appeal to the S.C.C. refused (1979), 42 C.P.R. (2d) 33n.

114 See *Valmet Oy*, above note 112 at 14.

115 Harold G. Fox, *The Canadian Law and Practice Relating to Letters Patent for Inventions*, 4th ed. (Toronto: Carswell, 1969) at 409.

116 *Cardwell v. Leduc and Pelletier* (1962), 41 C.P.R. 167 at 175 & 76 (Ex. Ct.). The defendants were two former employees of the plaintiff. The first defendant set up a competing business that infringed by passing off (*Trade-marks Act*, above note 6, s. 7(b)) as the plaintiff's business/product. The second defendant was "sales agent" for the first defendant and thereby "aided and abetted" the first defendant.

117 *Robert Simpson Co. Ltd. v. Simpson's-In-The Strand Ltd.* (1980), 49 C.P.R. (2d) 16 at 19 (Ont. H.C.). The proceedings were interlocutory and the facts had yet to be established.

118 *Ibid.*

119 *Inwood Laboratories, Inc. v. Ives Laboratories, Inc.*, 456 U.S. 844 at 854 & 855 (1982) [*Inwood*].

120 See *Tiffany (NJ), Inc. v. eBay, Inc.*, 576 F. Supp. 2d 463 at 502 (S.D.N.Y. 2008) [*Tiffany*].

121 *Inwood*, above note 119 at 854; and *Tiffany*, *ibid.*

the defendant generic pharmaceutical drug manufacturers had marketed pills intentionally with the same appearance (shape, size, and colour) as brand-name drugs but had not directly induced pharmacists to mislabel and mis-supply generic drugs for brand-name drugs. Pharmacists were said to be doing so, without passing on the savings to the purchaser. The decision was determined procedurally,[122] but the principle of aiding or inducing was established.

The Supreme Court majority noted the existence of a broader formulation of "reasonably have anticipated,"[123] but Justices White and Marshall concurring rejected this broader standard and criticized the majority for "silently acquiesc[ing]" in this dilution of the requisite standard.[124] Although this broader test has been accepted in the *Restatement*,[125] it is frequently rejected.[126]

Focusing only on the two-pronged *Inwood* test, therefore, the knowledge criterion in the second prong may be more readily established when combined with a proximity to the ability to control or terminate the infringing activities and the prospect of some gain or benefit to the alleged contributor. Contextually this may exist with a refocusing of contribution on owners of market facilities hired for independently organized flea and swap markets that include transactions in counterfeit or infringing merchandise.[127] This extension beyond that of suppliers or distributors of products has been found to be within the principle of contributory infringement and equally applicable to Internet-based electronic markets.[128] Control is usually through contract and may reflect a relationship of franchisor and franchisee,[129] subject to a continued emphasis on "intentionally inducing" or "knowingly participating."[130]

---

122 The Supreme Court found the Second Circuit Court of Appeals to have erroneously substituted its own factual determination for that of the District Court. *Inwood, ibid.* at 855 & 856.
123 *Ibid.* at 856 and 617.
124 *Ibid.* at 862 and 620–21.
125 *Restatement (Third) of Unfair Competition*, above note 43, § 27.
126 See *Tiffany*, above note 120 at 502 & 503 citing a significant body of caselaw to this effect and declining to apply the test from the *Restatement (Third) of Unfair Competition, ibid.*
127 *Hard Rock Cafe Licensing Corp. v. Concession Services, Inc.*, 955 F.2d 1143 (7th Cir. 1992); *Fonovisa, Inc. v. Cherry Auction, Inc.*, 76 F.3d 259 (9th Cir. 1996); and *Polo Ralph Lauren Corp. v. Chinatown Gift Shop*, 855 F. Supp. 648 (S.D.N.Y. 1996).
128 *Tiffany*, above note 120 at 504–6.
129 *Mini Maid Service Co. v. Maid Brigade Inc.*, 967 F.2d 1516 at 1519 (11th Cir. 1992).
130 *Ibid.* See also *Perfect 10, Inc. v. Visa International Service Association*, 494 F.3d 788 at 807 (9th Cir. 2007) [*Perfect 10, Inc.*], where the Ninth Circuit denied

One commentator has described the second prong of *Inwood* as encompassing "willful blindness" to the infringing activities when combined with the further elements of control and benefit from the hireage of the facilities, including Internet-related facilities.[131] Such cases are, nevertheless, fledgling. Granting a domain name is an insufficient connection to find liability against an issuing registry.[132] Liability has been mooted against search engine owners who permit and encourage listed entities to utilize keywords that may infringe trademark interests for the purpose of enabling banner advertisements or sponsored links,[133] but this has recently been rejected as "fair use," even if the generating of sponsored links is a "use" under US trademark law.[134]

The comprehensive analysis of the District Court in 2008 in *Tiffany (NJ), Inc. v. eBay, Inc.*[135] is the leading Internet-related US authority. Although an appeal is filed,[136] the District Court found an online auction market intermediary to have no obligation to bear the overall financial burden of policing its site for postings and trade in counterfeit or trademark infringing products, as the primary obligation to protect a mark rests with the trademark owner.[137] Given that items bearing a genuine trademark can be lawfully resold (for example, second-hand sales),[138] neither a general knowledge that some counterfeiting or infringing activity is occurring on the site nor any assumption with respect to the

---

contributory infringement by credit card companies for processing payments to websites that allegedly infringed the plaintiff's trademarks.

131 Deborah J. Peckham, "The Internet Auction House and Secondary Liability — Will eBay Have to Answer to *Grokster*?" (2005) 95 The Trademark Reporter 977 at 986. Peckham's article is given emphasis in McCarthy, above note 82 , vol. 4, s. 25(20).

132 *Lockheed Martin Corp. v. Network Solutions, Inc.*, 194 F.3d 980 (9th Cir. 1999).

133 See *Playboy Enterprises, Inc. v. Netscape Communications Corp.*, 354 F.3d 1020 (9th Cir. 2004); and *Google, Inc. v. American Blind & Wallpaper Factory Inc.*, 2005 U.S. Dist. LEXIS 6228 (N.D. Cal. 2005). See also *Gucci America, Inc. v. Hall & Associates*, 135 F. Supp. 2d 409 (S.D.N.Y. 2001), leaving open the potential of ISP liability.

134 *Tiffany*, above note 120 at 501.

135 *Ibid.*

136 *Ibid.* Appeal 08-3947-CV was filed in the Second Circuit (2008) but not heard as of March 2010.

137 *Ibid.* at 470 and 527.

138 *Ibid.* at 496, 509, and 512. This is the principle of "first sale" or "exhaustion" of proprietary rights upon the first release of a trademarked item in a marketplace. It is commonly seen in a context of parallel importation. See Robert G. Howell & Khaw Lake Tee, "Parallel Importation of Wares and Reputation Spillover: Examples of Transnationalization of Law" in D.M. Johnston & G. Ferguson, eds., *Asia-Pacific Legal Development* (Vancouver, BC: UBC Press, 1998) at 87 & 88 (regarding exhaustion of proprietary protection).

effect from higher quantities of items in particular listings is sufficient to meet the level of knowledge necessary under the second prong of the *Inwood* test — "knows or has reason to know." Knowledge must be contextual, fact specific, and individualized to the particular incidence.[139] The inclusion of "willful blindness,"[140] in the sense of to "suspect wrongdoing and *deliberately* fail to investigate" [emphasis added], was acknowledged but found inapplicable by the systems in place by the defendant to counter infringement.[141]

The test in *Inwood* is consistent with the Canadian formulation of "inducing or procuring," but whether the US developments might prevail in Canada is entirely speculative. No "market proprietor" or Internet-related contexts have yet been presented. A comparison with "authorization" in Canadian copyright, as most recently interpreted by the Supreme Court, would bring a standard of actual knowledge by notification together with control and inaction.[142] However, infringement by authorization in copyright has express statutory recognition, and there is no recognition of any tort-focused contributory infringement in Canadian copyright law. In the United States, a link between contributory infringement in copyright and that in trademark has been rejected because of the differences between these areas and the origin of third-party liability in each instance. Contributory infringement of trademarks is determined to be "more narrowly circumscribed" than that for copyright.[143]

Tiffany also presents contributory infringement in a context of trademark dilution proceedings.[144] This is even more speculative in Canada as relief against trademark dilution is itself entirely fledgling.[145]

---

139 *Tiffany*, above note 120 at 508–11.
140 See text accompanying note 131, above in this chapter.
141 *Tiffany*, above note 120 at 513–15.
142 Chapter 5, text accompanying notes 236–37.
143 *Perfect 10, Inc.*, above note 130 at 807. See also *Tiffany*, above note 120 at 510.
144 *Tiffany, ibid.* at 521–26.
145 In Canada, dilution was recognized under s. 22, *Trade-marks Act*, above note 6, by the Supreme Court of Canada in *Veuve Clicquot*, above note 18 at para. 38ff. See Robert G. Howell, "A Watershed Year for Well Known or Famous Marks" in Ysolde Gendreau, ed., *An Emerging Intellectual Property Paradigm: Perspectives from Canada* (Cheltenham, UK: Edward Elgar, 2008) at 27–34; and Robert G. Howell, "Depreciation of Goodwill: A 'Green Light' for Dilution from the Supreme Court of Canada in an Accommodating Infrastructure" (2008) 17 Transnat'l L. & Contemp. Probs. 689 at 706–11. Contrast Michael Darling, "Depreciation in Canadian Trade-Mark Law: A Remedy in Search of a Wrong" (2007) 21 I.P.J. 49.

C. TRADEMARKS AND DOMAIN NAMES OR ASSIGNED NUMBERS

The location or address of a computer or host on the Internet is presented by a unique identifier that comprises two broad features. First, at a machine or technical level there is an Internet Protocol (IP), expressed numerically (for example, 203.267.194.58). This is what the system will identify in a communication, whether by e-mail or Internet connection. It is combined with the program that assembles the transmission, the Transmission Control Protocol (TCP), being then described as the TCP/IP program.[146] Second, there is the human-readable address depicted in Uniform Resource Identifiers (URIs), of which the most common is the Uniform Resource Locators (URLs) of the World Wide Web (www), the system of Internet servers supported by most web browsers, including Microsoft's Internet Explorer, Mozilla Firefox, and Netscape.[147] The IP numerical sequence is allocated through five regional Internet registries (RIRs), each covering a geographical area and coordinated by the Internet Assigned Numbers Authority (IANA).[148] The UDIs/URLs are allocated by separate domain name registries. It is the UDIs/URLs that present trademark and domain name issues.

1) Domain Names

The URL will first refer to the protocol format of the system of the Internet servers. For example, http://www. refers to Hyper Text Transfer Protocol, the protocol that is used by the World Wide Web. The URL then refers to a domain name, being the location of the particular resource or website. For example, law.uvic.ca/, refers to the Faculty of Law at the University of Victoria in Canada. The whole URL is therefore http://www.law.uvic.ca/.

---

146 See the definitional database Search SBM.com Definitions, online: http://whatis. techtarget.com.

147 Mozilla is an open source browser developed collectively by Internet users under the Mozilla Foundation. In April 2005, the Mozilla Firefox brand had a 6.8 percent market share in the United States but higher outside the country. Microsoft's Internet Explorer had an 89 percent US market share. Netscape, a Mozilla-based browser, had a 2.2 percent market share. See online: www.broad-bandreports.com/shownews/63555. As of 2008, Internet Explorer had dropped to a 68.15 percent market share in the United States with Firefox at 24 percent and Safari at 7.93 percent, online: www.dslreports.com/forum/remark,21671936 ?hilite=ie+market+share.

148 This is described more fully in the text accompanying notes 174ff., below in this chapter.

The domain name is an essential feature of the address. It is divided into two parts, reflecting the two levels of domain name allocation. The top level is the suffix. It can be of two types, a generic top-level domain (gTLD) or a geographic suffix or country code top-level domain (ccTLD). The generic suffix has progressed through various phases. It was initially limited to the following:

.com (commercial entities)
.edu (US educational entities)
.net (computer network providers)
.int (international organizations)
.org (miscellaneous non-profit organizations)
.gov (US governmental organizations)
.mil (US military organizations).[149]

The suffixes .int., .edu, .gov, and .mil are not available for allocation to the public, being reserved for the particular organizations to which they relate. The suffixes .com, .net, and .org are available for public allocation, and the demarcation between them reflects the nature of the organization concerned.[150]

A second phase in the development of gTLDs brought an expansion of these domains, essentially:[151]

.aero (air transporatation)*
.asia (entities in the Asia-Pacific region)
.biz (businesses)
.cat (Catalan language and culture)
.coop (cooperatives)*
.info (no specific user)
.jobs (employment related)
.mobi (mobile devices)
.museum (museums)*
.name (families or individuals)
.pro (professionals)

---

149 See WIPO, *The Management of Internet Names and Addresses: Intellectual Property Issues*, Final Report of the WIPO Internet Domain Name Process, Pub. No. 92-805-0779-6, Part 1 at para. 6 (Geneva: 1999), online: WIPO www.wipo.int/amc/en/processes/process1/report/finalreport.html#IV [WIPO Final Report].

150 The recognition of additional gTLDs coincided with the encouragement of an expanded use in the United States of the ccTLD .us domain, as discussed in the U.S., Department of Commerce, *Management of Internet Names and Addresses* (Doc. No. 980212036-8146-02) (1998) at paras. 11 and 13, online: www.ntia.doc.gov/ntiahome/domainname/6_5_98dns.htm.

151 See online: www.iana.org/domains/root/db/ for a frequently updated list.

.tel (telephone – Internet connections)
.travel (travel industries).

The first four along with the earlier seven gTLDs are "unsponsored." The three marked with an asterisk are "sponsored" in the sense that a sponsor is appointed by stakeholders to operate the TLD for the benefit of the specific category of entities, the "Sponsored TLD Community." The sponsor is to create policies for the use of the particular TLD, select the registry for the domain, and establish the relationship between it and the registry.[152]

A third phase was approved in June 2008 by the Internet Corporation for Assigned Names and Numbers (ICANN), the authority overseeing assigned names since 1999,[153] and has proceeded under various planning stages through 2010.[154] After wide consultations, ICANN has decided to open the scope of gTLDs to allow choice and creation by applicants. The result will reflect complete diversity. Meanwhile, in June 2010, approval was given to the long sought after, but politically contentious, .xxx top level domain for sites providing pornographic material.[155]

A geographic suffix corresponds to the recognized abbreviations for countries. Both generic and geographic suffixes[156] originated in the United States, where the Internet and domain name system was

---

152 These gTLDs were approved in November 2000 and the unsponsored gTLDs were publicly available through 2001 to 2002. See Internet Corporation for Assigned Names and Numbers (ICANN), online: ICANN www.icann.org/tlds/. See also, Scott W. Johnston, Sandra Epp Ryan, & Gregory C. Golla, "News from the United States: Trademarks; Patents; Copyrights; Cyber Law" (2002) 16 I.P.J. 152, s. 4 (Cyber Law Update). For information concerning activities for the sponsored gTLDs: (1) re .Aero see online: WIPO www.wipo.int/amc/en/domains/gtld/aero/; (2) re .coop see online: www.nic.coop/about.asp; and (3) re .museum see online: about.museum/.

153 See note 165 and text accompanying notes 163–68, below in this chapter, for historical and current governance of the Internet domain name system.

154 See ICANN, *New gTLD Program*, online: ICANN www.icann.org/en/topics/new-gtld-program.htm. This site has links to documentation from June 2008. See ICANN, Explanatroy Memorandum, *New gTLD Program* (15 February 2010), which is still expressed to be a draft and that "details of the new gTLD program [remain] subject to further consultation and revision." The memorandum is more easily accessed by a direct Google search.

155 See ICANN News Release, "ICANN . . . Also Moves Forward on .xxx Domain Application,": online: www.icann.org/en/release-25june10-en.pdf.

156 The geographic suffixes are two-letter codes set according to the "ISO 3166 Standard" of the International Organization for Standardization (ISO). See WIPO Final Report, above note 149, Part 1 at para. 7.

developed,[157] but with geographic suffixes, the allocation of subsequent second-level or sub-domain features is delegated to the particular country. In Canada, the second-level allocation was performed until fall 2000 by a volunteer organization, "CA domain," at the University of British Columbia.[158] An attempt was made to ensure that the rightful owners received registration of a domain name relevant to their business. The applicant could obtain only a single-level .ca domain name, which also had to resemble its name (corporate or business) or registered trademark. A structure of sub-domain allocation in Canada was also provided.[159] Since fall 2000, the oversight organization for the .ca domain has been the Canadian Internet Registry Authority (CIRA),[160] created in December 1998 following a Government of Canada White Paper 1997.[161] In December 1999, CIRA contracted with an Ottawa-based agency, CANARIE Inc.,[162] to set up operational plans for the assumption of responsibility for .ca registrations through registrars recruited for this purpose.[163]

Domain name registration was originally an unrestrained "first come, first served" procedure. This presented some conflicts. First, a practice popularly described as "cybersquatting" developed. Applicants gained domain names with a second-level name of a well-known entity and would not release that domain name until well remunerated by that entity.[164] Second, personal and business disputes arose between holders of similar domain names and between holders of domain names and holders of trademarks or similar interests in indicia of identity protected as registered trademarks or at common law. Historically, the allocation of gTLDs was performed exclusively by the Internet Network Information Centre (InterNIC), administered by Network Solutions Inc. (NSI) under an agreement with the US government. A system of

---

157 See Cybertelecom, *History of DNS*, online: www.cybertelecom.org/dns/dns.htm.

158 The CA domain website was www.cdnnet.ca, but this URL now links automatically with CIRA, online: CIRA www.cira.ca.

159 See *ibid.* (CA domain rules).

160 The CIRA website, above note 158, provides a history of the creation and development of this non-profit entity.

161 Industry Canada, Information and Communications Technologies, "White Paper on Internet Protocol Number Allocation in Canada" by Rayan Zachariessen, representing the Internet Protocol Discussion Group of the Association of Internet Providers (CAIP) (25 March 1997), online: http://web.archive.org/web/20000325004526/strategis.ic.gc.ca/SSG/it04030e.html.

162 The website for CANARIE Inc. is www.canarie.ca.

163 See CIRA website, above note 158 (Facts).

164 See WIPO Final Report, above note 149, Part 3 (dispute resolution) at paras. 170–79 regarding "Abusive Registration" or "cybersquatting."

dispute resolution was operated enabling an objector to the allocation of a domain name to present evidence of an identical registered trademark from the United States or elsewhere. Priority was set according to the time of registration of the objector's trademark and the allocation of the domain name. If the dispute could not be resolved, neither party could have the domain name until adjudication (by a court or arbitrator) or settlement.

The current system was established from 1999 by the US Department of Commerce, in consultation with the World Intellectual Property Organization (WIPO).[165] It is overseen by ICANN, which is a non-profit international corporation[166] created in September 1998. ICANN also performs management functions formerly exercised by the US government, contractors, or volunteers. ICANN is assisted by a number of supporting organizations (SOs) and a government advisory council (GAC) with international membership. The SOs consider areas of protocol standards, policy, and rationalization of the system of Internet operation and domain name structures. The principal oversight is in relation to the allocation of the gTLDs. A shared registration system (SRS) in these domains was established in October 1998, introducing a competitive allocation service through entities accredited by ICANN as registrars in the United States and other countries, including Canada.[167] These accredited registrars use one shared, central registry that continues to be under the administration of NSI and, operationally, InterNIC.[168] Geographic domains are enabled to continue to be allocated nationally.

2) Assigned Numbers

Once a domain name has been allocated, the holder must, for operating reasons, obtain from the applicable RIR the numerical translation that will constitute the IP. The five registries that together provide a global coverage are:

---

165 See *ibid.*, Part 3 at paras. 129–244.
166 The website for ICANN is www.icann.org.
167 The introduction of this competitive system quickly resulted in significantly reduced registration fees for top level domains. For current domain pricing see www.icann.org.
168 See ICANN, *About Registrar Accreditation [Shared Registration System]*, online: ICANN www.icann.org/registrars/accreditation.htm.

1) American Registry for Internet Numbers (ARIN),[169] covering Canada and the United States;
2) Réseaux IP Européens/RIPE Network Coordination Centre (RIPE NCC),[170] covering Europe and the Middle East;
3) Asia Pacific Network Information Centre (APNIC),[171] covering Asia-Pacific;
4) Latin American and Caribbean Internet Addresses Registry (LACNIC),[172] covering Mexico and Central America; and
5) AfriNIC registration service (AfriNIC)[173] for African registrations.

AfriNIC was approved as the fifth RIR on 8 April 2005 by ICANN and became operative on 17 May 2005.[174] A transition of registrations for Africa from ARIN and RIPE to AfriNIC was set in place.

The RIRs are supervised and coordinated by IANA, which has overall authority, under ICANN, for Internet numerical addresses and their allocation and assignment to the five RIRs. IANA also coordinates numerical addresses determining the parameters of the Internet.[175]

3) Dispute Resolution Policy

Parties seeking domain names within the SRS framework for specified gTLDs must also agree to a process for arbitration of disputes, under ICANN's Uniform Domain Name Dispute Resolution Policy (UDRP), conducted in accordance with its "Rules for Uniform Domain Name Dispute Resolution Policy."[176] The UDRP is incorporated by reference

---

169 The website for American Registry for Internet Numbers (ARIN) is www.arin.net/.
170 The website for Réseaux IP Européens/RIPE Network Coordination Centre (RIPE NCC) is www.ripe.net/.
171 The website for Asia Pacific Network Information Centre (APNIC) is www.apnic.net/.
172 The website for Latin American and Caribbean Internet Addresses Registry (LACNIC) is lacnic.net/sp/.
173 The website for AfriNIC registration service is www.afrinic.net/.
174 ICANN, Resolution of the Board (8 April 2005), online: ICANN www.icann.org/minutes/resolutions-08apr05.htm.
175 See The TCP/IP Guide, *Internet Registration Authorities and Registries (IANA, ICANN, APNIC, ARIN, LACNIC, RIPE NCC)*, online: www.tcpipguide.com/free/t_InternetRegistrationAuthoritiesandRegistriesIANAIC-2.htm. IANNA existed prior to ICANN.
176 See ICANN, Uniform Domain Name Dispute Resolution Policy [UDRP] and Rules for Uniform Domain Name Dispute Resolution Policy, online: ICANN www.icann.org/udrp/udrp.htm. This policy applies to registrations in the gTLD categories of .biz, .com, .info, .name, .net, and .org and essentially requires that "most types of trademark based domain-name disputes . . . be resolved by

in a domain name holder's registration agreement.[177] It contains warranties by the holder of (1) accuracy of the holder's statements in its registration agreement, (2) no known infringement by the holder of any rights of third parties, (3) no illegality of purpose in registering the domain name, and (4) no knowingly unlawful use of the domain name.[178]

Paragraph 3 of the UDRP sets out the circumstances in which a registration may be cancelled, transferred, or changed, being principally the receipt of an order from "a court or arbitral tribunal" of competent jurisdiction,[179] or the receipt of a decision of an administrative panel under paragraph 4 deciding a dispute to which the holder was a party.

4) Cybersquatting

The protection of trademarks against cybersquatting is remedial under the UDRP. It may also be remedial through proceedings under the *Trade-marks Act*[180] or at common law as passing off, but this is problematic. In the United States, the federal trademark statute, the *Lanham Act*,[181] was amended in 1999 with the addition of section 43(d) by the *Anticybersquatting Consumer Protection Act (ACPA)*.[182] No such provision exists in Canada.

---

agreement, court action, or arbitration before a registrar will cancel, suspend, or transfer a domain name." The arbitration process is determined expeditiously by electronic administrative proceedings before "an approved dispute-resolution service provider."

177 UDRP, *ibid.* at para. 1 (adopted 26 August 1999), online: ICANN www.icann.org/udrp/udrp-policy-24oct99.htm.

178 *Ibid.* at para. 2.

179 The reference to the court or arbitral tribunal being "of competent jurisdiction" seems to refer to a competency to deal with the dispute *between the parties* concerned, so that a dispute between Canadian parties, dealt with before a Canadian court, would mean that a resulting court order might be acted upon under the ICANN Policy by an SRS registrar, even if that registrar were extraterritorial of Canada. Recommendation 47 of the WIPO Final Report, above note 149, would require an applicant for a domain name "to submit, without prejudice to other potentially applicable jurisdictions, to the jurisdiction of the courts of: (i) the country of domicile of the domain name applicant; and (ii) the country where the registrar is located." A domain name may itself be a trademark (if registered) or indicia under passing off if it meets the requirements in these contexts. As such it would be subject to litigation in the regular courts. See *Law Society of British Columbia*, above note 31.

180 *Trade-marks Act*, above note 6.

181 *The Trademark Act of 1946*, 15 U.S.C. 1051 (the *Lanham Act*).

182 *Anticybersquatting Consumer Protection Act*, 15 U.S.C. § 1125(d) (1999) [*ACPA*].

Proceedings under the Canadian *Trade-marks Act* or at passing off will not deal effectively with cybersquatting *simpliciter*. The requirement of "use" for statutory infringement, which involves the sale or transfer of wares or advertising of services,[183] is ordinarily not present. Likewise, for passing off to occur there needs to be a misrepresentation causing public (consumer) confusion as to some connection between the businesses or products of the parties,[184] commonly not established in pure cybersquatting but essentially a question of fact. *Easyjet Airline Co. Ltd. v. Dainty*[185] demonstrates that dissimilar businesses and domain names can be found to involve passing off when accompanied by other indicia such as distinctive get-up for websites and an intent to confuse.[186] In pure cybersquatting, a defendant who has utilized a plaintiff's trademark or indicia in its domain name registration is ordinarily not in business with respect to that trademark or indicia and is therefore not using the domain as a trademark under section 4, *Trademarks Act* or to show origin of the wares in passing off.[187] It is most often being held simply with the prospect that the plaintiff will be obliged to purchase it from the holder or that the holder has some other unrelated reason for holding the registration. This was the position in *1215757 Ontario Inc. (Saxon Chocolates) v. Zhadan*, where infringement was rejected.[188] The court in that case also considered an application of the tort of "Interference With Economic Interests," requiring an intention by a defendant to injure the plaintiff, the suffering of economic or related loss by the plaintiff, and use of unlawful means.[189] These elements were not established, but a properly determined UDRP finding against a defendant was considered to ordinarily meet the third requirement of illegality.[190]

The *ACPA*[191] in the United States overcomes the limitations of trademark infringement and passing off by providing relief for mere use or misappropriation in a domain name of a trademark (actual or confusingly similar) protected under section 43, including the dilution of a

---

183 See text accompanying notes 9–15, above in this chapter.
184 See text accompanying notes 28ff., above in this chapter.
185 *Easyjet Airline Co. Ltd. v. Dainty* (2001), [2002] F.S.R. 6 (Ch. D.) [*Easyjet Airline*] involving domain names easyjet.com and easyRealestate.co.uk. The court found the word "easy" to not be protected in itself (*ibid.* at para. 16).
186 *Ibid.* at paras. 13–17.
187 See text accompanying note 16, above in this chapter.
188 *1215757 Ontario Inc. (Saxon Chocolates) v. Zhadan*, [2003] O.J. No. 3068 at paras. 19 and 44 (S.C.J.).
189 *Ibid.* at para. 42ff.
190 *Ibid.* at paras. 61 & 62.
191 *ACPA*, above note 182.

famous mark,[192] if the usurper has a "bad faith intent to profit from that mark." Non-exclusive factors to consider in determining a bad faith intent are listed.[193] The factors seek to balance the domain name registrant's interests, including a reflection of the registrant's own name, any prior use by the registrant, any non-commercial fair use, and non-distinctiveness or lack of fame in the domain name. An overall defence is that the registrant "believed and had reasonable grounds to believe that the use of the domain name was a fair use or otherwise lawful."[194]

An important remedy under the Act is an *in rem* civil action against a domain name. Under stipulated conditions, it may be brought in the judicial district in which the domain name registrar, registry, or other authority is located.[195] Such proceedings are proprietary, determining rights in the item itself, rather than any position between the parties.

The juristic nature of a domain name outside of the *ACPA* is unclear. The Ninth Circuit stayed proceedings claiming that the tort of conversion might apply to a domain name and certified the proceeding to the California Supreme Court for determination.[196] Historically, conversion and bailment have concerned only tangible property, but there is recognition in the *Restatement (Second) of Torts* in the United States of intangible interests being remedial in conversion if the intangible is merged with a tangible document that has been converted, thereby preventing the exercise of the intangible rights.[197] The *Restatement* in this respect is not, however, followed in all states.[198] An intangible domain name has not, to date, been accepted within this principle. Indeed, the documentation for a domain name is not converted. It remains untouched with the registry.[199] Nevertheless, a property right in a domain name was accepted by the court.[200] The dissent considered this to be sufficient, relying on a second ground in the *Restatement* that conversion also lies for the prevention of the exercise of intangible rights merged

---

192 *Ibid.*, § 1125(d)(1)(A)(ii)(1).
193 *Ibid.*, § 1125(d)(1)(B)(i).
194 *Ibid.*, § 1125(d)(1)(B)(ii).
195 *Ibid.*, § 1125(d)(1)(E)(2)(A).
196 *Kremen v. Cohen*, 314 F.3d 1127 (9th Cir. 2003) [*Kremen*] concerning a deregistration and transfer of a domain name by a registry.
197 *Restatement (Second) of Torts*, § 242 (St. Paul, MN: American Law Institute, 1965–). An example is a share certificate.
198 See *AdVnt Biotechnologies, LLC v. Bohannon*, 2007 U.S. Dist LEXIS 47160 (S. Ariz. 28 June 2007), distinguishing *Kremen*, above note 196, on this basis.
199 *Kremen, ibid.* at para. 40, n. 13, Kozinski J dissenting.
200 *Ibid.* at paras. 14, 26, and 29.

in a document not itself converted.[201] Additionally, a domain name is clearly and discretely defined and when usurped a holder is denied its use entirely.[202]

The position in Canada with respect to property in, conversion of, and *in rem* proceedings (in the absence of a statutory provision similar to the *ACPA* in the United States) for domain names is undetermined, although the tort of conversion has been found appropriate to protect a commercial chose in action.[203] However, *Easyjet Airline* in the United Kingdom[204] involved the same situation as that before the Ninth Circuit, the transfer of the domain name from the defendant to the plaintiff.[205] Chancery, in *Easyjet Airline*, ordered the transfer as part of the relief granted, even though the defendant's use of the domain name itself (i.e., apart from the get-up of the website) may not have supported passing off, a feature that had existed in an earlier instance granting relief of this nature.[206] The possibility of the domain name being used "as an instrument of fraud" (waiting to be bought out) was enough even without a potential of passing off.[207] The order was designed to prevent the defendant from re-registering a variation of the domain name or transferring it to a third party.[208] Conceptually, this constitutes proprietary relief.

---

201 *Ibid.* at para. 40, n. 13 citing *Restatement (Second) of Torts,* above note 197, § 242(2).

202 *Kremen,* above note 196 at para. 41. The position was contrasted with situations in which an intangible remains, after usurpation, for use by the first party, such as a trade secret. Compare *R. v. Stewart,* [1988] 1 S.C.R. 963, denying the inclusion of confidential information within the crime of "theft" under the *Criminal Code,* R.S.C. 1985, c. C-46, s. 322(1) [s. 283(1) at the time].

203 See *HZPC Americas Corp v. True North Seed Potato Co.* (2007), 271 Nfld. & P.E.I.R. 79, [2007] P.E.I.J. No. 29 at para. 21 (S.C.) concerning True North's use of HZPC's potato seeds without permission and in contravention of the limited licence. HZPC claimed irreparable damage to its property interest of commercial quality in its potato varieties.

204 *Easyjet Airline,* above note 185.

205 The domain name had been transferred by the registry, giving rise to the claim of conversion – *Kremen,* above note 196.

206 *British Telecommunications plc v. One in a Million Ltd.,* [1998] EWCA Civ 1272.

207 *Easyjet Airline,* above note 185 at paras. 21–27.

208 *Ibid.* at para. 23.

D. INTERFERENCE WITH WEBSITES AND MEDIA

1) Trespass

Earlier reference to *Pro-C Ltd.*[209] in Ontario, involving the overwhelming of a website by electronic inquiries, presented the possibility of general tortious relief should instances of this nature be intentionally designed to damage the plaintiff's website or business (described as "denial of service" (DoS) activity) or if the defendant is negligent in carrying out its legitimate activities with a foreseeable consequence of damage to another,[210] as well as for other activities of varying interference or impact. These included viruses,[211] worms,[212] spyware,[213] or perhaps less serious intrusions such as cookies, spam, and surreptitiously deposited pop-up programs.

---

209 *Pro-C Ltd.*, above note 1.
210 See text accompanying notes 1–2, above in this chapter. A DoS is an electronic interference that overwhelms resources in a system, causing it to cease to function and thereby preventing its use by the owner and legitimate users. A common method of attack is to transmit a multitude of transmissions (packets) simultaneously to the target to block the entire capacity of the system. See Jennifer A. Chandler, "Security in Cyberspace: Combating Distributed Denial of Service Attacks" (2003–4) UOLTJ 231 at 261, paras. 11 & 12.
211 A computer virus is a self-replicating program that spreads by attaching itself to other programs or code and destroys programs or data or simply by replication that overwhelms the capacity of the infected system. See Microsoft, "*What is a Computer Virus?*", online: www.microsoft.com/nz/protect/computer/basics/virus.mspx.
212 A computer worm is a self-replicating program that can operate without being attached to other programs. It is downloaded surreptitiously and may, in addition to deletions and other damage, cause an infected computer to be used as a vehicle of transmission for the benefit of the worm operator (e.g., sending of spam). The infected computer is then often referred to as a "Zombie" transmitter. See Microsoft Security, "*What Is a Worm?*", online: www.microsoft.com/security/worms/whatis.aspx. See also Chandler, above note 210 at para. 13, referring to types of "worms."
213 Spyware is software that is surreptitiously downloaded and at best merely monitors and reports on a user's web-browsing activities, allowing commercial targeting for products or services. At worst, browser requests are rerouted, personal information is misappropriated, and a recipient's computer is manipulated for the benefit of the spyware operator. Spyware may be consented to within the terms of a licence of software that is made available and downloaded. In this context, the purpose is to ensure compliance with the terms of the licence. See Microsoft Security, "*What Is Spyware?*", online: www.microsoft.com/security/spyware/whatis.aspx. See also David Dubrovsky, "Protecting Online Privacy in the Private Sector: Is There a Better Model?" (2005) 18 R.Q.D.I. 171 at para. 8.

These interferences present a spectrum of justifications from some to none. The area is ripe for the creation of a remedial civil process, in addition to any criminal process that might be appropriate. While legislative measures, within federal or provincial constitutional competence, would allow a customizing of relief to the particular interference, common law or *Civil Code* measures might be adapted in the meantime. Common law has, through the centuries, presented a tool of creativity and adaptability to social and contextual change. There is no reason for it to now fall fallow. In the United States, there is a focus on trespass to chattels.[214] Perhaps, there may also be scope for conversion, privacy, or other torts. The choice of trespass or conversion is one of degree or scope of interference. Additionally, some of the interferences present dimensions that may be characterized as an infringement of privacy, presenting the potential for alternative relief as described in Chapter 4.

Historically, the torts of trespass to chattels and conversion were restricted to protecting tangible items of personal property (chattels) from physical interference. This may simply have reflected the contemporary absence of valuable intangible interests that could be the subject of interference in a manner similar to that of tangibles, and that the time has now arrived to develop beyond this limitation. However, even without this, depending on the particular interference, an electronic entry to digitized media may be conceptualized as producing immediate physical consequences to the system. Loss of bandwidth, memory, and resources is disruptive, slowing the medium in its operation as well as disrupting (or even preventing) physical usage of the hardware of the medium, for example by use of screen space with repetitive and disruptive pop-up messages. The direct and instantaneous nature of the interference, with the interferer intending the downloaded code to have the precise consequences that do actually eventuate, readily distinguishes other contexts of intangible interferences (historically treated as nuisance rather than trespass), such as noise, smell, or vibrations. Furthermore, the ability of some intrusive code to remain active within the recipient's system, in some instances evading detection or deletion,

---

214 The late 1990s saw a number of cases in different contexts, but frequently involving spam. See note 236ff., below in this chapter. Recent leading cases are: *Intel Corporation v. Hamidi*, 71 P.3d 296 (Sup. Ct. Cal. 2003) [*Intel*] and *Sotelo v. Directrevenue, LLC*, 384 F. Supp. 2d 1219, U.S. Dist. LEXIS 18877 (N.D. Ill. 2005) [*Sotelo*]. See also Robert V. Hale, "Wi-Fi Liability: Potential Legal Risks in Accessing and Operating Wireless Internet" (2005) 21 Santa Clara Computer & High Tech. L.J. 543; Daniel Kearney, "Network Effects and the Emerging Doctrine of Cybertrespass" (2005) 23 Yale L. & Pol'y Rev. 31; and Ashley L. Rogers, "Is There Judicial Recourse to Attack Spammers?" Note (2004) 6 Vand. J. Ent. L. & Prac. 338.

is a further feature that can distinguish more traditional interferences that have not been treated as trespass.[215]

Although trespass to chattels is one of the five intentional torts that developed from the ancient writ of trespass, as opposed to the action on the case, thereby suggesting it is actionable *per se*, or without proof of damage, it has, in fact, been limited by a requirement of proof of damage.[216] It may also require some measure of "directness" in the sequence of causation.[217] These features avoid the potential of liability for trivial interference as well as for consequences of a more remote nature[218] and will provide some solace to fears that trespass is too strict and inflexible to be suitable for application to multi-functional digital media. Current authority in the United States would limit trespass to instances involving physical injury or damage, impairment of the software, or the inability to use it for a significant period.[219] This is consistent with the *Restatement (Second) of Torts*.[220]

Conversion is notoriously difficult to define, with the relationship between trespass and conversion being in the scope or extent of interference.[221] If an interference were to destroy for all practical purposes the use of the computer or medium to the owner, or if it were taken over significantly by a usurper (for instance, to send spam or messages on behalf of the usurper), or if the intrusive code could not be readily removed, then conversion might be appropriate.[222] The benefit of establishing conversion lies in the measure of damage. It is the replacement cost of the chattel (i.e., the medium or system) if there is a complete

---

215 See *Sotelo, ibid.* at 1224 describing in the context of "spyware" the many intrusive features of such software code.

216 See Gerald H.L. Fridman, *The Law of Torts in Canada,* 2d ed. (Toronto: Carswell, 2002) at 32–34. See also *Everitt v. Martin,* [1953] N.Z.L.R. 298, where Adams J notes ". . . I would hesitate to be the first to hold that there is a right of action for the mere touching of another's good without damage or asportation."

217 Fridman, *ibid.* at 30–32.

218 *Ibid.* at 28–30.

219 *Intel,* above note 214 at 21 where the majority (4:3) of the Supreme Court of California emphasized that trespass protects an interest in the computer system (as a chattel) in itself. It does not encompass lost time or personal distress in reading an unwanted message, nor time spent by computer owners in an attempt to block messages. See also *Sotelo,* above note 214 (wasted resources and impaired bandwidth).

220 *Restatement (Second) of Torts,* above note 197, § 218.

221 The scope of the tort of conversion is imprecise, requiring many examples to demonstrate potential limits. See William L. Prosser, "The Nature of Conversion" (1957) 42 Cornell L.Q. 168.

222 See *Sotelo,* above note 214 at 1229–30.

destruction or substantial loss of use. Otherwise the measure is simply actual loss.[223]

Utilizing theories of conversion or trespass beyond physical damage or impairment will necessarily involve some conceptual and policy expansion. Yet why should this not occur? In related contexts, flexible conceptual development can be seen,[224] including the earlier discussed usurpation of the persona of another for marketing purposes and the potential of use of *in rem* proprietary process to control use of domain names.[225] It simply reflects the well-recognized analytical and policy expansion by judicial determination to encompass new situations: in the current context, interests in intangible assets in cyberspace. Beyond this issue, the modern focus of trespass in Canada may be quite accommodating, as it preserves the option of relief upon simple "direct" interference,[226] as well, of course, as the modern focus of intent of

---

223 See John G. Fleming, *The Law of Torts*, 9th ed. (Sydney, NSW: LBC Information Services, 1998) at 76–78 discussing the time at which the "full market value" is assessed. Historically, conversion value is assessed at the time of the conversion, on the theory that the owner had immediately replaced the lost item. On the other hand, the tort of detinue (the refusal without justification to return an item, otherwise lawfully acquired, to the owner) allowed the assessment to be made at the date of judgment, on the theory that the return of the item was expected. See *Steiman v. Steiman* (1982), 18 Man. R. (2d) 203 (C.A.), leave to appeal to S.C.C. granted (1983), 52 N.R. 236, but not pursued.

224 For example, computer programs when intertwined with hardware or when sold as prepackaged computer hardware and software or as "complete systems" have been defined as "goods" (defined as tangible terms) under sale of goods legislation. See, for example, *Burroughs Business Machines Ltd. v. Feed-Rite Mills (1962) Ltd.* (1973), 42 D.L.R. (3d) 303 (Man. C.A.), aff'd (1976), 64 D.L.R. (3d) 767 (S.C.C.). This topic is discussed extensively across many jurisdictions in Barry B. Sookman, *Computer, Internet and Electronic Commerce Law*, looseleaf (Toronto: Carswell, 1989, updated to 2010) at para. 2.17. In a related but not identical context, hidden electrical impulses have been recognized as a "literary work" for the purpose of copyright protection. Literary works are, of course, intangible, but ordinarily had been presented in a manner that enabled the product to be read by humans. In *Apple Computer, Inc. v. Mackintosh Computers Ltd.*, [1990] 2 S.C.R. 209, the inability to humanly observe or perceive the impulses was of no consequence in establishing liability. In identical proceedings in Australia, the majority of the High Court reached the opposite conclusion. See *Computer Edge Pty. Ltd. v. Apple Computer Inc.* (1986), 65 A.L.R. 33 at 39 (H.C.A.).

225 See text accompanying notes 44 (personality) and 199–208 (domain names), above in this chapter.

226 See *Cook v. Lewis*, [1951] S.C.R. 830 at 833–34 and 840, discussed in Allen M. Linden & Bruce Feldthusen, *Canadian Tort Law*, 8th ed. (Toronto: LexisNexis/ Butterworths, 2006) at 277–81. The position in Canada is seen as avoiding the rationalization in the United Kingdom that emphasizes the distinction between

the wrongdoer. Electronic interference is both intentional and direct in most instances.

Alternative approaches include recognition of a tort of intentional interference with the business of another[227] or recognition of a new tort in the nature of intentional interference with digital media. These new formulations are more likely to flow from legislative measures, however, even though Canadian common law has seen fit to create new torts, from the venerable "action on the case."[228] New torts have included a short-lived recognition of a tort of discrimination developed at common law drawing on the public policy expressed in legislation,[229] and, more significantly, that of appropriation of personality,[230] analogizing directly with the tort of conversion,[231] to protect a celebrity's interest in the economic value attaching to his or her persona.[232] There is therefore no conceptual or principled reason why Canadian courts should not develop common law and equitable relief in response to the need for protection of identifiable intangible interests in cyberspace, namely websites and other electronic digital media, as part of an ongoing common law response to new societal contexts. Specifically focused legislative regulatory or penal measures are also desirable and could form the basis for judicial recognition of a civil breach of statutory duty, proceeding upon any breach of such measures, if the legislation does

---

"intent" (trespass) and "carelessness" (negligence) rather than notions of "directness." See *Fowler v. Lanning*, [1959] 1 Q.B. 232; *Letang v. Cooper*, [1965] 1 Q.B. 232 (C.A.).

227 See Gerald H.L. Fridman, "Interference with Trade or Business" Part 1 (1993) 1 Tort Law Review 19 at 99.

228 The "action on the case" has been looked to in a "residual" sense as the juridical theory, or historical authority, for the creation of new torts. See Fleming, above note 223 at 21–27 discussing the historical position, noting a "residual" capacity in both "trespass" and "case." Fleming (at 27) distinguishes the position in Canada from the modern English rationalization set out above in note 226. See also Dale Gibson, "The New Tort of Discrimination: A Blessed Event for the Great Grandmother of Torts" (1980) 11 C.C.L.T. 141. The conceptual linkage to these residual resources simply provides an historical framework for what essentially is a policy choice by the court.

229 *Seneca College v. Bhadauria*, [1979] 27 O.R. (2d) 142 (C.A.), rev'd [1981] 2 S.C.R. 181 [*Seneca College*]. The S.C.C. reversed on the basis that the Ontario human rights legislation provided exclusive relief for human rights violations and this precluded any scope for common law development. Otherwise the Court "commended" the attempt to advance the common law (at 194).

230 *Krouse v. Chrysler Canada* (1973), 1 O.R. (2d) 225 (C.A.).

231 *Ibid.* at 237 characterizing the tort as within "an action on the case, or in more recent legal history in an action for trover or conversion in its modern form."

232 See above note 44.

not itself grant or reject such relief;[233] or of a new category of common law relief paralleling the statute.[234]

2) Spam

Spam raises particular features. As an expression, spam has many meanings, but today is used to mean unsolicited bulk electronic mail.[235] Unlike viruses, worms, spyware, or denial of service, individual spam messages do not cause harm to the computer or communications medium in itself. It is the cumulated quantity of such messages from many sources that causes interference to a user in the nature of nuisance. It is similar to telemarketing: unsolicited telephone calls selling products, seeking donations, or seeking completion of surveys. From 2005, telemarketing in Canada has been the subject of legislative measures enabling potential recipients to be listed to not receive such calls.[236] Similar legislation for spam is found in Bill C-27, *Electronic Commerce Protection Act*, providing for multi-agency protection as well as enabling private relief for compensation.[237] Legislation exists elsewhere,[238] and

---

233 See, for example, *Whistler Cable Television Ltd. v. IPEC Canada Inc.* (1992), 75 B.C.L.R. (2d) 48 (S.C.) re breach of rights under the *Broadcasting Act,* S.C. 1991, c. 11. See Chapter 2, note 342 and accompanying text.

234 See, for example, *Seneca College,* discussed in above note 229 and accompanying text; *Joseph v. Daniels* (1986), 4 B.C.L.R. (2d) 239 at 145-46, [1986] B.C.J. No. 3231 at para. 16 (S.C.); *Gould Estate v. Stoddart Publishing Co.* (1996), 30 O.R. (3d) 520 at paras. 14–15, 19–20, and 30 (Gen. Div.), aff'd on other grounds (1998), 39 O.R. (3d) 545 (C.A.).

235 See Jeremiah Kelman, "E-Nuisance: Unsolicited Bulk E-Mail at the Boundaries of Common Law Property Rights" (2004) 78 S. Cal. L. Rev. 363 at 369–70.

236 Sections 41(1)–41(7) and 72(01)–72(15) were inserted in the *Telecommunications Act* (1993) in 2005 to enable the CRTC to administer databases to prohibit or regulate the use by any person of the telecommunications facilities of a Canadian carrier for the purpose of unsolicited telecommunications. See *Telecommunications Amendment Act,* S.C. 2005, c. 50 [National Do Not Call List].

237 Re private right of action, Bill C-27, *Electronic Commerce Protection Act,* 2d Sess., 40th Parl., 2009, cl. 47–55. See also Industry Canada, "Stopping Spam," *Report of the Task Force on Spam,* online: www.ic.gc.ca/eic/site/ecic-ceac.nsf/vwapj/stopping_spam_May2005.pdf/$file/stopping_spam_May2005.pdf at 13–15.

238 See, for example, Australia: *Spam Act 2003* (Cth.), online: AustLII www.austlii. edu.au/au/legis/cth/num_act/sa200366/; EC, *Commission Directive 2002/58/EC of 12 July 2002 on Privacy and Electronic Communications,* [2002] O.J. L 201/31(7) at 37; EC, *Commision Regulation (EC) 2426/2003 of 11 December 2003 the privacy and electronic communications (EC directive) regulations 2003,* [2005] O.J. L Regs. 22 & 23; and in the United States, *Controlling the Assault of Non-Solicited Pornography and Marketing Act of 2003,* Pub. L. No. 108-187, 117 Stat. 2699.

has received significant academic attention in Canada.[239]

The difficulty presented in controlling spam lies in the need to identify and regulate secondary features that will control the cumulative nuisance yet still recognize that unsolicited communication is inherent in any communication system.[240] Legislation in jurisdictions seeking to regulate this practice is therefore necessarily lengthy and complex, involving multiple definitions and an infrastructure designed to accommodate an entirely new area of regulation. In general, electronic commercial advertising messages are prohibited, in the absence of prior consent, with definitional exclusions of permitted communications. Sender identification and functional unsubscribe features are usual requirements.

The extraterritorial origin of spam presents further jurisdictional and other issues of private international law.[241] The Australian legislation provides an example. It is expressly extraterritorial in application[242] and includes a definitional element of an "Australian link" within the meaning of the prohibited commercial electronic messages.[243] This serves the purpose of ensuring a link, in the nature of a "real and substantial" connection, of the communication with Australia.[244] Transnational cooperation exists between Australia, the United Kingdom, and the United States in enforcement of commercial anti-spam legislation and other e-mail matters.[245]

---

239 See Karen Ng, "Spam Legislation in Canada: Federalism, Freedom of Expression and Regulation of the Internet" (2005) 2 UOLTJ 447, and Andrea Slane, "Home Is Where the Internet Connection Is: Law, Spam and the Protection of Personal Space" (2005) 2 UOLTJ 225.

240 Compare entry onto land to knock on the occupier's door. In the absence of prior notice forbidding entry, this could not constitute trespass. See Benjamin Adida et al., "The Future of Trespass and Property in Cyberspace" (1998), online: http://groups.csail.mit.edu/mac/classes/6.805/student-papers/fall98-papers/trespass/final.html. See also Richard Warner, "Border Disputes: Trespass to Chattels on the Internet" (2002) 47 Vill. L. Rev. 117 at 163 (implied consent).

241 See Chapter 6 for an analysis of private international law (conflict of laws) nuanced to issues of telecommunications.

242 Spam Act 2003, above note 238, ss. 13 & 14.

243 Ibid., ss. 7 and 16.

244 Compare the test of "real and substantial connection" in Canadian conflict of laws or private international law, in Chapter 6, text accompanying notes 21–25.

245 See Memorandum of Understanding on Mutual Enforcement Assistance in Commercial E-mail Matters, online: www.ftc.gov/os/2004/07/040630spammoutext.pdf. See also Industry Canada, above note 237 at 29 on international bilateral and multilateral arrangements concerning spam.

Although an application of common law proceedings for trespass to chattels[246] or nuisance focusing on the potential of interference with the use and enjoyment of land[247] have been suggested, the prospects are remote. The requirement that trespass be limited to damage to, or impairment of, the medium or software system itself[248] will be difficult to meet with respect to spam. Indeed, even for a claim in nuisance there are difficulties of identifying individual causation, given that the interference by spam most often lies in the cumulative impact from many spammers.[249] Perhaps legislation providing for "joint and several liability" might be available to a plaintiff so long as the legislation in the particular jurisdiction is expressed broadly to encompass "fault" as opposed to just "negligence."[250]

In the United States, the federal anti-spam legislation[251] has been found to pre-empt any state legislative initiative specific to e-mail messages,[252] although not state common law of torts in general (i.e., not specifically focused on e-mail messages) so that the potential for trespass, nuisance, or conversion remains if these causes can be established.[253] Spamming has been recognized as contrary to Canadian appropriate Internet practice ("netiquette"), enabling an ISP to terminate an account.[254]

---

246   See *CompuServe v. Cyber Promotions*, 962 F. Supp. 1015 (S.D. Ohio 1997) and *America Online, Inc. v. IMS*, 24 F. Supp. 2d 548 (E.D. Va. 1998) (spam as trespass to chattels).

247   See Kelman, above note 235. Compare *Motherwell*, above note 3, in which a cause in nuisance was recognized for an overwhelming daily number of telephone calls to an occupier of land, but this situation was more personally intrusive in volume, kind, and circumstance than any spam e-mail.

248   See text accompanying note 219, above, and *Omega World Travel, Inc. v. Mummagraphics, Inc.*, 469 F.3d 348 at 358–59 (4th Cir. 2006) [*Omega World Travel*].

249   See P.J. Kozyris, "Abusive Advertising on the Internet through Spam: Problems and Solutions" (2007) 11:3 E.J.C.L. 20.

250   See *Bell Canada v. Cope (Sarnia) Ltd.* (1980), 11 C.C.L.T. 170 (Ont. H.C.), aff'd (1980), 31 O.R. (2d) 571 at paras 24–30 (C.A.), where Linden J suggests that the *Negligence Act* will encompass both negligence and trespass. See also Fleming, above note 223 at 306–9 for an overview of apportionment.

251   See above note 238.

252   *Omega World Travel*, above note 248 at 350–56.

253   *Ibid.* at 358. See also Katherine Wong, "The Future of Spam Litigation after *Omega World Travel v. Mummagraphics*" (2007) 20 Harv. J.L. & Tech. 459.

254   See *1267623 Ontario Inc. v. Nexx Online Inc.* (1999), 45 O.R. (3d) 40 (S.C.J.).

3) Cookies

Particular features also exist with cookie technology,[255] the depositing of small text files on an accessor's computer hard drive when an accessor links to a website. This text is embedded in a website's supply of a webpage requested by an accessor. After the cookie has been placed, each occasion that the accessor re-accesses the particular website causes the cookie to be attached to the request for access. This enables the website server to modify and update the cookie text to reflect current browsing within the accessed website. On exiting the website, an updated cookie is returned to the accessor's computer, for which trespass to chattels has been suggested as a common law response.[256]

Information gained from the cookie enables an operator to customize its site and advertising to a particular accessor's interests. This may reflect product type or geographic location. If an accessor has previously given his or her name, then personalized welcomes may be given by name.[257] The placement of cookies may be precluded, however, by an appropriate setting on an accessing computer that gives the accessor ultimate control subject to some websites being inaccessible if cookie technology is not enabled. An entirely appropriate element of choice is exercised by an accessor in these instances. While an unawareness of cookie technology may preclude an exercise of choice, knowledge of the process with passive response would logically constitute consent to or acceptance of the consequence. Indeed, cookies may be seen as simply part of the broader technology of the Internet. Cookie technology has survived legal challenge under a variety of causes, including claims in privacy.[258] Trespass to chattels has not been contemplated judicially.

4) Web Crawlers

Web crawler programs search for information on the World Wide Web, proceeding from server to server, through hypertext links, index-

---

255 Referred to simply as a "cookie," an "HTTP Magic Cookie" is applicable to servers of the World Wide Web. Cookie technology was invented by Lou Montulli, a founder of Netscape. See "The Unofficial Cookie FAQ," online: www.cookie-central.com/faq/, and Andrew Stuart, "Mysteries of the Internet: Where Cookie Comes From," *DominoPower Magazine* (July 2002), online: DominoPower www.dominopower.com/issues/issue200207/cookie001.html.

256 See Michael R. Siebecker, "Cookies and the Common Law: Are Internet Advertisers Trespassing on Our Computers?" (2003) 76 S. Cal. L. Rev. 893 at 898.

257 *Ibid.* at 898–99.

258 Siebecker, *ibid.*, provides a comprehensive analysis of a series of cases concerning cookies, various US statutory provisions, and privacy.

ing, and copying web pages according to the criteria of the requested search. They are commonly known as "web spiders," "ants," or "bots" (for "robots").[259] Ordinarily, the search for information is within the usual context of Internet usage. If, however, through intentional or negligent design a crawler bot overloads a server, causing malfunction and therefore a denial of service, there is no reason why the provider of a server could not recover for tortious injury as discussed earlier.[260] The difficulty in this context may be to identify and link causatively to a particular initiator of a crawler when actual damage is the cumulative effect of many such programs.

Activities contextually related to web crawling have been recommended for remedial legislation, including "dictionary attacks" and "harvesting."[261] The former is the practice of systematic use of words and variations of words in an attempt to discover a password to a protected source.[262] The latter is the gathering of e-mail addresses for the gatherer's use or sale to others. Both situations present *prima facie* lawful activities and may proceed in the absence of legislative proscription. Continuous accessing, taking, and reusing of information on the recipient's competing business website has, however, been found remedial in the United States as trespass to chattels.[263] However, the website is publicly available and any taking and reuse that does not damage or impair the system itself is not likely to be remedial in trespass.[264] The appropriation of data for use in a competing site may constitute misappropriation of business values or unfair competition, which is given limited recognition in the United States but not yet recognized in Canada, and has been rejected in some other Commonwealth jurisdictions.[265]

---

259 See MSDN, *WebCrawler Technology Sample*, online: MSDN msdn.microsoft.com/en-us/library/t7w4afa2.aspx. See also John C. Butler, "Another Node on the Internet" (1996) 22:2 Computers & Geosciences 193–94.

260 See text accompanying notes 1, 2, and 212, above in this chapter, and text accompanying note 263, below in this chapter.

261 See Industry Canada, above note 237 at 14 & 15.

262 See TopBits.com Tech Community, *Dictionary Attack*, online: www.tech-faq.com/dictionary-attack.shtml.

263 *E-Bay, Inc. v. Bidder's Edge, Inc.*, 100 F. Supp. 2d 1058 (N.D. Cal. 2000).

264 See *TicketMaster Corp. v. Tickets.com, Inc.*, 2000 U.S. Dist. LEXIS 4553 (C.D. Cal. 28 March, 2000). See Laura Quilter, "Regulating Conduct on the Internet: The Continuing Expansion of Cyberspace Trespass to Chattels" (2002) 17 Berkeley Tech. L.J. 421 at 439–44. See also text accompanying notes 216–20, above in this chapter.

265 See above notes 40–44.

5) Pop-Ups

"Pop-ups" are advertisements or notices that appear spontaneously on an accessor's computer screen when he or she visits websites on the Internet. They arise in two situations. First, the owner of the website that is being accessed may have implanted them on the website, usually for advertising revenue. There can be little legal relief for intrusions from such a source. Websites must be taken as an accessor finds them, apart from situations causing harm to an accessor's equipment through viruses or other disruptive intrusions flowing to an accessor. If too disruptive, the website should be avoided or technical measures taken to block incoming pop-ups. Second, a pop-up program may be installed on the accessor's computer. The objective of these programs is to monitor the user's activities and to provide timely information for the user of alternative sources to consider. A host, who may desire comprehensive information and to be acquainted with alternatives, may have purposely installed such a program. In such circumstances, only an owner of a website that has been accessed and had its presentation disrupted and, perhaps, business diverted, would be the source of complaint. However, should a host user have involuntarily installed the pop-up program through the deception or subterfuge of the pop-up program owner[266] and the effective operation of the host's equipment be seriously disrupted, then that host should reasonably be entitled to relief for this disruption.[267]

The interests of website owners whose displays on an accessor's screen are disrupted by pop-ups have been tested in the United States for infringement of trademark and passing off as well as for copyright infringement. To date there have been no reported proceedings elsewhere. The context of such proceedings is similar to that discussed earlier of use of another's meta-tags.[268] Entities responsible for generating pop-ups, in whatever context, often use the trademarks of the accessed website as identifiers to cause the pop-ups to occur. This may not, however, be a "use" as required by section 4, *Trade-marks Act*.[269] Infringement has been denied in the United States on an equivalent principle,

---

266 The subterfuge may occur by a mimicking of notices from the server that cause the download of the pop-up program to occur by a mouse click ordinarily designed to close a window or pop-up. Many pop-up programs are, however, downloaded voluntarily as part of a "bundle" of voluntarily downloaded programs.

267 See text accompanying note 222, above in this chapter.

268 See text accompanying note 64ff., above in this chapter.

269 *Trade-marks Act*, above note 6, s. 4. See text accompanying notes 15 and 16ff., above in this chapter.

being seen as purely machine or technically purposed, rather than as a trademark use in commerce[270] of identifying the source of a business or product. A contrary position might find use as a trademark by causing confusion as to the source of the wares or services presented in the pop-up alongside those of the website owner, or of their respective businesses, in a manner similar to confusion by "framing."[271] Use of a website address, as opposed to a trademark, is not an infringement.[272]

Copyright infringement is also claimed. Pop-ups cause a plaintiff's copyright-protected website to be presented to an accessor differently from the manner intended by the owner.[273] Copyright claims in the United States have concerned the right to prepare derivative works and the right to display them publicly.[274] Those situations are not distinct categories of infringement in Canada. Infringement by reproduction was, however, discussed in the United States, but rejected. Nothing from the plaintiff's website is reproduced or copied. In effect, the pop-ups are simply superimposed on the website, without any additional copy of the plaintiff's website. The position would probably be decided similarly in Canada.[275]

E. SUMMATION AND PROGNOSIS

This chapter is focused primarily on the new telecommunications media in cyberspace, which has produced *media-specific* dimensions within the areas discussed. Domain name creation, registration, use, and misuse developed almost overnight as a major area of indicia-related confusion of businesses and products, necessitating the creation of an electronic dispute resolution process surrounding domain names in conflict with other such names as well as with trademarks and trade names.[276] Trademark infringement and passing off proceedings before

---

270 See *U-Haul International, Inc. v. WhenU.com, Inc.*, 279 F. Supp. 2d 723 at 727 (E.D. Va. 2003); and *Wells Fargo*, above note 56 at 762.

271 See text accompanying notes 55–56, above in this chapter.

272 *1-800 Contacts, Inc. v. WhenU.com*, 309 F. Supp. 2d 467 (S.D.N.Y. 2003), rev'd and remanded, 414 F.3d 400, 75 U.S.P.Q.2d 1161 at para. 12 (2d Cir. 2005).

273 See Robert G. Howell, "Recent Copyright Developments: Harmonization Opportunities for Canada" (2003–4) 1 UOLTJ 151 at 156, para. 18.

274 *Copyright Act of 1976*, Pub. L. No. 94-553, §§ 106(2) and (5), 90 Stat. 2541.

275 See *Théberge v. Galerie d'Art du Petit Champlain*, [2002] 2 S.C.R. 336, 2002 SCC 34 at para. 42, requiring an *additional copy* in order to constitute a reproduction. See also Howell, above note 273 at 156–57 considering copyright and moral rights liability.

276 See text accompanying notes 176–180, above in this chapter.

the courts have also brought media-specific dimensions. The most significant is the use of meta-tags that allow search engine identification of potentially relevant websites to accessors. Are meta-tags trademarks? Is the inclusion in meta-tags of the code of a registered trademark sufficient? Do meta-tags depict origin of wares or services? Is the use of a meta-tag a "use" for trademark purposes under section 4 of the Act, or a misrepresentation causing confusion at common law? Is passing off the appropriate remedial measure for what is essentially a ranking of search results, or a diversion of an accessor from the site of origin of the meta-tags to that of another, but without the accessor seeing or even being aware of the meta-tags?

These issues are far from resolved, but for present purposes it is noted that an accessor familiar with the plaintiff's website is, at most, only initially confused upon opening a different but higher ranked site. An accessor with no familiarity with the plaintiff's site is not at all confused, but simply opens available results. In the first instance, any misrepresentation or confusion is entirely ephemeral. In the second, there is no misrepresentation, no real confusion, only misappropriation by the defendant usurper of the mega-tags. It is accordingly problematic as trademark infringement or passing off, and even upon a dilution theory would need to meet the non-confusion requirements of "use" under the Act.

Likewise, causing a website to crash or be rendered inoperable or to be simply damaged through a multiplicity of accessing (denial of service) as a result of an advertising campaign by another website operator with a substantially in common trademark is not comfortably remedial as trademark infringement or passing off.[277] The fact that no other form of relief may be available for the destruction or damage ought not to encourage the amelioration of trademark infringement or passing off by seeking to accommodate what has occurred. Instead, if policy compels relief, consideration should be given to other, more appropriate causes or to the structuring of entirely new relief, tailored specifically to circumstances that the new technology has presented.

In a broader context, but toward achieving this objective, this chapter has examined fledgling initiatives in the United States to apply causes primarily in trespass and conversion to myriad interferences with new media communications. These include serious intrusions of viruses, worms, and spyware, as well as less serious situations of cookies, spam, and surreptitiously placed pop-up programs. If the mode

---

277 This was the position in *Pro-C Ltd.*, above note 1, where passing off was denied by the Ontario Court of Appeal.

of interference includes the gathering and reporting of information or data from a website, an alternative remedy could be developed through privacy, a topic dealt with in Chapter 4.

While trespass and conversion will present a court with the choice of extending these causes from their historical context of the physical and tangible to today's world of the intangible, this should not pose too much difficulty, as courts of common law jurisdiction are not ordinarily foreclosed to developing and crafting the common law to encompass new manifestations of valuable interests. Nor should the global dimensions of cyberspace inhibit any such development. Private international law or conflict of laws is another rapidly developing area of Canadian jurisprudence, expanding jurisdictional grounds as well as recognition and enforcement of judgments interprovincially and internationally. These matters are examined in Chapter 6. Even if the global and largely anonymous environment of cyberspace renders common law initiatives impossible in some instances, enforcement will be possible in many others, and development ought not to fail upon despair of an inability to encompass all damage and injury. Finally, specifically crafted legislation, particularly if the product of interprovincial and international cooperation and uniformity, is most beneficial, but the current absence of legislative initiatives ought not inhibit common law development. Indeed, historically, it has justified and enhanced recognition of common law measures and may do so today in the environment of cyberspace.

PRIVACY

A. PERSPECTIVES OF A DIGITAL AGE

Historically, the concept of privacy was relatively peripheral to tele-communications law. The traditional point-to-point media of princi-pally telephone communications by a Canadian carrier is essentially a matter of "carriage," and section 36, *Telecommunications Act* (1993) pro-vides: "Except where the [CRTC] approves otherwise, a Canadian car-rier shall not control the content or influence the meaning or purpose of telecommunications carried by it for the public."[1] Noted in other contexts,[2] section 36 prohibits a Canadian carrier from interfering with the content of a communication, but it may also be interpreted to imply exemption of a Canadian carrier from liability for content provided by others.[3] Additionally, other regulatory provisions may be relevant.[4]

---

1   *Telecommunications Act,* S.C. 1993, c. 38, s. 36.
2   See Chapter 2, text accompanying note 47.
3   See Chapter 2, text accompanying notes 228–30 and Chapter 5, text accom-
    panying notes 259–60 and 261–65, reporting the CRTC to have purported to
    exempt a Canadian carrier from liability for defamation or copyright infringe-
    ment in any communication it carries. Such an exemption may present a
    constitutional and jurisdictional challenge to the exercise of what might be seen
    as provincial jurisdiction (common law tort or *Civil Code* delict) under s. 92(13),
    Constitution Act, 1867 (U.K.), 30 & 31 Vict., c. 3, reprinted in R.S.C. 1985, App.
    II, No. 5, "Property and Civil Rights in the Province" in respect of defamation
    and an excess of jurisdiction concerning copyright where the position of pro-
    viders of the means of communication is addressed in the *Copyright Act*, R.S.C.
    1985, c. C-42.
4   See, for example, Chapter 2, text accompanying notes 90–94.

These situations aside, a Canadian carrier would be responsible under any federal legislative provisions concerning privacy, as well as provincial legislation, tort, or delict for privacy violation. In Quebec, legislative and *Civil Code* provisions provide significant privacy protection, and similarly, four common law provinces have enacted statutory privacy protection.[5] In the ordinary course of operations, however, a carrier is unlikely to violate these provisions unless it is a direct party to the dissemination of the *content* of any message.[6] On the other hand, point-to-mass broadcast media carry a higher risk of content-related liability. This would include any recognized privacy interest.

Today, the digitized media of telecommunications has significantly increased the scope of privacy protection within telecommunications. Two broad dimensions are revealed. The first is the principal focus of this chapter: the development of Canadian law to accommodate issues of privacy contextually with digitized transactions and related links to the analysis of interference with communications equipment, data and information discussed in Chapter 3, copyright enforcement issues in MP3 file sharing and the corresponding balancing of user privacy interests by Internet Service Providers (ISPs) discussed in Chapter 5, and private international law presented in Chapter 6. While many aspects of privacy law are encompassed within these and other contexts, the most significant is the protection of personal information under the federal *Personal Information Protection and Electronic Documents Act (PIPEDA)*[7] and equivalents in three provinces, enacted specifically in response to privacy risks in the private sector collection of data and especially during Internet telecommunications, though *PIPEDA* is not limited to this or any particular medium. The second broad dimension is still largely political, and any legal and policy response is more speculative. Features of this dimension are simply identified in this chapter, with a warning of the potentially erosive impact to interests in privacy that digitized media bring to individuals from the facilitation the afford governments and other organizations to maintain surveillance and to acquire information concerning individuals. Given the nature and global scope of digitized media, both national and international responses will be needed if, indeed, there is the political will to take

---

5   See *Civil Code of Quebec*, S.Q. 1991, c. 64, arts. 35–41; and notes 69–72, below in this chapter.

6   See, for example, *Dominion Telegraph Company v. Silver* (1882), 10 S.C.R. 238, discussed in Chapter 5, text accompanying notes 263–65.

7   *Personal Information Protection and Electronic Documents Act*, S.C. 2000, c. 5, concerning "Protection of Personal Information in the Private Sector" [*PIPEDA*].

significant privacy-related measures. Security and law enforcement interests may discourage a response that is too focused on privacy.

Additionally, both dimensions must reflect societal attitudes, which are ambivalent with respect to the use of technology. Commentator Jonathan Shaw provides an illustrative example. A person who waves to a friend and has a photograph taken by a high-resolution camera of his or her finger prints is likely to call for privacy, but the taking of finger prints to gain entry to a popular event without delay may present a preference for the convenience of the technology.[8] This may be especially so with younger people who have embraced digital communications technologies as a "social network" through cellphone voice and photographic wireless transmissions and the Internet media of Facebook or MySpace, or other similar blogs, including the practice termed "sexting," noted as common among young persons, involving the sharing of nude self-photographs.[9] The result often is voluntary, irretrievable disclosure of highly personal information. This may lead to the conclusion that these users do not value the type of privacy protection that older generations have traditionally sought. Whether such a conclusion is accurate or not,[10] it has led to high-profile advice to young people encouraging a protection of their privacy interests.[11]

Projections of the plight or otherwise of individual privacy in a future reflecting the embrace of technologies and related communi-

---

8   Jonathan Shaw, "Exposed: The Erosion of Privacy in the Internet Era" *Harvard Magazine* (September–October 2009), online: Harvard Magazine http://harvard-magazine.com/2009/09/privacy-erosion-in-internet-era.

9   See "U.S. Poll Finds Sexting Common among Young People" *CTV News* (3 December 2009), online: CTV www.ctv.ca/CTVNews/TopStories/20091203/sexting_poll_091203/.

10 A survey reported in the United Kingdom in September 2009 that 54 percent of the young people (age eleven to sixteen) wanted advice "about how to retain privacy and not share personal information" and a further 28 percent about "how to retain security of information." See Ipsos Mori, *Children and Young People's Access to Online Content on Mobile Devices, Games Consoles and Portable Media Players*, Report prepared for Ofcom (September 2009), commented on at Becta Emerging Technologies for Learning, "Half of young people want personal privacy advice," online: http://emergingtechnologies.becta.org.uk/index.php?section=etn&rid=14823.

11 See warning given by President Barack Obama to American school children and teenagers to be cautious about posting personal information on Facebook and other blogs in cyberspace: "Obama Warns Teens about Facebook Risks" *Reuters* (9 September 2009), online: www.internetnews.com/breakingnews/article.php/3838231/Obama+Warns+Teens+About+Facebook+Risks.htm.

cations media have been made in both the United States[12] and Canada.[13] *PIPEDA* in Canada is seen as affording an ameliorating measure through the concept of an ongoing consent to the holding of personal information that may be subsequently withdrawn by the supplier of that information or may expire, as opposed to the act of consent being simply a one-time transactional event.[14] Other commentators have pursued this dimension of a new social process centred upon technology and media, and report young people to have a privacy perspective that reflects the process itself. It is not one of strict control of information, as this would preclude social networking, but instead one of confidentiality within the social network. Disclosure outside of the network, or intrusion upon the network, is seen as a privacy violation.[15]

An application of privacy control to such a process is, indeed, now illustrated in the acceptance in 2009 by the US-based global social networking medium Facebook, Inc. of recommendations of the Privacy Commissioner of Canada,[16] providing a positive example of regulatory originated changes to improve the privacy of users of this new technology medium, said by the Commissioner to have a user base in Canada of nearly 12 million and over 200 million globally.[17] The complaint was multi-faceted and substantial. Some features were determined to be "not well-founded," whereas others were resolved by measures agreed during the proceeding. The remainder were those subsequently agreed between the Commissioner and Facebook, Inc.[18] This positive conclusion does, however, also provide a glimpse at the extraterritorial legal difficulties that might have ensued if Facebook, Inc. and the Commis-

12   Daniel J. Solove, *The Digital Person: Privacy and Technology in the Digital Age* (New York: New York University Press, 2004); Jerry Berman & Deirdre Mulligan, "Privacy in the Digital Age: Work in Progess" (1999) 23 Nova L. Rev. 549.

13   Jennifer Barrigar, Jacquelyn Burkell, & Ian Kerr, "Let's Not Get Psyched out of Privacy! Reflections on Withholding Consent to the Collection, Use and Disclosure of Personal Information" (2007) 44 Can. Bus. L.J. 54.

14   Barrigar, Burkell, & Kerr, *ibid.* at 59–61.

15   See Avner Levin & Patricia Sánchez Abrill, "Two Notions of Privacy on Line" (2009) 11(4) Vand. J. of Ent. & Tech. Law 1001.

16   Privacy Commissioner of Canada, *Report of Findings into the Complaint Filed by the Canadian Internet Policy and Public Interest Clinic (CIPPIC) against Facebook Inc.*, (Ottawa: 2009) [Facebook Report].

17   *Ibid.* at para. 8.

18   See Privacy Commissioner of Canada, News Release, "Facebook agrees to address Privacy Commissioner's concerns" (27 August 2009), online: www.priv. gc.ca/media/nr-c/2009/nr-c_090827_e.cfm; Privacy Commissioner of Canada, News Release, "Letter from OPC to CIPPIC, Outlining its Resolution with Facebook" (25 August 2009), online: www.priv.gc.ca/media/nr-c/2009/let_090827_e. cfm [Letter from OPC].

sioner had not reached an accord.[19] Aspects of the Facebook proceeding are referred to variously in this chapter.

A further example of successful influence by the Privacy Commissioner (and provincial Commissioners) concerns Google Maps Street View.[20] This digital medium provides a 360-degree quality colour snapshot at street level of Google Map streets, using multiple images to present the scene as a person would see it if physically on the street. The images are recorded from camera-equipped vehicles traversing streets in numerous cities. They are accessible from any Internet connection, and Street View enables zooming in to, rotating, and panning across the images, as well as the capacity to view specific sites, buildings, or homes. A Street View of several Canadian cities, towns, and communities became accessible from 7 October 2009.[21] Photographing commenced in the United States in 2007 and has already covered a significant portion of the world.[22] Useful, educational, entertaining, and popular, this medium has also afforded a significant measure of individual safety and privacy after US-based Google Inc. accommodated privacy concerns of the federal and provincial Privacy Commissioners[23] leading to blurring of images of human faces and vehicle licence plates and the provision of digital means for users to ask Google Inc. to remove inappropriate images or images of the user, his or her family, vehicle, or home.[24] Google Inc. also posts the locations of vehicle camera operations.[25]

The Supreme Court of Canada has attributed constitutional significance to privacy,[26] and in 2006 reiterated a "quasi-constitutional status attributed to privacy" specifically for the protection of personal information.[27] Significantly, the defence was raised by the Court itself

---

19   See Chapter 6, text accompanying notes 18–19 and 130–38, discussing private international law enforcement issues in this context.

20   See Google Maps Canada, "Street View: Explore the world at street level" (home page), online: maps.google.ca/intl/en_ca/help/maps/streetview/.

21   See Shaw, "Google Street View Live in Canada," online: SHAW www.shaw. ca/2009/10/07/google-street-view-live-in-canada/.

22   See Google Maps Canada, above note 20, "Where is Street View?".

23   Information and Privacy Commissioner of Alberta, Information and Privacy Commissioner for British Columbia, Commission d'accès à l'information du Québec, & Privacy Commissioner of Canada, *Captured on Camera: Street-level Imaging Technology, the Internet and You* (2009), online: Fact Sheet www.priv. gc.ca/fs-fi/02_05_d_39_prov_e.pdf.

24   Google Maps Canada, above note 20, "Privacy."

25   *Ibid.*, "Where is Street View?".

26   See, for example, *Dagg v. Canada*, [1997] 2 S.C.R. 403 at 434; *Lavigne v. Canada* 2002 SCC 53 at para. 25; and *H.J. Heinz Co. v. Canada*, 2006 SCC 13 at para. 28.

27   *Pro Swing Inc. v. Elta Golf Inc.*, 2006 SCC 52, [2006] 2 S.C.R. 612 at para. 60.

in the context of a public policy defence to the enforcement of a foreign judgment ordering the disclosure of personal information in contempt proceedings. In another context, in 2007, the Ontario Superior Court, for reasons of infringement of privacy, quashed Ontario legislation granting adopted children and birth parents access to personal information in adoption records. Belobaba J found privacy to be "undeniably a fundamental value in Canadian society."[28]

This broad constitutional dimension for privacy, as a principle in itself, has developed from expectations of privacy inherent in specific contexts under the *Canadian Charter of Rights and Freedoms*.[29] These include protections principally against unreasonable search and seizure,[30] and rights to life, liberty, and security of the person.[31] Freedom of thought, belief, religion, expression, and association[32] may also reflect more indirectly a privacy protection to belief and association.[33] Contextually, privacy within these constitutional principles has been informationally focused on retention or exclusion by an accused, or disclosure by others in criminal or public law proceedings. The apparent expansion of a privacy expectation from these specific protections to a more generalized, quasi-constitutional proposition is significant and will facilitate the balancing of a privacy dimension in wider situations. The *Charter* is applicable only in governmental contexts involving the state and the citizen, most commonly within the application and interpretation of statutes, but common law and *Civil Code* provisions in Quebec may also be developed in conformity with "Charter values."[34]

Today's digitized, electronic, and interactive global telecommunications media are entirely informationally focused, involving data supplied to, or gathered by, governmental authorities, business entities, or

---

28 *Cheskes v. Ontario (Attorney General)* (2007), 87 O.R. (3d) 581 at para. 112 (S.C.J).
29 *Canadian Charter of Rights and Freedoms*, Part 1 of the *Constitution Act, 1982*, being Schedule B to the *Canada Act 1982* (U.K.), 1982, c. 11, ss. 1–34 [*Charter*].
30 *Ibid.*, s. 8. See *Hunter v. Southam Inc.*, [1984] 2 S.C.R. 145.
31 *Charter*, *ibid.*, s. 7. See *R. v. Hebert*, [1990] 2 S.C.R. 151; and *R. v. Broyles*, [1991] 3 S.C.R. 595.
32 *Charter*, *ibid.*, s. 2. See *R. v. Big M Drug Mart*, [1985] 1 S.C.R. 295; and *Syndicat Northcrest v. Amselem*, [2004] 2 S.C.R. 551.
33 See Louise Potvin, Robert G. Howell, & Tom McMahon, "Canada" in Michael Henry, ed., *International Privacy and Personality Laws* (London: Butterworths, 2001) at 76, para. 7(08). See also *ibid.* at 76–79 concerning substantive criminal law situations involving a dimension of privacy.
34 *Hill v. Church of Scientology of Toronto*, [1995] 2 S.C.R. 1130 at 1169. The Preliminary Provision of the *Civil Code of Quebec*, above note 5, expresses the Code to be "in harmony with the Charter of human rights and freedoms."

makers of databases. In Canada, the privacy of information accumulated by governments has for some time been protected both federally[35] and provincially.[36] However, historically only Quebec[37] provided legislative privacy protection specifically for personal information supplied to, or collected by, the private sector, the field now occupied nationally by the federally enacted *PIPEDA*.[38]

For the first three years, *PIPEDA* applied only to organizations that "collect, use or disclose" personal information in connection with a "federal work, undertaking or business"[39] or disclosed the information "outside the province for consideration." However, at the expiry of the three years in 2004, *PIPEDA* became applicable to all organizations in Canada.[40] The legislative intention is that provinces are to have an opportunity to enact equivalent legislation, but if this is not done there cannot be a vacuum of regulation.[41] The constitutional dimensions of this formulation are considered in Chapter 1.[42]

The provinces of British Columbia,[43] Alberta,[44] and Quebec[45] have enacted personal information protection measures (PIPAs) that meet the requisite substantial similarity with *PIPEDA*.[46] Ontario has simi-

---

35   *Privacy Act*, R.S.C. 1985, c. P-21.

36   See, for example, *Freedom of Information and Protection of Privacy Act*, R.S.B.C. 1996, c. 165; *Freedom of Information and Protection of Privacy Act*, R.S.A. 2000, c. F-25; *Freedom of Information and Protection of Privacy Act*, R.S.O. 1990, c. F.31.

37   Specific legislative protection was in place in Quebec from 1993. See *An Act respecting the protection of personal information in the private sector*, S.Q. 1993, c. 17.

38   *PIPEDA*, above note 7.

39   This expression is defined in *ibid.*, s. 2(1) as "means any work, undertaking or business that is within the legislative authority of Parliament. It includes [a significant list of express inclusions follows]".

40   *Ibid.*, s. 30. See Chapter 1, notes 233 and 234 and accompanying text. The three-year period ended three years after *PIPEDA*; s. 30 came into effect on 1 January 2001. References to relevant *Canada Gazette* notices are given in Chapter 1, note 233.

41   For the process for determining whether a province has provisions "substantially similar" to *PIPEDA*, see Chapter 1, note 243, in the context of constitutional issues.

42   See Chapter 1, text accompanying notes 224–65.

43   *Personal Information Protection Act*, S.B.C. 2003, c. 63.

44   *Personal Information Protection Act*, S.A. 2004, c. P-6(5).

45   *An Act respecting the protection of personal information in the private sector*, R.S.Q., c. P-39(1).

46   For compliance by Alberta, see Chapter 1, note 243. For compliance by British Columbia, see *Organizations in the Province of British Columbia Exemption Order*, S.O.R./2004-220 (12 October 2004), P.C. 2004-1164 (12 October 2004), C. Gaz. 2004.II.1640. For compliance by the province of Quebec, see *Organizations in*

larly legislated in the context of personal health information,[47] meeting
the substantial similarity requirement in this sector.[48] Provincial legislation applies only to provincially regulated organizations operating
within the province.[49] The privacy regulation of the telecommunications industry and media will, therefore, be substantially federal under
PIPEDA.[50]

Internationally, a political and philosophical division is reflected
between the United States and the European Union. The United States
favours voluntary privacy policies implemented by businesses and
industries engaged in electronic transactions under a "Safe Harbor"
scheme.[51] The European Union has stipulated through its personal data
Directive[52] a legislated system of protection. The position afforded in
Canada by *PIPEDA* is in between, being the enactment in a legislative
schedule of a standards guideline initially created by industry sources.
These infrastructional differences could have been of considerable consequence as the EU Directive stipulates that foreign jurisdictions lacking a substantially equivalent system of protection will be excluded
from access to European databases.[53] Conflict has been avoided. The
European Union has approved both *PIPEDA* in Canada[54]and the US Safe

---

the *Province of Quebec Exemption Order*, S.O.R./2003-374 (19 November 2003),
P.C. 2003-1842 (19 November 2003), C. Gaz. 2003.II/2917.

47   *Personal Health Information Protection Act*, S.O. 2005, c. 3.
48   For compliance by Ontario, see Chapter 1, note 258.
49   Investigation Report P2005-IR-007; *Rick Arsenault Enterprises Inc. (Re)*, [2005]
A.I.P.C.D. No. 45 at para. 2 (Information and Privacy Commissioner); Decision
P07-03, *British Columbia (Constituency Office of a Federal Member of Parliament)*,
[2007] B.C.I.P.C.D. No. 29 (Information and Privacy Commissioner).
50   See Chapter 1, Section C, concerning the constitutional dimensions of telecommunications.
51   See Export.gov, *Welcome to the U.S.-EU & Swiss Safe Harbor Frameworks*, online:
www.export.gov/safeharbor/.
52   EC, *Commission Directive 95/46/EC of the European Parliament and of the Council
of 24 October 1995 on the protection of individuals with regard to the processing of
personal data from 24 October 1995*, [1995] O.J. L 281/31, online: http://ec.europa.
eu/justice_home/fsj/privacy/docs/95-46-ce/dir1995-46_part1_en.pdf. (Note also
EC, *Commission Directive 2002/58/EC on telecommunications prohibition on spamming without consent from 12 July 2002*, [2002] O.J. L 201/37, art. 13.
53   EC, *Directive 95/46/EC, ibid.*, art. 25(1).
54   EC, *Commission Decision 2002/2/EC of 20 December 2001 pursuant to Directive
95/46/EC of the European Parliament and of the Council on the adequate protection
of personal data provided by the Canadian Personal Information Protection and
Electronic Documents Act*, [2002] O.J. L 2/13 online: http://eur-lex.europa.eu/
LexUriServ/LexUriServ.do?uri=OJ:L:2002:002:0013:0016:EN:PDF.

Harbor approach[55] as meeting the criteria to enable reciprocality of data usage to proceed. Significantly, however, the US Safe Harbor framework is essentially an accord between the United States and the European Union to meet the reciprocality requirements of the European Union. The framework enables a US business to self-certify to the US Commerce Department that it has gained membership in a self-regulatory organization that imposes on its members principles of privacy of information that are identified in the US/EU accord. The Commerce Department then certifies that business as being within the Safe Harbor framework. The Federal Trade Commission (FTC) may bring proceedings against a business that has gained certification but has violated the requisite privacy principles. The framework reflects the US policy goal of self-regulation by industry.[56]

Canadian commentators have assessed the US privacy philosophy as grounded in "liberty" (avoidance of government intrusion), that of the European Union as "dignity" and "public image," and that of Canada as "individual autonomy" and "person control of information." The middle Canadian ground has been urged on the United States.[57]

Privacy and *PIPEDA* issues are presented in all Internet contexts, including the cooperation of intermediaries such as Internet service providers (ISPs), which is required to identify users who may be infringing the rights or interests of a third party, such as copyright infringement by the unauthorized downloading of sound recordings.[58] In the absence of an order from a court of competent jurisdiction, the intermediaries may be liable for infringing *PIPEDA*, other privacy laws, or their contracts with subscribers by disclosing subscriber information to rights holders.[59] A similar situation would prevail in other contexts

---

55   EC, *Commission Decision 2000/520/EC of 26 July 2000 pursuant to Directive 95/46/EC of the European Parliament and of the Council on the adequacy of the protection provided by the safe harbour privacy principles and related frequently asked questions issued by the US Department of Commerce*, [2000] O.J. L 215/4 online: http://eurlex.europa.eu/LexUriServ/LexUriServ.do?uri=CELEX:32000D0520:EN:HTML.

56   U.S., Federal Trade Commission, *US/EU Safe Harbor Agreement: What It Is and What It Says About the Future of Cross Border Data Protection*, by Mozelle W. Thompson (Federal Trade Commissioner) & Peder van Wagonen Magee (of the F.T.C.) (Washington, DC: Federal Trade Commission, 2003), online: www.ftc.gov/speeches/thompson/thompsonsafeharbor.pdf.

57   Avner Levin & Mary Jo Nicholson, "Privacy Laws in the United States, the EU and Canada: The Allure of the Middle Ground" (2005) 2 UOLTJ 357.

58   See Chapter 5, text accompanying notes 291–93.

59   See *BMG Canada Inc.* v. *John Doe*, [2004] 3 F.C.R. 241 at paras. 36–42 (Fed. Ct.). The Federal Court of Appeal affirmed but placed less emphasis on privacy in

when enforcement or suit requires disclosure of identification, or other information, held by intermediaries.[60]

Before considering the detailed requirements of *PIPEDA*, the scope of privacy protection existing apart from *PIPEDA* should be considered in its potential application to the telecommunications sector.

B. PROVINCIAL TORT OR DELICT

Common law and state legislative measures in the United States, have long recognized a right to privacy, flowing from the seminal 1890 article by Warren and Brandeis.[61] Canadian and the other Commonwealth common law has not directly protected interests in privacy. Fledgling but disputed moves in this direction[62] may today be assisted by the recent trend of a quasi-constitutional dimension to privacy.[63] Historically, however, privacy interests have been protected at common law only indirectly through other torts or by contract.[64] Some recognition

---

contexts involving infringement of third party rights, such as copyright. See *BMG Canada Inc.* v. *John Doe*, [2005] 4 F.C. 81 at paras. 41 and 42 (C.A.).

60   Those contexts include security-related issues, criminal law matters (for example, transmission or possession of child pornography), and common law situations such as defamation. These contexts would ordinarily be within procedural rules for disclosure or discovery against third parties. See, for example, the "equitable bill of discovery" principle in federal civil procedure detailed in *BMG Canada Inc.* v. *John Doe*, *ibid.* at para. 13 (Fed. Ct.).

61   Samuel Warren & Louis D. Brandeis, "The Right to Privacy" (1890) 4 Harv. L. Rev. 193.

62   See *Saccone* v. *Orr* (1981), 34 O.R. (2d) 317 (Co. Ct.); *Roth and Roth* v. *Roth, Roth and Stephens* (1991), 4 O.R. (3d) 740 (Gen. Div.) [*Roth and Roth*]; and *MacDonnell* v. *Halifax*, 2009 NSSC 187, recognizing a tort for invasion of privacy. See also *Somwar* v. *McDonald's Restaurants of Canada Ltd.* (2006), 263 D.L.R. (4th) 752 at 760 (Ont. S.C.J.): "[T]he time has come to recognize invasion of privacy as a tort in its own right." Against, see *Parasiuk* v. *Canadian Newspaper Co.*, [1988] 2 W.W.R. 727 (Man. Q.B.) [*Parasiuk*]; and *Turton* v. *Butler* (1987), 85 A.R. 193 at 195 (Q.B.) [*Turton*].

63   See text accompanying notes 26–27, above in this chapter.

64   Nuisance, trespass to land, and intentional infliction of mental suffering are the likely available causes. See, for example, *Motherwell* v. *Motherwell* (1976), 73 D.L.R. (3d) 62 (Alta. S.C. (A.D.)); *Roth and Roth, ibid.*; *Weingerl* v. *Seo* (2005), 256 D.L.R. (4th) 1 (Ont. C.A.); *Saelman* v. *Hill*, [2004] O.J. No. 2122 at paras. 37–38 (S.C.J.). A major resource is 2008 British Columbia Law Institute, "Report on the *Privacy Act* of British Columbia" (2008) BCLI Rep. No. 49, online: www. bcli.org/bclrg/publications/49-report-privacy-act-british-columbia [2008 British Columbia Law Institute].

of privacy may be seen within employment relations[65] and recently, in the United Kingdom, within the breach of confidence proceeding.[66]

Prosser categorized US caselaw as involving four contexts: (1) intrusion into private situations; (2) public disclosure of private facts; (3) casting another to the public in a false light;[67] and (4) appropriating the name or likeness of another for commercial gain.[68] All such matters can occur in telecommunication transactions, but the categories of "intrusion" and "public disclosure of private facts" are of particular relevance for electronic interference with Internet-related systems and the collection and storage of private data.

Legislation in the common law provinces of British Columbia,[69] Saskatchewan,[70] Manitoba,[71] and Newfoundland[72] creates in the respective provinces statutory torts for the violation of privacy, an expression that is not statutorily defined. Judicial interpretation has proceeded on a case-by-case basis. The nature, incidence, and occasion are to be taken into account,[73] together with a balancing of circumstances and the interests of others.[74] Injuries ordinarily remedial under privacy are expressed in terms of mental distress, embarrassment, annoyance: in general, personal suffering or loss of dignity in having one's private area invaded or disclosed to others.[75] However, while Saskatchewan, Manitoba, and Newfoundland have a single statutory tort,[76] British Columbia provides separately for a tort of appropriation of one's name or

---

65   See, for example, *United Foods and Commercial Workers International Union Local 1000A v. Janes Family Foods* (2006), 156 L.A.C. (4th) 304 (Ont. Lab. Arb.); and *Teamsters, Local 419 v. Securicor Cash Services*, [2004] O.L.A.A. No. 99 (Lab. Arb.).

66   See 2008 British Columbia Law Institute, above note 64 at 30–31, especially n. 94 listing the UK authorities. See also Tanya Aplin, "The Future of Breach of Confidence and the Protection of Privacy" (2007) 7 O.U.C.L.J. 137 at 165.

67   This sub-cause is very close to defamation but provides protection beyond simply "reputation."

68   See William L. Prosser, "Privacy" (1960) 48 Cal. L. Rev. 383 at 389–91. See also *Restatement (Second) of Torts* (St. Paul, MN: American Law Institute, 1977–) §§ 652A–652E.

69   *Privacy Act*, R.S.B.C. 1996, c. 373, s. 1 [BC].

70   *Privacy Act*, R.S.S. 1978, c. P-24, s. 2 [SK].

71   *Privacy Act*, C.C.S.M. c. P125, s. 2(1) [MB].

72   *Privacy Act*, R.S.N.L. 1990, c. P-22, s. 3(1) [NL].

73   See, for example, BC, above note 69.

74   *Ibid.*, s. 1(2).

75   See John G. Fleming, *The Law of Torts*, 9th ed. (Sydney: LBC Information Services, 1998) at 664ff.; and Linda D. Rainaldi, ed., *Remedies in Tort*, vol. 3 (Toronto: Carswell, 1987) c. 24, ss. 2 and 12.

76   SK, above note 70, s. 6(2)(b); MB, above note 71, s. 4(2)(b); NL, above note 72, s. 3(1).

likeness, essentially in a commercial context, presenting a proprietary dimension.[77] Of course, the use of the name or likeness of another can be equally encompassed within the single statutory privacy tort of the other three provinces, as well as a privacy conception at common law.[78] Nevertheless, a reformulation as a property interest in Ontario,[79] by analogy with the US proprietary principle "right of publicity," [80] is facilitating for relief of purely economic or proprietary loss. It reflects the relationship of this dimension to the unfair competition or business perspectives of passing off.[81] It also provides an ability to deal with interest in a proprietary manner, including the inheritability of the interest,[82] or in balancing the scope of exclusivity with the public interest.[83]

To date, there has been little express use of Prosser's US categorization. In British Columbia, a comparison was drawn at trial but deemphasized on appeal,[84] and has been rejected elsewhere in Canada.[85] Prosser's categorization has, however, been drawn upon in New Zealand.[86] Nevertheless, the perspectives recognized in the United States must necessarily be similar, at least contextually, in Canada. Recent instances might be characterized as presenting contexts involving

---

77   BC, above note 69, s. 3.

78   See *Dowell v. Mengen Institute* (1983), 72 C.P.R. (2d) 238 (Ont. H.C.); and *Joseph v. Daniels* (1986), 4 B.C.L.R. (2d) 239 (S.C.) discussed by Robert Howell, "Publicity Rights in the Common Law Provinces of Canada" (1998) 18 Loy. L.A. Ent. L.R. 487 at 495–97.

79   See *Krouse v. Chrysler Canada Ltd.* (1973), 13 C.P.R. (2d) 28 (Ont. C.A.) [*Krouse*] discussed by Howell, *ibid.* at 491–93.

80   See *Zacchini v. Scripps-Howard Broadcasting Co.*, 433 U.S. 562 (1977) (Ohio common law), finding the "Right of Publicity" proceeding to constitute a discrete category of the general proceeding for "misappropriation of business values" (*ibid.* at 572–73 and 576) for which relief may be "unjust enrichment" (*ibid.* at 576). See Howell, above note 78 at 493–94.

81   *Krouse*, above note 79 at 26 found passing off to be inapplicable given that the plaintiff football player was not engaged in the same business as the defendant car manufacturer (i.e., no confusion as to origin or business between the parties). The possibility of *Krouse* being interpreted as a hybrid of passing off and misappropriation is discussed by Howell, above note 78 at 493.

82   See Howell, *ibid.* at 504–8.

83   See *ibid.* at 502–4.

84   *Davis v. McArthur* (1969), 10 D.L.R. (3d) 250 (B.C.S.C.), rev'd (1970), 17 D.L.R. (3d) 760 (B.C.C.A.) [*Davis*].

85   See *Parasiuk*, above note 62 at 727; and *Turton*, above note 62 at 195.

86   See *Hosking v. Runting*, [2005] 1 N.Z.L.R. 1 (C.A.), discussed in 2008 British Columbia Law Institute, above note 64 at 31.

intrusion,[87] disclosure of true facts,[88] disclosure in a false light,[89] and use of name or image.[90]

Proceedings in tort, whether statutory or common law, for intentional interference have yet to be utilized with respect to telecommunication systems or data, although telephone tapping, recording, and distribution of content[91] and unauthorized access to a computer[92] have been considered. In Chapter 3, attention was given to civil relief through trespass-related torts of Internet-related telecommunication systems. Interferences of an intentional and unsolicited nature can include pop-ups, viruses, worms, spyware, denial of service, spam, cookies, and web crawlers. Consideration might also be given to characterizing some of these non-physical interferences with an individual's autonomy as a breach of privacy.[93] Privacy infringement is *prima facie* more probable in instances of intrusion upon, interference with, or disclosure of information, especially if it is utilized in some way by the taker, as would be the position with spyware;[94] or if the communication involves some harassing feature as may be presented by spam and pop-ups.[95]

Each situation must be analyzed individually. For instance, the damage from spam is the cumulative impact from many sources, ren-

---

87   See, for example, *Watts v. Klaemt* (2007), 71 B.C.L.R. (4th) 362 (S.C.) [*Watts*]; *Lord v. McGregor* (2000), 50 C.C.L.T. (2d) 206 (B.C.S.C.) [*Lord*]; and *Milner v. Manufacturers Life Insurance Co.*, 2005 BCSC 1661 [*Milner*].

88   *Lord, ibid.*; *B.M.P. Global Distribution Inc. v. Bank of Nova Scotia* (2005), 8 B.L.R. (4th) 247 (B.C.S.C.), var'd (2007), 63 B.C.L.R. (4th) 214 (C.A.); *Peters-Brown v. Regina District Health Board*, [1995] S.J. No. 609, [1996] 1 W.W.R. 377 (Q.B.), aff'd [1997] 1 W.W.R. 638 (Sask. C.A.).

89   *St. Pierre v. Pacific Newspaper Group Inc.*, 2006 BCSC 241.

90   *New Flyer Industries Ltd. and Canadian Auto Workers, Local 3003* (2000), 85 L.A.C. (4th) 304 (Man. Arb. Bd); *Poirier v. Wal-Mart Canada Corp.*, 2006 BCSC 1138.

91   See *Watts*, above note 87 and accompanying text (interception recording and distribution of cellphone communication).

92   *Tilbury v. Tilbury*, 2006 MBQB 134. See also *Cole v. Prairie Centre Credit Union Ltd.*, 2007 SKQB 330 at paras. 40–46 concerning the discarding of computers containing personal information, but not done "willfully."

93   In effect this approach would present privacy as an umbrella for a variety of interferences and as such is the theory articulated by Warren & Brandeis, above note 61 at 194.

94   Chapter 3, text accompanying note 213. Ordinarily this would occur upon opening an attachment to an e-mail message, but the potential for infection is much broader. See Jay Munro, "Picture Peril" *PC Magazine* (30 November 2004) 76, noting the technological ability to invade computers by code in a JPEG image from websites.

95   Chapter 3, text accompanying notes 235–54 (spam) and 266–75 (pop-ups).

dering problematic an individual causative link. Additionally, the implied invitation to receive mail, just as with a letter box, would further ameliorate any claim of privacy violation. There may also be difficulty in establishing the usual element of privacy damage: personal distress as opposed to business injury. Similarly, cookies have been seen as simply part of the operational value of the medium, and may, with an appropriate setting, be excluded by a system user.[96] Pop-ups, if part of a website that is accessed, are simply a price of using that website as created by its owner, but pop-up programs structured to be stealthily or surreptitiously downloaded, along with spyware similarly implanted, may more readily meet a theory of privacy infringement. A determination of a right of privacy involves an assessment of the reasonable expectation of the plaintiff to privacy in the circumstances of the allegedly infringing event.[97] Regular operational processes of the particular medium, even if intrusive, are likely to negate any reasonable expectation of privacy in the use of the medium. However, drawing a comparison, an expectation that one's home may be broken into ought not ordinarily deny an expectation of privacy in one's home, subject to taking reasonable precautions against these potential intrusions. An omission to take such precautions (say, by failing to install security or defensive software) may be seen as diminishing the expectation of privacy, although the carelessness of a victim of violation has been challenged as relevant to an expectation of privacy.[98]

The practice of "phishing"[99] may present issues of this nature. Phishing involves sending an e-mail intentionally and deceptively disguised as originating from an official, legitimate, or trusted source, with the objective of persuading the user to disclose personal private information, such as passwords, user access names, or account numbers. Certainly the practice is fraudulent, but if it does not involve depositing malicious code or spyware, it is difficult to characterize it as trespass. It may, however, be characterized as an invasion of the privacy of the user by the intentional and intrusive deceptiveness to gain access to recognized categories of personal and private information, subject to an expectation of care and discernment on the part of users.

---

96 *Ibid.*, text accompanying notes 255–58 (cookies).
97 The position is summarized and applied in *Milner*, above note 87 at paras. 74–87.
98 *Ibid.* at para. 90.
99 The expression and practice is described as the phonetic equivalent to "fishing" and is explained in detail in Paul McFredries, "Word Spy: The Word Lover's Guide to New Words," online: www.wordspy.com/words/phishing.asp.

Surveillance or tracking has been recognized as infringing,[100] but justifications have generally been found.[101] A fledgling common law recognition of tracking and harassing exists with respect to secretly planted electronic devices.[102] Spyware structured to be stealthily or surreptitiously downloaded is the essential equivalent in a digitized context.[103] The key privacy focus ought to be on how the code or program came to be installed. Downloading surreptitiously or by stealth denies choice of acceptance or rejection and is the intrusive event, even if the program is seen to benefit the user, as may be the position with respect to a pop-up program. The requirement of "wilful" violation,[104] interpreted as the subjective or objective knowledge of the violation of the privacy of the plaintiff,[105] should be readily met in this context.

Quebec has been noted as the only province that provided, prior to federal *PIPEDA* in 1999, legislative protection directed specifically to the protection of personal information supplied to, or collected by, the private sector.[106] In addition, Quebec included broad and general privacy protections in the Quebec *Charter of Human Rights and Freedoms*, in which section 4 safeguards individual dignity, honour, and reputation, and section 5 provides that every person "has a right to respect for his private life."[107] Although only a legislative measure, the *Quebec Charter* was from 1987 given supremacy in application and interpretation over all other provincial legislation, requiring any measure purporting to derogate from this to expressly stipulate that it applies

---

100 BC, above note 69, s. 1(4); *Heckert v. 5470 Investments Ltd.*, 2008 BCSC 1298 at para. 86; and *Milner*, above note 87 at para. 82.

101 See, for example, *Milner, ibid.* at para. 84 re insurance claim by, and credibility of, the plaintiff; *Davis*, above note 84, justification in the conducting of a private investigation process; and *Cam v. Hood*, 2006 BCSC 842, film of plaintiff playing volleyball to disprove the plaintiff's claim of disability.

102 See *Saccone v. Orr* (1981), 34 O.R. (2d) 317 (Co. Ct.) and *Roth and Roth*, above note 62.

103 In British Columbia, spyware surreptitiously downloaded might also be interpreted as an electronic version of "eavesdropping," BC, above note 69, s. 1(4).

104 *Ibid.*, s. 1(1). See also SK, above note 70, s. 2; and NL, above note 72, s. 3. In Manitoba, the phrase "substantially, unreasonably" is used, MB, above note 71, s. 2(1).

105 *Hollinsworth v. BCTV* (1998), 59 B.C.L.R. (3d) 121 at 127 (C.A.); *Milner*, above note 87 at para. 80.

106 See *An Act respecting the protection of personal information in the private sector*, above note 37.

107 *Charter of Human Rights and Freedoms*, R.S.Q. 1977, c. C-12, as am. by *An Act to Amend the Charter of Human Rights and Freedoms*, S.Q. 1982, c. 61, which replaced the original 1975 statute (S.Q. 1975, c. 6) [*Quebec Charter*].

despite the *Quebec Charter*.[108] In addition, the *Civil Code of Québec*, Article 35, provides: "Every person has a right to the respect of his reputation and privacy. No one may invade the privacy of a person without consent of the person or his heirs unless authorized by law."[109] Article 36 expressly includes as privacy violations the interception of private communications,[110] keeping a person's "private life under observation by any means,"[111] and using a person's "correspondence, manuscripts, or other personal documents."[112] These contexts have been broadly interpreted[113] and can be readily applied to Internet-related technology. They may also provide a useful comparative source for courts in the common law provinces interpreting the scope and content of "privacy" within the provincial enactments and any development at common law.

1) Privacy of Personal Information in the Public Sector

PIPEDA[114] brought to the private sector a broad equivalency of privacy protection for personal information that had been afforded in the 1980s and '90s to public sector informational collections in federal[115] and provincial sources.[116] These public sector legislative schemes provide a correlation between preservation of privacy and the provision of access to the information collected and held by the relevant public sources. Enactment was prior to the imprint of Internet-related technology and electronic storage that was the impetus for *PIPEDA* in 1999. Public contexts concern simply government collection and retention of information, inclusive of an electronic medium. The structure and scheme of these provisions present a broad public sector equivalence to *PIPEDA*.

The federal *Privacy Act* will serve to illustrate the essential features. Protection is given to "personal information," defined in section 3 as information concerning an "identifiable individual" and that is "recorded in any form."[117] A non-exclusive list follows of the categories of such information, including: race, national or ethnic origin, colour,

---

108 *Ibid.*, s. 52, enacted in 1975. See, generally, Potvin, Howell, & McMahon, above note 33 at 84–85 regarding privacy and the *Quebec Charter*.
109 *Civil Code of Québec*, above note 5, Art. 35 C.C.Q.
110 *Ibid.*, Art. 36(2) C.C.Q.
111 *Ibid.*, Art. 36(4) C.C.Q.
112 *Ibid.*, Art. 36(6) C.C.Q.
113 See Potvin, Howell, & McMahon, above note 33 at 85–88.
114 *PIPEDA*, above note 7.
115 *Privacy Act*, above note 35.
116 See note 36, above, for examples.
117 *Privacy Act,* above note 35, s. 3.

religion, age, marital status, educational, medical, criminal or employment history, financial dealings, various locators such as address, finger prints or blood type, numbers or identifying symbols relevant to
the individual, opinions or views of the individual and of others about
the individual, explicitly or implicitly confidential correspondence sent
by the individual to a government institution covered by the legislation. The scheme of the Act requires that the covered personal information be collected directly from the individual concerned[118] and only
for the purpose of an operating program of the collecting government
institution.[119] The institution must inform the individual as to the purpose of the collection.[120] After use, the information must be retained
by the institution for a period to allow access to it by the individual.[121]
The institution must reasonably ensure that the information is kept as
current and as accurate as possible[122] and, ultimately, disposed of under
a controlled system.[123] While such information is under the control of
a government institution it can be used only for the purpose for which
it was obtained, unless otherwise consented to by the individual or
otherwise allowed under the Act.[124] Unless consented to by the individual, it can be disclosed only as provided in the Act.[125] An individual's
right of access to the information and the process for giving access are
prescribed.[126] It will be seen that those enactments do provide a broad
equivalence to the privacy aspects of *PIPEDA*.

2) The *Personal Information Protection and Electronic Documents Act*

Part I of this federal enactment, in effect from 1 January 2001,[127] concerns the protection of personal information in the private sector. The
basic obligations are set out in Schedule 1, being the Canadian Standards Association's 1966 national "Model Code for the Protection of

---

118 *Ibid.*, s. 5(1). A non-direct collection may be authorized by the individual or may
be permitted by other provisions in the Act.
119 *Ibid.*, s. 4.
120 *Ibid.*, s. 5(2).
121 *Ibid.*, s. 6(1).
122 *Ibid.*, s. 6(2).
123 *Ibid.*, s. 6(3).
124 *Ibid.*, s. 7.
125 *Ibid.*, s. 8.
126 *Ibid.*, ss. 12–18.
127 *PIPEDA*, above note 7, Part I, *Order Fixing the Dates of the Coming into Force of
Certain Parts of the Act*, S.I./2000-29 (26 April 2000), P.C. 2000-584 (14 April
2000), C. Gaz. 2000.II.914.

Personal Information."[128] This Code, now with legislative effect, comprises ten "Principles" imposed on an organization with respect to the collection and control of personal information.

The nature and scope of privacy protection is identified; rights of access to and correction of personal information are granted to individuals to whom the information relates; and an administrative enforcement structure under the Privacy Commissioner is established.[129] Supervisory jurisdiction under both public and private measures should enable the Commissioner to coordinate policies, procedures, and responses between the sectors. Consistently, the Federal Court of Appeal has recognized the structure of the Act and the essentially non-legal drafting of Schedule 1, requiring a flexible and pragmatic approach in interpretation to achieve a dual legislative objective of privacy protection and facilitation of collection, use, and disclosure.[130]

a) Scope of Protection

The application of *PIPEDA*, beyond federal works, undertakings, or businesses and the constitutional issues that this presents have been discussed earlier.[131] Beyond this, the scope of the legislation must be considered. Section 3 and applicable definitions in section 2(1) of the Act describe the purpose of the legislation as being

> to establish, in an era in which technology increasingly facilitates the circulation and exchange of information, rules to govern the collection, use and disclosure of personal information in a manner that recognizes the right of privacy of individuals with respect to their personal information and the need of organizations to collect, use or disclose personal information for purposes that a reasonable person would consider appropriate in the circumstances.[132]

A distinction is made between "personal health information" and the more general category of "personal information." Only the latter is considered here. The essential focus is the collection, use, and disclosure of personal information in the carrying on of a commercial activity. A balance is sought between the legitimate privacy interests of individuals

---

128 *Ibid.*, Sch. 1, clause 5.

129 *Ibid.*, s. 2 defines the reference to "Commissioner" as the Privacy Commissioner appointed under the *Privacy Act*, above note 35, for the public sector.

130 *Englander v. Telus Communications Inc.*, 2004 FCA 387, 247 D.L.R. (4th) 275 [*Englander*].

131 See text accompanying notes 39–42, above in this chapter, and Chapter 1, text accompanying notes 224–65.

132 *PIPEDA*, above note 7, s. 3.

and the need of organizations to collect, use, and disclose personal information as part of legitimate commercial activity.[133] An organization includes "an association, a partnership, a person and a trade union."[134] The expression "person" is, by the *Interpretation Act*, to include a corporation.[135] A commercial activity is broadly defined to encompass single transactions and courses of dealing of a commercial character, including "the selling, bartering or leasing of donor, membership or other fundraising lists."[136] The information must be "personal information," defined as information about an "identifiable"[137] individual but not the individual's name, title, or business address[138] or telephone number as an employee of an organization.[139] In addition, an organization that collects, uses, or discloses personal information about an employee is included within the Act even if not engaged in a "commercial activity," but this provision is specifically limited to organizations connected with a federal work, undertaking, or business,[140] even though Part I of the Act is now applicable beyond federally regulated organizations.[141]

---

133 *Ibid.*, s. 4(1)(a). An unsuccessful attempt to surreptitiously record (by a device placed under a table) a conversation is not a "collection" of information. See *Morgan v. Alta Flights (Charters) Inc.*, 2005 FC 421, aff'd 2006 FCA 121.

134 *PIPEDA*, above note 7, s. 2(1). A non-commercial, recreational fish and game club operating only on membership fees is not included in "commercial activity." See *Rodgers v. Calvert* (2004), 244 D.L.R. (4th) 479 (Ont. S.C.J.).

135 *Interpretation Act*, R.S.C. 1985, c. I-21, s. 35(1).

136 *PIPEDA*, above note 7, s. 2(1) definition of "commercial activity." See *PIPEDA Case Summary* #2006-345, [2006] C.P.C.S.F. No. 22 (Canada Privacy Commissioner), excluding from this category a private school providing educational services. See also *PIPEDA Case Summary* #2005-305, [2005] C.P.C.S.F. No. 19 at para. 6 (Canada Privacy Commissioner), which found a private website for selling dogs to be a commercial activity.

137 The expression "identifiable," rather than "identified" is used, meaning that it is sufficient if an individual is rendered capable of being identified. See *PIPEDA Case Summary* #2006-343, [2006] C.P.C.S.F. No. 20 at para. 11 (Canada Privacy Commissioner).

138 This expression has been found to not include a business e-mail address, so such is *prima facie* personal information. See *PIPEDA Case Summary* #2005-297, [2005] C.P.C.S.F. No. 44 (Canada Privacy Commissioner).

139 *PIPEDA*, above note 7, s. 2(1) definition of "personal information."

140 *Ibid.*, s. 4(1)(b). An employee's home phone number is not within the s. 2(1) exclusion from coverage and, *prima facie*, would be personal information. It was nevertheless found not to be sufficiently "sensitive" personal information and therefore could be disclosed. See *Via Rail Canada Inc. v. CAW-Canada, National Council 4000* (2003), 116 L.A.C. (4th) 407 (Can. Arb. Bd.) [*Via Rail*]. As for the need for sensitivity with respect to the information, see text accompanying notes 171–72, below in this chapter.

141 See text accompanying notes 40–47, above in this chapter.

Interpretations have included as "personal information" video surveil-lance in the workplace,[142] a spouse's employment history and citizen-ship status,[143] and a user's Internet Protocol (IP) address, including the IP dynamic address that changes on each "log on."[144] A personal name and unpublished telephone number, if displayed on a call recipient's cellphone screen, is likely to be included if the subscriber is within a call-blocking service that permanently blocks the subscriber's name and telephone number.[145]

The privacy features of *PIPEDA* have primacy over subsequently en-acted legislation, unless such other legislation is expressly declared to the contrary.[146] There are three broad exclusions from *PIPEDA*: govern-ment (public sector) institutions to which the federal *Privacy Act*[147] ap-plies; the collection, use, and disclosure of personal information by an *individual* solely for that collector's "personal or domestic purposes";[148] and the collection, use, and disclosure of personal information by an *organization* solely for "journalistic, artistic or literary purposes."[149] The latter two exclusions present considerable uncertainty.

Sections 3 and 5(3)[150] stipulate the need for collection, use, or dis-closure of personal information to be what a reasonable person would consider to be "appropriate in the circumstances," being those existing at the time of the collection, rather than hypothetical risks or those flowing from future technological changes.[151] The Federal Court of Ap-peal has approved the Privacy Commissioner's four-part test requiring: (1) the measure to be demonstrably necessary to meet the specific need; (2) the measure to be effective in meeting this need; (3) the benefit

---

142 *Telus Corp. v. Telecommunications Workers Union (Fenske Grievance)* (2005), 46 B.C.L.R. (4th) 315 (S.C.).

143 *Ontario Power Generation Inc. v. Society of Energy Professionals*, [2004] O.L.A.A No. 28, 128 L.A.C. (4th) 265 (Ont. Arb. Bd.) [*Ontario Power Generation*].

144 See *PIPEDA* Case Summary #2005-319, [2005] C.P.C.S.F. No. 33 (Canada Privacy Commissioner); and *PIPEDA* Case Summary #2001-25 (2001), online: www.priv.gc.ca/cf-dc/2001/cf-dc_011120_e.cfm.

145 *PIPEDA* Case Summary #2002-75 (2002), online: www.priv.gc.ca/cf-dc/2002/cf-dc_021010_1_e.cfm.

146 *PIPEDA*, above note 7, s. 4(3), giving primacy to Part I of the Act.

147 See text accompanying notes 35 and 115, above in this chapter.

148 *PIPEDA*, above note 7, s. 4(2)(b). The expression "personal or domestic pur-poses" is not defined in the Act. Surveillance of a plaintiff in a malpractice suit qualified as "personal or domestic" in *Ferenczy v. MCI Medical Clinics* (2004), 70 O.R. (3d) 277 at 283 (S.C.J.).

149 *PIPEDA*, ibid., s. 4(2)(c). This expression is not defined in the Act.

150 *Ibid.*, ss. 3 and 5(3).

151 See *Wansink v. Telus Communications Inc.*, 2007 FCA 21 [*Wansink*] (employees to provide voice samples for voice recognition technology).

gained and privacy lost to be proportional; and (4) any less invasive means to be considered.[152] These tests are crucial, as Schedule 1 itself contains no limit or definition of purposes for which information may be collected. It deals simply with how the organization is to proceed with any purpose. In a telecommunications context, requiring photographic identification and a valid credit card from a customer seeking to purchase satellite telecommunications equipment is reasonable in order to alleviate the unauthorized taking of a telecommunications satellite signal.[153] Similarly, the need to provide photographic identification (driver's licence or passport) is reasonable when asking a domain name registrar to amend or change the administration e-mail address for a website domain name in order to prevent taking of the domain name for the site without consent.[154]

b)   The Principles of Privacy in Schedule 1

i)   Principle 1: Accountability

Responsibility is imposed on an organization for personal information under its control.[155] A person or persons within the organization must be designated to be accountable for its compliance with the ten principles of the legislation, even though the collection and processing is done by others within the organization.[156] The organization must, upon request, make known the identity of this designated and accountable individual. The responsibility of an organization extends to personal information transferred to a third party for processing. The organization is obliged to utilize "contractual or other means" to ensure that any third party provides "a comparable level of protection" during processing.[157] A general obligation is imposed to implement procedures and policies to ensure compliance with the ten principles.

---

152 *Eastmond v. Canadian Pacific Railway*, 2004 FC 852.

153 *PIPEDA* Case Summary #2004-280, [2004] C.P.C.S.F. No. 25 (Canada Privacy Commissioner), although the provider was asked by the Commission to consider alternative measures.

154 *PIPEDA* Case Summary #2006-363, [2006] C.P.C.S.F. No. 40 (Canada Privacy Commissioner).

155 *PIPEDA*, above note 7, Sch. 1, clause 4.

156 Organizations should instruct all employees of the need for compliance with *PIPEDA* through the person designated to be accountable. See *PIPEDA* Case Summary #2007-367, [2007] C.P.C.S.F. No. 3 (Canada Privacy Commissioner).

157 This requirement is reinforced in a number of determinations. See, for example, *PIPEDA* Case Summaries #377, [2007] C.P.C.S.F. No. 13 at para. 14 (Canada Privacy Commissioner); and *PIPEDA* Case Summaries #386, [2007] C.P.C.S.F. No. 22 (Canada Privacy Commissioner).

ii) Principle 2: Identifying Purposes

At or before the time of collection of personal information,[158] the organization must identify the purposes[159] for which the information is being collected.[160] This Principle provides the foundation for a number of later, more specific, principles that themselves are predicated on the purposes for which the information has been collected.[161] Information may be collected only for the purposes that the organization has identified and notified. The means of giving notice will depend on the manner of collecting the information. It may be oral or in writing, including on an application form, and the standards recommend that the person collecting the information be able to explain the purposes for which the information is collected. Any use of information beyond the purposes identified at the time of collection requires a further identification and notification of the new purpose and, unless otherwise permitted by law, obtaining consent from the individual to whom the personal information relates.

All of these factors reflect a primary policy objective underlying this Principle, that a formal notification of purposes will enable an organization to identify more accurately just what information is *needed* and to collect only such information,[162] as opposed to making a general or unrestricted collection from which a selection of desired information is subsequently made.

iii) Principle 3: Consent

This Principle[163] is correlative to Principle 2. An individual must *know* what he or she is consenting to before any purported consent can be a "meaningful consent," as is required. The Principle is described as requiring the purposes being presented in a way that enables an in-

---

158 The stipulation "at or before" is set out expressly in the opening paragraph but is later given as a "recommendation," in *PIPEDA*, above note 7, Sch. 1, clause 4.2.3. See *PIPEDA*, *ibid.*, s. 5(2) concerning the interpretation to be given to the expression "should" in Sch. 1. See text accompanying note 168, below in this chapter.

159 *PIPEDA*, above note 7, Sch. 1, clause 4.2.

160 See *PIPEDA* Case Summary #2005-300, [2005] C.P.C.S.F. No. 14 (Canada Privacy Commissioner).

161 These are: Principle 3 – Consent; Principle 4 – Limiting Collection; Principle 5 – Limiting Use, Disclosure, and Retention; Principle 8 – Openness; and Principle 9 – Individual Access.

162 In effect, this reflects Principle 4, limiting collection "to that which is necessary for the purposes identified by the organisation" (*PIPEDA*, above note 7, Sch. 1, clause 4.4).

163 *Ibid.*, clause 4.3.

dividual to "reasonably understand how the information will be used or disclosed."[164] In this context, the Commission has determined that there must be precision as to the type and sources of personal information, rather than an open-ended request.[165] This may require a compiler to advise an individual of an alternative option to disclosure that might be available.[166] Additionally, all secondary or consequential purposes must be advised.[167] However, there is in Principle 3 some literal inconsistency or, perhaps, amelioration of Principle 2, requiring identification of the purposes for which the information is required, by the stipulation in Principle 3 that organizations "shall make a reasonable effort" to advise the purposes. This qualifier is not present in Principle 2.[168]

---

164 *Ibid.*, clause 4.3.2. See, for example, *PIPEDA* Case Summary #2007-384, [2007] C.P.C.S.F. No. 20 (Canada Privacy Commissioner) requiring notification for the recording "for quality assurance" of both incoming and outgoing calls from and to customers; and *PIPEDA* Case Summary #2003-180, [2003] C.P.C.S.F. No. 147 at para. 7 (Canada Privacy Commissioner), where notification by a bank call centre that a customer's call "might be recorded for quality monitoring purposes" did not sufficiently convey to the caller, nor obtain his consent to, the recording (containing personal information) being accessible audibly to all employees for call training purposes. See also, *PIPEDA* Case Summary #2002-61 (2002), online: www.priv.gc.ca/cf-dc/2002/cf-dc_020719_2_e.cfm, concluding that a reasonable person would not consider pursuit of a third-party debtor to be a reasonable or contemplated use of his or her long-distance telephone records held by a telephone service provider; and Facebook Report, above note 16, s. 1 concerning the provision of greater explanation by Facebook of *why* a user's date of birth must be given and *how* it is to be used.

165 See *PIPEDA* Case Summary #2003-203 (2003), online: www.priv.gc.ca/cf-dc/2003/cf-dc_030805_01_e.cfm.

166 See *Englander*, above note 130 at 316 (D.L.R.), finding no effective consent when Telus made no effort to advise of an option not to have a listing in the White Pages. See also *PIPEDA* Case Summary #2002-104 (2002), online:www.priv.gc.ca/cf-dc/2002/cf-dc_021219_9_e.cfm

167 *Englander, ibid.* at 313–14, requiring notice of listing or use functions consequential upon a White Page listing, for example, usage in a reverse look-up function. In Facebook Report, above note 16, s. 3, Facebook, Inc. agreed to describe more clearly the nature of the advertising to which users would be subject.

168 Similarly, the need for the consent to be given at the time of the collection is expressed in non-mandatory terms. Compare note 158 and accompanying text, above in this chapter, concerning the purposes for which the information is required being given "at or before" the time of collection of the information.

Indeed, considerable flexibility is presented concerning the giving of consent. First, consent may be express[169] or implied.[170] Second, the way of obtaining consent must reflect "the *circumstances* and the *type* of information collected," with particular attention to whether the information is "sensitive" information. A characterization of "sensitivity" may be met by the information being of an inherently sensitive nature.[171] Otherwise, the characterization will depend on the particular context or the nature of the particular information.[172] Third, the "reasonable expectations" of the individuals supplying the information are to be considered in determining whether consent has been given. A requirement of consent must not be imposed as a condition of providing a product or service, beyond that required to fulfil legitimate purposes.[173]

These criteria allow considerable flexibility but also substantial scope for uncertainty in a situation in which consent is not express. In effect, a determination whether a consent, as a subjective act, has been given is decided upon objective criteria of a reasonable person's expectations in the circumstances. This reflects an application of societal standards or norms from which the subjective consent is implied.[174] The examples given in the Schedule are appropriate,[175] but outside of

---

169 Express consent may be given in broadly purposed documents such as a "Consent/Screening Form" that refers to objectives or agencies from whom it is implicit checks will be made: *Ontario Power Generation*, above note 143 at para. 10, or from a reference to an "independent source" (*Thomas v. Robinson* (2001), 21 B.L.R. (3d) 96 (Ont. S.C.J.)).

170 Consent is implied in the filing of court proceedings under PIPEDA: *Englander*, above note 130 at 310 (D.L.R.), or in other proceedings: *Ferenczy v. MCI Medical Clinics*, above note 148 at 285 (plaintiff who sued doctor for medical malpractice had to expect surveillance). Compare the position under provincial privacy tort legislation: see above note 36.

171 Examples given are medical records and income records. See *PIPEDA*, above note 7, Sch. 1, clause 4.3.4. See also above note 140, concerning a lack of sensitivity in an employee's home phone number in the circumstances there prevailing.

172 See *ibid.*, clause 4.3.4, drawing a distinction between information (names and addresses) about subscribers to a general news magazine and information about subscribers to a "special interest magazine."

173 *PIPEDA* Case Summary #2005-316, [2005] C.P.C.S.F. No. 30 (Canada Privacy Commissioner).

174 Compare the regular inquiry in tort or delict as to when a consent can be implied. See Gerald H.L. Fridman, *The Law of Torts in Canada* (Toronto: Thomson Canada, 2002) at 50–51.

175 See above note 171. With respect to a personal address, a distinction is drawn between a permissible use of a name and address for mailing of routine correspondence (such as billing or subscription renewal) and an impermissible

these relatively certain situations there is considerable room for divergence.[176]

The Schedule explicitly excludes a consent obtained by deception[177] and the making of the supply of a product or service conditional on the supply, use, or disclosure of information beyond that legitimately relevant to such supply.[178] Conversely, the need to obtain consent does not apply if considered to be "inappropriate." Examples given in the Schedule include situations in which "legal, medical or security reasons" make the obtaining of consent "impossible or impractical"; and for the purposes of law enforcement or the detection and prevention of fraud.[179] Additionally, when an organization without "a direct relationship" with an individual seeks a mailing list from another organization, the latter is assumed to have obtained the consent of the listed individuals before supplying the list.[180] This suggests that the scope of this practice is narrow and that ordinarily information disclosed to one organization must be limited to the purposes of that organization.

The Schedule also addresses the manner in which an express consent may be given, but notes only examples, including: through completing and signing an application form; using a negative "check off box" system (check to *preclude* the transfer of information to third parties); oral consent if the information is collected by telephone; and consent at the time of using a product or service.[181] Surprisingly, no example is included of a consent given on the Internet. However, some comparison may be drawn with the formulation of contracts in this medium.

---

disclosure to sellers of health care products of information provided by patients to health care professionals (see *PIPEDA*, above note 7, Sch. 1, clause 4.3.5).

176 For example, should subscription details to every "special interest" magazine be considered "sensitive" information (see above note 171). Sensitivity may exist for magazines containing content that might be embarrassing to any subscriber (such as a sexually explicit magazine) or revealing of the subscriber's political or religious persuasion or of some personal situation (such as a medical condition).

177 *PIPEDA*, above note 7, Sch. 1, clause 4.3.5.

178 *Ibid.*, clause 4.3.3. This provision is to be interpreted in a reasonable and contextual manner.

179 *Ibid.*, clause 4.3. Reference is included to the difficulty of obtaining consent from an infant or minor who is "seriously ill, or mentally incapacitated." However, see clause 4.3.6, allowing consent to be given by an authorized representative, which should surely be obtained in such circumstances.

180 *Ibid.* No guidance is given as to the circumstances that will cause an individual included on a mailing list to be in "a direct relationship" with a third-party organization seeking that list, to enable it to be supplied without the consent of the individual.

181 *Ibid.*, clause 4.3.7.

A user's click in an "I Accept" box may be all that is necessary to give a consent to purposes that are reasonable, indicated in the frame being viewed or perhaps in earlier frames. Consideration is likely to be given to the "custom" of Internet usage or "netiquette."[182] Some consideration may also be given to the level of Internet knowledge and experience of the particular user and the extent to which the notification of purposes, or what it is that the user is consenting to, has been brought to his or her attention.[183]

Although preferring a mechanism of "opting in" rather than "opting out" of consent to secondary marketing, the Privacy Commissioner stipulated the following conditions that must be met in instances of an "opt-out" form of consent: (1) the personal information must be "demonstrably non-sensitive in nature and context"; (2) information sharing must be "limited and well defined" in terms of the nature of the personal information and the intended use or disclosure; (3) the collecting organization's purposes must also be "limited and well defined" and clearly communicated to the supplier at the time of collection; and (4) there must be a convenient procedure for easily and inexpensively withdrawing consent and this procedure must be advised to the supplier at the time of collection.[184]

In the Facebook proceedings, the Privacy Commissioner accepted "opt out" default settings if this met users' reasonable expectations. In two respects, this was not met: first, the default setting that photo albums would be sent to "everyone"; and second, the consent to personal information being open to search engines. In response, Facebook, Inc. agreed to make available a spectrum of high, medium, and low privacy settings and to allow users to choose such settings on individual photographs and certain other features of content.[185]

Under the Schedule, consent may be withdrawn upon reasonable notice, but this is naturally subject to any contractual or other legal obligations that have been assumed. The organization is required to provide information about the consequences of any withdrawal of consent.

---

182 See *1267623 Ontario Inc. v. Nexx Online Inc.* (1999), 45 O.R. (3d) 40 (S.C.J.) where an application of Internet usage, custom, or "netiquette" was judicially recognized.

183 *PIPEDA*, above note 7, Sch. 1, clause 4.4.

184 See, *PIPEDA* Case Summary #2003-203, above note 165; and *PIPEDA* Case Summary #2003-207 (2003), online: www.priv.gc.ca/cf-dc/2003/cf-dc_030806_02_e.cfm.

185 Facebook Report, above note 16, s. 2.

Section 7 of the Act provides significant exceptions to Schedule clause 4.3 consent requirements by allowing collection without knowledge or consent in a number of specified contexts, including journalistic, artistic, or literary purposes,[186] collection for the purpose of a disclosure "required by law,"[187] the material being publicly available, disclosure made to a barrister or solicitor or (in Quebec) advocate or notary,[188] and for collection of a debt owed by the individual to the organization.[189] Rejecting the determination of the Trial Division,[190] the Federal Court of Appeal expressed section 7 to be exhaustive, preventing the court from recognizing other situations of non-consent.[191]

The Commission has determined transborder transfer of personal information by a Canadian entity outsourcing to a foreign-based service provider to be permissible under *PIPEDA*, notwithstanding that the storage of personal information, electronic or otherwise, within a foreign jurisdiction is subject to the law of that jurisdiction and that this may allow lawful access to a Canadian's personal information by foreign authorities. The scope of control by *PIPEDA* is simply to require the Canadian entity to provide transparency with respect to its practices of handling personal information (that is, to notify customers of its practice of transborder outsourcing of personal information) and to protect by contract or other lawful means the confidentiality of personal information under the control of foreign parties.[192]

---

186 *PIPEDA*, above note 7, s. 7(1)(c).

187 *Ibid.*, ss. 7(1)(e)(ii) and 7(3) identifying a number of contexts. See *Via Rail*, above note 140 at para. 17 (Collective Agreement); *Fishing Lake First Nation v. Paley*, 2005 FC 1448 (Adjudicator labour issues); and *R. v. Anderson*, 2005 ABPC 99 (ISP providing to police source identification for Internet Protocol (IP) re child pornography).

188 *PIPEDA*, *ibid.*, s. 7(3)(a).

189 *Ibid.*, s. 7(3)(b).

190 (*Sub nom.*)*Turner v. Telus Communications Inc.* (2005), 284 F.T.R. 38 at paras. 49–51 (Fed. Ct.).

191 *Wansink*, above note 151 at 23.

192 *PIPEDA* Case Summary #2007-365, [2007] C.P.C.S.F. No. 1 (Canada Privacy Commissioner), concerning Canadian financial institutions providing to the Society for Worldwide Interbank Financial Telecommunication (SWIFT) (based in the United States) the personal information of Canadian customers, enabling the US Department of the Treasury to access such information under US law. The focus of the determination by the Commission was *PIPEDA*, above note 7, s. 7(c) and Sch. 1, clause 4.1.3. See also *PIPEDA* Case Summary #2008-394, [2008] C.P.C.S.F. No. 7 (Canada Privacy Commissioner).

Foreign-based entities operating in Canada, including Internet or online operations into Canada, must comply with *PIPEDA*.[193] A Canadian-based entity may share customer personal information with a foreign-based parent company if the disclosure is within the original purpose for which consent was given, or if a further purpose is specified and consent contained. The Canadian-based entity is required under Principle 4.1.3 to use contractual or other means to ensure a comparable level of protection for personal information that has been so disclosed. The Commission has accepted that between a foreign parent and a Canadian subsidiary, other means of protection include the foreign-based parent's adhering to the same levels of data protection as the Canadian entity.[194] There is no general prohibition in *PIPEDA* against sharing personal information with a foreign-based entity, even though that foreign entity will be subject to compliance with foreign territorial laws that may require disclosure to a foreign government or its agencies.[195]

iv) *Principle 4: Limiting Collection*

The collection of personal information must not be indiscriminate.[196] The *quantity* and *nature* of information collected is limited to what is *necessary* to meet the notified purposes.[197] Guidelines and implementation procedures required under this principle should specify minimum and maximum retention periods.[198] The means of collection must be

---

193 *PIPEDA* Case Summary #2008-388, [2008] C.P.C.S.F. No. 1 at para. 29 (Canada Privacy Commissioner). See also Facebook Report, above note 16.

194 *PIPEDA* Case Summary #2006-333, [2006] C.P.C.S.F. No 10 at para. 20 (Canada Privacy Commissioner).

195 *Ibid.* at paras. 22–24.

196 *PIPEDA*, above note 7, Sch. 1, clause 4.4.

197 See *PIPEDA* Case Summary #2005-297, above note 138 at para. 9, collection of a business e-mail address for the purpose of marketing the addressee, against explicit instructions of the addressee, contravenes Principle 4.3. In this instance, a distinction was drawn between the marketing and the selling organizations. The latter received personal information only of customers who had expressed an interest in its products (*ibid.* at para. 21). In *PIPEDA* Case Summary #2005-288, [2005] C.P.C.S.F. No. 2 (Canada Privacy Commissioner), requiring more than two pieces of identification on application for a special cellular telephone service was found to be excessive for the purposes of establishing credit worthiness. However, collection of personal information (credit card or social insurance details) was acceptable for extending credit for cellphone usage. See *PIPEDA* Case Summary #2002-104, above note 166; and *PIPEDA* Case Summary #2003-204 (2003), online: www.priv.gc.ca/cf-dc/2003/cf-dc_030805_02_e.cfm.

198 *PIPEDA* Case Summary #2003-252 at para. 8 (2003), online: http://www.priv.gc.ca/cf-dc/2003/cf-dc_031215_e.cfm.

non-deceptive, in the sense that there must be no misleading over the purposes of the collection. Collected information must be retained at a security level appropriate to the sensitivity of the information.[199]

v)   Principle 5: Limiting Use, Disclosure, and Retention

This Principle[200] reiterates that the use, disclosure, and retention of personal information are limited to the purposes for which the information was collected, except if further consent is given by the individual to whom the information relates. The Principle adds that once the purposes of the collection are fulfilled, the organization must destroy the personal information. Organizations are recommended to implement procedures with guidelines for the management, including the destruction, of all personal information that it has collected. The system of management should facilitate the ability of individuals to ascertain the minimum and maximum retention periods for the information. Any personal information used in relation to a decision concerning an individual must, however, be retained for a sufficient time after the decision to allow the individual to exercise his or her right of access under Principle 9.

vi) Principle 6: Accuracy

Personal information must be "accurate, complete and up-to-date" to the extent necessary, having regard to the use or purpose of the information and the "interests of the individual," but particularly if a decision concerning the individual is being made with reference to the information.[201] Again, the emphasis is on an organization's need. Personal information can be updated only to the extent necessary for the notified purpose. The Schedule recommends that personal information used, or disclosed to third parties, on a continuing basis always be updated. Presumably, there must be either an initial consent to the process of updating or a consent at the time of each update.

vii) Principle 7: Safeguards

An organization must provide appropriate security for personal information in its possession. Although not referred to within this Principle,[202] the obligation of accountability imposed in Principle 1 with respect to

---

199 *PIPEDA*, above note 7, Sch. 1, clauses 4–9. See *PIPEDA* Case Summary #2003-137 (2003), online: www.priv.gc.ca/cf-dc/2003/cf-dc_030306_6_e.cfm.

200 *PIPEDA, ibid.*, clause 4.5.

201 *Ibid.*, clause 4.6.

202 *Ibid.*, clause 4.7.

transferring personal information to third parties[203] is likely to impose some similar security obligation on organizations with respect to the third party's possession, at least if the information is given on a temporary basis, for example for processing purposes.[204] However, transfer to a third party for that party's own and separate use is likely to constitute an entirely new purpose, requiring compliance with Principle 2.[205]

Attention is directed to the level, scope, and methods of achieving security of personal information. The *level* of security relates primarily to the level of sensitivity of holding that personal information[206] but is also relevant with respect to the quantity of the information, the scope of any distribution, the format in which the information is held (but format as a factor cannot be taken to negate the obligation for protection),[207] and the method of storage. The *scope* of security is to encompass "loss or theft, as well as unauthorized access, disclosure, copying, use, or modification,"[208] with special attention to security upon disposal or destruction of the information. Recommended *methods* of protection are said to include physical measures, organizational measures (clearances and "need to know" access), technological measures (passwords and encryption), and security awareness training for employees. The Privacy Commissioner accepted in the Facebook proceedings that Facebook, Inc. could monitor the site "for anomalous behaviour" so long as it reasonably informed users that it was doing so.[209]

viii) Principle 8: Openness

Principles 8 to 10[210] present a change in direction from privacy and security to information and access to the personal information by the individual to whom the personal information relates, and the ability of

---

203 See *ibid.*, clause 4.1.3, referring specifically to the supply of personal information to a third party for "processing."

204 See note 157 and accompanying text, above in this chapter.

205 See text accompanying notes 158ff., above in this chapter.

206 *PIPEDA*, above note 7, Sch. 1, clause 4.7. See notes 171 and 176 and accompanying text, above in this chapter, concerning sensitivity of personal information. See Facebook Report, above note 16, s. 9, where the Privacy Commissioner accepted that Facebook, Inc. was providing an acceptable level of safeguard to users.

207 See *PIPEDA*, *ibid.*, clause 4.7.1, providing that organizations must protect personal information "regardless of the format in which it is held." Compare clause 4.7.2 noting format as a factor relevant to the extent of the security or safeguards to be afforded.

208 *Ibid.*, clause 4.7.1.

209 Facebook Report, above note 16, s. 10.

210 *PIPEDA*, above note 7, Sch. 1, clause 4.8.

that individual to challenge compliance by the organization with the Principles in the Schedule.

The requirement of "openness" concerns an individual's ability "without unreasonable effort" to ascertain, in an "understandable form," details of an organization's policies and practices with respect to its managing of personal information. The advice to this effect by an organization must be "specific." It must identify the employee accountable for these policies and practices[211] and to whom inquiries or complaints can be made or other means of gaining access to the personal information; provide a description of the type of personal information that the organization holds and how it is used; must explain how the individual may access this information; and must detail the distribution of the information within subsidiaries of the organization. If the organization provides brochures or other sources of information about its privacy policies or standards, these should be made available. The means of making information available may include toll-free telephone numbers and online services.

ix) Principle 9: Individual Access

The essential features of this Principle[212] are information, access, and challenge:

a.   Information

An individual must receive advice as to the existence of personal information held by the organization, the use that is being made of the information, and to whom (as third parties) the information has been disclosed. To effect this process, the individual must provide the organization with sufficient information to enable the organization to provide a response that complies with this Principle. Such information can be used only for this purpose. In complying with this Principle, an organization must respond within a reasonable time and largely at the expense of the organization. Only minimal cost may be sought from an individual seeking information and access. The Commission has distinguished access to information from access to a record that may have contained the information. If available in other sources, a specific document need not be retained.[213] Overall, personal information itself is to be retained only for so long as the purpose for which it was collected is unfulfilled.[214]

---

211 Ibid., clauses 4.8.1 and 4.8.2.a.
212 Ibid., clause 4.9.
213 PIPEDA Case Summary #2003-252, above note 198 at para. 10.
214 See text accompanying notes 197–99, above in this chapter.

The information must be provided in a style that is understandable to the individual. This will involve the organization in translating or decoding any internal terminology or codes used with respect to the information. However, organizations are merely "encouraged" to provide to the individual the source of acquisition of this personal information. Likewise, while an organization *must* provide details of third parties to whom the individual's personal information has been disclosed,[215] it is only recommended that this information be as specific as possible, and if specific information cannot be provided the organization may give a generalized response about parties to whom a disclosure *may* have been made.[216]

b.   Access

Access to personal information must be given to the individual unless there is a valid exception to such access, for which reasons should be given. The schedule is not conclusive about applicable exceptions, noting merely that they may include cost, the existence of reference to other persons' information for which "legal, security or commercial proprietary" reasons prevent disclosure, and information subject to solicitor–client or other privilege. If the information is of a medical nature and is considered to be sensitive, an organization may choose to make it available through a medical practitioner.

c.   Challenge

This element enables an individual to correct any "inaccuracy or incompleteness." An organization is required to amend by correction, deletion, or addition any personal information that it holds and to advise such amendment to third parties with access to the information. It is unclear whether the reference in the schedule to "third parties having access"[217] includes those to whom the information has been previously disclosed or whether this provision covers only situations of current or temporary access by third parties to an organization's collection of personal information. It is suggested that perhaps subject to a suitable time limitation (say, five years) from the notification of personal information to a third party, an organization ought to be responsible for notifying amendments to that information.[218] Certainly, if personal information

---

215 *PIPEDA*, above note 7, Sch. 1, clause 4.9.1.
216 *Ibid.*, clause 4.9.3.
217 *Ibid.*, clause 4.9.5.
218 Support for this interpretation can be found in *ibid.*, clause 4.9.1, which requires an account of the third parties to whom information has been disclosed, that is, previously disclosed. Compare the requirement (Principle 1) concerning the

is disclosed to third parties on a continuing basis, the Schedule else-where recognizes the need for updating.[219] This should therefore apply to inaccuracies established by an individual's challenge.

The onus is on the individual to "successfully demonstrate" any inaccuracy. However, if not successful, or if the challenge is otherwise unresolved to the satisfaction of the individual, the organization must record the substance of the unresolved challenge and "when appro-priate" notify third parties who have access to the information of the existence of the dispute. No guidance is given as to when this would be appropriate, but it is suggested that third parties should be notified as a matter of course if they have access to the information. It appears that only the fact of an unresolved challenge, rather than the content of the challenge, must be so indicated.[220]

x) Principle 10: Challenge Compliance
This Principle[221] overlaps the preceding discussion of Principle 9 and a challenge by an individual with respect to the accuracy of his or her personal information held by an organization. However, Principle 10 is of broader application. It concerns a challenge by an individual to any non-compliance with any of the Principles set out in the Schedule. It is a general dispute resolution provision in accordance with accessible, and simple to use, complaint procedures that an organization must es-tablish and inform individuals about. Initial access is to be through the person designated under Principle 1[222] for the organization's com-pliance with the ten Principles. All complaints must be investigated. Additionally, if other complaint procedures exist, for example through a regulatory body, complainants must be so advised.[223]

---

need for security measures by a third party to whom personal information is disclosed for processing. See text accompanying notes 157 and 204, above in this chapter. However, the position concerning information transferred for a third party's benefit has been noted as more problematic. See text accompany-ing notes 158ff. (re purposes of collection) and 205, above in this chapter.

219 See text accompanying note 201, above in this chapter, concerning Principle 6 – Accuracy.
220 *PIPEDA*, above note 7, Sch. 1, clause 4.9.6.
221 *Ibid.*, clause 4.10.
222 See text accompanying notes 155–57, above in this chapter.
223 *PIPEDA*, above note 7, Sch. 1, clause 4.10.3.

C. THIRD PARTIES, EXTRATERRITORIALITY, AND SURVEILLANCE

The practice of passing personal information on to third parties is relevant to several of the Principles of privacy and has been noted variously in this chapter.[224] It deserves a dedicated reference as it is necessarily a sensitive topic given the more extended line of control and, when sent extraterritorially, the application of laws of the territorial sovereign that may require disclosure notwithstanding any confidentiality agreement between the Canadian holder of the personal information and the extraterritorial recipient. Contextually, this merges with broader issues, including that of government access to data and surveillance of media usage, being not only Canadian measures but foreign as well. The *Uniting and Strengthening America by Providing Appropriate Tools Required to Intercept and Obstruct Terrorism (USA PATRIOT) Act (Patriot Act)* in the United States[225] has been criticized as overly intrusive,[226] but this potential has not brought any reconsideration of the position under *PIPEDA* regarding the supply of personal information to a US-based holder. The Privacy Commissioner has reiterated the usual rule that *PIPEDA* does not prohibit organizations from outsourcing extraterritorially. The risks that a customer might be injured in the transfer of his or her personal information must, however, be considered, and a formal means by contract or otherwise with the foreign organization must be implemented. The customer must be notified that his or her personal information will be available to a foreign government should it be sought under the law of that jurisdiction. A change in an extraterritorial service provider utilizing the personal information does not require further consent if the purpose has not changed from that of the earlier consent.[227]

---

224 See text accompanying notes 157, 180, 192–95, 203–5, and 218–19, above in this chapter.

225 *Uniting and Strengthening America by Providing Appropriate Tools Required to Intercept and Obstruct Terrorism (USA PATRIOT) Act of 2001,* Pub. L. No. 107-56, 115 Stat. 272 (2001), renewed *USA PATRIOT Improvement and Reauthorization Act of 2005,* Pub. L. No. 109-177, 120 Stat. 192 (2006).

226 See, for example, Sharon H. Rackow, "How the *USA Patriot Act* will Permit Governmental Infringement upon the Privacy of Americans in the Name of 'Intelligence" Investigations'" (2002) 150 U. Pa. L. Rev. 1651; and Steven A. Osher, "Privacy Computers and the *Patriot Act*: The Fourth Amendment Isn't Dead, But No One Will Insure It" (2002) 54 Fla. L. Rev. 521.

227 *PIPEDA* Case Summary #2008-394, above note 192.

The Privacy Commissioner's recommendations in the Facebook proceedings,[228] subsequently agreed to by Facebook, Inc.,[229] concerned the disclosure of user's personal information to third-party developers of applications (task or function options). Technological changes will now limit developers' access. Meaningful consent will be obtained from users, and users will be told of the specific item or items of personal information and the purpose or purposes for which the information is needed by the developer of an application.[230]

A different dimension of third parties, also discussed in the Facebook proceedings, is the posting by users of personal information of other persons ("non-users"), including by "tagging": the identifying of others in a photograph, video, or statement. Facebook, Inc. was found to have no responsibility under *PIPEDA* for the actions of users, unless Facebook itself used the information that users provided.[231] Facebook, Inc. is now prepared to advise non-users that they have been tagged and to provide a means for them to remove the tag.[232] It will also require users to have the permission of the third party concerned.[233]

While an Internet host such as Facebook, Inc. may not directly violate *PIPEDA* by the activities of users who post personal information of third parties, it is feasible that the acts, or omissions, of a host be seen as so closely related to those of the users that, in general, a relationship of joint or concurrent tortfeasor may be articulated under a general privacy tort[234] or, indeed, under *PIPEDA*. This proposition is presented analogously in other, but related, contexts.[235] In effect, the actions of the users, if condoned by the host, or certainly if encouraged, may conceivably be seen as actions of the host itself.

Facebook, Inc. may not have reached this position, given its resolution with the Privacy Commissioner. However, the Internet medium YouTube (Google), was involved in a US copyright infringement con-

---

228 Facebook Report, above note 16, s. 4.
229 See Letter from OPC, above note 18.
230 Facebook Report, above note 16, s. 4.
231 *Ibid.*, s. 9.
232 See Tom Occhino, "Tag Friends in Your Status and Posts" *Facebook blog* (2009), online: http://blog.facebook.com/ blog.php?post=109765592130. .
233 See Letter from OPC, above note 18.
234 The potential of general tort recovery for violation of privacy is discussed in the text accompanying note 61ff., above in this chapter.
235 See Chapter 3, notes 106–7. See also Chapter 5, Section C(5), concerning a similar situation for copyright infringement but under specifically focused legislation.

cerning postings by users of video tapes.[236] From a privacy perspective, the court ordered that all data from the YouTube "logging" database be disclosed. This included the IP address and "login ID," so that an identification of a user's computer and videos accessed would be revealed.[237] The Privacy Commissioner's blog notes that no geographic limits were set by the court and therefore Canadian users will have been identified.[238] An order of this nature, granting disclosure to establish alleged copyright infringement without regard to the privacy of users' IP addresses, may bear some comparison with a Canadian balance weighted toward copyright enforcement rather than privacy of users.[239]

Disclosure or discovery under regular civil process is permitted under *PIPEDA*.[240] In addition, *PIPEDA* allows collection, use, and disclosure of personal information in a variety of circumstances without the knowledge or consent of the individual to whom the personal information relates. Included is *collection* "for purposes related to investigating … a contravention of the laws of Canada or a province."[241] Investigation of the breach of laws of "a foreign jurisdiction" is added with respect to *use* and *disclosure* of personal information.[242] In the case of use, the contravention must be in progress or imminent,[243] and for disclosure, an investigation "or gathering intelligence for the purpose of enforcing any [federal or provincial] law"[244] or upon suspicion that the information concerns national security, defence, or international affairs.[245] For collection and use, the organization may proceed of its own initiative.[246] However, disclosure may be to a government institution only upon its request, "identifying its lawful authority" and confirming the purpose for which the information is needed.[247]

---

236 See *Viacom International Inc., v. YouTube, Inc.* 253 F.R.D. 256 (S.D.N.Y. 2008), available at Office of the Privacy Commissioner of Canada, *YouTube Could Reveal a Lot about You* (4 July 2008), online: http://blog.privcom.gc.ca/index.php/2008/07/04/youtube-could-reveal-a-lot-about-you/. See Chapter 5, Section C(7).

237 *Ibid.*, Part 4 at 11–12.

238 Office of the Privacy Commissioner, above note 236.

239 See Chapter 5, text accompanying notes 291–93.

240 *PIPEDA*, above note 7, s. 7(3)(c).

241 *Ibid.*, s. 7(1)(b). It must be "reasonable to expect" that availability or accuracy would be compromised to proceed with knowledge or consent.

242 *Ibid.*, ss. 7(2)(a) and (3)(c. 1)(ii).

243 *Ibid.*, s. 7(2)(a).

244 *Ibid.*, s. 7(3)(c.1)(ii).

245 *Ibid.*, s. 7(3)(c.1)(i).

246 *Ibid.*, ss. 7(1)(b) (collection) and 7(2)(a) (use) (if it has "reasonable grounds to believe").

247 *Ibid.*, s. 7(3)(c.1).

The contexts described are appropriate and demonstrate safeguards. More problematic is the access by a government to a sampling of millions of Internet searches made by users through search engines. Such access was sought by the US Department of Justice to assist in the defence of a constitutional challenge of legislation designed to protect children online.[248] The search engine organizations were not party to the proceeding. Google Inc. resisted the US government, which sought the information to indicate how often users were linked to pornographic sites and thereby demonstrate a need for the legislation, rather than a reliance on filtering programs.[249] Ultimately, the court ordered access to a smaller sample without any identifying personal information.[250]

Search engine organizations themselves are criticized for retaining the IP addresses of users and their search logs for too long. Google Inc. has agreed with EU regulators that it will reduce this period from eighteen to nine months, at which time personal indicators will be removed but the search data itself will remain.[251] Of the other principal search engine proprietors, Yahoo Inc. has opted for ninety days,[252] and Microsoft has indicated that it would be prepared to adopt a period of six months if that becomes an industry standard. It also reports that its system of separating identifying information from the search query itself provides greater privacy protection than that available from simply a shorter period.[253]

---

248 The legislation was the *Child Online Protection Act*, 47 U.S.C § 231 (1998), found to be unconstitutional. See *Ashcroft, Attorney General v. American Civil Liberties Union*, 542 U.S. 656 (2004).

249 For a full description of the proceedings see silicon.com, *Google Fights US Gov't Request for Search Data,* online: www.silicon.com/management/cio-insights/2006/01/20/google-fights-us-govt-request-for-search-data-39155785/. Copies of documentation are provided, online: SearchEngineWatch http://blog.searchenginewatch.com/060119-161802.

250 Declan McCullagh, *Google Must Capitulate to DoJ, Says Judge* (15 March 2006), online: www.silicon.com/management/cio-insights/2006/03/15/google-must-capitulate-to-doj-says-judge-39157220/.

251 See Search Engine Land, *Google Halves Data Retention Time against Backdrop of EU Pressure, US Regulatory Scrutiny,* online: http://searchengineland.com/google-halves-data-retention-time-against-backdrop-of-eu-pressure-us-regulatory-scrutiny-14706.

252 Arnold Zafra, *Yahoo Reduces Data Retention Limit to 3 Months* (18 December 2008), online: www.searchenginejournal.com/yahoo-reduces-data-retention-limit-to-3-months/8165/.

253 See Microsoft, "Comparing Search Data Retention Policies of Major Search Engines before the EU" *Microsoft Privacy and Safety* (10 February 2009), online: http://blogs.technet.com/privacyimperative/archive/2009/02/10/comparing-search-data-retention-policies-of-major-search-engines-before-the-eu.aspx.

D. SUMMATION AND PROGNOSIS

The loss of personal privacy need not be an inevitable consequence of new technologies in telecommunications. Yet in many respects it is. Even the traditional telephone in one's home is the target of persistent computer-assisted telemarketing, in a manner more intrusive than e-mail spam.[254] The prime focus, however, is upon the Internet, a para-doxical medium. Decentralized in operation, and of global, borderless dimension, it can afford substantial but not total anonymity for users, even to the extent of shielding illicit conduct such as unauthorized file sharing of copyrighted music,[255] or trading in illegal child pornog-raphy or security-related crimes. Yet this very nature and scope of the medium can cause personal information, once uploaded, with consent or otherwise, to be available to millions of users at the click of a mouse and to be largely irretrievable, even if removed from the site of initial uploading. Beyond this, digitized systems in themselves are engineered to record and store, creating a footprint ripe for sifting, surveillance, and hacking to an extent impossible with manual recording and stor-age. In effect, situations that were inherently and systemically limited in accessibility now present significant risk of intrusiveness from the breadth and means of digitized access.

The essential response, nationally and internationally, has been to alert and warn users and to systematize the collection of personal in-formation, essentially requiring consent. Necessarily this requires the disclosure of contextually related purposes for which the acquisition is required, the granting of access to the provider, and the need to destroy the information when the purposes are achieved. In Canada, the prin-cipal focus is the federal legislative measures in *PIPEDA* and the recog-nized equivalent measures approved by the Governor in Council and enacted in British Columbia, Alberta, Ontario (health information), and Quebec with respect to entities within provincial jurisdiction. Other provinces have not enacted equivalent measures, and the federal legislation applies in these provinces to all entities, including provin-cially controlled entities, under a formulation to this effect in *PIPEDA*. Constitutional objections may remain with respect to a formulation of this nature.

Although the global dimensions of the Internet render national measures problematic in outcome, the success of the Privacy Commis-sioner in the claim of privacy infringement by Facebook, Inc., the US-

---

254 Chapter 3, text accompanying notes 236–39.
255 See text accompanying note 239, above in this chapter.

based owner of the popular social networking medium Facebook,[256] and in negotiating with Google Inc. concerning its Street View service[257] demonstrates an efficiency and purposiveness of the *PIPEDA* process in an international context.

Outside of *PIPEDA*, the existing legal framework of privacy protection in Canada may afford tort-related relief against intrusion and interference with telecommunications media, essentially the Internet and related connections and interests. These matters have been considered at common law and under provincial legislation. A necessary linkage has been drawn with Chapter 3 concerning US-led development in this context of utilizing trespass and related torts, but privacy relief has the potential to encompass more than simply interference or impact injury. It can provide a more accurate conceptual framework with respect to the implantation of devices or code that are ordinarily delivered by stealth or deception to an unsuspecting user of a host computer and then operate to collect and utilize information from that unwilling host.

The future protection of privacy in digital communications technologies may ultimately depend on a global governmental will to value and protect individual privacy, but more particularly to address the still fledgling, but probably intrusive, access to data and the surveillance or monitoring that the Internet enables, at least after an initial identification of an individual's IP address. Ordinarily, governmental access or surveillance concerns security and crime detection and prevention. In these contexts, governmental and societal interests will often justify the intrusions upon an individual's expectation of privacy in media usage and data storage. However, the *process* by which these measures are achieved will provide the context of success or failure. A process similar to that in current law involving authorities having reasonable cause to suspect a violation of law is, of course, entirely appropriate. In this sense, digitized electronic media should be treated no differently from any other medium, such as the telephone, which may be subject to wiretapping. The digital media, however, readily allow word searches that may trigger electronic recognition and flagging of a communication, leading to a "drift net" style of surveillance. This could conceivably follow from governmental access to search engine data of the nature described earlier as sought against Google Inc. and other search engine providers. The checks, balances, and accountability through the judicially controlled subpoena process has to date en-

---

256 See text accompanying notes 16 and 18, above in this chapter.
257 See text accompanying notes 20–25, above in this chapter.

sured that a government purpose is achieved without the disclosure of personal identification of users, and it is hoped that this shield will continue to be effective.

In very many respects, however, these governmental dimensions are beyond the present purposes and scope of this work. Their focus is that of security and criminal violation as opposed to the transactional contexts.

CHAPTER 5

COPYRIGHT

A. INTRODUCTION

The ability to convert visual and aural expression and information into a digital format has merged the historically distinct areas of computer technology and telecommunications to constitute what is today often described by industry as "telematics," reflected principally in Internet communications. Indeed, the Internet itself is the prime example of a telematic technology.[1] Many of the categories of law applicable to computer technology could therefore be encompassed within a treatment of telecommunications. Necessarily, however, only those that present dimensions or issues *specific to the media* are included. Features of copyright law are of considerable significance in this regard, presenting issues at the centre of public policy controversy with respect to the nature, purpose, and scope of Internet usage, especially involving downloading and peer-to-peer swapping of music, video, or motion picture productions. Copyright also presents media-specific features with respect to the traditional media. However, the designed decentralization of the Internet stands in sharp contrast to television networks, cable companies, and radio stations. Decentralization not only presents difficulties in attempting any regulation[2] but also renders the application and enforcement of the general law, including copyright, problematic.

---

1   Look Up Tech Terms, "telematics," online: http://searchnetworking.techtarget.com/sDefinition/0,,sid7_gci517744,00.html.
2   See Chapter 2.

This has led to a focus on the liability and role of system providers or intermediaries, such as Internet service providers (ISPs) or owners of host websites, raising systemically focused issues, including those of balancing the interests of content owners with the privacy and access rights of users and the public interest in full and effective utilization of media as sources of information. It has also brought to prominence substantial issues of private international law (conflict of laws), including jurisdiction, choice of law, and enforcement of judgments within those areas.[3]

A holder's copyright exclusivity to communicate protected subject matter to the public by telecommunication[4] and the authorization of others to make such a communication are of key significance. It is the authorization right, in particular, that enables a copyright owner to proceed against a third party who is not the immediate infringer, on the basis that the third party has "authorized" the infringement in the sense that it has "sanctioned, approved, and countenanced" the communication.[5] The operative factor is the level of facilitation or contribution that has enabled the infringement to occur. A narrow formulation favours the third party. A broad formulation favours the copyright holder. The medium of the Internet brings this matter into particular focus for telecommunications.[6]

The need to properly define the scope of copyright as a significant economic monopoly in today's marketplace of intangible, information-based products is manifest. While strictly an issue of statutory interpretation,[7] a 2002 decision of the Supreme Court that was re-affirmed unanimously by the Court in 2004, adopted an incentive theory of balancing a just reward for an author against "promoting the public interest in the encouragement and dissemination of works of the

---

3   See Chapter 6.

4   The right to communicate to the public by telecommunication is applicable to works (s. 3(1)(f)) and a performer's performance (ss. 15(1)(a)(i) and 26(1)(a)), *Copyright Act*, R.S.C. 1985, c. C-42.

5   This classic phrase from *Falcon v. Famous Players Film Co.*, [1926] 2 K.B. 474 at 486 was adopted by the Supreme Court of Canada in *Muzak Corporation v. Composers, Authors & Publishers Association of Canada Ltd.*, [1953] 2 S.C.R. 183 at 193 [*Muzak*]; and recently in *Society of Composers, Authors and Music Publishers of Canada v. Canadian Association of Internet Providers*, [2004] 2 S.C.R. 427 at para. 124 [*Tariff 22* (SCC)].

6   See text accompanying note 220ff., below in this chapter.

7   See, for example, *Compo Co. v. Blue Crest Music Inc.* (1979), [1980] 1 S.C.R. 357 at 373; and *Bishop v. Stevens*, [1990] 2 S.C.R. 467 at 477 [*Bishop*].

arts and the intellect,"[8] that may provide a contextual perspective for interpretations, particularly those balancing holder and user interests. The Court drew upon the 1769 judgment of Willes J in *Millar v. Taylor* ("to encourage letters").[9] It is a formulation in substance identical to the constitutional requirement in the United States that copyright shall "promote the progress of science."[10] No doubt the judgment of Willes J was available to the drafters of the US Constitution in 1789.

1) Essential Principles

Copyright is provided universally within member countries of the *Berne Convention*,[11] the *Universal Copyright Convention*,[12] or the World Trade Organization (WTO)[13] as long as an author meets the qualifying requirements of being, at the time of making a work, "a citizen or subject of, or a person ordinarily resident in, a treaty country" or, in the case of a published work, to have first published in a treaty country.[14] Publication is "making copies of a work available to the public"[15] in a quantity that is sufficient to meet reasonable demands given the nature

---

8   *Théberge v. Galerie d'Art du Petit Champlain*, [2002] 2 S.C.R. 336, 2002 SCC 34 at para. 30 [*Théberge*]; and *CCH Canadian Ltd. v. Law Society of Upper Canada*, [2004] 1 S.C.R. 339 at para. 23 [*CCH* (SCC)]. See also *Euro-Excellence Inc. v. Kraft Canada Inc*, 2007 SCC 37 [*Euro-Excellence Inc.*], dividing the Court between a more literal interpretation (Rothstein J with Fish J concurring at para. 3, and McLachlin CJ and Abella J dissenting at para. 113) and a more purposive, contextual interpretation focused on balancing policy perspectives (Bastarache, LeBel, and Charron JJ at paras. 74–76).

9   *Millar v. Taylor* (1769), 4 Burr. 2303 (K.B.).

10   U.S. Const. art. I, § 8, cl. 8.

11   *Berne Convention for the Protection of Literary and Artistic Works*, 9 September 1886, 828 U.N.T.S. 221, as last rev'd by the *Paris Act*, 24 July 1971, 1161 U.N.T.S. 3, online: www.wipo.int/treaties/en/ip/berne/trtdocs_wo001.html [*Berne Convention*]. See *Copyright Act*, above note 4, s. 91. Unless otherwise stated, statutory references hereinafter are to the *Copyright Act, ibid.*

12   *Universal Copyright Convention*, 6 September 1952, 216 U.N.T.S. 132, concluded at Geneva, as last rev'd by the *Paris Act 1971*, 943 U.N.T.S. 178.

13   *Marrakesh Agreement Establishing the World Trade Organization*, 15 April 1994, 1867 U.N.T.S. 154, 33 I.L.M. 1144. See *World Trade Organization Agreement Implementation Act*, S.C. 1994, c. 47, s. 2(1) [*WTOAIA*]. Article 9 of the *Agreement on Trade-Related Aspects of Intellectual Property Rights* [*TRIPs Agreement*], Annex 1C of the *Marrakesh Agreement Establishing the World Trade Organization*, requires WTO members to comply with arts. 1–21 of the *Berne Convention* (Paris 1971), above note 11, except for art. 6*bis* concerning moral rights.

14   *WTOAIA, ibid.*, s. 5(1)(a).

15   *Ibid.*, s. 2.2(1)(a)(i).

of the work.[16] Members of treaty countries are protected within every treaty country to the extent provided by the copyright law of that country — the principle of national treatment.[17]

Copyright in Canada is an exclusively federal constitutional jurisdiction and entirely legislative. Common law copyright was abolished in 1924. Despite the substantial term of protection,[18] copyright covers only the expression created by an author that is fixed in a material form having a relatively permanent endurance.[19] An idea, fact, or story itself is not protected by copyright and may be presented in another author's expression. Copyright precludes copying and other usages of an author's expression. A purely literal, or textual, copying presents little difficulty, but the division between expression and idea or content is difficult to draw in "non-literal" copying.[20] It concerns the copying of the plot or the structure, sequence, and organization of the author's work without using the author's literal expression. With few authorities, it is difficult to pinpoint the degree of abstraction at which the line between idea and expression is crossed in a non-literal, or non-textual, context.[21]

Nevertheless, non-literal copying is utilized in the context of software protection. In an attempt to provide a workable framework, courts in both the United States and Canada have reached a position of filtering or "weeding out" from the works of competing parties those aspects that cannot be said to be original to the respective authors. A comparison is then made of matters original to the authors. Expressions from the public domain or dictated by industry or common practice or by the particular medium are excluded. Likewise, matters that can be expressed in only one or limited ways might also be excluded.[22]

---

16   *Ibid.*, s. 5(1)(c)(i).
17   The principle "national treatment" requires that nationals (by citizenship or habitual residence) of a "treaty country" enjoy in other treaty countries the same rights that the copyright law of those countries provides to its own nationals, subject to meeting the "minimum requirements" of copyright law established under the relevant international conventions or treaties.
18   Section 6 provides a term of the life of the author, the remainder of the calendar year of the author's death plus fifty years.
19   See *Canadian Admiral Corporation Ltd. v. Rediffusion, Inc.*, [1954] Ex. C.R. 382, 20 C.P.R. 75 at 86 [*Canadian Admiral*].
20   In the United Kingdom the expressions "textual" and "non-textual" have been used. See *Baigent v. Random House Group Ltd*, [2007] EWCA Civ 247, [2008] E.M.L.R. 7.
21   The classic authority is that of Learned Hand CJ in *Nichols v. Universal Pictures Corp.*, 45 F.2d 119 (2d Cir. 1930).
22   See *Delrina Corp. v. Triolet Systems Inc.* (2002), 58 O.R. (3d) 339 (C.A.); and *Computer Associates International Inc. v. Altari Inc.*, 982 F.2d 693 (2d Cir. 1992).

In addition to attempting to preserve the distinction between expression and idea, this identification of copyrightable subject matter reflects the standard of originality now required in Canada. In 2004, the Supreme Court addressed the divergence in appellate decisions of whether originality should be established by the traditional English test of sweat of the brow (industrious effort) or by the qualitatively higher element of creativity from the United States. It rejected both tests, expressing the adoption of an intermediate formulation: skill and judgment involving intellectual effort. Defining skill as "the use of one's knowledge, developed aptitude or practiced ability" and judgment as "the use of one's capacity for discernment or ability to form an opinion or evaluation by comparing different possible options,"[23] the test might literally be seen as more stringent than that of creativity. This was not intended. The term "creativity" was avoided as it was seen to suggest novelty or uniqueness. The practical application of skill and judgment in Canada is likely to differ little from that of creativity in the United States.

Copyright protection encompasses two broad areas: "works" and "other subject matter" (otherwise termed "neighbouring rights"). Works must qualify within one of the categories of literary, dramatic, musical, or artistic. These categories are broadly interpreted, although there is some definitional uncertainty. The area of "other subject matter," or neighbouring rights, generally concerns secondary creations derived from or predicated upon works. They are performer's performance rights, the rights of sound recording makers, and the rights of broadcasters in communication signals. The category of performer's performance may involve a performance that is not based on an underlying work, presenting an exception to the general position of predication on underlying works.

The division between works and other subject matter reflects consequences within the overall structure of copyright. Works receive the full measure of economic rights stipulated in section 3 of the *Copyright Act*. Other subject matter is protected only to the extent provided for the particular subject matter. For example, the protection afforded sound recording makers does not include the right of public performance of the sound recording. This right pertains only to the owner of the underlying musical work. However, both the sound recording maker and the owner of musical work can prevent reproduction.[24] Protection by way of moral rights is available only to works, and exclusively to the *authors*

---

23   *CCH* (SCC), above note 8 at para. 16.
24   Section 18(1)(b) (sound recording) and s. 3(1) (musical work).

of the works. Lastly, the term of protection for other subject matter is not defined by reference to life of an author, as is the case for works. It is fixed at fifty years from creation of the subject matter.

Economic rights applicable to works consist of reproduction; performance in public; publication if the work is unpublished; specific enumerated rights, including the right to communicate a work to the public by telecommunication; and the right to authorize any of the foregoing rights. Economic rights are vested in the *owner* of the copyright. Ordinarily, the owner is the author but may be the author's employer, if a work arises from the author's employment, or may be vested in an assignee or transferee of the copyright, such as a publisher.[25] Moral rights, on the other hand, are vested in the author and cannot be the subject of an *inter vivos* (between living persons) assignment or transfer,[26] but can pass by testamentary disposition or upon intestacy to persons entitled.[27] Moral rights may be waived *inter vivos*, meaning that a holder may agree to non-enforcement.[28]

Moral rights in Canada have three features. First is the right of integrity, which allows an author to prevent "distortion, mutilation and other modification" to the work or to prevent it being used in conjunction (usually promotionally) with "a service cause or institution." The alleged infringement must be such as to prejudice the honour or reputation of the author. Second is the right of association (i.e., attribution) of the author by name or pseudonym "where reasonable in the circumstances." Third is the right of the author to remain anonymous.[29] There has been little judicial interpretation of moral rights in Canada and many uncertainties exist over their scope and application. However, moral rights are a significant feature of copyright law and are discussed contextually later in this chapter.[30]

Economic rights have received considerable attention. The reproduction right and the right to perform in public are both subject to a substantiality test. An insubstantial interference by reproduction or performance in public is not an infringement. Substantiality is a question of fact and has quantitative and qualitative elements; the latter is the more significant. Accordingly, a quantitatively small portion of a work may still be substantial if it is qualitatively important. An ex-

---

25   Sections 13(3) & (4).
26   Section 14.1(2).
27   Section 14.2(2).
28   Section 14.1(2).
29   Sections 14.1(1) and 28.2(1).
30   See text accompanying notes 183ff., below in this chapter.

ample is a short but popular chorus in a song.[31] Judicial determinations have interpreted broadly the requirement for performance to be "in public." Only domestic or private situations are excluded.[32] The publication right includes making copies of an unpublished work available to the public in sufficient number to satisfy a reasonable demand,[33] but might possibly also include something less, such as "making public" the work or subject matter.[34]

The Supreme Court has reinvigorated user interests through the "fair dealing" provision, which is described as an integral part of the Act that affords a "user right" as opposed to a defence or excuse for infringement.[35] Literally, the Act simply excludes fair dealing from copyright protection.[36]

B. TELEVISION, RADIO, AND CABLE

1) Communication to the Public by Telecommunication

The communication right, enacted in *Copyright Act*, s. 3(1)(f), is of primary significance in a telecommunications context. Legislatively defined ("means") as "any transmission of signs, signals, writing, images or sounds or intelligence of any nature by wire, radio, visual, optical or other electromagnetic system," the right affords a copyright exclusivity for the telecommunication of a work to the public.[37] While a "communication" must involve a sender and a receiver and is not complete until it is received,[38] there is no requirement that it be heard or perceived by a

---

31 See, for example, *Grignon v. Roussel* (1991), 38 C.P.R. (3d) 4 at 16 (F.C.T.D.) noting the qualitative feature as "often the attractive part, commonly referred to as 'the hook' which identifies a song, sets it apart and sometimes makes it a popular and commercial success."

32 See *Jennings v. Stephens*, [1936] 1 Ch. 469 (C.A.) [*Jennings*]; *Canadian Admiral*, above note 19 at 99–102 (C.P.R.).

33 Sections 5(1)(c)(i) and 2.2(1)(a)(i).

34 See *Robert D. Sutherland Architects Ltd. v. Monty Investments Inc.* (1995), 61 C.P.R. (3d) 447 at 459–60 (N.S.S.C.); and *Infabrics Ltd. v. Jaytex Ltd.*, [1982] A.C. 1, [1981] 1 All E.R. 1057 at 1067 (H.L.): "'[P]ublishing the work' . . . means making public in the United Kingdom [or other Treaty Country]" (Lord Scarman). See also David Vaver, *Copyright Law* (Toronto: Irwin Law, 2000) at 122–123, n. 20.

35 *CCH* (SCC), above note 8 at para. 48.

36 Sections 29, 29.1, & 29.2 ("Fair dealing for the purpose of . . . does not infringe copyright").

37 Section 3(1)(f).

38 See text accompanying notes 145–52, below in this chapter.

recipient simultaneously, or with some immediacy, with the transmission. Rather, it is simply the passing of information, including in the form of a digital audio file, between persons,[39] with the recipient being part of the public to whom the communication is made. In this context, a royalty tariff certified by the Copyright Board was held to be applicable to ringtones sent from a wireless telephone provider to a cellphone owner and user of the provider's service at the request of that owner.[40]

The chequered history of the communication right has led to many amending legislative measures. First enacted in 1931, the communication right responded to the recognition in the *Berne Convention* of the technology of radio communication, which provided in article 11*bis*(1), in French and English:

> (1) Les auteurs d'oeuvres littéraires et artistiques jouissent du droit exclusif d'autoriser la communication de leurs oeuvres au public para la radiodiffusion.

> (1) Authors of literary and artistic works shall enjoy the exclusive right of authorizing the communication of their works to the public by radiocommunication.[41]

The translation to English of the French-language *Berne Convention* and the legislative implementation in Canada of this provision have presented considerable difficulty with television and radio broadcasts and cable retransmissions. Many current provisions of the *Copyright Act* derive their origin from these difficulties.

The translation was criticized in 1968 by the Supreme Court of Canada: "[W]here the Convention speaks of 'radiodiffusion' i.e. radio broadcasting, the unfortunate translation reads 'radiocommunication'. The error in translation of the Convention was obviously carried into the statute [*Copyright Act*, s. 3(1)(f)] intended to implement it. . . ."[42]

The decision before the Court was the first in a series of cases from 1968 to 1993 interpreting the scope of this right. The Court was concerned with the operation of television networks and the payment

---

39   *Canadian Wireless Telecommunications Association v. Society of Composers, Authors and Music Publishers of Canada*, [2008] 3 F.C. 539, 64 C.P.R. (4th) 343 at paras. 17–20 leave to appeal to S.C.C. refused, 2008 Can LII 46984 [*Canadian Wireless*].

40   *Canadian Wireless*, *ibid.* See text accompanying notes 56–59, below in this chapter, as to the requirement of being "to the public."

41   *Copyright Amendment Act, 1931*, SC 1931 (21–22 Geo. V.), c. 8, s. 3; *Berne Convention*, above note 11, Art. 11*bis*(1).

42   *Composers, Authors and Publishers Association of Canada Limited (CAPAC) v. CTV Television Network Limited*, [1968] 1 S.C.R. 676 at 681 [*CAPAC v. CTV*].

of royalties for the transmission of musical works. Royalties were assessed as a percentage of advertising revenues earned by television stations. The Canadian Television Network (CTV) affiliate stations held the licences necessary to perform the works in public and paid royalties linked with their advertising revenue. Royalties were not, however, paid by the network itself on the advertising revenues it earned. Did the transmission by the network to its affiliates constitute a communication by radio communication?[43] Notwithstanding that the Court considered that a public performance was contemplated under article 11*bis*(1) of the *Berne Convention*, the limited scope of the legislation denied this recognition. It referred only to the communication of a musical work without reference to the *performance* of that work. A musical work itself was defined as the graphic presentation (i.e., the written score) of the music, which of course was not transmitted. Additionally, the Act did not include reference to the communication being "to the public."[44] Infringement, therefore, could not be established against the network.[45]

Legislative changes in 1988 implementing the *Canada–United States Free Trade Agreement (FTA)*[46] introduced the current definition of the communication right, including the phrase "to the public." Not until 1993, however, was the definition of "musical work" amended to include performance of the work.[47] Even then, a network did not communicate the work "to the public" but to its affiliates.[48] Section 2.4(1)(c), however, had since 1988 provided that a network, as defined in the *Broadcasting Act*, or a "programming undertaking"[49] whose operations cause the communication of works or other subject matter to the public other than by a cable retransmission (through a cable company)[50] is li-

---

43   The transmission to affiliates within the network was "in some cases by shipping a copy of the videotape," although generally by telephone cable and microwave. *Ibid.* at 678–79.

44   *Ibid.* at 681–83.

45   For subsequent proceedings, see *CTV Television Network Ltd. v. Canada (Copyright Board)*, [1993] 2 F.C. 115 at 120, n. 1 (C.A.) [*CTV v. Copyright Board*].

46   *Canada–United States Free Trade Agreement Implementation Act*, S.C. 1988, c. 65, s. 62(1) [*Canada–US FTAIA*].

47   *Copyright Amendment Act*, S.C. 1993, c. 23, s. 1 [*Copyright Amendment Act, 1993*], amending the definition to read "'musical work' means any work of music or musical composition, with or without words."

48   See *CTV v. Copyright Board*, above note 45 at para. 134.

49   The expression "programming undertaking" is not defined for the purpose of this provision. Nor is there an express referencing of this expression to its meaning under the *Broadcasting Act* as is the position for the expression "network," but the relevant meaning is logically that provided in the *Broadcasting Act*, S.C. 1991, c. 11, s. 2.

50   Sections 2.4(1)(c)(ii) and 31(1) (definition of "retransmitter").

able for an infringing transmission from a member of the network to the public on a joint and several basis.[51]

A cable retransmitter directly infringed the copyright in a musical work after the 1993 amendment to the definition of "musical work." Unlike a network, which transmits to affiliates, a cable retransmitter transmits "to the public."[52] Since 1988, persons occupying apartments and rooms situated in the same building are part of the public and a communication intended to be received by them is a communication to the public,[53] even though the occupants may not be "in public" under section 3(1).[54] Accordingly, the position concerning copyright infringement by telecommunication of protected subject matter is consistent with the requirement of signals being "to the public" from a "broadcasting undertaking" under the *Broadcasting Act* (1991), discussed in Chapter 2.[55]

Recent determinations have drawn a fine but sustainable distinction between a request-based photocopy service provided by a law society library to society members (as not constituting a communication to the public)[56] and a request-based transmission of a ringtone from a wireless telephone provider to a cellphone owner and user of the provider's service (as constituting a communication to the public).[57] While both instances involved a request leading to a subsequent one-to-one transmission, a particular ringtone would be requested by many users, leading to many transmissions of the same musical work over a period of time to many different users, together constituting members of the

---

51 *Canada–US FTAIA*, above note 46, s. 62(2) inserted provisions to this effect as ss. 3(1.4) & (1.5). At the time, reference was made only to the communication of "works." The inclusion of "other subject-matter" was effected by the *Copyright Amendment Act*, S.C. 1997, c. 24, s. 2 [*Copyright Amendment Act, 1997*], which also renumbered the provision as s. 2.4(1)(c).

52 See *Canadian Cable Television Association v. Copyright Board (Canada)*, [1993] 2 F.C. 138 at 152–54 (C.A), leave to appeal to S.C.C. refused, [1993] 4 S.C.R. v [*CCTA v. Copyright Board*].

53 Now s. 2.4(1)(a). A provision to this effect was first enacted by *Canada-US FTAIA*, above note 46, s. 62. Compare *Telstra Corporation Ltd. v. Australasian Performing Rights Association Ltd.* (1997), 146 A.L.R. 649, 71 A.L.J.R. 1312 (H.C.) [*Telstra*], concerning the playing of musical works to telephone users "placed on hold."

54 The test of "openly and without concealment" that had been stipulated in interpreting the expression "in public" is not applicable to the expression "to the public": *Canadian Wireless*, above note 39 at para. 42.

55 See text accompanying note 161, below in this chapter, and Chapter 2, notes 300–1 and 323–34.

56 See *CCH* (SCC), above note 8 at paras. 77–79.

57 *Canadian Wireless*, above note 39 at paras. 33–39.

public or a significant portion of the public.[58] Of course, this could also occur with a photocopy service (for example, numerous requests for a particular, recently given judicial decision), but it is suggested the difference lies in the nature of the photocopy service,which involves more happenstance than the wireless operator's storage of a limited number of ringtones for the sole intended purpose of providing them by transmission to users, as members of a segment of the public. Customers of the wireless telephone provider were found as "a group [to be] sufficiently large and diverse that it may be characterized as 'the public.'"[59]

2) Performance in Public

Apart from the communication right in section 3(1)(f), cable retransmitters were held in 1993 to infringe the right of "performance in public" in section 3(1), despite the expression "in public" being narrower than that of "to the public."[60] Networks escaped.[61] Section 2.3 subsequently excludes a telecommunication transmission *simpliciter* from this category, reflecting a legislative preference for cable transmissions to be included within section 3(1)(f) without invoking the general right of performance in public under section 3(1).

3) Authorization Right

Network affiliates paid royalties for transmission of musical works. The network could not, therefore, be found to have infringed copyright by authorizing the affiliates to infringe.[62] Again, however, this was not the position with cable retransmitters. In addition to the transmissions constituting direct infringement of copyright by performance *in public*, the cable retransmitters were found to have authorized any infringement that might be attributed to a viewer or listener upon activating a television or radio receiving set and gaining a performance of the work.[63] Section 2.3 has similarly removed this potential liability.[64]

---

58 *Ibid.* at para. 39.
59 *Ibid.* at para. 32.
60 See *CCTA v. Copyright Board,* above note 52 at 148–49 and 155–56 (F.C.).
61 See *CTV v. Copyright Board,* above note 45 at 134–35.
62 *CAPAC v. CTV,* above note 42 at 680 and 683.
63 See *CCTA v. Copyright Board,* above note 52 at 155.
64 Section 2.3 provides that a communication "by that act alone" is not a performance in public.

4) Fixation

The element of fixation[65] brought some uncertainty over how this principle might be applied to a work communicated to the public by telecommunication. In early television development, a live telecast involved no prior recording or other fixation. It therefore did not create any copyrightable subject matter.[66] Since 1988, fixation in a telecommunication to the public can be met by a recording made simultaneously with the transmission.[67]

5) Retransmission Right

In Chapter 1, attention was given to broadcasting issues arising from the reception by Canadian cable television distributors of signals originating in the United States for retransmission by cable to Canadian subscribers. The proceedings before the courts and the Canadian Radio-television and Telecommunications Commission (CRTC) concerned regulatory matters, essentially whether a particular reception and redistribution constituted that entity as a "broadcasting undertaking" under the *Broadcasting Act* (1991), operating without a licence to do so. From that perspective, the signals from the United States were perceived as interfering with Canada's attainment of the broadcasting policy or attempt to preserve a national cultural identity distinct from that of the United States.[68]

However, the opposite perspective is that of Canadian viewers receiving television signals from the United States without paying of royalties to copyright holders of works or other protected subject matter included in the programs contained in the signals received by microwave antennae reception; cable reception from a Canadian distribution undertaking (cable company); and direct-to-home (DTH) reception by individual satellite dishes of unencrypted signals.

To establish liability under Canadian copyright law, an infringing act must occur in Canada.[69] Microwave and DTH reception by individual persons, viewed in the receivers' domestic circumstances and involving no retransmission, will not in itself amount to an infringe-

---

65   See text accompanying note 19, above in this chapter.
66   See *Canadian Admiral*, above note 19 at 86–87 (C.P.R.).
67   Section 3(1.1) inserted as by *Canada–US FTAIA*, above note 46, s. 62(2).
68   See Chapter 1, text accompanying notes 100 and 135–47, and Chapter 2, text accompanying notes 231–32.
69   This is the traditional situation under the principle of "national treatment" in international copyright law.

ment by the recipient. However, the historical absence in Canada of a retransmission right caused uncertainty in circumstances involving retransmission. These might include general cable retransmissions or reception by a building or hotel owner followed by retransmission to residential units or suites in the building.[70]

These uncertainties led copyright owners, particularly of television feature programs and motion pictures, to lobby the US government to secure in the negotiations leading to the *FTA* the enactment in Canadian copyright law of a "retransmission" right. Canada agreed. The *FTA* provides for such a right,[71] and the *Copyright Act* was amended accordingly. However, the provisions represent a compromise, setting out a system of regulation of copyright and communications. Section 31[72] excludes copyright infringement from any communication to the public by telecommunication of any literary, dramatic, musical, and artistic work, if the requirements set out in the provision are met. The communication must be a retransmission of a local or distant signal containing the work that has initially been transmitted "by a terrestrial radio or terrestrial television station" to be received free by the public. Qualifying signals are classified as either "local" or "distant."[73] A "local" signal is one for which the receiving retransmission system and its service area is within a transmission area of thirty-two kilometres from the signal contour of the television, or from the principal studio of an AM radio station, or within the field-of-strength contour of an FM radio station. A local signal may be retransmitted without payment of a royalty, but retransmission of a "distant" signal will require payment.[74]

To qualify, a retransmission must also be lawful under the *Broadcasting Act* (1991) and must be retransmitted "simultaneously and in its entirety" unless otherwise permitted under Canadian law — for ex-

---

70 Section 2.4(1). The communications by the building or hotel owner would be "to the public," rather than to affiliates within a network. The operation is analogous to that of a cable retransmitter. See text accompanying notes 52–55, above in this chapter.

71 *Free Trade Agreement between the Government of Canada and the Government of the United States of America* (22 December 1987) Can. T.S. 1989 No. 3 at 526, online: www.worldtradelaw.net/nafta/CUSFTA.pdf at 218.

72 Section 31 inserted as s. 28(01) by *Canada–US FTAIA*, above note 46, s. 63.

73 Section 31(3)(a) empowers the Governor in Council to make regulations defining "local" and "distant" signals.

74 Section 31(3); and *Local Signal and Distant Signal Regulations*, S.O.R./89-254, as am. by S.O.R./2004-33.

ample, the retransmission of a signal with advertisements substituted with Canadian advertisements when so authorized by the CRTC.[75]

The royalties to be paid for the retransmission of "distant" signals are set by the Copyright Board under the procedures set out in Part VII of the *Copyright Act*.[76] They are collected by the cable operator through the cable service fees charged to subscribers.

The exempting and regulating measures in section 31 encompass only regular systems of cable retransmission[77] of microwave broadcast signals, that is, television and radio retransmitters. DTH satellite signals are not within the terrestrial source and signal definitional requirements. Internet and other new media-related retransmissions are excluded from 2002 by legislative amendment.[78] Without this intervention, retransmission via the Internet would have been included under section 31 as these transmissions are a lawful broadcast under the *Broadcasting Act* (1991) by reason of the 1999 exemption for new media.[79] The amendment reflected transborder influences.[80]

Section 31(2), enacted in 1988, provides that there is no "infringement of *copyright* for a retransmitter to communicate to the public by telecommunication any literary, dramatic, musical or artistic work" [emphasis added]. Legislative amendment in 1997 added a definition of the term "copyright"[81] to include protection of "other subject matter" (neighbouring rights) in a performer's performance,[82] a sound

---

75   See Chapter 1, text accompanying notes 135–36.

76   See ss. 68, 68.1, & 68.2. See also *Retransmission Royalties Criteria Regulations*, S.O.R./1991-690.

77   See the definition of "retransmitter" in s. 31(1).

78   *An Act to Amend the Copyright Act*, S.C. 2002, c. 26, s. 2 revised s. 31 to exclude Internet retransmitters from the definition of "retransmitter" and empower the Governor in Council to prescribe conditions applicable to some or all retransmitters. See also Broadcasting Public Notice CRTC 2003-2 (17 January 2003), online: www.crtc.gc.ca/eng/archive/2003/pb2003-2.htm.

79   *Exemption Order for New Media Broadcasting Undertakings*, Public Notice, CRTC 1999-197, Appendix A, online: www.crtc.gc.ca/eng/archive/2003/pb2003-2.htm. See Chapter 2, text accompanying notes 33, 204, and 314.

80   See Chapter 6, text accompanying note 154, citing *Twentieth Century Fox Film Corporation v. iCraveTV*, 2000 WL 255989 (W.D. Pa. 2000) [*iCraveTV*].

81   Section 2 "copyright" inserted by *Copyright Amendment Act, 1997*, above note 51, s. 1(5).

82   Section 15 (with respect to countries party to the *Rome Convention*, below note 89) and s. 26 (with respect to countries that are members of the WTO). Provisions in what is now s. 26 were first enacted as s. 14(01) by *WTOAIA*, above note 13, s. 58. This provision was amended, and s. 15 was enacted, by the *Copyright Amendment Act, 1997*, ibid., ss. 12 and 14.

recording,[83] and a broadcaster's communication signal.[84] From 1997, the position under section 31(2) is therefore that copyright in both works and other subject matter is not infringed by a communication to the public by telecommunication. A performer's performance specifically includes a right to communicate the performance to the public by telecommunication,[85] but this right will accordingly be subject to section 31(2), being within the general definition of "copyright."

Section 31 requires any retransmission to be simultaneous with the original broadcast and to be without alteration.[86]

6) Neighbouring Rights/Other Subject Matter

Copyright in "other subject-matter" is significant in a context of telecommunications. These rights, although usually deriving from a primary copyright, are separate copyright interests. A telecommunication may involve infringement of copyright in both the underlying work and in the neighbouring right or subject matter.

The scope of protection for subject matter, other than works, is limited to specific rights provided for each category.[87]

a)   A Performer's Performance
This right is vested in the person who is performing the work. There are two categories of performer's performance. First, section 15[88] affords national treatment protection to citizens or permanent residents of member countries of the *Rome Convention* of 1961.[89] Second, section 26 affords national treatment protection to a performer's performance

---

83   Section 18 enacted by *Copyright Amendment Act, 1997, ibid.*, s. 14.

84   Section 21 enacted by *Copyright Amendment Act, 1997, ibid.*

85   See ss. 15(1)(a)(i) and 26(1)(a).

86   Section 31(2)(c).

87   The general economic rights provision for "works" is s. 3(1). The economic rights of "other subject-matter" or neighbouring rights are set out in the sections for the respective subject matter: ss. 15 and 26 (performer's performance), s. 18 (sound recordings), and s. 21 (broadcaster's communication signals).

88   Section 15 was inserted by *Copyright Amendment Act, 1997,* above note 51, s. 14, and the definition of "performer's performance" in s. 2 was amended by *ibid.*, s. 1(2).

89   *International Convention for the Protection of Performers, Producers of Phonograms and Broadcasting Organizations,* 26 October 1961, 496 U.N.T.S 43 (signed at Rome), online: www.wipo.int/treaties/en/ip/rome/trtdocs_wo024.html [*Rome Convention*]. See *Copyright Act,* above note 4, s. 2 (definition) and s. 91(b).

that occurs in a WTO member country.[90] The scope of protection under section 26 is less than that under section 15.

Sections 15 and 26 both stipulate that if a performance is not fixed, the performer has the sole right of communicating the performance, or a substantial part of it, to the public by telecommunication.[91] Both sections afford a right to fix any performer's performance in a sound recording and to reproduce any unauthorized fixation or any substantial part of the fixation. Section 15 rights, however, are not limited to fixing in a sound recording. A performer has a right of first fixation of any type of performance "in any material form."[92] A visual fixation, for example, by videotape or motion picture would be included, as would any fixation in any storage medium.

Additionally, section 15 gives a performer an exclusivity to perform in public by telecommunication any unfixed performance. It is limited to a transmission by artificial guide, such as cable transmission. Transmissions by wireless radio waves are excluded.[93] Wired Internet media (telephone lines or high-speed access cable) seem to be included, but wireless Internet would be excluded as likely to constitute a transmission of "radio waves." The difficulty with the global reach of the Internet is that a transmission is likely to be a mixture of both wire-line (artificial guide) and wireless.

Common situations within section 15 include the performing of a performer's performance in public by cable through a television set, say in a club or bar; the transmission by wire to a sound system in a shopping mall (for example, background music); or the transmission of a performer's performance by wired telephone through a "caller on hold" system.[94]

No "arificial guide" limitation applies to the right to communicate any unfixed performance outside of a sound recording (for example, a "live" performance) to the public by telecommunication in any transmission by television, radio, or cable.[95] A performer's performance covered by section 15 and incorporated within a sound recording is subject

---

90   Section 26 was enacted as s. 14(01) by *WTOAIA*, above note 13, s. 58, and amended and renumbered as s. 26 by *Copyright Amendment Act, 1997*, above note 51, ss. 12 and 14.

91   Sections 15(1)(a) and 26(1)(a).

92   Section 15(1)(a)(iii).

93   Section 2 definition of "communication signal." Compare Chapter 2, Figure 2 and note 327 and accompanying text, regarding the expression "without artificial guide."

94   Compare *Telstra*, above note 53.

95   Section 15(1)(a)(i) and section 26(i)(a).

to a rental right of that sound recording in favour of the performer.[96] Sections 15 and 26 both include an authorization right within the scope of each provision.[97]

b) Sound Recordings

Section 18 protects "the maker" of a sound recording. The rights stipulated do not include transmission to the public by telecommunication or performance in public. However, the right to reproduce the sound recording in any material form is included and is the focus of the continuing battle between the recording industry and proponents of digitized file sharing of recordings.[98] This right is also significant to broadcasters in a context of the practice of making an ephemeral recording in the process of broadcasting a sound recording.[99]

c) Broadcaster's Communication Signals

A "communication signal" means "radio waves transmitted through space without any artificial guide, for reception by the public."[100] This encompasses both microwave and satellite transmissions.[101] The requirement that the signal be "to the public" will preclude encrypted signals to particular subscribers.[102] A broadcaster must be an operator of a broadcasting undertaking[103] lawfully operating in the country of its location. However, if the "primary activity" of the entity is retransmission then that entity is not included.[104] Cable retransmitters of television and radio broadcasts are therefore excluded. Television and radio stations are the primary beneficiaries. The broadcaster must, however,

---

96   Section 15(1)(c).

97   Sections 15(1) and 26(1).

98   See text accompanying notes 285–95, below in this chapter.

99   See *Bishop*, above note 7, discussed in the text accompanying notes 113ff., below in this chapter.

100 Section 2 definition of "communication signal," see above note 93.

101 See Chapter 2, note 327 and accompanying text, concerning the meaning to be given to the expression "without any artificial guide" and the inclusion within that phrase of "down links" or signals from a satellite to earth.

102 See Chapter 2, text accompanying notes 328–34, concerning the meaning of "to the public" in the related context of an unencrypted pay television signal that is *accessible* by the public constituting a signal "to the public" from the accessibility alone.

103 The expression "broadcasting undertaking" is not defined for the purpose of this provision of the *Copyright Act*, but the definition "broadcaster" requires that the broadcast communication signal be lawful. This would necessitate that the broadcaster comply with the provisions of the *Broadcasting Act*, above note 49 (see Chapter 2).

104 Section 2 definition of "broadcaster."

be located by its headquarters in Canada, a WTO member country, or member country of the *Rome Convention* at the time of the broadcast, which must occur from that country.[105]

The content or scope of the right involves a right to fix the communication signal; to reproduce any unauthorized fixation of the communication signal; to perform the communication signal "in a place open to the public on payment of an entrance fee"; to authorize any of the preceding three acts; and to authorize the retransmission of the communication signal to the public by another broadcaster "simultaneously with its broadcast."[106]

Typical broadcast situations to which this provision would apply include the showing of a television broadcast (say, of a popular sporting event) in a bar or club where patrons are charged a cover or entrance fee, or the unauthorized exchange of video or film clips between broadcasters. Significantly, an originating broadcaster can control the retransmission of its communication signal by another broadcaster simultaneously with that broadcaster's own broadcast signal. The policy objective is to prevent subsequent broadcasters from fusing their own broadcasts with those of the originator.

7) Ephemeral Recordings

Communications technology and copyright law have been intertwined from the advent of the printing press. The development of radio communication in the early twentieth century gave rise not only to the need for international agreements concerning the allocation of frequencies[107] but also to the economic or copyright interests in the communication. Although a copyright in a broadcaster's communication signal in itself was not afforded international treaty recognition until 1961, enacted in Canada from 1997,[108] the protection of works transmitted by radio communication was included in the *Berne Convention* as article 11*bis* and incorporated in Canadian copyright law from 1931.[109] Although

---

105 Section 21(2).

106 Section 21(1). With respect to the right to perform the communication signal "in a place open to the public on payment of an entrance fee" (s. 21(1)(d)), the federal Minister of Industry, by notice in the *Canada Gazette*, is enabled to deny such protection to any broadcaster headquartered in a *Rome Convention* or WTO country that the Minister believes does not itself grant such a right to broadcasters.

107 See Chapter 1.

108 See text accompanying notes 81 and 100–5, above in this chapter.

109 *Copyright Amendment Act, 1931*, above note 41 and accompanying text. See *Berne Convention* (Rome 1928), above note 11.

difficulties of interpretation that ensued in Canada were problematic with respect to musical works,[110] the international community had recognized the rights of copyright holders in works transmitted by radio-communication.

Technological development in radio broadcasting equipment, brought the addition of paragraph 3 to article 11*bis* in the *Berne Convention* (Brussels). This provision was designed to deal with broadcasting equipment *recording* before *communicating* a work to the public. The purpose was to ensure that permission for a work to be *communicated* to the public did not of itself imply permission to prerecord the work, even ephemerally. Any such prerecording would violate the *reproduction* right of copyright (section 3(1) as well as section 3(1)(d) "to make any sound recording . . . or other contrivance"), and each right of copyright is considered to stand separately and independently. After Brussels (1948) and with textual refinement in Paris (1971), article 11*bis*, paragraph 3, reads:

> (3) In the absence of any contrary stipulation, permission granted [to communicate a work to the public by telecommunication] shall not imply permission to record, by means of instruments recording sounds or images, the work broadcast. It shall, however, be a matter for legislation in the countries of the Union to determine the regulations for ephemeral recordings made by a broadcasting organization by means of its own facilities and used for its own broadcasts. The preservation of these recordings in official archives may, on the ground of their exceptional documentary character, be authorized by such legislation.[111]

Canada did not adhere to this provision until 1997.[112] In 1990, the Supreme Court of Canada in *Bishop v. Stevens*[113] considered whether the making of an ephemeral recording prior to broadcast would be included within a licence to broadcast the performance as part of that process in reliance on the standard practice in the industry. If not, would the granting of a licence to broadcast a performance carry an implied

---

110 See text accompanying notes 37–64, above in this chapter.

111 *Berne Convention*, above note 11, art. 11*bis*.

112 Section 91(a), inserted by the *Copyright Amendment Act, 1997*, above note 51, s. 50, secured the adherence of Canada to the *Berne Convention* as revised by the *Paris Act* of 1971, above note 11, thereby including the Brussels (1948) additions.

113 *Bishop*, above note 7 at 477.

consent to making an ephemeral recording, again relying on industry practice?[114]

Both questions were answered in the negative. The Court confirmed the separate and distinct nature of rights in copyright. The right of communication to the public in a broadcast is a "right to perform" and radiocommunication (now telecommunication) is within the definition of "performance" in the Act.[115] This is distinct from any right to record or "reproduce." Ordinarily, there can be no implied consent to the contrary. The particular licensing societies had jurisdiction to licence only a performance, not a reproduction.[116]

The Court declined to imply an exception as such would cause a loss of control over the work by a copyright owner once a recording or reproduction is made, in contrast to the position upon a mere public performance of the work, or, in this respect, to contemplate a judicially determined balancing of the respective interests.[117] The Court further acknowledged implementation of an international convention to be a legislative function, not to be achieved by judicial interpretation.[118]

The *Copyright Amendment Act, 1997* did respond to the question of ephemeral recordings enacting sections 30.8 and 30.9 of the *Copyright Act*.[119] These provisions provide a system of regulation. Section 30.8 enables an ephemeral fixation to be made of a performer's performance and an ephemeral reproduction to be made of a work (other than a cinematographic work), that is performed live or of a sound recording "that is performed at the same time as the performer's performance or [the performance of] the work." Section 30.9 enables an ephemeral reproduction of a sound recording (including "a performer's performance or work that is embodied in a sound recording") that is prerecorded.

Rights under section 30.8 may be exercised by a "programming undertaking," defined for the purpose of this provision as that under the *Broadcasting Act* (1991), including "distribution undertakings" under that Act (essentially cable retransmitters),[120] and a broadcast-

---

114   *Ibid.* at 485.
115   *Ibid.* at 477.
116   *Ibid.* at 486. For a reaffirmation of this approach, see *Canadian Wireless*, above note 39 at para. 15, concerning the separate rights of "reproduction" and "communication to the public by telecommunication."
117   *Ibid.* at 481–83.
118   *Ibid.* at 484.
119   *Copyright Amendment Act, 1997*, above note 51, s. 18.
120   Sections 30.8(1) and (11). See Chapter 2, Figure 2 and text accompanying notes 299–313, concerning "programming undertaking" and "distribution undertakings" under the *Broadcasting Act,* above note 49.

ing undertaking (as defined in the *Broadcasting Act* (1991))[121] within a network when the fixation or reproduction has been made by a programming undertaking within that network. Additionally, a programming undertaking must first hold a broadcasting licence issued by the CRTC under the *Broadcasting Act* (1991),[122] and second be authorized to communicate to the public by telecommunication a performance of the subject matter.[123] Several conditions are imposed,[124] including that a licence to make the fixation or reproduction is not available from a collective society.[125] The latter would afford a means of obtaining consent upon payment of an appropriate tariff.[126] This demonstrates the essential policy that royalty payments should be negotiated whenever possible.

Sections 30.8(2)–(7) provide the essential balance contemplated by article 11*bis*, paragraph 3, of the *Berne Convention*, reserving for member countries, as stated above, the right to regulate the making of recordings in this context, and to authorize "[t]he preservation of these recordings in official archives . . . on the ground of their exceptional documentary character. . . ."

It also reflects the discussion by the Supreme Court of Canada that a reproduction of a work (and similarly a fixation of a performer's performance) presents a loss of control by the copyright holder and increased facilitation of further infringement by the copier or others.[127] To balance the competing interests, the section stipulates that the fixation or recording can lawfully exist for only thirty days after it is made. Retention after this period may be authorized by the copyright holder. The fixation or recording may, however, be deposited in an archive as provided in the section without requiring authorization from the copy-

---

121 Section 30.8(9) and *ibid.* with respect to the meaning of "broadcasting undertaking" under the *Broadcasting Act, ibid.*

122 Section 30.8(11).

123 Sections 30.8(1) and (9). Note that a maker of a sound recording does not have a copyright to any performance or communication of the recording (s. 18(1)), but does have a right to prevent any reproduction in a material form (s. 18(1)(b)).

124 Section 30.8(1). The performer's performance of work must be "live" or, if in a sound recording, performed with a performance of the sound recording; the fixation or reproduction is to be made by the programming undertaking itself, for the purpose of its own broadcasts; the fixation or reproduction is not to be synchronized "with all or part of another recording"; the fixation or reproduction is not to be "used in an advertisement intended to sell or promote . . . a product, service, cause or institution."

125 Section 30.8(8).

126 The provision cannot reasonably be interpreted as allowing a reproduction if a licensing authority is available but refuses to grant a licence.

127 See text accompanying note 117, above in this chapter.

right holder. Otherwise, the programming undertaking must destroy the fixation or recording.[128] A record must be kept of the dates of the making and destruction and any other relevant information. Access to this record must be given to copyright holders or their representatives within twenty-four hours of a request.[129]

Archival deposits may be made to Library and Archives Canada or any provincial "official archive" established by provincial law. A fixation or reproduction may be deposited if the programming undertaking considers it to be "of an exceptional documentary character," and if the official archive consents. This consent will reflect to some extent the opinion of the official archive as to the qualifying nature of the fixation or reproduction.[130]

Section 30.9 concerns prerecorded sound recordings or a performer's performance or work embodied in the recordings.[131] Rights under this provision may be exercised by a broadcasting undertaking (as defined in the *Broadcasting Act* (1991)) holding a licence issued by the CRTC under that Act.[132] A prerecorded sound recording (or performer's performance or work embodied in the sound recording) may be reproduced if the broadcasting undertaking owns an authorized copy of the sound recording and is authorized to communicate it to the public by telecommunication.[133] Beyond this, the requirements and infrastructure of record keeping, access, and destruction are substantially the same as those under section 30.8.[134]

C. THE INTERNET

From 2002 to 2007, the Supreme Court of Canada gave judgment in six copyright-related proceedings, five of which involved significant developments in interpretation and application of copyright law in Can-

---

128 Section 30.8(4).

129 Sections 30.8(2) & (3).

130 Sections 30.8(6) & (7).

131 The expression "pre-recorded sound recording" refers to "a sound recording, or a performer's performance or work that is embodied in a sound recording" (s. 30.9(1)).

132 Section 30.9(7).

133 Sections 30.9(1)(a) & (b).

134 The thirty-day period with respect to reproductions of "pre-recorded recordings" does not apply if the broadcasting undertaking within that period ceases to possess the sound recording or copy of the performer's performance or work embodied in the sound recording. See s. 30.9(4).

ada.[135] One of these, *Society of Composers, Authors and Music Publishers of Canada v. Canadian Association of Internet Providers (Tariff 22)*, concerned the Internet and the telecommunication right in section 3(1) (f). Many other categories of copyright infringement can occur on the Internet.

Two primary locations should be considered for infringement purposes: the place of origin of the transmission and the place of receipt. At the former, the focus is on unauthorized uploading. At the latter, it is on unauthorized downloading or display. Other locations, such as "mirror sites" where a work or subject matter may be located, are also relevant.

1) The Place of Origin or Uploading

An unauthorized uploading of a work or other subject matter will inevitably constitute infringement by reproduction. The digitized version of the item now on a website is an additional copy in a material form,[136] even if the site is not accessed by a user. Uploading an unpublished work or sound recording may infringe the right "to publish" the work or subject matter. This may be broader than, but is at least inclusive of, the meaning of "publication" in sections 2.2(1)(a) (works) and (b) (sound recordings)[137] as requiring the making available of copies of a work or sound recording to the public for the first time. For a work, section 5(1)(c)(i) specifies that these available copies must be in a sufficient quantity "as to satisfy the reasonable demands of the public" assessed in the context of the nature of the work.[138] No similar requirement is specified for a sound recording. Unlike television or radio transmissions, which are performance focused, the presentation of a work on the Internet causes a copy to be made in the random access memory

---

135 *Théberge*, above note 8; *CCH* (SCC), above note 8; *Tariff 22* (SCC), above note 5; *Robertson v. Thomson Corp.*, 2006 SCC 43, [2006] 2 S.C.R. 399; and *Euro-Excellence Inc.*, above note 8. A further decision was *Desputeaux c. Éditions Chouette (1987) Inc.*, 2003 SCC 17, [2003] 1 S.C.R. 178, involving arbitration in an intellectual property context.

136 See *Apple Computer, Inc. v. Mackintosh Computers Ltd.*, [1990] 2 S.C.R. 209 [*Apple Computer*] (finding a digitized "machine language" version of a computer program to constitute a reproduction of the source code of the program). In *Théberge*, ibid. at para. 42, the S.C.C. found that an additional copy must be produced in order to constitute an infringement by "reproduction."

137 Sections 3(1) and 18(1)(a). See text accompanying notes 33 and 34, above in this chapter.

138 Sections 2.2(1)(a) and 5(1)(c)(i).

(RAM)[139] of the receiving or accessor's computer, and provides the capacity to download or to print. A "publication" therefore appears to be feasible simply by making a work available on an Internet website.

However, in defining publication, section 2.2(1)(c) excludes "the communication to the public by telecommunication" of a work or sound recording; if section 2.2 (defining "publication") is seen to control the meaning of the economic right "to publish," a literal application of this exclusion may preclude the possibility of publication by the Internet, or by any other electromagnetic system, such as a facsimile.[140] However, electronic publication is widespread and is entirely contemplated as an essential publication means.[141] An interpretation that allows this to be achieved is to read these exclusions as concerning only "performance," "display," or "exhibition," which would not afford the ability to make a copy. Television and radio transmissions fall into this category and were no doubt the intended object of this exclusion. The dimension of the Internet that allows copies to be taken should present a sufficient distinction.[142] A consequence of this, however, might be the obsolescence of the qualifying requirements for receiving copyright protection. Protection is granted on the basis of either an author being a citizen or subject of, or being ordinarily resident in, a treaty country,[143] or to have first published the work in a treaty country regardless of citizenship or residency.[144] If merely placing a work on the Internet can constitute publication by the ability of an accessor to make a copy, then publication within a treaty country will be automatic.

The position may also be influenced by the interpretation to be given to the communication right. The current position in Canada is to deny a communication upon simply making a work or subject matter available for accessing. Arguably, however, the two categories are distinct. The Act expressly stipulates "making available" as the essence

---

139 RAM is temporary storage for the duration of the connection only.

140 See the meaning of "telecommunication" in s. 2.

141 See Information Highway Advisory Council Secretariat (IHAC), *Copyright and the Information Highway*, Final Report of the Copyright Sub-committee (Ottawa: IHAC, 1995) at 10–11 [IHAC Report]; and Michel Racicot *et al.*, *The Cyberspace is Not a "No Law Land": A Study of the Issues of Liability for Content Circulating on the Internet* (Ottawa: Industry Canada, 1997) at 227, online: www.ic.gc.ca/epic/site/smt-gst.nsf/vwapj/1603118e.pdf/$FILE/1603118e.pdf.

142 See Racicot *et al.*, *ibid.* at 226, discussing briefly whether availability on the Internet may amount to a "distribution" under s. 42(1)(c) with consequent criminal liability.

143 Section 5(1)(a).

144 Section 5(1)(c).

of publication.[145] This is exclusively an action of the uploader or supplier. There is no requirement of advertising or informing prospective acquirers of the availability of the work.[146] However, with respect to a "communication" (section 3(1)(f)), emphasis has been placed on there being at least two persons, a sender and a receiver. The recognition in the 1996 *WIPO Copyright Treaty*[147] of infringement by "making available" has not to date been legislatively implemented but has received support in Canadian studies.[148] The distinction was emphasized by the Copyright Board of Canada in *Tariff 22*.[149] However, once accessed, the communication would be complete even if the accessor did not use, play, or view the material, and the communicator is the person who uploaded the material and who has taken "all the required steps to make the work available for communication," bringing responsibility to the uploading person for transmissions not only from the source but also from any cache or "mirror" server.[150] This interpretation was seemingly approved by the Federal Court of Appeal[151] but was not discussed by the Supreme Court of Canada.[152]

There is, therefore, little practical difference between making available a work by posting to a website and having communicated the work once it is accessed by a user. A proposition that an actual transmission comprises a "packet" of data rather than a musical work or a performance of a musical work was rejected. The data transmission, once "reassembled," enables the performance or copying to occur.[153] This conclusion is supported by the statutory meaning of telecommunication as including "intelligence of any nature."[154]

---

145 Section 2.2(1)(a)(i).

146 Text accompanying note 34, above in this chapter.

147 *WIPO Copyright Treaty* (1996), 36 I.L.M. 65, art. 8, online: www.wipo.int/treaties/en/ip/wct/trtdocs_wo033.html [WCT].

148 See IHAC Report, above note 141 at 11; and Racicot *et al.*, above note 141 at 210–22.

149 *Statement of Royalties to be collected for the Performance or the Communication by Telecommunication, in Canada, of Musical or Dramatico-Musical Works (Tariff 22 — Transmission of Musical Works to Subscribers Via a Telecommunications Service Not Covered under Tariff Nos. 16 or 17)* (27 October 1999), 1 C.P.R. (4th) 417, Part IIIB (Copyright Board), online: www.cb-cda.gc.ca/ [*Tariff 22* (Copyright Bd.)].

150 *Ibid.*, Part IIIC at para. 1.

151 *Society of Composers, Authors and Music Publishers of Canada v. Canadian Association of Internet Providers*, 2002 FCA 166, [*Tariff 22* (FCA)].

152 *Tariff 22* (SCC), above note 5.

153 *Tariff 22* (Copyright Bd.), above note 149, Part IIIA at para. 5; and *Tariff 22* (FCA), above note 151 at paras. 13 and 26.

154 Section 2 definition of "telecommunication."

Accessing by even one person will constitute a communication "to the public" if the posting was intended for the public.[155] Point-to-point e-mail is probably not a communication to the public if it is confined between specifically identified persons, such as a limited group of interconnected persons.[156] This may, however, depend on the nature of the group and the qualification for joining. For example, an electronic newsletter made available to any person who wishes to subscribe would be "to the public" even if prior registration and passcodes are utilized. The recipients would be in the nature of a public audience to the copyright holder. This is the classic test for determining the related issue of performance "in public" under section 3(1).[157] The broader meaning of the expression "to the public" compared with that of the expression "in public" is discussed earlier in the context of broadcasts.[158] The High Court of Australia has similarly emphasized the commercial setting and the nature of the copyright owner's audience in a context of the playing of music to telephone callers placed on hold.[159] Likewise, recall the transmission to subscribers of ringtones stored for this purpose by a wireless cellphone provider.[160] The consistency of this situation with that under the *Broadcasting Act* (1991) has been noted.[161]

An unauthorized uploading is unlikely to cause the uploader to infringe by a *performance in public*. Despite the finding in 1993 by the Federal Court of Appeal that cable television operators were performing in public the musical works that were being transmitted to subscribers,[162] section 2.3 precludes finding a performance in public from the mere act of transmitting a work to the public by telecommunication.[163] Perhaps more than a mere act of transmission to the public is involved in an Internet context, given that the uploading necessarily involves a repro-

---

155   Compare radio, television, and cable signals, which are transmissions whether or not a listener or viewer activates the receiving apparatus. See *CCTA v. Copyright Board*, above note 52 at 155 (F.C.).

156   See IHAC Report, above note 141 at 10; *CCH* (SCC), above note 8 at paras. 77–79.

157   See *Jennings*, above note 32 at 416–17 (Romer LJ) and 418–21 (Greene LJ). The passage from Romer LJ was applied in *Canadian Admiral*, above note 19 at 405–7 (Ex. C.R.).

158   See text accompanying notes 52–61, above in this chapter.

159   *Telstra*, above note 53 at 657–59 and 698 (A.L.R.).

160   See *Canadian Wireless*, above note 39 and text accompanying notes 56–59, above in this chapter.

161   See text accompanying note 55, above in this chapter. See also Racicot *et al.*, above note 141 at 220–21.

162   *CTA v. Copyright Board*, above note 52.

163   Section 2.3 is set out, above note 64.

duction of the works in question. However, any presentation in public (say, playing in a bar to patrons) at the place of receipt is more likely to be at the instance of the accessor. Historically, the meaning of "performance" has been limited to *acoustic* presentation or visual depiction of "dramatic action" or a "dramatic work,"[164] but from 1997 any visual depiction has been sufficient.[165]

Infringement by *authorization* is significant in an Internet context. The relative anonymity of identity and location of a user is contrasted with the identifiable presence of Internet intermediaries or centralized host sites. This has caused the authorization right to present considerable prospects to copyright holders. The scope of liability by authorization has been considered by the Supreme Court of Canada in *CCH Canadian Ltd. v. Law Society of Upper Canada* (CCH) and *Tariff 22* and is discussed later.[166]

Some additional rights may be applicable. The making of a sound recording or a cinematograph and the exhibition right deserve some attention. Essential elements of a sound recording in the Act are "a recording, fixed in any material form, consisting of sounds, whether or not a performance of a work."[167] The digitization of a musical work for transmission on the Internet (e.g., MP3 audio disc compression)[168] may well constitute a sound recording and thereby infringe the right of the owner of the musical work to make any sound recording.[169] Likewise,

---

164 Prior to 1994, the definition of "performance" referred to any "dramatic action" as the visual component. In 1994, this requirement was amended to "dramatic work" by *North American Free Trade Agreement Implementation Act, 1993*, S.C. 1993, c. 44, s. 53(2) [*NAFTA Implementation Act*].

165 The current definition of "performance" in s. 2, amended by *Copyright Amendment Act, 1997*, s. 1(2), refers to "any acoustic or visual representation of a work" or other subject matter including "a representation made by means of any mechanical instrument, radio receiving set or television receiving set."

166 *CCH* (SCC), above note 8; *Tariff 22* (FCA), above note 151. See text accompanying notes 234–38, below in this chapter.

167 Section 2 definition of "sound recording"; the sound track of a cinematographic work is excluded "where it accompanies the cinematographic work."

168 The expression "MP3" refers to a digital video compression standard developed by an expert group known as the Moving Picture Expert Group (MPEG) of the International Organization for Standardization (ISO) and the International Telecommunication Union (ITU), international organizations establishing international communications standards. The MP3 standard compresses audio or visual data. The MPEG Audio Layer 3 standard compresses audio data by a 12:1 ratio, enabling substantial *quantitative* transmission with CD quality sound. See Alan Freedman, *Computer Desktop Encyclopedia*, 2d ed. (New York: American Management Association, 1999) s.v. "MP3."

169 Section 3(1)(d).

any digitization and transmission of a visual presentation may infringe the owner's right to make a cinematographic work, especially after the meaning of this category was extended with effect from 1994 to include "any work *expressed* by any process analogous to cinematography."[170]

The right to present an artistic work "at a public exhibition, for a purpose other than sale or hire"[171] may be infringed by an Internet display of such works.[172] This provision, however, is narrow. It does not mirror the "right to display in public" in the United States.[173] A specific event of public exhibition — a virtual art exhibition as opposed to a display in public — is needed.

Rental rights of sound recordings[174] or computer programs[175] and importation rights[176] have been said to be inapplicable to the medium of the Internet, attributing a physical perspective to these rights and requiring the transfer of the rented or imported copy rather than the making of an additional digitized copy for transmission with the original remaining at the point of origin.[177] However, a wider interpretation may be more appropriate to embrace changing technology.

2) The Place of Receipt

The most likely infringement by an accessor or receiver is reproduction.[178] This is clear in the case of downloading to a hard drive or disk or any printing. It is an additional copy "in a material form."[179] There

---

170 Section 2 definition of "cinematograph" [emphasis added] inserted by *NAFTA Implementation Act*, above note 164, s. 53(2). Prior to 1994, the focus was not upon how the work was *expressed* but how it was *produced*. This narrower concept emphasized exposure of a negative to light and chemical processing, not an electromagnetic or digitized process.

171 Section 3(1)(g). The work must be created after 7 June 1988. A map, chart, or plan is excluded.

172 See IHAC Report, above note 141 at 11.

173 *Copyright Act 1976*, 90 Stat. 2541, 17 U.S.C. § 106(5). Section 101 defines "display" of a work as "mean[ing] to show a copy of it, either directly or by means of a film, slide, television image or other device or process." See US Patent and Trademark Office, *Intellectual Property and the National Information Infrastructure*, Report of the Working Group on Intellectual Property Rights (Washington, DC: US Patent and Trademark Office, 1995) (Chair: Bruce A. Lehman) at 72.

174 Section 3(1)(i).

175 Section 3(1)(h).

176 Sections 27(2)(e), 27(1), and 44–45.

177 See IHAC Report, above note 141 at 12.

178 Sections 3(1) (works) and 18(1)(b) (sound recordings).

179 See *Apple Computer*, above note 136, where the S.C.C. found a digitized "machine language" version of a computer program to amount to a "reproduction" of the source code version of the program.

may be issues with respect to the parameter of the work in order to establish an infringement. If the component files on a website are determined to be one overall work (like a book with chapters) by the same author, then the boundaries demarcating the work may be those of the website as a whole, thereby lessening the likelihood of one or two downloaded frames constituting "a substantial part" of the work.[180] However, if component files or frames in a website are written as separate pieces (like poems in a published collection) and are written or drawn by different persons, then the website is likely to involve a copyright in each component part as a distinct and separate work. The overall website may be a collective work or a compilation.[181] The content and depictions on a screen will be protected as a manifestation of the underlying program. However, a screen display might also attract an artistic copyright distinct from that of the underlying literary work.[182]

3) Moral Rights

Moral rights were noted earlier.[183] Essentially European in origin, international recognition was provided in article 6bis of the *Berne Convention*, and this minimum level was enacted in Canadian law in 1931.[184] The current format and content were prescribed in 1988.[185] The bicultural nature of Canadian jurisprudence, of French civil law and English common law, has enabled Canada to be seen as "bridge between the approach to moral rights in common law and civil law systems."[186] Inherent within this comment is the ambivalence of com-

---

180 Section 3(1) gives "the sole right to produce or reproduce the work *or any substantial part thereof* in any material form" [emphasis added]. The element of "substantiality" has both a *quantitative* and a *qualitative* dimension. Qualitative factors are more significant, but the two dimensions are inseparable. Other factors are also considered, including the relative effort between the parties in preparing their respective works and impact on the plaintiff's market. See David Vaver, *Intellectual Property Law* (Concord, ON: Irwin Law, 1997) at 80–83; and Barry B. Sookman, *Sookman Computer Law: Acquiring and Protecting information Technology*, looseleaf (Toronto: Carswell, 1989) (updated to 2010) at paras. 3-7(a) and 3-189ff.

181 See s. 2 for the meaning of these expressions.

182 See Vaver, above note 34 at 27–28.

183 See text accompanying notes 26–30, above in this chapter.

184 *Berne Convention* (Rome 1928), above note 11; *Copyright Amendment Act, 1931*, above note 41, s. 12 and Sch. A; *Copyright Act*, R.S.C. 1970, c. C-30, s. 12(7); and *Copyright Act*, above note 4, ss. 14(1), 14(2), 28(1), & 28(2).

185 *Copyright Amendment Act, 1988*, R.S.C. 1985 (4th Supp.), c. 10, ss. 4, 6, and 8.

186 Gerald Dworkin, "Moral Rights in the Common Law Countries" in *The Moral Right of the Author, Association littéraire et artistique internationale* (Paris: ALAI,

mon law jurisdictions to the recognition of moral rights. Historically, common law jurisdictions have claimed that common law principles, presented in various torts and *ad hoc* statutory provisions, are sufficient to meet obligations under article *6bis* of the *Berne Convention*.[187] Express moral rights provisions are of recent origin in, for example, the United Kingdom,[188] New Zealand,[189] and Australia.[190] In the United States, federal statutory moral rights protection is available only for "works of visual art," being static art works.[191] This divergence of ideology accentuates the difficulties presented in systems of global, digitized, and decentralized communication.

The moral right most applicable in a digitized context is the right to the integrity of the work. It concerns the manipulation and alteration ("distortion, mutilation or other modification") of a work, or the use of a work "in association with a product, service, cause or institution."[192] The essence of digitization is the capacity to make changes. The public interest in utilizing this capacity has caused some contemplation of whether moral rights ought to apply to digitized works.[193] There is no reason in principle to deny an application of moral rights to authors with respect to digitized or Internet-related media. No consent or waiver of moral rights should be implied by reason alone of an Internet or digitized context. An alteration or distortion or an involuntary use of an author's work to promote a "product, service, cause or institution" cannot be said to be integrally linked to the operational process of the Internet and is likely to be the very last thing an author wants. The requirement that any modification or usage be "to the prejudice of the honour or reputation of the author"[194] is seen as sufficient to set a balance between the right of an author to the integrity of the work and a public interest in a utilization of the work.[195]

Moral rights in Canada lack significant judicial analysis and are subject to many uncertainties. For example, do moral rights extend beyond physical modifications to the *original* work to encompass a re-

---

1994), Congress of Antwerp 19–24 September 1993 (Paris: ALAI, 1993) at 93.

187   *Ibid.* at 83–84.

188   Enacted in 1988, *Copyright Designs and Patents Act 1988* (U.K.), 1988, c. 48, ss. 77–89.

189   *Copyright Act 1994* (N.Z.), 1994/143, ss. 94–110.

190   *Copyright Act 1968* (Cth.), ss. 189–195, as am. by *Copyright Amendment (Digital Agenda Act) 2000* (Cth.).

191   *Visual Artists Rights Act of 1990*, 17 U.S.C. § 106A (1990).

192   Sections 28(2)(1)(a) & (b).

193   See IHAC Report, above note 141 at 18–20.

194   Section 28(2)(1).

195   See *Théberge*, above note 8 at paras. 57 and 60.

flection on this work by an alteration or modification to a copy of the original? Many digitized works will be a copy of an original. If an original is unaffected, to what extent is there liability for alterations to the digitized copy? The Information Highway Advisory Council (IHAC) Copyright Sub-committee found this to be of significance in the context of digitization of paintings, sculptures or engravings, for which prejudice is deemed to have occurred upon any alteration or modification in itself.[196] The Sub-committee recommended legislative amendment to ensure that any deeming of prejudice be limited to interference with the original.[197] Second, does a non-physical distortion, such as to the theme of a work, constitute an infringement?[198] Third, what is the scope and relevance of any subjective opinion of the author when determining the likelihood of prejudice to that author's honour and reputation? Initially, considerable but not absolute weight was given to an author's subjective opinion.[199] More recently, a greater balance with objective perspectives has been applied.[200]

Moral rights are rights of the author of a work, often seen as inherently personal.[201] An author is ordinarily the first owner of the copyright (economic rights),[202] but not necessarily so. The work may have been prepared in the course of employment, in which case the copyright owner is the employer and the employee is the holder of moral rights.[203] Similarly, the copyright (economic rights) may have been assigned, for example to a publisher.[204] As mentioned earlier in this chapter, moral

---

196 Section 28(2)(2) noted in the IHAC Report, above note 141 at 19.

197 The Sub-committee considered the policy behind the statutory deeming of prejudice to be the public interest in the preservation of art, *ibid.*

198 See *Pollock v. CFCN Productions Ltd.* (1983), 26 Alta. L.R. (2d) 93 at 95–96 (Q.B.) (subsequently settled).

199 See *Snow v. The Eaton Centre Ltd.* (1982), 70 C.P.R. (2d) 105 at 106 (Ont. H.C.) [*Snow*] referring to "a certain subjective element or judgment on the part of the author so long as it is reasonably arrived at."

200 See *Prise de parole Inc. v. Guérin Éditeur Ltée* (1995), 66 C.P.R. (3d) 257 at 265 (F.C.T.D.) finding, in addition to any subjective evaluation, "an objective evaluation of the prejudice based on public or expert opinion."

201 Section 14.1(1). See David Vaver, "Authors' Moral Rights – Reform Proposals in Canada: Charter or Barter of Rights for Creators?" (1987) 25 Osgoode Hall L.J. 749 at 752–54, attributing the philosophy of moral rights to Kant and Hegel. From this perspective, moral rights reflect the author's personality or personal identity. Vaver has further suggested an economic dimension to moral rights. See David Vaver, "Can Intellectual Property Be Taken to Satisfy a Judgment Debt?" (1991) 6 B.F.L.R. 255 at 279.

202 Section 13(1).

203 Section 13(3).

204 Section 13(4).

rights cannot be assigned or transferred *inter vivos* but may be waived in particular instances,[205] and may pass to beneficiaries upon death.[206]

Moral rights are limited to "works."[207] They have no application to "other subject matter": neighbouring rights of a performer's performance, a sound recording, or a broadcaster's communication signal.[208] The term of moral rights protection is the same as for economic rights,[209] and the infringement of moral rights will invoke substantially the same remedies as for the infringement of economic rights.[210]

4) Neighbouring Rights/Other Subject Matter

The nature and scope of neighbouring rights has been described in the context of television and radio broadcast signals.[211] While there has not yet been a judicial interpretation of the scope of these rights in an Internet context, Internet transmissions can fall within the rights granted specifically to each category of subject matter. Examples include an Internet communication of an unfixed performer's performance; fixation of a performer's performance in an MP3 compression transmission as a sound recording[212] or any visual compression transmission, being a fixation in a material form;[213] and the reproduction by uploading or downloading of a sound recording.[214] Broadcast communication signal rights[215] are defined as meaning "radio waves transmitted through space without artificial guide, for reception by the public."[216] This covers television and radio broadcasts by microwave and satellite transmission,[217]

---

205 Sections 14.1(2)–(4).

206 Sections 14.2(2) & (3).

207 Section 14.1(1) grants moral rights to "[t]he author of a work."

208 See, however, Bill C-60, *An Act to amend the Copyright Act*, 1st Sess., 38th Parl, 2005, cl. 9 [Bill C-60]; Bill C-61, *An Act to amend the Copyright Act*, 2nd Sess., 39th Parl., 2008, cl. 8 [Bill C-61]; and Bill C-32, *An Act to amend the Copyright Act*, 3d Sess., 40th Parl., 2010, cl. 10 [Bill C-32], providing for moral rights to be available to performers' performances.

209 Section 14.2(1).

210 Section 34(2). Statutory damages (s. 38(1)) are available only to a copyright owner and relate to only infringement of economic rights.

211 See text accompanying notes 100ff., above in this chapter.

212 Sections 15 and 26.

213 Section 15(1)(a)(iii).

214 Section 18.

215 Section 21.

216 Section 2.

217 See Chapter 2, Figure 2 and note 327 and accompanying text. See also note 93, above in this chapter.

and to the extent that Internet transmissions are by wireless radio wave, an Internet broadcaster would be included.[218]

Internet broadcasting is likely to infringe several of the rights of the original broadcaster of the communications signal that is received and retransmitted by an operator of an Internet site. The original broadcaster, and the "communication signal" itself, must meet the qualifying criteria to gain protection under this right.[219] Ordinarily, television and radio stations broadcasting by microwave or satellite signals to the public will qualify. First, when a broadcast communication signal is received by the Internet site operator, a digitized copy of the signal is made. This infringes the *right to fix* the communication signal.[220] Second, only the broadcaster of the communication signal can *reproduce* the unauthorized fixation.[221] Accordingly, any subsequent reproduction in an Internet context, say on uploading or on downloading by an accessor, would infringe the broadcaster's copyright in the communication signal. Third, if the operator of the Internet site is itself considered to be "broadcasting" and thereby transmitting a "broadcast" signal of its own, any interpolation in this signal of the original broadcaster's communication signal may infringe the broadcaster's right to authorize a retransmission of its signal simultaneously with the broadcast signal of another.[222] Fourth (and subject to specific exemptions), if the original signal of the broadcaster is a television signal,[223] any accessibility of this signal through an Internet retransmission "in a place open to the public on payment of an entrance fee" (such as an entertainment setting, conference, or classroom) would constitute an infringement as amounting to a performance of the broadcaster's signal in such a location.[224]

In addition, a broadcaster has an overall *right to authorize* the first, second, and fourth situations noted above. This may be of some significance in establishing liability against a third-party intermediary.[225]

---

218 For example, a broadcast such as presented in the proceedings in early 2000 involving the "iCrave TV" retransmission from a Canadian website of broadcast microwave signals received from the United States. See *iCraveTV*, above note 80.

219 See text accompanying notes 100ff., above in this chapter.

220 Section 21(1)(a). This provision does not specify the need for fixation "in any material form," but this may be implied.

221 Section 21(1)(b).

222 Section 21(1)(c).

223 The term "television" is not specifically defined in the *Copyright Act*.

224 Section 21(1)(d).

225 With respect to third-party intermediaries, see text accompanying notes 244ff., below in this chapter.

5) The Authorization Right

The availability of an authorization right or, in the United States, a concept of common law contributory infringement,[226] assumes substantial importance in Internet transmissions, for which the direct infringer is not ordinarily identifiable and may be located extraterritorially with the attendant jurisdictional difficulties.[227] The ability to fix liability on an intermediary, identifiable and possibly present within the territorial jurisdiction, is attractive. This was illustrated effectively in the 2001 *A & M Records, Inc., v. Napster, Inc.* proceeding, in which despite efforts to depict the centralized music exchange site as a system operated by users, sufficient facilitation occurred centrally to warrant Napster, Inc.'s liability as a contributor.[228]

The conceptual difficulty lies in determining when the acts or omissions of the alleged authorizer are sufficient to constitute an independent infringement. Within the Commonwealth there is a spectrum of formulation. In England, a narrow test requires that the authorizer must have, or purport to have, authority to make the authorization.[229] An Australian test is broad and expansive, reflecting mere facilitation through control over the means of infringement, or the party directly infringing, and with knowledge that infringement is occurring, but with insufficient action to prevent the infringement.[230] In Canada, in *de Tervagne v. Beloeil*, a middle formulation was articulated,[231] but doubt remained from earlier decisions in the Supreme Court of Canada[232] and

---

226 An "authorization right" does exist in the United States. See *Copyright Act 1976*, above note 173, s. 106 providing "the owner of copyright . . . has the exclusive rights to *and to authorize* any of the following [enumerated rights]" [emphasis added]; and Aden Allen, "What's in a Copyright? The Forgotten Right 'To Authorize'" (2008) 9 Colum. Sci. & Tech. L. Rev. 87, online: www.str.org/volumes/volume-ix-2007-2008/allen/. Ordinarily, however, indirect liability of third parties is actionable under a theory of tortuous "contributory infringement." See Melville B. Nimmer & David Nimmer, *Nimmer on Copyright*, looseleaf, vol. 3 (New York: Matthew Bender, 1996) ss. 1204[A][1] & [2] (re the "authorization right") & [3] (re "contributory infringement").

227 See Chapter 6.

228 *A & M Records, Inc., v. Napster, Inc.*, 239 F.3d 1004 at 1027 (9th Cir. 2001).

229 See Whitford J in *CBS Inc. v. Ames Records & Tapes Ltd.*, [1981] 2 All E.R. 812 at 821 (Ch.), approved in *CBS Songs Ltd. v. Amstrad Consumer Electronics Plc.*, [1988] 1 A.C. 1013 (H.L.).

230 See *University of New South Wales v. Moorhouse* (1975), 6 A.L.R. 193 (H.C.A.) [*Moorhouse*]; and *RCA Corp. v. John Fairfax & Son Ltd.*, [1982] R.P.C. 91 at 100 (N.S.W.S.C.).

231 See *de Tervagne v. Beloeil*, [1993] 3 F.C. 227 at 239–41 (T.D.), where Joyal J expressly rejects both the English and Australian formulations [*de Tervagne*].

232 *Muzak*, above note 5 at 189, 192, and 197.

the Privy Council on appeal from Canada.[233] The latter had emphasized the criterion of control, presenting a broader perspective. The former concerned primarily service *ex juris*, but included a discussion of authorization in terms closer to the English test.

The current position is reflected in the judgments of the Supreme Court of Canada in *CCH* and *Tariff 22* as an apparent middle position, but still with a measure of uncertainty. In *CCH*, the Court rejected the Australian approach as too broad and inconsistent with earlier Canadian and British decisions.[234] The Court, however, appears to accept *de Tervagne*, which had rejected both the Australian and the English formulations.[235] In *Tariff 22*, the Supreme Court emphasized relational and control features, considerably removed from the narrow English test.[236] A reconciliation with *CCH* is based on the criterion of *knowledge*. Infringement was only a possibility in *CCH*, but should actual notice be given to an intermediary then its failure to respond may establish sufficient indifference to constitute authorization.[237] This result and formulation is closer to the earlier rejected Australian approach. The knowledge criterion in *Tariff 22* led the Court to reflect upon a "notice and take down" process for Internet intermediaries, especially ISPs, that exists elsewhere.[238]

6) An Intent to Infringe

In the United States, the focus on contributory infringement at common law, as opposed to an application of a principle of authorization within the statute itself, has led to a distinction between an *imputed* intent to enable infringement and an *actual* intent to do so. In the latter situation, a provider of an infringing means is liable for contributory infringement even if the means encompasses substantial non-infringing uses.[239] The absence of evidence of intent focuses the inquiry on

---

233 *Vigneux v. Canadian Performing Right Society*, [1945] A.C. 108 (P.C.).

234 See *CCH* (SCC), above note 8 at para. 41. The Australian test (*Moorhouse*, above note 230) had been applied by the Federal Court of Appeal majority in *CCH Canadian Ltd. v. Law Society of Upper Canada* (2002), 212 D.L.R. (4th) 385 at para. 114 [*CCH* (FCA)].

235 *de Tervagne*, above note 231, was accepted in *CCH* (SCC), *ibid.* at para. 38.

236 *Tariff 22* (SCC), above note 5 at para. 122.

237 *Ibid.* at paras. 126 & 127.

238 *Ibid.* at para. 127. See text accompanying note 285, below in this chapter.

239 *Metro-Goldwyn-Mayer Studios Inc., v. Grokster, Ltd.*, 545 U.S. 913 (2005). On this issue Souter J gave judgment for a unanimous Supreme Court.

the substantiality of non-infringing uses.[240] Canadian law has not developed any similarly focused principles at common law with respect to copyright infringement. Yet while the position is trite that mere supply of equipment or means is not in itself authorization of infringement,[241] an *actual intent* to infringe through supply of the means of infringement could well constitute authorization in a manner similar to a provider of a means receiving notice of an infringing activity within the provider's power to control.[242] Bill C-32 (2010)[243] would provide in this regard by inserting in the *Copyright Act*, sections 27(2.3) & (2.4), a new ground of secondary infringement that will occur should a person provide an Internet or other digitized service that the person "knows or should have known is designed primarily to enable acts of copyright infringement" if such an infringement is attributable to that service and occurs by the Internet or other digitized means (section 27(2.3)). Section 27(2.4) provides factors to consider in reaching this determination.

7) Liability of Intermediaries

Intermediaries include, first, an ISP, being an entity that provides access to the Internet by supplying to a user a software package that will connect the user's computer, through the user's modem, to an Internet browser service; and, second, the proprietor or operator of a website that receives information or material uploaded or supplied by others through a process it provides. Although the present context is that of copyright, other areas of civil liability, including defamation and privacy infringement, might be rationalized in this way with respect to concurrent liability.[244]

The infringement provisions of the *Copyright Act* were reformulated in 1997.[245] Section 27 provides for primary and secondary infringement. A primary infringement involves a person doing without consent any of the exclusive statutory rights given to the copyright owner.[246]

---

240 With respect to this issue, contrast the diverging opinions of Ginsburg J (concurred in by Rehnquist CJ and Kennedy J) (*ibid.* at 942–49) and Breyer J (concurred in by Stevens and O'Connor JJ), *ibid.* at 949–66.

241 See *de Tervagne*, above note 231 at 236–47 (F.C.R.) for a comprehensive review of the historical authorities in this context in both Canada and the United Kingdom.

242 See text accompanying notes 237–38, above in this chapter.

243 See Bill C-32, above note 208, cl. 18.

244 See Racicot *et al.*, above note 141 at 33–109 and 124–99.

245 *Copyright Amendment Act, 1997*, above note 51, s. 15, repealing and substituting *Copyright Act*, s. 27.

246 Section 27(1).

This provision is therefore linked directly with the economic rights of copyright as set out in section 3 (for "works") and sections 15, 18, 21, and 26 (for "other subject-matter" or neighbouring rights). Secondary infringement is focused on specified activities performed with a copy of a work or other subject matter. An infringer must, or should, know that the copy being dealt with is an infringing copy. If the copy has been made outside of Canada, it will still constitute an infringing copy if it would have infringed copyright had it been made by the copier in Canada. This element of knowledge is not a requirement of primary infringement.[247]

An intermediary is potentially liable for both primary and secondary infringement. Authorizing another to infringe copyright, as discussed earlier, is an exclusive right of the copyright owner. When done by someone else it constitutes primary infringement. Additionally, if the intermediary has become too closely involved in the uploading process, or in the material content, it may be liable as a concurrent or (if there is a common design) a joint tortfeasor[248] infringer of an exclusive right of the copyright owner. The expression "content-neutral" was utilized by the Supreme Court in *Tariff* 22 to demarcate activities as a conduit of the message from the provision of the message itself.[249] The Court distinguished an embedded hypertext link, for which activation is automatic without any "clicking" by a user, from a link required to be activated by the user. The former would cause the provider of the link to move into content; the latter would not.[250] The Copyright Board found the provision of content to include having a business relationship with the uploader or content provider, moderating a news group, creating a cache for reasons beyond simply improvement of performance of the system, modifying the content of cached material, or interfering with the means of obtaining information about the number of "accesses" or "hits" to cached material.[251]

The position is further illustrated by two cases from the United States. In the first, an ISP and a bulletin board operator were found

---

247 See, however, s. 39, providing that if an infringer "was not aware and had no reasonable ground for suspecting" the existence of copyright in the work or other subject matter, and the copyright is not registered, then the only remedy that may be granted to a copyright owner is an injunction.

248 See Chapter 3, text accompanying notes 103–5, discussing the distinction between "joint" and "concurrent" tortfeasors and noting that joint tortfeasors are "responsible for the same tort," whereas concurrent tortfeasors commit separate torts but cause the same damage.

249 *Tariff* 22 (SCC), above note 5 at para. 92.

250 *Ibid.* at para. 25.

251 *Tariff* 22 (Copyright Bd.), above note 149, Part III(c)(3) at para. 134.

not to have infringed copyright for temporary storage on a website of infringing material uploaded by others. The defendants were mere conduits selling *access* to the Internet.[252] In the second, the website operator provided adult-oriented images for a subscription fee. It obtained fresh supplies of images by joining "news groups" from which it received digital files of new images. It was found liable for direct infringement because it had taken "affirmative steps to cause the copies to be made" and was selling *images*, not access.[253]

The liability of an intermediary for primary copyright infringement (including infringement by authorization) will affect website owners rather than ISPs, which would rarely do more than merely provide access.

As for secondary infringement, sections 27(2)(a) and (c) (and therefore (d), which is predicated on (a) and (c)) require that a secondary infringer have some trade or commercial purpose concerning the copy of the work or other subject matter and its sale or hire, including the distribution, exposure, or offering for sale or hire. This would encompass a website selling images. Section 27(2)(c) is broader, by the phrase "or exhibit in public," without the qualifying expression "by way of trade" and it also is separated from the context of "sale or rental."[254] Likewise, 27(2)(b) refers simply to a distribution to an extent prejudicial to the owner of the copyright without any qualifier as to trade, sale, or rental. An ISP would, if anything, be within only the non-trade provisions concerning prejudicial *distribution*.[255] Section 27(2)(d) refers to the *possession*, and section 27(2)(e) to the *importation*, into Canada of a copy of an infringing work or other subject matter, in each instance for the purpose of doing anything referred to in the preceding sections 27(2) (a) to (c). The receipt by a territorial website or e-mail addressee of any extraterritorial transmission may be contemplated as an importation,

---

252 *Religious Technology Centre v. Netcom On-Line Communication Services, Inc.*, 907 F.Supp. 1361 at 1372–73 (N.D. Cal. 1995).

253 *Playboy Enterprises Ltd. v. Webbworld Inc.*, 991 F.Supp. 543 (N.D. Tex. 1997), aff'd 168 F.3d 486 (5th Cir.1999).

254 Section 27(2)(c) reads "by way of trade distribute, expose or offer for sale or rental, *or exhibit in public*" [emphasis added]. The separation of the emphasized phrase from the preceding portions appears to be justified by the double use of the word "or."

255 It is difficult to conceptualize an ISP as exhibiting in public any work or other subject matter. Display on a website is necessary to achieve any exhibition of the material. An ISP does not create the websites of persons utilizing the Internet. Furthermore, the transmissions by an ISP, while made "to the public" (in individual places of reception) are not presentations "in public."

although the concept of electronic importation has been queried.[256] Any element of possession would most likely be met by a website operator but would be indirect and ephemeral for an ISP.

Most instances constituting secondary infringement depend on the infringer knowing, or being reasonably considered as knowing, of the infringing nature of the copy of the work or other subject matter.[257] This criterion is unlikely for an ISP but probable for a website owner. Once either the ISP or website owner *has been informed* of the presence of the infringing copy, this element will be established.

In addition to the general exceptions to copyright liability, in particular that of fair dealing,[258] are exceptions that relate to the medium of communication itself. First, if an ISP is a "Canadian carrier" as defined in the *Telecommunications Act* (1993) it may be subject to section 36 of that Act, which provides: "Except where the [CRTC] approves otherwise, a Canadian carrier shall not control the content or influence the meaning or purpose of telecommunications carried by it for the public."[259]

This inquiry involves some speculation. The provision has not to date been invoked in any Internet context. To be relevant, section 36 must be interpreted as impliedly *exempting* the Canadian carrier from liability for content, rather than merely *prohibiting* interference with content. Conversely, the prohibition against interference may preclude an ISP from disconnecting a user even upon receiving reasonable information of copyright infringement activities by the user. If so, a user may have a civil remedy under section 72,[260] even if the carrier ISP has a contractual provision with a subscriber purporting to allow such a disconnection. The contractual provision itself might be seen as interfering with, or attempting to control, content.

Apart from section 36, the CRTC has regulated that a Canadian carrier shall "not be liable for: (b) defamation or copyright infringement arising from material transmitted or received over the carriers facilities."[261] If this regulation is within the constitutional and regula-

256 See IHAC Report, above note 141 at 12.
257 Section 27(2). Note s. 27(3) providing that for any infringement under ss. 27(2) (a)–(d) of a copy imported to Canada under s. 27(2)(e), whether the importer knows the copy was an infringement is irrelevant.
258 See text accompanying notes 35–36, above in this chapter.
259 *Telecommunications Act*, S.C. 1993, c. 38, s. 36. The potential of an ISP to be included within the meaning of "Canadian carrier" is discussed in Chapter 2, in the text accompanying notes 228–30.
260 See Chapter 2, text accompanying notes 229–30.
261 *Review of the General Regulations of the Federally Regulated Terrestrial Telecommunications Common Carriers* (26 March 1986), Telecom Decision CRTC 86-7,

tory jurisdiction of the CRTC[262] and is found to be applicable to ISPs, it will provide an immunity for all potential copyright infringements by an ISP. Perhaps section 36 and the CRTC Regulation can be seen as limiting the effect of an 1882 Supreme Court of Canada decision declining to exempt the providers of telegraph services from liability for defamation.[263] This decision implicitly denies in Canada any common law rule in the nature of that in the United States granting a "common carriers" exemption from liability for telephone and telegraph transmissions.[264] The decision is distinguishable, however, as the majority of the Supreme Court proceeded on the basis that the particular carrier telegraph company itself initiated the defamatory communication as part of an operation of gathering news and supplying it to newspapers in the region.[265] It was therefore acting as a content supplier, not a mere provider of infrastructure for the communication.

A second legislative exemption is found in sections 2.4(1)(b) & (c) of the *Copyright Act*. It is limited to infringement of the communication right and does not include an exemption for *authorizing* such a communication or for the other categories of copyright infringement, such as reproduction. Yet because the communication right is the principal economic right of copyright in a telecommunications context, in practice the provision presents a significant exemption. The 2005 lapsed Bill C-60, the 2008 lapsed Bill C-61, and Bill C-32 (2010) to amend the *Copyright Act* would extend this exclusion to any and all rights of copyright in the case of persons providing Internet or other digital network services.[266] Given the definition of "copyright" within the Act, these provisions would not encompass moral rights, but there is no structure

---

as am. by Telecom Order 86-593 (22 September 1986), online: www.priv.gc.ca/information/pub/sub_crtc_090320_e.cfm.

262 See Chapter 1, text accompanying notes 130–59, discussing how far regulation of content might be said to be exercisable by the CRTC. See also Racicot *et al.*, above note 141 at 262, quoting Michael H. Ryan, *Canadian Telecommunications Law and Regulation*, looseleaf (Scarborough, ON: Carswell, 1993), doubting the existence of any such jurisdiction. Note also Racicot *et al.*, *ibid.* at 128.

263 *Dominion Telegraph Company v. Silver* (1882), 10 S.C.R. 238 (4:2 majority) [*Dominion Telegraph*].

264 The "common carriers" rule in the United States is discussed in Racicot *et al.*, above note 141 at 260–65.

265 *Dominion Telegraph*, above note 263 at 255–56. The dissenting Taschereau and Gwynne JJ considered that the telegraph company (defendant) transmitted the material on behalf of the newspapers, rather than of its own initiative. See *ibid.* at 269–70.

266 See Bills C-60 (cl. 20); C-61 (cl. 21); and C-32 (cl. 35), all above note 208. All bills proposed s. 31.1(1) to this effect.

of authorization or contributory infringement of moral rights within the Act.

The potential application of section 2.4(1)(b) in the context of an Internet transmission was considered in *Tariff 22* by the Supreme Court.[267] Being simply not an infringement[268] avoids any implication of narrow interpretation that might flow if the provision were a defence to an infringement. The scope of a copyright holder's right within this section is to be read in a fair and balanced manner.[269] While Internet intermediaries are not seen as "users" of either the copyrighted material or of the physical substrata containing the copyrighted material, in the sense articulated by the Court in *CCH* and *Théberge*,[270] a balance is presented by section 2.4(1)(b) between copyright holders and intermediaries[271] that reflects a public interest in the facilitation of use of the Internet and the technological innovation that it provides in the dissemination of "works of the arts and intellect."[272] This underpinning of section 2.4(1)(b) is consistent with the overall incentive theory of copyright articulated by the court in *Théberge*.[273] Internet intermediaries are not concerned with incentives, as they are content neutral. The legislative objective is to distinguish those who provide the communication medium from content providers, holders of copyright, and users. Protection for providers of the medium itself is seen as essential to the national economy.[274]

Analytically, section 2.4(1)(b) contains several key phrases. The first is the meaning of "the means of telecommunication." This is not limited to physical features but includes any means of communication, including Internet-related software connections.[275] The provision of a cache by an ISP presented issues concerning the scope of what was *necessary* to effect a communication.[276] The majority in the Federal Court

---

267 *Tariff 22* (SCC), above note 5 at paras. 100–3. The provision was also considered by the Federal Court of Appeal in *Tariff 22* (FCA), above note 151 and the Copyright Board of Canada in *Tariff 22* (Copyright Bd.), above note 149.

268 *Tariff 22* (SCC), above note 5 at para. 87.

269 *Ibid.* at para. 88.

270 *Ibid.* at para. 132.

271 *Ibid.* at para. 89.

272 *Ibid.* at para. 40.

273 See text accompanying note 8, above in this chapter.

274 *Tariff 22* (SCC), above note 5 at para. 131.

275 *Ibid.* at para. 92.

276 Section 2(4)(1)(b) refers to "the means of telecommunication *necessary* for another person to so communicate" [emphasis added]. The section also refers to the provider's "only act" being the provision of the means of telecommunication.

of Appeal had found the process of caching to be an enhancement and therefore to be beyond what is necessary for communication.[277] Shalow JA and the Copyright Board reached an opposite conclusion focusing on economic and cost effectiveness.[278] The Supreme Court agreed with Shalow JA and the Copyright Board. The provision and convenience of a cache did not cause the ISP to move from conduit to content.[279] The Court approved of the consistency of this result with the position in the United States and the European Union.[280]

Bill C-32 (2010)[281] would incorporate these measures, inserting section 31.1 in the Act. This provision covers persons providing Internet or another digitized network service and excludes such providers from copyright liability for providing the means for the telecommunication of works or other subject matter, unless proposed section 27(2.3) is infringed.[282] Conditions for the application of section 31.1 are imposed,[283] in particular, if the person who first made the work or other subject matter available by telecommunication has given directions as to caching and these directions may be effected by automation, then the directions must be applied.[284]

In *Tariff 22*, the Supreme Court noted the absence in Canada of legislative implementation of the 1996 *WIPO Copyright Treaty* and the *WIPO Performances and Phonograms Treaty* and, therefore, of any implementation of a legislative framework determining the relationship of ISPs and other intermediaries for copyright infringement by Internet users, and noted the "notice and take down" process in the United States and the European Union.[285] Both the 2005 and 2008 lapsed copyright reform Bills provided for a system that might be described as "notice and retain," considerably less than a "notice and take down" process. Bill C-32 (2010) provides similarly. The copyright owner must proceed directly against the alleged infringer with the attendant expense and time that is entailed. This would present a process advantage for an alleged infringer and would lack harmony with the United States and the European Union. Bill C-32 (2010) would require providers of services related to the Internet or other digital networks or those providing

---

277 *Tariff 22* (FCA) above note 151 at para. 135, Evans and Linden JJA.
278 *Tariff 22* (FCA), *ibid.* at para. 196, Shalow JA dissenting; *Tariff 22* (Copyright Bd.), above note 149, Part IIIC at para. 2.
279 *Tariff 22* (SCC), above note 5 at paras. 113–19.
280 *Ibid.* at paras. 117–18.
281 See Bill C-32, above note 208, cl. 35.
282 *Ibid.*, proposed section 27(2.3) is discussed above, text accompanying note 243.
283 *Ibid.*, proposed sections 31.1(4)–(6).
284 *Ibid.*, proposed section 31.1(4).
285 *Tariff 22* (SCC), above note 5 at 127.

digital memory or an information location tool, on receiving notice of claimed infringement, to forward electronic notice to an alleged infringer and to report back to the claimant that this had been done, or to explain why it had not been done, and to *retain* for specified periods records identifying the person owning the electronic location of the alleged infringement.[286]

The absence of a statutory mechanism led representatives of the Canadian recording industry to seek under existing law the disclosure from five ISPs of the identity of users considered to be illegally trading in music by peer-to-peer sharing. The procedure under the *Federal Court Rules*[287] is in the nature of a discovery process against alleged wrongdoers who are unknown.[288] The proceedings were unsuccessful. An evidentiary basis had not established a *bona fide* claim.[289] The Federal Court of Appeal left the position open to the plaintiffs to pursue a further claim, but there is no published indication that this has taken place. The proceedings have received detailed analysis.[290] Significantly, the Court of Appeal rebalanced the positions of Internet users and copyright holders from the motions judge, who had weighed the interests toward Internet users. A standard of a *bona fide* claim was substituted for that of a *prima facie* case.[291] The relationship between a user's interest in privacy under the *Personal Information Protection and Electronic Documents Act*[292] and the copyright owner's interest in preventing infringement was weighted more toward the copyright interest.[293] The determination by the motions judge that copyright infringement would not have occurred was found to have been a premature finding.[294]

---

286 Bill C-32, above note 208, cl. 47, proposing s. 41.26 to this effect.

287 The principal focus was on *Federal Court Rules, 1998*, S.O.R./98-106, Rule 238.

288 Hence the proceedings are brought against "John and Jane Doe" representing the unknown defendants. See *BMG Canada Inc. v. John Doe*, [2004] 3 F.C.R. 241 (F.C.), aff'd [2005] 4 F.C.R. 81 (C.A.) [*BMG (FCA)*].

289 Significantly, the evidence used to link Internet Protocol IP addresses with user pseudonyms was hearsay. See Chapter 3 at notes 146–48 re IPs and *BMG (FCA)*, *ibid.* at para. 21.

290 See, for example, Jane Bailey, "The Substance of Procedure: Non-Party Disclosure in the Canadian and U.S. Online Music Sharing Litigation" (2005–6) 43 Alta. L. Rev. 615 at 625ff.; and Amy Min-Chee Fong, "Unmasking the John Does of Cyberspace: Surveillance by Private Copyright Owners" (2005) C.J.L.T. 169, online: http://cjlt.dal.ca/vol4_no3/pdfarticles/fong.pdf.

291 *BMG (FCA)* above note 288 at paras. 31–34. Contrast Fong, *ibid.* at 176 suggesting a much higher standard — that "*Charter* values" be applied.

292 S.C. 2000, c. 5 [*PIPEDA*], discussed in Chapter 4.

293 *BMG (FCA)*, above note 288 at paras. 36–45.

294 *Ibid.* at paras. 46–54.

Applications of this nature, utilizing existing rules of procedure and presenting a significant balancing of interests between Internet users and copyright holders, reiterate the need for and importance of contextually specific legislative measures.[295]

8) 1996 WIPO Treaties

In 1996, the World Intellectual Property Organization (WIPO) concluded two copyright treaties,[296] to which Canada committed itself:[297] the *WIPO Copyright Treaty* (*WCT*); and the *WIPO Performances and Phonograms Treaty* (*WPPT*). The terms of the treaties are the same *mutatis mutandis*. The primary objective is to strengthen copyright protection and enforcement in a digital age. The following features should be noted.

a) Technological protection measures
Article 11 (*WCT*) and Article 18 (*WPPT*) impose obligations on member states to implement "adequate legal protection and effective legal remedies against the circumvention of effective technological measures that are used by authors" or performers or producers of phonograms to prevent copyright infringement. The types of measures are not set out in the treaty, but examples given in a federal report include "data encryption, signatures, access codes and asymmetric key systems."[298] Bill C-32 (2010) defines "technological protection measure" as meaning

---

295 In different contexts involving the Internet and applications of this nature to ISPs, see *Irwin Toy Ltd. v. Doe*, [2000] O.J. No. 3318 (S.C.J.) (alleged defamation, privacy recognized but application granted); *Warman v. Wilkins-Fournier*, [2009] O.J. No. 1305 (S.C.J.) (posting hate speech, disclosure ordered); and *R. v. Kwok*, [2008] O.J. No. 2414 (Ct. J.) (Internet-related child sexual exploitation, warrant needed).

296 *WCT*, above note 147; and *WIPO Performances and Phonograms Treaty*, 20 December 1996, 36 I.L.M. 76, online: www.wipo.int/treaties/en/ip/wppt/trtdocs_wo034.html [*WPPT*].

297 Minister of Canadian Heritage & Minister of Industry, News release/Communiqué, "Canada Commits to Sign International Copyright Treaties" (18 December 1997). More recently, see Minister of Canadian Heritage & Minister of Industry, "Government of Canada Proposes Update to Copyright Law: Balanced Approach to Truly Benefit Canadians" (12 June 2008), online: www.ic.gc.ca/eic/site/icl.nsf/eng/04204.html.

298 Johanne Daniel & Leslie Ellen Harris, "Discussion Paper on the Implementation of the WIPO Copyright Treaty" (commenting on *WCT*, Art. 11 at 5–6) (17 July 1998), online: Industry Canada, www.strategis.ic.gc.ca/pics/ip/wipodp_e.pdf; Johanne Daniel & Leslie Ellen Harris, "Discussion Paper on the Implementation of the WIPO Performances and Phonograms Treaty" (commenting on *WPPT*,

"any effective technology, device or component that in the ordinary course of its operation" controls access to, or restricts activities concerning, copyright protected subject matter.[299]

Bill C-32[300] would insert into the *Copyright Act* as sections 41 to 41.24 technical prevention measures covering economic rights in a work, a sound recording, and a performer's performance fixed in a sound recording. Applicable relief is similar to that available to a copyright owner.[301] Proceedings may be brought by the copyright owner[302] against any person circumventing the technological measure;[303] against a person offering to the public or providing a service to circumvent if that service is primarily of use or marketed for the purpose of circumvention;[304] and against a person who deals in enumerated ways such as manufacturing, selling, renting, distributing, or importing any technology, device, or component of primary design or use for, or marketed for, the purpose of circumvention.[305]

b) Electronic Rights Management Information

Article 12 (*WCT*) and Article 19 (*WPPT*) require member states to ensure that legal provisions are enacted to preserve what is known as rights management information. This information includes details of copyright ownership in any work or subject matter or authorship of any work or terms and conditions relating to the use of the work or subject matter. The details must be attached to a copy of the work or must appear with the communication to the public of the work.

Criminal sanctions are contemplated with a requirement that the offender know, or have "reasonable grounds to know," any civil remedies.[306]

Bill C-32[307] would insert in the *Copyright Act*, as section 41.22, protection of rights management information concerning a work, a sound recording, and a performer's performance fixed in a sound recording. It would cover only economic rights, not moral rights. An owner of the

---

Art. 18 at 10–11) (17 July 1998), online: Industry Canada, www.strategis.ic.gc.ca/pics/ip/wipopt_e.pdf.

299 Bill C-32 (2010) above note 208, cl. 47, proposing s. 41 to this effect.

300 *Ibid.*, cl. 47.

301 Statutory damages (s. 38.1 would, however, not be available. Bill C-61, *ibid.*, proposed s. 41.1(3).

302 *Ibid.*, proposed ss. 41.1(2)–(4).

303 *Ibid.*, proposed s. 41.1(1)(a).

304 *Ibid.*, proposed s. 41.1(1)(b).

305 *Ibid.*, proposed s. 41.1(1)(c).

306 *WCT*, above note 147, art. 12(1); and *WPPT*, above note 296, art. 19(1).

307 Bill C-32, above note 208, cl. 47, proposed s. 41.22.

designated subject matter would have obtained relief against a person
who knowingly removed or altered any rights management information. An alleged infringer would have had to have reasonably known
that the removal or alteration would facilitate or conceal infringement
of copyright or adversely affect a sound recording owner's right of remuneration under section 19.[308] Additionally, an infringement would
have followed from any dealing in enumerated ways with the material
form of a protected matter by a person who knew, or ought to know, of
the removal, or alteration of, rights management information.[309]

c)   Telecommunications to the Public

Article 8 (WCT) stipulates that the right to communicate a work to
the public by telecommunication (section 3(1)(f), *Copyright Act*) may
be "by wire or wireless means, including the making available to the
public [by authors] of their works in such a way that members of the
public may access these works from a place and at a time individually
chosen by them."

This provision would enable the mere *making available* of a work for
accessing by others to constitute a communication to members of the
public.[310] Bill C-32 (2010) would enact this accordingly.[311]

d)   Performer's Performances

The *WPPT* includes various enhancements of the performer's performance rights, including the recognition of moral rights of identification
as performer and a right of integrity for any "distortion, mutilation or
other modification of [the performer's] performance . . . prejudicial to
[the performer's] reputation" (Article 5).[312] Economic rights recognized

---

308   *Ibid.*, proposed s. 41.22. *Copyright Act*, above note 4, s. 19 (subject to s. 20)
      provides for equitable remuneration to be paid to the performer and the maker
      of a published sound recording when the recording is being performed in public
      or is communicated to the public by telecommunication, otherwise than by
      retransmission (s. 31). Bill C-32, *ibid.*, would also amend s. 19 to also exclude
      from s. 19 a communication under proposed ss. 15(1.1)(d) and 18(1.1)(a).
309   Bill C-32, *ibid.*, proposed s. 41.22(3). The stipulated dealings would encompass
      renting, selling, distributing (to an extent that the copyright owner is prejudi-
      cially affected), importing, or communicating material to the public by telecom-
      munication, or (by way of trade) distributing, exposing, or offering for sale or
      rental or exhibiting in public.
310   See text accompanying notes 136ff., above in this chapter, especially at note 148
      concerning the publication right of copyright.
311   See Bill C-32, above note 208, cl. 3 proposing to amend *Copyright Act*, s. 2.4 by
      inserting s. 2.4(1.1).
312   *WPPT*, above note 296, art. 5(1).

in the treaty include the exclusive right of authorizing reproduction, directly or indirectly, of the performer's performance (Article 7) and of making the performance available to the public in an electronically accessible format (Article 10).

In effect, the performer is given an exclusive right to control public access, including Internet access, to a performance fixed in a sound recording. Therefore, as between the performer and the owner of the sound recording, the performer would gain a greater measure of control over the uploading of sound recordings to the Internet.[313]

e)   Implementation Controversy

Canadian implementation of the WIPO treaties was recommended unanimously by a Parliamentary Committee in 2004.[314] Implementation, however, presents differing scopes, options, and dimensions. Kim[315] provides a comparison of anti-circumvention measures in the United States, European Union, Japan, and (as at 2002) Australia.

The overall objective is the reinforcement of copyright and the means of enforcement. In this sense the treaties establish an additional layer of protection. A work or subject matter is protected by copyright; in turn the copyright is protected by anti-circumvention and rights management technologies; these measures are then afforded legal protection against interference. The United States implemented the treaties in the *Digital Millennium Copyright Act 1998 (DMCA)*.[316] The European Community approved the treaties[317] and incorporated implementing

---

313 The owner of a copyright in the sound recording would also have to consent to any reproduction of the sound recording by uploading to the Internet. Compare *WPPT, ibid.*, art. 8, concerning the measure of control given to a performer with respect to making available to the public a phonogram that includes a fixation of the original or a copy of the performer's performance.

314 See Canada, House of Commons, Standing Committee on Canadian Heritage, *Interim Report on Copyright Reform* (May 2004) at 5 (recommending "that the Government of Canada ratify the *WIPO Copyright Treaty* (WCT) and the *WIPO Performances and Phonograms Treaty* (WPPT) immediately"), online: http://cmte. parl.gc.ca/Content/HOC/committee/373/heri/reports/rp1350628/herirp01/ herirp01-e.pdf.

315 Selena Kim, "The Reinforcement of International Copyright for the Digital Age" (2002–3) 16 I.P.J. 93 with useful charts at 121–22.

316 *Copyright Act*, 17 U.S.C. 1201, inserted by *Digital Millennium Copyright Act*, 112 Stat. 2860, (1998) [*DMCA*].

317 EC, *Council Decision 2000/278 of 16 March 2000 on the approval, on behalf of the European Community, of the WIPO Copyright Treaty and the WIPO Performances and Phonograms Treaty*, [2000] O.J. L. 089/6 (Justis: Celex).

provisions into the 2001 EC Copyright Directive.[318] A state can, of course, provide for anti-circumvention measures without actually joining the treaties. A state's laws can simply be in compliance. This was the position in Australia[319] until accession to the WIPO treaties was required by the *Australia–United States Free Trade Agreement.*[320]

Considerable controversy has attended the enactment in Canada of anti-circumvention provisions. The right of fair dealing in copyright is seen to be impinged upon by technical measures that prevent access or copying and by legal protection of such measures.[321] This presents a difficult issue. Fair dealing does not ordinarily provide an affirmative right of access to expressions of information but is simply an exception to copyright. Since *CCH*, fair dealing is no longer to be interpreted as a defence; instead, the Court described it as a user right — but even as such, it is a right wholly within a copyright context.[322] More accurately, it should be neither a defence nor a right but rather, a matter not covered by the *Copyright Act.*[323] By way of analogy, physical access to a published book cannot be demanded through the fair dealing provision. Why should a digital work protected by encryption or other technical measures be treated differently? Logically, it should not. Therefore, any general right of access to electronic expressions of information ought to be found in some other and broader source than simply the fair dealing provision in copyright. A contrary position has

---

318 EC, *European Parliament and Council Directive 2001/29 of 22 May 2001 on the harmonisation of certain aspects of copyright and related rights in the information society,* [2001] O.J. L. 167/10 (Justis: Celex) [EC Copyright Directive].

319 See *Copyright Amendment (Digital Agenda Act) 2000* (Cth.).

320 *Australia–United States Free Trade Agreement* (18 May 2004, effective 1 January 2005), art. 17(1)(4), online: Department of Foreign Affairs, Australia www.dfat. gov.au/trade/negotiations/us_fta/final-text/ [*Australia–US FTA*]. See Australia, Commonwealth, Attorney General, *WIPO Copyright Treaty Adopted by the diplomatic Conference at Geneva on 20 December 1996,* National Interest Analysis (22 June 2004), online: www.austlii.edu.au/au/other/dfat/nia/2004/15.html.

321 There are several criticisms of the proposed amendments. See, for example, Michael Geist, "Anti-Circumvention Legislation and Competition Policy: Defining a Canadian Way?" in Michael Geist, ed., *In the Public Interest: The Future of Canadian Copyright Law* (Toronto: Irwin Law, 2005) at 211–50. More generally, consider the theoretical and conceptual positions presented by US professor Larry Lessig in, among other works, "The Path of Cyberlaw" (1995) 104 Yale L.J. 1743; *Code and Other Laws of Cyberspace* (New York: Basic Books, 1999); *The Future of Ideas* (New York: Random House, 2001); and "Law of the Horse, What Cyberspace Might Teach" (1999–2000) 113 Harv. L. Rev. 501.

322 *CCH* (SCC), above note 8 at paras. 48–49.

323 Sections 29, 29.1(1), and 29.2(1) all provide "Fair dealing for the purpose of . . . *does not infringe copyright*" [emphasis added].

been presented. Described as "prescriptive parallelism," it envisages the balance of holder and user interests presented in the fair dealing (or, in the United States, fair use) relationship as being of general application to the accessibility of works and subject matter in a digital environment. It is of US origin, but has been evaluated in a Canadian context.[324] Bill C-32 (2010) includes a number of exemptions from the technological protection measures[325] and the writer suggests that specifically focused statutory exemptions of this nature present a more logical and appropriate response to user interests.

Neither WCT nor WPPT include any express balancing of interests between creators and users. However, Article 10 (WCT) and Article 16 (WPPT) do enable implementing states to "provide for the same kinds of limitations or exceptions" as that jurisdiction provides for copyright infringement, so long as such limitations or exceptions do not conflict "with a normal exploitation" of the work or subject matter and "do not unreasonably prejudice the legitimate interests" of the copyright holder. An appropriate balance can therefore be struck in any implementing legislation. Difficulties may, however, be found in achieving this in the largely self-help environment of the Internet. The effectiveness of the anti-circumvention measures would be destroyed by allowing a unilateral right of access. Access ought, it is suggested, to be made available for specific purposes by application and (time-limited) passcodes. Such a system would more effectively balance the interests of holder and user.

f) Constitutional Jurisdiction

Whether anti-circumvention measures are, or are not, part of copyright law might present constitutional perspectives. If anti-circumvention measures are outside of copyright, the federal legislative jurisdiction to enact such measures must be contemplated.[326] Federal legislative jurisdiction for "copyright" is expressly allocated.[327] There was little conceptual or analytical consideration on the two earlier occasions that

---

324 J.H. Reichman, G.B. Dinwoodie, & P. Samuelson, "A Reverse Notice and Take-down Regime to Enable Public Interest Uses of Technically Protected Copyrighted Works" (2007) 22 Berkeley Tech. L.J. 981. For the Canadian evaluation, see Carys J. Craig, "Digital Locks and the Fate of Fair Dealing in Canada: In Pursuit of 'Prescriptive Parallelism'" [forthcoming] Journal of World Intellectual Property.

325 See Bill C-32, above note 208, cl. 47, proposed ss. 41.11–44.18.

326 See J. deBeer, "Constitutional Jurisdiction over Paracopyright Laws" in Geist, ed., above note 321 at 89–124. See also Chapter 1 for a discussion of constitutional issues concerning the Internet.

327 Constitution Act, 1867 (U.K.), 30 & 31 Vict., c. 3, s. 91(23), reprinted in R.S.C. 1985, App. II, No. 5.

challenged the extent and meaning of copyright. First, the disjointed relationship between economic and moral rights casts a doubt of constitutional validity over the latter.[328] Second, Part VIII of the *Copyright Act*, concerning private copying and levying of a fee on blank audiorecording media, was argued to be constitutionally *ultra vires* the federal legislative jurisdiction for various reasons, including being not, in pith and substance, copyright law.[329]

The validity of both areas, as within the concept and principles of copyright, has been sustained.[330] *Canadian Private Copying Collective v. Canadian Storage Media Alliance* applied the prevailing tests,[331] more recently reiterated by the Supreme Court in *Kirkbi AG v. Ritvik Holdings Inc.*,[332] to determine constitutional validity. The objective and legal effect of the private copying and levy regime is to compensate rights holders for reproduction of music for private use. The provisions were seen to be sufficiently linked to achieving this objective, even if persons who do not copy are also levied.[333]

The technological protection measures and those to protect electronic rights management information, originating in the 1996 WIPO treaties, must be considered within the three stages of analysis confirmed in *Kirkbi*. First, the impugned provisions must be characterized in isolation from the rest of the statute.[334] Second, the statute as a whole must be validly federal,[335] as is the situation under the specific enumeration for "copyrights."[336] Third, the impugned provision must be sufficiently integrated into the statute.[337] This last criterion requires an examination of the implementing legislation, but the proposals to date in Bills C-60 (2005), C-61 (2008), and C-32 (2010)[338] are likely

---

328 See Robic Richard Léger, "Protection des artistes — droit d'auteur — Droit voisin — Une autre approache constitutionelle" (1992) 5 C.P.I. 7, arguing that moral rights are *ultra vires* the federal legislative jurisdiction.

329 See *Canadian Private Copying Collective v. Canadian Storage Media Alliance*, [2005] 2 F.C.R. 654 at paras. 32–38 [*Private Copying*].

330 See *Snow*, above note 199 at 106, concerning moral rights; and *Private Copying*, *ibid.* at paras. 37–38.

331 *General Motors of Canada Ltd. v. City National Leasing*, [1989] 1 S.C.R. 641; *Global Securities Corp. v. British Columbia (Securities Commission)*, 2000 SCC 21, [2000] 1 S.C.R. 494.

332 *Kirkbi AG v. Ritvik Holdings Inc.*, [2005] 3 S.C.R. 302 at paras. 14–32 [*Kirkbi*].

333 *Private Copying*, above note 329 at paras. 34–38.

334 *Kirkbi*, above note 332 at para. 23.

335 *Ibid.* at para. 28.

336 *Constitution Act, 1867*, above note 327.

337 *Kirkbi*, above note 332 at para. 32.

338 See text accompanying notes 300–305, above in this chapter, describing the implementation that was proposed in Bill C-32, above note 208.

to be seen as sufficiently integrated into the scheme of protection and available relief provided by the *Copyright Act*.

Characterization of an impugned provision examines whether and to what extent the provision intrudes into a provincial head of power, namely section 92(13), property and civil rights in the province.[339] This said, difficulties are presented under this head of rights "in the province." Characterizing anti-circumvention and rights management measures as provincial would present the anomaly of provinces being asked to enact laws designed to ensure efficient enforcement of the enumerated exclusive federal jurisdiction for copyright law,[340] principally in the context of a medium that at least operationally and systemically is most certainly exclusively federal jurisdiction, operating well beyond even national boundaries, let alone provincial.[341]

Comparatively, technological protection measures and those to protect electronic rights management information are more integrated with copyright protection than are the regime of private copying and fee levies and even moral rights. The underlying purpose and legal effect is to protect digital works and subject matter from copyright infringement. Digital media necessitates technical measures and rights management procedures. Legal protection of these measures assists in achieving their efficacy.[342] A government is not bound to use copyright law to implement these provisions,[343] but having other options of implementation cannot in itself render the matter *ultra vires* the copyright power. In *Private Copying*, the *practical* nature of levies and private copying to achieve the copyright objective was acknowledged.[344] Technical measures and rights management information, together with the legal protection of such measures, are essentially the only practical means of preserving copyright in a digital, Internet-focused context.

Bills C-60 (2005), C-61 (2008), and C-32 (2010) present attempts to implement the WIPO treaties. Key provisions of these, particularly those of Bill C-32, were noted earlier.[345] While a comprehensive assessment of all measures proposed in Bill C-32 would not be within present purposes, other proposals linked with telecommunications include (1) an economic right enabling a copyright owner of a work that can

---

339 *Constitution Act, 1867*, above note 327.

340 *Ibid.*, s. 91(23).

341 *Ibid.*, s. 92(10)(a). See Chapter 1, Section C(1).

342 See deBeer, above note 326 at 100 to the contrary, that the pith and substance is "more of a technological, contractual, or commercial matter."

343 See *ibid.* at 94.

344 *Private Copying*, above note 329 at paras. 28, 51–52, and 72.

345 See text accompanying notes 266, 286, and 299–311, above in this chapter.

be put into circulation as a tangible object (such as a CD or DVD) to control the sale or transfer of that object if it has not been previously transferred with the authority of the copyright owner;[346] (2) allowing a previously published sound recording to be communicated to the public by telecommunication so long as equitable remuneration is afforded, in effect a compulsory licence with a right of remuneration;[347] (3) allowing under specified conditions and in specified circumstances the reproduction of certain works or subject matter, including a video cassette[348] or a sound recording[349] onto another medium or device and fixing a broadcast communication signal from radio or television and reproducing a work or sound recording that is being broadcast in order to listen to or watch it at a later time,[350] but this is not to include a work or subject matter received under an "on demand service," being a service that allows reception at times of a user's choosing;[351] and (4) providing for an exception to copyright, under detailed circumstances and conditions, for education-related online activities.[352]

Overall, the provisions are designed to enforce copyright, technological protection measures, and rights management provisions, but with exceptions that balance the interests of copyright holders and users, including for broadcasting undertakings circumventing a technological protection measure for the purpose of making an ephemeral reproduction.[353]

9) Regulated Royalties

The essence of proprietary exclusivity is the ability to exclude others from utilizing the particular item or interest to which that exclusivity relates. Subject to stipulated exceptions and the application of other laws, such as competition or anti-trust laws,[354] copyright is in most respects a proprietary interest of exclusivity.

---

346 Bill C-32, above note 208, cl. 4, providing s. 3(1)(j).
347 *Ibid.*, cl. 12, providing s. 19(1).
348 *Ibid.*, cl. 22, providing s. 29.21–29.22.
349 *Ibid.*, providing s. 29.23.
350 *Ibid.*, providing s. 29.23(1).
351 *Ibid.*, providing s. 29.23(3).
352 *Ibid.*, cl. 27, providing ss. 30.01–30.04. In addition, cl. 21 proposes to amend s. 29 (fair dealing) to include the additional purposes of "education, parody or satire" and includes as proposed s. 29.21 situations of dealings with non-commercial user-generated content.
353 *Ibid.*, cl. 47, providing s. 41.17. See also text accompanying notes 107ff., above in this chapter.
354 *Competition Act*, R.S.C. 1985, c. C-34, ss. 32 and 79(5). See Vaver, above note 34 at 239, n. 35; and Geist, above note 321 at 215ff.

Enforcement difficulties and a policy interest in balancing copyright holders and users in ensuring accessibility for the public have qualified this proposition. Administrative systems designed to ensure the flow of royalty payments through tariff and private copying schemes, while enabling users to exercise otherwise infringing activities, lead to a partial conceptualization of copyright as a quasi-public good that may be readily acquired for a prescribed fee or royalty.

This has been the case particularly in the music and recording industry. The system of tariff setting by administrative tribunal, the Copyright Board of Canada, has the consequence of the value of the tariff being the limit of recovery by all copyright holders of that category of work or subject matter.[355] In effect, this presents a compulsory licence for a prescribed royalty. Even more, the system of private copying, expressed to be an exclusion from copyright,[356] may, after *CCH*, be interpreted as a "user right."[357] In return, the copyright holder participates in proceeds from a government-sponsored and collectively administered levy on manufacturers and importers of "blank audio recording media." These administrative mechanisms redefine the copyright holder's interest from proprietary exclusivity to simply an entitlement to remuneration.[358]

Private copying is limited to infringement by reproduction[359] and covers only authors of musical works, performers of musical works embodied in a sound recording, and owners of sound recordings in which a musical work or a performer's performance is embodied. Schemes of this nature have been widely utilized to deal with the impossibility of enforcement against private copying.[360] Downloading from the Internet

---

355   Sections 68.2(2) and 70.17.

356   *Ibid.*, s. 80.

357   *CCH* (SCC), above note 8. See text accompanying notes 35–36, above in this chapter.

358   The scheme of private copying is usefully summarized by deMontigny J in *Canadian Private Copying Collective v. Z.E.I. Media Plus Inc.*, 2006 FC 1546 at paras. 4–10.

359   Section 80(1) authorizes only reproduction. Additionally, s. 80(2) specifically excludes activities including communication to the public by telecommunication and performing, or causing to be performed, in public. Sale or renting out or by way of trade, exposing or offering for sale or rental as well as distribution, whether for trade or otherwise, are expressed as beyond the private copying exception.

360   See, generally, Ysolde Gendreau, ed., *Copyright Administrative Institutions* (Cowansville, QC: Les Éditions Yvon Blais, 2002); and Australian Copyright Council, *Remuneration for Private Copying in Australia*, Discussion Paper (September 2001), online: www.copyright.org.au/pdf/acc/articles_pdf/PrivCopDiscPprAV.

and then file sharing for private use is likely within this exception,[361] but uploading for the purpose of access by others to the work or subject matter is not, nor is the making of a copy for another.[362]

A regime of private copying presents a mechanism that affords a pragmatic balance between copyright holders and users. The current scheme, however, is predicated on the older technologies of cassette tapes and prerecorded CD-ROMs, predominant in the recording industry in 1997, the time of implementation.[363] Audio musical transmissions and recordings were then at the cusp of Internet MP3 digital technology, which has subsequently outpaced the perimeters of the private copying scheme. The Private Copying Tariff, 2008–9, effective 6 December 2008, is levied on blank audiocassette tapes of forty minutes or more (twenty-four cents per tape) and on CD-R, CD-RW, CD-R Audio, CD-RW Audio, and MiniDisk (twenty-nine cents per disk).[364] Attempts by the Copyright Board to apply the tariff levy to the memory disk permanently embedded in digital audiorecorders (MP3 format recorders) have been rejected.[365] The Copyright Board had accepted that no levy could be made on a recorder itself as a recorder is seen as a *device* rather than a blank audiorecording *medium*,[366] but contemplated that this outcome could be avoided by focusing separately on the implanted memory disk. In effect, the court's conclusion finds the memory component embedded permanently in a recording device to be part of the device itself.[367] The Copyright Board, supported by the court, had al-

---

pdf. Part 4 canvases private copying schemes in several international jurisdictions starting at 9.

361 See *BMG* (FCA), above note 288 at 241, para. 25 (Motions Judge, cited to F.C.). See, however, text accompanying note 294, above in this chapter.

362 See s. 80(2)(c) excluding from the "private use" any communication to the public by telecommunication, or distribution (whether or not for the purpose of trade), which would include private distribution.

363 *Copyright Amendment Act, 1997*, above note 51, s. 50.

364 Tariff of Levies to Be Collected by CPCC [Canadian Private Copying Collective] in 2008 and 2009 on the Sale of Blank Audio Recording Media, In Canada, In Respect of the Reproduction for Private Use of Musical Works Embodied in Sound Recordings, of Performers' Performances of Such Works or of Sound Recordings in Which Such Works and Performances are Embodied, C. Gaz.2008.1.4 at para. 3. A copy of this tariff for 2010 is available from the Canadian Private Copying Collective, online: www.cpcc.ca/english/currentTariff.htm.

365 *Private Copying*, above note 329 at paras. 148–64.

366 *Ibid.* at paras. 148–63.

367 More abstractly, this joining of items, with one subsumed into the other, is simply the law of accessions of items of personal property or of fixtures between chattels and land.

ready determined that removable memory cards and removable micro hard drives, as well as "recordable or rewritable DVD's," could not be levied as they were determined as not ordinarily used for the personal copying of music.[368]

Bill C-32 does not address the meaning of a medium to which the private copying regime applies ("blank audio recording media") but does confirm that the "medium or device" to which copying may be made, includes MP3 player devices and, under specified conditions, exempting reproduction of a musical work (and performer's performance) embodied within a sound recording when copied to any such "medium or device."[369] This measure may correspond consistently with a further proposed exemption of fixing communication signals and recording broadcast programs for later listening or viewing[370] but ought to be more precisely and definitionally correlated with the private copying regime using digital technology that today is largely Internet based.

The memory disk embedded in digital audiorecorders, or the recorders themselves, ought to be subject to a copyright levy with respect to private copying, given the capacity of such devices to record musical works. Indeed, perhaps all exclusions from copyright infringement of musical works and performers' performances embodied within sound recordings should be within the private copying regime rather than within a new and separate category. Certainly, however, memory cards or recording devices are used for purposes other than private copying within this context, and some users will, therefore, be paying for private copying when they are not themselves engaged in this activity. However, any levy scheme is incapable of precise correlation between persons doing actual copying and purchasers of media or devices that enable this to be done. Rather than exclude media that have purposes other than the copying of sound recordings or digital musical communications, the scope of "other uses" of a medium may be correlated more accurately by differing levels in the tariff. Media that present few other purposes should logically bear a heavier tariff. This may still be perceived critically,[371] but it would ensure an optimal level of pragmatic efficiency without too great an imposition on all concerned.

---

368 *Private Copying*, above note 329 at para. 137.
369 Bill C-32, above note 208, cl. 22, providing s. 29.22.
370 See above text accompanying note 350 in this chapter.
371 The opinion of retailers and consumers is, overall, critical of the private copying regime. See online: www.cbc.ca/consumer/story/2008/01/11/levy-recorders. html. Yet, the connection between "blank audio recording media" and private copying is substantially met.

What seems to inhibit an expansion of the private copying regime is not only consumer opposition but also the policy or political concern that such an extension to MP3 digital recording devices would blur the distinction between a reproduction of a lawfully acquired sound recording and a reproduction from one acquired by infringement. The proposed exemption in Bill C-61 for copying to simply a "medium or device" (i.e., outside of the private copying regime) would have been limited to lawfully acquired recordings.[372] This limitation is not explicitly stipulated in the private copying regime,[373] but there is no reason why it could not be.

D. SUMMATION AND PROGNOSIS

While the contained, centrally organized and controlled traditional media of radio, television, and cable distribution do provide a context for media-specific dimensions in copyright law, the circumstances and consequences are relatively incidental to telecommunications in a systemic sense. Historically, copyright infringement in telecommunications has also been somewhat peripheral to commerce and the socioeconomic dimensions of society overall. Today, however, technology and globalized economic and trade enhancement have brought swift and dramatic change. Digitized computer technology, first in industrial and business use and then in personal desktop and laptop devices, laid the foundation for an information-based economy. Copyright was elevated in commercial and market significance as the IPR of choice in protecting the software products. This was a contained step, but quickly evolved as the industrial computer industry combined with the communications industry. Digitized communication in a telematic environment of political, philosophic, and commercial globalization has caused copyright to become of systemic importance in the telecommunications sector.

The medium of the Internet in its broadly based mass usage from the early 1990s was the dramatic new medium that decentralized both expression and access, rendering impossible any sense of traditionally styled regulation. The relationship of this medium to information and

---

372 See Michael Geist, "Fearing Legalized P2P Downloading, CRIA Declares War on Private Copying Levy" (15 September 2007), online: www.michaelgeist.ca/content/view/2238/125. In this context, the Canadian Recording Industry Association (CRIA) appears to differ from the Canadian Private Copying Collective (CPCC), the latter favouring the levy on digital devices for recording music.

373 Section 80.

that of copyright to visual and aural information, now packaged digitally, thrust copyright to the centre of contention between protection of and access to information.

Bills C-60 (2005), C-61 (2008), and C-32 (2010) present attempts to set an appropriate balance between owners of copyrighted subject matter and users. Broadly speaking, passage of legislation of this nature is crucial to achieving this balance and to meeting international obligations, especially the 1996 *WIPO Copyright Treaty* and *WIPO Performances and Phonograms Treaty*, which directly address copyright and the digitized telecommunications media. These treaties provide the framework within which Canada must set its own standard to encourage and protect creation and ownership, give appropriate access to users, but foreclose the opportunistic pure taking of intellectual product. In the latter respect, in the medium of the Internet, relief must engage with ISPs as the only entities capable of implementing measures of control. However, this engagement in itself presents corresponding issues of user privacy and significant issues of private international law, given the often extrajurisdictional locations of hosting ISPs. These perspectives are dealt with in Chapters 4 and 6 and call for some measure of international harmonization and compliance. It is sufficient to note here first, *BMG Canada* and the balance of privacy and copyright enforcement through an ISP,[374] and second, the preparedness of the Supreme Court to allow copyright royalty tariffs to be assessed on musical works transmitted on the Internet from servers outside of Canada so long as the particular transmission presents a real and substantial connection with Canada.[375] This test is taken directly from current developments in Canadian private international law (conflict of laws), an area directly relevant to any extraterritorial server and copyright tariffs and of particular significance in telecommunications today. It is discussed in Chapter 6.[376]

---

374 See text accompanying notes 287–94, above in this chapter, and, generally, Chapter 4 concerning *PIPEDA*.

375 *Tariff 22* (SCC), above note 5 at paras. 60 and 77.

376 Chapter 6, text accompanying notes 1 and 139–45.

PRIVATE INTERNATIONAL LAW

A. INTRODUCTION

The global dimensions of telecommunications media present significant issues of jurisdiction, enforcement of extraterritorial judgments, and choice of law. The hemispheric footprint of a transmission signal from a broadcast satellite presents significant transborder dimensions, but the decentralized and largely anonymous operation of Internet transmissions is even more demanding in the context of private international law. In most contexts, effective control of Internet content rests with the provider of the server hosting a site or user. That provider is jurisdictionally situated, yet rights and liabilities arising from the transmission are multijurisdictional. An example, given in Chapter 5, is the 2004 decision of the Supreme Court of Canada enabling a Canadian copyright tariff to be levied on musical works transmitted on the Internet, even with respect to a transmission from a server hosted outside Canada. The transmission need only have a "real and substantial connection" with Canada.[1] This meets the primary requirement for a Canadian court to take jurisdiction. However, the effectiveness of any resulting order, particularly if injunctive or otherwise non-monetary,

---

1   *Society of Composers, Authors and Music Publishers of Canada v. Canadian Association of Internet Providers*, [2004] 2 S.C.R. 427, 2004 SCC 45 [*Tariff 22*]. Noted in Chapter 5, text accompanying note 375, but discussed below in this chapter, text accompanying notes 139–45.

will depend on the ability to enforce the order in the jurisdiction hosting the server. That jurisdiction will apply its own principles of private international law and may decline to recognize or enforce the Canadian order.

In addition, the principles of Canadian private international law are under considerable judicial development after landmark decisions over recent years by the Supreme Court in *Morguard Investments Ltd. v. De Savoye*,[2] *Hunt v. T&N, plc*,[3] *Tolofson v. Jensen*,[4] *Beals v. Saldanha*,[5] and *Pro Swing Inc. v. ELTA Golf Inc.*.[6] Two further decisions by the Court in 2009 need also to be considered.[7] The ultimate scope and impact of these decisions is continuing to evolve, but the consequences are considerable and will continue to be so. *Morguard* and *Hunt* imposed constitutional requirements in interprovincial private international law. Without any constitutional element, *Beals* and *Pro Swing* have applied, or have set the stage to apply, these principles internationally, moving Canadian law well beyond the traditional common law position reflected in the Commonwealth. The Canadian common law position is today more reflective of features prevailing in the United States.[8]

An extraterritorial element of telecommunications has always existed. Radio and television signals do not respect jurisdictional boundaries. Radio or microwave transmissions and connections by telegraph and telephone demonstrated an early recognition of the need for some international cooperation and organization, such as the al-

---

2   *Morguard Investments Ltd. v. De Savoye*, [1990] 3 S.C.R. 1077, 76 D.L.R. (4th) 256 [*Morguard*].

3   *Hunt v. T&N, plc*, [1993] 4 S.C.R. 289 [*Hunt*].

4   *Tolofson v. Jensen*, [1994] 3 S.C.R. 1022 [*Tolofson*].

5   *Beals v. Saldanha*, [2003] 3 S.C.R. 416, 2003 SCC 72 [*Beals*].

6   *Pro Swing Inc. v. ELTA Golf Inc.*, 2006 SCC 52, [2006] 2 S.C.R. 612 [*Pro Swing*].

7   *Teck Cominco Metals Ltd. v. Lloyds Underwriters*, [2009] 1 S.C.R. 321, 2009 SCC 11 [*Teck Cominco*]; and *Canada Post Corporation v. Lépine*, [2009] 1 S.C.R. 549, 2009 SCC 16 [*Canada Post Corporation*].

8   See *Restatement of the Law Third, Foreign Relations Law of the United States* (St. Paul, MN: American Law Institute, 1987) § 481, Recognition and Enforcement of Foreign Judgments. See also Wanda Ellen Wakefield, Annotation, *Judgement of Court of Foreign Country as Entitled to Enforcement or Extraterritorial Effect in State Court*, American Law Reports, 13 A.L.R. (4th) 1109 (1982), discussing the recognition and enforcement of foreign judgments across the United States. It is clear from this provision that the US position, although reflecting diversity between state jurisdictions, includes the enforcement of foreign non-monetary judgments in certain circumstances; see, for example, *Siko Ventures Limited v. Argull Equities, LLC*, 2005 U.S. Dist. LEXIS 21257 at paras. 4 and 7 (W.D. Tex.), concerning a Hong Kong order in the nature of an injunction "to enjoin the selling of further shares of corporate stock" being enforced by the Texas court.

location of the radio frequencies, and led to the early determination of exclusive federal constitutional jurisdiction for telecommunications media.[9] Since then, national jurisdiction has coped for the most part with the relatively contained international or transborder elements of radio and television microwave signals.

The hemispheric footprint of satellite broadcasting brought change, not only by providing a greater range in the actual signal communication but by diminishing regulatory control. The grey market for satellite broadcast decoders of unlicensed signals in Canada was litigated by the Canadian licence holders *ex juris* against US providers of decoders to Canadian viewers.[10] However, the multifarious scope and decentralization afforded by the Internet, together with its influence in so many aspects of human existence, present even greater international elements and create demands of such magnitude that they may overwhelm private international law, in the absence of an international accord stipulating an infrastructure. Writing in 2006, a US commentator, relying on US business survey evidence, found a primary business concern to be the divergence of national laws over the illegality of content of websites and the corresponding likelihood of states claiming jurisdiction for a tort "committed in" that state from simple accessibility.[11]

International agreement, however, has been elusive,[12] though still a matter for possible future discussion.[13] The European Union has internal regulation with respect to "information society services"

---

9   Chapter 1, text accompanying notes 46–52 and 75–93.

10   *United States Satellite Broadcasting Co. v. WIC Premium Television Ltd.*, 2000 ABCA 233.

11   Holger P. Hestermeyer, "Personal Jurisdiction for Internet Torts: Towards an International Solution?" (2006) 26 Nw. J. Int'l L. & Bus. 267 at 267–68.

12   Hague Conference on Private International Law, *Preliminary Draft Convention on Jurisdiction and Foreign Judgments in Civil and Commercial Matters*, Preliminary Document No. 11 (August 2000), online: www.hcch.net/upload/wop/jdg-mpd11.pdf. Not being responsive to Internet communications (the negotiations had taken place while the Internet was in its relative infancy) the proposals collapsed, despite attempts to coordinate the recommended terms to the new media. See Avril D. Haines, *The Impact of the Internet on the Judgments Project: Thoughts for the Future*, Preliminary Document No. 17 (February 2002), submitted by the Permanent Bureau for the attention of the Special Commission of April 2002 on general affairs and policy of the Conference, online: www.cptech.org/ecom/hague/hague17feb2002-ah-internet.rtf. See Hestermeyer, *ibid.* at 287–88.

13   See Hague Conference on Private International Law, *Annual Report 2007* at 27, para. 7(a), retaining on the Conference's agenda: "questions of private international law raised by the information society . . . ," online: www.hcch.net/upload/annualreport2007.pdf.

(eCommerce).[14] This provides for jurisdiction at the location of source[15] and differs from television and radio broadcasting,[16] for which signals do not involve a user accessing and requesting a particular item.[17] An infrastructure is developing by judicial determination in both Canada and the United States to provide some limits on the taking of jurisdiction in an Internet-focused context. It is consistent with the general dimensions of private international law, which are experiencing similarly rapid development in Canada toward a global interdependent reciprocity of expanding jurisdiction that remains reflective of jurisdictional self-restraint. If restraint is not universally accepted, the only available control may be a restructuring of principles of recognition and enforcement.

After the taking of jurisdiction, there is a need to determine choice of law. It is possible for choice of law determinations to dispense with some of the impact flowing from divergence in national laws. If choice of law theory dictates application of one system of law, that should be applied by all courts that have taken jurisdiction. Alas, however, even this is not straightforward. Each jurisdiction has its own choice of law theory. Of course, there is some measure of similarity among jurisdictions, but not of uniformity. Interprovincial approaches are significantly more uniform.

The extraterritorial potential of the regulatory features of telecommunications in a global environment may present further unexplored issues; the scope of recognition and enforcement of determinations of administrative or quasi-judicial tribunals within private international law is certainly a merely fledgling feature of private international law.[18]

---

14   EC, *Directive 2000/31 of the European Parliament and of the Council of 8 June 2000 on legal aspects of information society services, in particular electronic commerce, in the Internal Market*, [2000] O.J. L. 178/1 [EC Directive on Electronic Commerce]. See, generally, Y. Farah, "Allocation of Jurisdiction and the Internet in E.U. Law" (2008) 33 Ed. L. Rev 257.

15   EC Directive on Electronic Commerce, *ibid.* at para. 23.

16   EC, *Directive 89/552/EEC of the European Council of 3 October 1989 on the coordination of certain provisions laid down by law, regulation or administrative action in Member States concerning the pursuit of television broadcasting activities* [1989], O.J. L. 298/23, art. 2(1) [Consolidated Text, ANACOM 1997], online: www.anacom.pt/render.jsp?contentid=318395 [EC Satellite Broadcasting Directive].

17   EC Directive on Electronic Commerce, above note 14 at para. 28.

18   See Robert G. Howell, "Relevance of National Regulation in an Age of Borderless Transmission" in Ysolde Gendreau, ed., *Copyright Administrative Institutions* (Cowansville, QC: Éditions Yvon Blais, 2002) at 620–34. See also Edward Mazey, "The Enforcement of Labour Orders Outside the Jurisdiction of Origin" (2001) 59 U.T. Fac. L. Rev. 25 at 38–43, concerning enforcement of labour tribu-

In addition, most instances of tribunal assessment involve content or process of a public law and policy flavour. Might this be a further and separate ground for denying recognition and enforcement?[19]

Not within private international law but closely related in Internet communications is cross-border infringement of the criminal law of a jurisdiction hosting an accessed site. In effect, from his or her desk on one side of the world, a hacker can breach criminal or felony laws on the other side of the world. This is aptly illustrated by the ordering in 2008 of extradition from the United Kingdom to the United States of a UK resident for hacking from the United Kingdom into US data resources, with a consequent breach of US criminal law sanctions.[20]

B. JURISDICTION *SIMPLICITER* OR TERRITORIAL COMPETENCE

In *Morguard* and *Hunt*, the Supreme Court determined that jurisdiction can be taken if, within a framework of "order and fairness" and comity between provinces, a "real and substantial connection" exists between the jurisdiction and the alleged claim and parties. The interpretation of *Morguard* in *Hunt* adds a constitutional requirement interprovincially to this essential minimum requirement.[21] It has revolutionized both the taking of jurisdiction *simpliciter* and the enforcement of extraterritorial judgments, characterizing these features as interrelated. If jurisdiction is properly taken under this test, a constitutional imperative, predicated on interprovincial comity, will to an extent yet to be determined require another province to enforce the resulting judgment. This effectively establishes a full faith and credit recognition to interprovincial enforcement of judgments,[22] while meeting the constitutional requirement of a provincial jurisdiction grounded in "Property and Civil

---

nal decisions in a context of multinational companies integrated by technology and telecommunications (*Copyright Administrative Institutions, ibid.* at 31).

19 See text accompanying notes 132ff., below in this chapter, especially notes 139–43 with respect to royalties assessed by the Copyright Board.

20 *McKinnon v. Government of the United States of America*, [2008] 1 W.L.R. 1739 (H.L.).

21 See *Morguard*, above note 2 at paras. 47–49. *Hunt* determined that the rules in *Morguard* were constitutional imperatives, above note 3 at para. 56.

22 Somewhat unusually for a federation, the constitutional legislation for Canada contains no express provision to this effect.

Rights in the Province."[23] The extraprovincial reach of service *ex juris* meets this requirement by being, in pith and substance, *a matter within the province*,[24] if the real and substantial connection test is met.[25]

While the historical and current focus of private international law is demarcated as a provincial constitutional jurisdiction, a potential federal jurisdiction is envisaged interprovincially and internationally,[26] but has not to date been attempted. Instead, an initiative of the Uniform Law Conference of Canada[27] has been enacted by a number of provinces that have legislated substantially uniform principles concerning jurisdiction and the service of process extraterritorially (*ex juris* service), along with interprovincial recognition and enforcement of judgments.[28] In Ontario, the Court of Appeal[29] has significantly harmonized the province's common law and interpretation of the *Rules of Civil Procedure* concerning jurisdiction[30] with the Uniform Law Conference measures.[31] Using BC legislation as an example, the *Court Jurisdiction and Proceedings Transfer Act (CJPTA)*[32], section 3(e) grants "territorial competence" over a defendant if there is a real and substantial connection "between British Columbia and the facts on which the proceed-

---

23 *Constitution Act, 1867* (U.K.), 30 & 31 Vict., c. 3, s. 92(13), reprinted in R.S.C. 1985, App. II, No. 5.

24 *Hunt*, above note 3 at para. 60; see *Reference re Upper Churchill Water Rights Reversion Act*, [1984] 1 S.C.R. 297, 8 D.L.R. (4th) 1.

25 See John Swan, "The Canadian Constitution, Federalism and the Conflict of Laws" (1985) 63 Can. Bar Rev. 271 at 292–95.

26 See *Morguard*, above note 2 at 1098–1100 (S.C.R.); Peter W. Hogg, *Constitutional Law of Canada*, 5th ed., looseleaf (Toronto: Carswell, 2006 updated to 2009) at 13(20)–13(24); Ruth Sullivan, "Interpreting the Territorial Limitations of the Provinces" (1985) Sup. Ct. L. Rev. 511 at 551; E. Edinger, "*Morguard v. DeSavoye*: Subsequent Developments" (1993) 22 Can. Bus. L.J. 29 at 51–56; and Stevan M. Pepa, "Extraterritoriality and the Supreme Court's Assertion of the Economic Constitution" (2001) 34 Can. Bus. L.J. 231 at 251–52.

27 Uniform Law Conference of Canada, Selected Uniform Statutes in Alphabetical Order, online: www.ulcc.ca/en/us/index.cfm?sec=1&sub=1c4.

28 See, for example, in British Columbia, the *Court Jurisdiction and Proceedings Transfer Act*, S.B.C. 2003, c. 28 [*CJPTA*]; and *Enforcement of Canadian Judgments and Decrees Act*, S.B.C. 2003, c. 29

29 See *Van Breda v. Village Resorts Limited*, 2010 ONCA 84 [*Van Breda*].

30 *Rules of Civil Procedure*, R.R.O. 1990, Reg. 194, essentially r. 17(02) concerning service outside Ontario (*ex juris* service).

31 See Uniform Law Conference of Canada, above note 27. The harmonization measures are discussed in the text accompanying notes 70–83, below in this chapter.

32 *CJPTA*, above note 28.

ing is based."[33] Section 10 provides an inexhaustive list of situations in which the connection is assumed to exist.[34] A tort committed in the province is listed.[35] However, determining what constitutes the location of a tort is inherently difficult, made even more so by the nature of the technology in telecommunications media. The seminal decision of the Supreme Court of Canada in *Moran v. Pyle National (Canada) Ltd.* established jurisdictional flexibility in this respect.[36] Formal or pre-set rules were rejected.[37] In a product liability context, emphasis was placed on a manufacturer's reasonable contemplation of where the product might reach once released into commerce. Emphasis was placed on the location where the injury occurred, as damage is the requisite final element needed to constitute the tort of negligence.[38]

Cross-border transmission of radio and television signals containing musical works has been held by the Supreme Court to constitute an infringement at the place of *receipt*.[39] It is therefore a tort within that jurisdiction. A broadcast licence issued by the Canadian Radio-television and Telecommunications Commission (CRTC) affords to a Canadian provider of pay satellite service a right to provide that service within the area of the licence. An infringement of any exclusivity attaching to that right, most commonly by grey market provision and use of decoders for receiving foreign satellite pay television transmissions, is not only a violation of federal regulatory measures but also potentially a tort within the relevant licence area at the suit of the licence holder.[40] This focus on the place of *receipt* of the telecommunication signals is similar to that under the EC Satellite Broadcasting Directive.[41]

Inherently greater complications exist with respect to Internet transmissions. An early response in the United States accorded jurisdiction to a state if a website could be accessed from the forum state.[42] The courts sensibly resiled from this almost universal jurisdiction and stipulated the need for "minimum contacts" in the nature of some event or

---

33 *Ibid.*, s. 1 defines "territorial competence" more broadly by reference not only to the facts but also to a party to the proceedings.

34 See *Stanway v. Wyeth Pharmaceuticals Inc.*, 2009 BCCA 592 [*Stanway*].

35 *CJPTA*, above note 28, s. 10(g).

36 *Moran v. Pyle National (Canada) Ltd.*, [1975] 1 S.C.R. 393 [*Moran*].

37 *Ibid.* at 409.

38 *Ibid.*

39 *Composers, Authors and Publishers Association of Canada Ltd. v. International Good Music Inc.*, [1963] S.C.R. 136.

40 Chapter 2, text accompanying notes 341–42.

41 EC Satellite Broadcasting Directive, above note 16.

42 See, for example, *Inset Systems, Inc. v. Instruction Set Inc.*, 937 F. Supp. 153 at 160 (D. Conn. 1996).

activity that must be linked with the state, beyond mere accessing. The existence of sales made to persons in the state was high on a spectrum of connections. Interactive dialogue was mid-range.[43] Subsequent refinement de-emphasized the notion of a spectrum and interaction in itself in favour of a defendant's intent to "target" the jurisdiction by purposefully availing him or herself of the privilege of conducting activities within the particular state and in order to gain the protection of its laws, or of the scope, effect, or impact of the website in the particular state.[44]

These developments in the United States are consistent with the flexible formulation of the Supreme Court of Canada in *Moran* in locating tortious conduct.[45] They may also provide a useful comparison in applying the test of real and substantial connection in an Internet context.[46] The "targeting" test is particularly appropriate to sales or to the purposeful transmission of content (data, music products, or video) to persons in the jurisdiction. A website hosted outside of Canada but identifying and seeking viewership in Canada would also be likely to meet this test.[47] However, the Federal Court of Appeal declined to apply *Moran* to a claim of non-compliance with the federal *Competition Act* concerning false and misleading advertising[48] in the supply from a US source on a US server of free screensavers tainted with spyware.[49]

---

43 *Zippo Manufacturing Company v. Dot Com Inc.*, 952 F. Supp. 1119 at 1123–25 (W.D. Pa. 1997) [*Zippo*] is regarded as the leading US authority for the spectrum approach of "minimum contacts" in this context. See Jonathan D. Robbins, "Factors Affecting Online Jurisdictional Decisions" (2008) Advising eBusiness (ADVEBUS) § 9:32. See also *Cybersell, Inc. v. Cybersell, Inc.*, 130 F.3d 414 (9th Cir. 1997); and *Panavision International v. Toeppen*, 141 F.3d 1316 at 1320–21 (9th Cir. 1998) requiring "something more" than mere accessibility.

44 See Robbins, *ibid.*, noting the development by 2008 of more nuance to *Zippo*, *ibid.*, by reference to tests of "targeting," "deliberate action," and "effects."

45 See text accompanying notes 36–38, above in this chapter.

46 See, for example, *Pro-C Ltd. v. Computer City, Inc.* (2000), 7 C.P.R. (4th) 193, [2000] O.J .No. 2823 at paras. 102ff. (S.C.J.), rev'd (2000), 14 C.P.R. (4th) 441 (Ont. C.A.), leave to appeal to S.C.C. refused (2002), 294 N.R. 399 (note), [2002] S.C.C.A. No. 5. At para. 122, the court notes *Zippo*, above note 43, as the leading case on Internet jurisdiction and finds it to "echo" the real and substantial connection test. The Ontario Court of Appeal did not discuss this point; *Easthaven, Ltd. v. Nutrisystem.com Inc.* (2001), 202 D.L.R. (4th) 560, 55 O.R. (3d) 334 at paras. 28–29 (S.C.J.); and *Desjean v. Intermix*, 2006 FC 1395 at paras. 40–42, aff'd 2007 FCA 365.

47 See *R. v. Bahr*, 2006 ABPC 360. The facts in this instance (transmitting "hate" material) involved even greater connections with Canada but the principle set out in the text should qualify.

48 *Competition Act*, R.S.C. 1985, c. C-34, s. 36.

49 *Desjean v. Intermix Media Inc.* (2007), 66 C.P.R. (4th) 458 at para. 24 (F.C.A.) [*Desjean*].

The "effects test" is particularly appropriate with respect to defamation, when the greatest impact is likely to be at the place of the plaintiff's ordinary residence or business, so that a tort of libel or slander is committed in that jurisdiction.[50] This would also be the likely position for breach of privacy by way of *disclosure* of private information, although any act of *intrusion* to gain the private information will ordinarily occur at the *situs* of the information or data, or, perhaps, a third location from which an intrusive action was initiated, particularly by electronic accessing.

In some instances, the technology of the particular media may lead to tortious conduct at the place of origin as well as that of receipt of a communication and, perhaps, multiple intermediate locations. Copyright infringement is a useful example. It presents infringement (a tort) at the places of origin (uploading is a reproduction), receipt (reproduction by electronic or physical retention), and intermediate sites where an electronic copy may have been made.[51] The communication right[52] may be infringed equally at the place of origin or receipt, even if accessing must occur to establish a "communication,"[53] but the location of origin or source is likely for any infringement by "making available" when enacted,[54] or by "publication" (if a work is unpublished), as this is defined as a making available of copies to the public.[55]

Infringement of a registered trademark can occur only in the jurisdiction of the grant of the mark. A "use," as statutorily defined, must also occur within that jurisdiction. This may be established by the mere advertising of *services* with the mark,[56] or when the property or possession of *wares* passes to a purchaser.[57] Unregistered trademarks, however, are created by use rather than by any sovereign grant and are remedial under common law passing off, with the essential element of damage being at the location where the misrepresentation as to the origin of the product is effected. This may occur in multiple jurisdictions if a prior use of the mark has established goodwill attaching to the mark in those jurisdictions. Actual goodwill through use is the key focus at common law, as opposed to a sovereign grant of an exclusivity

---

50   *Dow Jones & Company Inc. v. Gutnick* (2002), 210 C.L.R. 575 at paras. 38–42 and 44 (H.C.A.) [*Dow Jones*].
51   See Chapter 5, text accompanying notes 135–82.
52   *Copyright Act*, R.S.C. 1985, c. C-42, s. 3(1)(f).
53   Chapter 5, text accompanying notes 149–52.
54   *Ibid.*, text accompanying note 148 (compare note 145 re publication).
55   *Copyright Act*, above note 52, s. 2.2(1)(a)(i).
56   *Trade-marks Act*, R.S.C. 1985, c. T-13, s. 4(2).
57   *Ibid.* s. 4(1). See Chapter 3, text accompanying notes 14–16.

under a statutory framework.[58] Infringement of common law interests in trademarks is, therefore, as much an application of an "effects test" at multiple locations of damage as is the case for products liability or defamation. Similarly, while tortious interferences with websites or Internet facilities can present tortious elements at the location of origin of the interference, the tort is not complete until an effect occurs at the place of receipt, by either impact or damage. However, the surreptitious installation of spyware from a US source without commercial or financial links with Canada was not a real and substantial connection.[59]

Jurisdictional issues in the United States are subject to an overall constitutional due process requirement that there be sufficient "minimum contacts" with a forum jurisdiction to afford a prerequisite of predictability as to where proceedings might reasonably be expected by a potential defendant in the ordinary course of his or her affairs.[60] The deliberate absence of a protection of property from section 7 of the *Canadian Charter of Rights and Freedoms* renders this provision problematic in affording a measure similar to that in the United States.[61] However, the principle of "minimum contacts" can be reflected in the flexible tests in *Moran* as to the location of a tort, and possibly in establishing an appropriate real and substantial connection with the forum.[62] The overall criterion is "order and fairness,"[63] but within this dimension one theory emphasizes public order and efficiency in the administra-

---

58 Use of a trademark must, however, exist (or follow) registration and continue with respect to a registered mark, if it is to remain valid. See *Trade-marks Act*, above note 56, s. 18(1)(c) (abandonment), s. 40(2) (declaration of use), and s. 45 (evidence of user).

59 *Desjean*, above note 49 at paras. 4–5. The US-based website did not "target" Canada. It simply made screensavers tainted with spyware universally available.

60 *International Shoe v. Washington*, 326 U.S. 310 (1945). The constitutional requirements are discussed in *Zippo*, above note 43 at 1122–23 in an Internet context.

61 *Morguard*, above note 2 at 1100 (S.C.R.) notes, without elaboration, s. 7 of the *Canadian Charter of Rights and Freedoms*, Part I of the *Constitution Act, 1982*, being Schedule B to the *Canada Act 1982* (U.K.), 1982, c. 11 [*Charter*]. The application of s. 7 was rejected in *Beals*, above note 5 at para. 78. See Garry D. Watson & Frank Au, "Constitutional Limits on Service *Ex Juris*: Unanswered Questions from *Morguard*" (2000) 23 Advocates' Q. 167 at 181.

62 Vaughan Black & John Swan "New Rules for the Enforcement of Foreign Judgments: *Morguard Investments Ltd. v. DeSavoye*" (1990–91) 12 Advocates' Q. 489 at 503 and 505.

63 *Morguard*, above note 2 at 1078 (S.C.R.). See Elizabeth Edinger, "The Constitutionalization of the Conflict of Laws" (1995) 25 Can. Bus. L.J. 38 at 64: "[A] principle of order and fairness has the potential to become the due process clause."

tion of justice within society, while the other is more focused on the position of the parties and the relationship between them, particularly the position of the defendant. The US due process approach tends toward this second category. The interpretation of real and substantial connection has tended toward the former,[64] though not exclusively so. Authorities reaffirmed in 2009 by the Nova Scotia Court of Appeal include "fairness to the parties," in a necessarily relative sense, within the real and substantial connection test.[65] The court rejected the idea that such a consideration is limited to the discretionary *forum non conveniens* inquiry.

Public order might well be the appropriate perspective in interprovincial proceedings but, it is suggested, a due process balancing perspective ought to be preferred internationally. The substantiality element of real and substantial connection has been emphasized internationally[66] and contextual differences between interprovincial and international proceedings have been well acknowledged.[67]

Canadian authorities that have considered jurisdiction in an Internet context have reached results consistent with the "targeting" and "effects" tests from the United States. Some have cited US authorities.[68] Others have relied on existing Canadian authorities outside of the Internet. In addition to extending the products liability analysis in *Moran* to Internet-related injury, particularly defamation,[69] reliance has been

---

64   See, for example, *Muscutt v. Courcelles* (2002), 60 O.R. (3d) 20, [2002] O.J. No. 2128 at paras. 56–74 (C.A.) (QL) [*Muscutt*], discussing these perspectives with reference to Joost Blom, "*Morguard*" (1991) 70 Can. Bar Rev. 733 and adopting an administration of justice approach. See also Vaughan Black, "The Other Side of *Morguard*: New Limits on Judicial Jurisdiction" (1993) 22 Can. Bus. L.J. 4 at 23.

65   *Bouch v. Penny*, 2009 NSCA 80, 310 D.L.R. (4th) 433 at para. 51 [*Bouch*].

66   *Beals*, above note 5 at para. 32.

67   *Morguard*, above note 2 at 1099–1101 (S.C.R.); *Spar Aerospace Ltd. v. American Mobile Satellite Corp.*, [2002] 4 S.C.R. 205, [2002] SCC 78 at paras. 51–54 [*Spar Aerospace*]; *Beals*, above note 5 at paras. 28 and 30; *Pro Swing*, above note 6 at para. 51.

68   See above note 46.

69   See *Barrick Gold Corp. v. Blanchard and Co.*, [2003] O.J. No. 5817 at paras. 43–45 (S.C.J.) (defamatory statement was placed in a "normal distribution channel designed for media attention and publication"); *Burke v. NYP Holdings, Inc.*, 2005 BCSC 1287 at para. 29 ("where the words are heard or read," it being foreseeable that a website would be accessed in British Columbia, the location of an incident referred to on the website); *Research in Motion Ltd. v. Visto Corp.* (2008), 93 O.R. (3d) 593, [2008] O.J. No. 3671 at para. 94 (S.C.J.) (normal distribution channel); and *Black v. Breeden* (2009), 309 D.L.R. (4th) 708, [2009] O.J. No. 1292 at paras. 46–48 (S.C.J.) ("[R]eplication of the defamatory material in the jurisdiction where the plaintiff resides . . . is the natural and probable consequence of the posting elsewhere": para. 47). See also *Disney Enterprises Inc.*

placed on the determination of the Ontario Court of Appeal in *Muscutt v. Courcelles*, involving person injury.[70] *Muscutt* was a consolidation of four appeals, all involving Ontario residents who had suffered serious personal injury in another province or country and then returned to Ontario, where they suffered continuing losses from medical treatment and depletion of income and amenities of life. *Muscutt* is, however, an extension of *Moran*, as the immediate damage (a motor vehicle accident), and therefore all elements of the tort in a causation sense, occurred outside of Ontario. The focus of *Muscutt* is the location of continuing consequential loss.

Although a leading authority in establishing a real and substantial connection, *Muscutt* has come under criticism,[71] and has been declared inapplicable in British Columbia after the enactment of the *CJPTA* in that province.[72] Subsequently, in *Van Breda v. Village Resorts Limited*,[73] a five-judge Court of Appeal panel in Ontario reviewed and modified the approach in *Muscutt* to afford significant harmonization with the structure recommended by the Uniform Law Conference for court jurisdiction. Key modifications are (1), that most categories enumerated in Ontario Rule 17.02 for *ex juris* service are now presumptive of a real and substantial connection,[74] in the same manner as found in British Columbia under section 10, *CJPTA*;[75] (2), that to establish a real and substantial connection, the connection between the forum and, respectively, the plaintiff and the defendant is of primary or "core" significance, and the remaining factors of *Muscutt* are merely "analytic tools" to assist in assessing the extent of the core connections;[76] and (3), that the categories of jurisdiction *simpliciter*, and *forum non conveniens* are not to be conflated into one test but are distinct tests to

---

70   *v. Click Enterprises Inc.*, [2006] O.J. No. 1308 at para. 28 (S.C.J.) (re copyright infringement).

70   *Muscutt*, above note 64.

71   See *Succession de feu André Gauthier v. Coutu*, 2006 NBCA 16, [2006] N.B.J. No. 38 at paras. 66–70, where in *obiter*, Drapeau CJ highlights several problems with the *Muscutt* analysis, most notably a blurring of the distinction between jurisdiction *simpliciter* and *forum non conveniens*.

72   *Stanway*, above note 34 at para. 73.

73   *Van Breda*, above note 29.

74   *Ibid.* at paras. 73–80. Enumerated categories in the *Rules of Civil Procedure*, above note 30, rr. 17.02(h) ("damages sustained in Ontario") and 17.02(o) ("a necessary and proper party") were excluded from the presumption as these categories have no equivalent in s. 10 of *CJPTA*, above note 28 (*Van Breda*, ibid. at paras. 74–79).

75   *Stanway*, above note 34 at paras. 21–22.

76   *Van Breda*, above note 29 at paras. 84–92.

be considered separately.[77] *Muscutt* had stipulated the following factors, of more or less equal application, to consider to establish a real and substantial connection for the taking of jurisdiction: (1) the connection between the forum and, respectively, the plaintiff and the defendant; (2) unfairness to either defendant or plaintiff in, respectively, taking or not taking jurisdiction; (3) the presence of other parties; (4) whether the court would recognize and enforce a foreign judgment given on the same jurisdictional basis; (5) whether the proceeding is interprovincial or international, jurisdiction being more readily assumed if interprovincial; and (6) comity, focused on standards elsewhere concerning jurisdiction, recognition, and enforcement.[78] In *Bangoura v. Washington Post*,[79] these *Muscutt* factors were considered in addition to an effects test involving defamation of the plaintiff in electronic versions of newspaper articles. Jurisdiction in Ontario, where the plaintiff moved three years after the publication, was denied. The Court of Appeal found insufficient connection with Ontario. Neither initial damage nor continuing consequential loss was suffered in the province. Rather, all damage had been sustained three years earlier, outside of Ontario.[80]

Overall, while the new telecommunications media readily lead to a plethora of potential forums for any one communication and present dimensions in format and operation that cause infringement situations beyond those of hard copy media, the application of jurisdictional criteria to the electronic media is essentially a nuance of the traditional tests developed in non-electronic contexts. In this respect, the significant harmonization in *Van Breda* of the *Muscutt* principles with those under *CJPTA* legislation, leaves a subtle difference. *Muscutt* and *Van Breda* describe as *core* the connection of *both* the defendant and the plaintiff with the forum,[81] with emphasis on the inclusion of the plaintiff's connection as a core element.[82] The *CJPTA* also includes the plaintiff in this relational role, but only through the enumerated categories or residually under section 10 by judicial inclusion within this real

---

77   *Ibid.* at paras. 81–82.

78   *Muscutt*, above note 64 at paras. 76ff. (paraphrased above). See *Schreiber v. Mulroney* (2007), 88 O.R. (3d) 605 (S.C.J.) for additional factors, specifically in the context of contracts law.

79   *Bangoura v. Washington Post* (2004), 235 D.L.R. (4th) 564, [2004] O.J. No. 284 (S.C.J.), rev'd (2005), 258 D.L.R. (4th) 341, [2005] O.J. No. 3849 (C.A.) [*Bangoura*].

80   *Ibid.* at paras. 22–25 (C.A.).

81   *Van Breda*, above note 29 at para. 84, discussed in the text accompanying note 76ff., above in this chapter

82   *Ibid.* at para. 88.

and substantial connection category. It is not expressly a core provision under *CJPTA*. In this sense, *CJPTA* legislation may be formulated closer to a personal subjection theory.[83] However, as long as a defendant has significant connections with the forum, the ability to protect a plaintiff citizen in the forum is appropriate.[84] The electronic media may be the crucible in testing the relational position of the parties to the forum, particularly the scope afforded to a plaintiff in circumstances in which the defendant's connection is insubstantial.

C. JURISDICTION *FORUM NON CONVENIENS*

While jurisdiction *simpliciter* allows jurisdiction upon *any* real and substantial connection as a minimal requirement,[85] and is likely to be established in typically several jurisdictions, especially with telecommunications media, *Morguard* recognized the additional principle *forum non conveniens* as available to restrain this multiplicity. This principle is discretionary. It seeks the jurisdiction that has the *most*, or *more*, real and substantial connection in the particular event. It does not enjoy universal international recognition and has no historical basis in civil law jurisdictions[86] but is now well established in Commonwealth and US conflict of laws theory. It has been of little significance interprovincially and post-*Morguard* jurisprudence appears to regard the test of real and substantial connection as all encompassing. However, the *CJPTA* (again using British Columbia as an example) has been held by

---

83 In *Stanway*, above note 34 at para. 78, the personal subjection theory is referred to and applied by the BC Court of Appeal in interpreting the *CJPTA*, above note 28.

84 This balancing requirement is emphasized by the Ontario Court of Appeal in *Van Breda*, above note 29 at paras. 86–89 and 95. In addition, interprovincial contexts may enhance the weight given to the position of a plaintiff more, given the relative uniformity of interprovincial administration of justice. See *Van Breda, ibid.* at paras. 104–6, emphasizing a differentiation between interprovincial and international proceedings "as a general principle of law that generally guides the analysis of real and substantial connection" (*ibid.* at para. 106).

85 *Braintech Inc. v. Kostiuk*, (1999), 63 B.C.L.R. (3d) 156 (C.A.) [*Braintech*].

86 In Quebec, the doctrine of *forum non conveniens* is codified in Art. 3135 C.C.Q. as follows: "Even though a Quebec authority has jurisdiction to hear a dispute, it may exceptionally and on application by a party, decline jurisdiction if it considers that the authorities of *another country* are in a better position to decide" [emphasis added]. The language suggests that Art. 3135 might not have interprovincial application.

the Supreme Court of Canada[87] to codify discretionary principles in the nature of those reflected in *forum non conveniens*.[88]

Interests in international comity in administration of justice form the essential policy dimension of the principle *forum non conveniens*, but with more emphasis on the relational interests of the parties. Since *Spiliada Maritime Corp. v. Cansulex Ltd.* in the House of Lords,[89] and *Amchem* in the Supreme Court of Canada,[90] the historical preference to preserve the plaintiff's "personal and juridical advantage"[91] in his or her choice of forum has passed. Instead, the interests of both (or all) parties are considered to determine the more appropriate or natural forum, having regard for not only the connections of the case and parties with the jurisdiction but other relevant circumstances.[92] The nomenclature "real and substantial connection" is sometimes used, perhaps indiscriminately, in this context. There is necessarily, however, a considerable overlap of factors between the test of real and substantial connection in jurisdiction *simpliciter* and the principle *forum non conveniens*. The codification in the *CJPTA* has brought some measure of focus to this relationship and the need to approach these two inquiries separately and not conflate them has been acknowledged.[93]

Section 11(1) of the *CJPTA* requires the court to consider both the interests of the parties and "the ends of justice" in determining whether the court of another jurisdiction is more appropriate to hear the proceeding. Section 11(2) requires "the circumstances relevant to the proceeding" be considered and then stipulates a non-exclusive list of six factors of relevance that must be considered. They include the comparative convenience to the parties and their witnesses, the choice of law to be applied, the avoidance of multiple proceedings with the potential for different results, and the enforcement of an eventual judgment. The fair and efficient working of the Canadian legal system as a whole is included.[94]

---

87 *Teck Cominco*, above note 7 at para. 22. See also *Bouch*, above note 65 at para. 78 to the same effect as to the whole of the *CJPTA* legislation.

88 *CJPTA*, above note 28, s. 11.

89 *Spiliada Maritime Corp. v. Cansulex Ltd.*, [1987] A.C. 460 (H.L.) [*Spiliada*].

90 *Amchem Products Inc. v. British Columbia (Workers' Compensation Bureau)*, [1993] 1 S.C.R. 897, 102 D.L.R. (4th) 96 [*Amchem*].

91 *Spiliada*, above note 89 at 476; *Amchem*, ibid. at 924 (S.C.R.).

92 *Amchem*, ibid. at 937–38.

93 The distinct assessments under jurisdiction *simpliciter* and *forum non conveniens* were expressly stipulated by the Ontario Court of Appeal in *Van Breda*, above note 29 at paras. 81 & 82.

94 *CJPTA*, above note 28, s. 11. In an international context, it is suggested that transnational efficiency of judicial resources might also be considered within

Principles of order and fairness within a framework of comity assume that a court will administer a restrained jurisdiction, staying proceedings when a more appropriate forum exists. This ideal may not always occur. Procedures for an anti-suit injunction (if a plaintiff is subject to forum personal jurisdiction) are available to the natural or more appropriate forum should it consider that an extraterritorial court has not properly restrained itself in proceeding with the case. It is an exceptional remedy as it presents an indirect but nevertheless adverse impact on comity. The English prerequisites of vexatiousness and abuse of process have been incorporated in Canada within a test of simple injustice to the defendant as the basis for the issue of this remedy.[95]

The Supreme Court in *Morguard* contemplated that a judgment of a foreign court, not properly restrained in taking jurisdiction, might not be enforced under the conflict of laws rules of the enforcing jurisdiction.[96] An Internet-related example of a refusal to enforce a foreign judgment from a court considered not to have been properly restrained in assumption of jurisdiction is *Braintech Inc. v. Kostiuk*.[97] The British Columbia Court of Appeal considered the state of Texas to fall short as the natural forum for determining a defamation suit between two BC residents. The only connection with Texas was the accessibility from Texas of the website containing the allegedly defamatory statement. This was held to be insufficient in terms of both *forum non conveniens* and any real and substantial connection.[98]

Braintech, however, must now be considered contextually with the 2009 decision of the Supreme Court of Canada in *Canada Post Corporation v. Lépine*[99] in its interpretation of Article 3135 of the *Civil Code of Québec*.[100] Class action proceedings were instigated by different plaintiffs in the same matter in three provinces. An Ontario judgment approved a settlement that purported to be binding on residents of certain other provinces, including Quebec.[101] The Superior Court and Court of Appeal in Quebec declined to recognize the Ontario judgment.[102] The Supreme Court upheld the Quebec Court of Appeal but rejected an application of the principle *forum non conveniens*, in Article 3135, as a

---

the reference to "the Canadian legal system as a whole."

95 *Amchem,* above note 90 at 936–37.

96 *Morguard,* above note 2 at 1103 (S.C.R.).

97 *Braintech,* above note 85.

98 *Ibid.* at paras. 61–69.

99 *Canada Post Corporation,* above note 7.

100 See above note 86.

101 *McArthur v. Canada Post Corporation,* [2004] O.J. No. 1406 (S.C.J.).

102 *Canada Post Corporation,* 2007 QCCA 1092 [unofficial English translation], aff'g [2005] Q.J. no 9806 (Sup. Ct.).

ground for declining to enforce the Ontario judgment. The Court distinguished the *existence* of jurisdiction in the judgment court from the manner in which the judgment court *exercised* such jurisdiction.

The Court examined two competing theories.[103] The first would utilize *forum non conveniens* (Article 3135) in assessing whether the judgment court properly assumed jurisdiction; the second would be limited to considering whether a Quebec court would have taken jurisdiction under only a substantial connection test: essentially (in common law terms) jurisdiction *simpliciter* requirements. The heart of the distinction between these competing interpretations of the *Civil Code* provisions was the prohibition of an enforcing court entering upon the merits of the proceeding (Article 3158). The opinion against utilizing *forum non conveniens* (Article 3135) characterizes the principle *forum non conveniens* as an exercise of discretion and, therefore, concerning the merits of the proceeding.[104]

While this proceeding turned on the interpretation of the *Civil Code*, LeBel J in giving the judgment of the Supreme Court described as basic the distinction between the *existence* and the *exercise* of jurisdiction, a feature similarly reflected in common law recognition and enforcement and earlier noted at common law by LeBel J in *Beals*, that *forum non conveniens* is a principle exercisable only by the judgment court.[105] However, LeBel J in his dissent in *Beals* did formulate extended defences to an enforcement proceeding and these readily reflect elements more familiar in a *forum non conveniens* inquiry.[106] The existence in the real and substantial connection test of criteria concerning "fairness to the parties" may also help mitigate against a too minimalist formulation of real and substantial connections.[107]

D. ENFORCEMENT OF FOREIGN JUDGMENTS

Foreign judgments *in rem*, concerning personal status (such as marriage) or proprietary title (such as to land), are not discussed. Communications situations primarily concern enforcement of *in personam* judgments. In this context, enforcement has historically been limit-

---

103 *Canada Post Corporation v. Lépine*, above note 7 at paras. 28–37. See also text accompanying notes 99–100, above in this chapter.

104 *Ibid.* at para. 33.

105 See *Beals*, above note 5 at paras. 185–86. See text accompanying notes 113–16, below in this chapter.

106 See below note 129.

107 See *Bouch*, above note 65 and accompanying text.

ed to *monetary* judgments and only if the defendant had been served within the originating jurisdiction, or had attorned or consented (say, by choice-of-forum clause in a contract) to the original jurisdiction. *Morguard* extended this to include an originating jurisdiction's *ex juris* service beyond the traditional categories so long as a real and substantial connection existed. As noted, the Court in *Hunt* gave *Morguard* a constitutional dimension interprovincially[108] and *Hunt* itself extended *Morguard* to the interprovincial enforcement of *in personam* non-monetary orders.[109]

Despite reference by LeBel J for the Court in 2002 noting that *Morguard* and *Hunt* could not be easily extended beyond an interprovincial context,[110] a majority in 2003 in *Beals* confirmed the extension of the *Morguard* real and substantial connection test to foreign *in personam* pecuniary judgments. The Court did, however, emphasize that the connection must be "significant" and "substantial," not "fleeting or relatively unimportant."[111] This test was distinguished from the principle *forum non conveniens*, which was referred to separately, even though the two are closely related.[112] The formulation is, therefore, directed to jurisdiction *simpliciter*. Historically, of course, the requirement of a foreign court acting within the limits of its rules of civil procedure has been of little significance to an enforcing court, given the enforcement prerequisites of presence, agreement, or attornment to that court's jurisdiction. Discarding these prerequisites in favour of the current broader principle of real and substantial connection necessarily enhances the prominence of the appropriateness or otherwise of the jurisdiction of the judgment court. The majority in *Beals* noted, "[D]efendants sued abroad can raise the doctrine *forum non conveniens* in the usual way."[113] LeBel J, in his dissent on other grounds, describes the majority in this passage as limiting an application of the principle *forum non conveniens* to the originating, rather than the enforcing, jurisdiction. In other words, raising the principle in the usual way means within an application to the originating court to "stay" the proceeding. LeBel

---

108 See above note 21 and accompanying text explaining that the decision of the S.C.C. in *Hunt* gave constitutional significance to the court's earlier determination in *Morguard*.

109 *Hunt*, above note 3, involved an order to produce documents in a discovery process.

110 *Spar Aerospace*, above note 67 at para. 51.

111 *Beals*, above note 5 at para. 32.

112 *Ibid.* at para. 35. In *Spar Aerospace*, above note 67 at para. 21, LeBel J (for the Court) approved commentary that found the *forum non conveniens* principle to be founded on a "real and substantial connection" test.

113 *Beals*, above note 5.

J also ultimately expresses this position,[114] and, as noted earlier, it has subsequently been confirmed by the Supreme Court interpreting the *Civil Code of Quebec*[115] and at common law by the Ontario Court of Appeal.[116]

It is suggested that a single test of real and substantial connection in a context merely of jurisdiction *simpliciter* may in some situations be too favourable to a plaintiff, especially if the acknowledged[117] differences between interprovincial and international contexts are not preserved. The unifying features of the Canadian constitutional and legal systems afford greater opportunities for a broad application of *ex juris* in interprovincial proceedings, recognition, and enforcement.[118] Internationally, however, these safeguards are absent.

Canadian constitutional law does not afford defendants a due process protection as provided in the United States, requiring sufficient predictability and thereby a narrowing in the scope of potential forum selection. The real and substantial connection test has been noted as possibly serving a similar function,[119] but only if it is applied with some measure of interjurisdictional conformity and objectivity to some significant level. Mere compliance with the rules of *ex juris* civil procedure in the originating jurisdiction will not always meet such a standard. The possibility in Canada of section 7 of the *Charter*[120] providing constitutional protection has been speculated[121] but is hampered by the absence from section 7 of a protection of an interest in property.[122]

This result produces some conceptual conflict with the *forum non conveniens* analysis in a context of an anti-suit injunction. These proceedings include an assessment of the most or more appropriate jurisdiction between the enjoining and the forum jurisdictions.[123] If such an injunction is issued but disregarded by a plaintiff, should recognition and enforcement of any resulting foreign judgment proceed on a less stringent test than that used in the anti-suit injunction proceedings? Logic suggests not.

---

114 *Ibid.* at paras. 185–86.
115 See text accompanying notes 99–104, above in this chapter, concerning *Canada Post Corporation v. Lépine*.
116 *United Laboratories, Inc. v. Abraham*, [2004] O.J. No. 3063 at para. 5 (C.A.), leave to appeal to S.C.C. refused, [2004] S.C.C.A. No. 414.
117 *Beals*, above note 5 at paras. 26, 30, 85, and 166–70.
118 *Ibid.* at para. 85.
119 See text accompanying notes 62–64, above in this chapter.
120 *Charter*, above note 61, s. 7.
121 *Beals*, above note 5 at para. 180.
122 *Ibid.* at para. 78.
123 See text accompanying notes 90–92, above in this chapter.

Likewise, in a context of parallel proceedings, the Supreme Court has upheld the continuation of domestic proceedings, notwithstanding active parallel proceedings before a foreign court, when the domestic jurisdiction is the more appropriate forum.[124] Difficulties over ultimate recognition and enforcement of any judgment of the foreign court were noted but left unresolved.[125]

The unusual facts in *Beals* and an unassailable recognition of the originating jurisdiction as, indeed, the only appropriate jurisdiction caused a significant division of judicial opinion. However, all judges of the Supreme Court were prepared to extend the real and substantial connection test of *Morguard* to recognition and enforcement of international *in personam* pecuniary judgments, subject to any legislation that might provide otherwise,[126] thereby denying *Beals* a constitutional dimension.

The majority in *Beals* also declined to re-evaluate the narrow and strictly interpreted defences developed historically in a context of traditional enforcement criteria. Yet that door is still open. Major J, for the majority, described the defences as representing "the most recognizable situations in which an injustice might arise [from enforcement] but they are not exhaustive."[127] Dissenting in the particular instance, Binnie and Iacobucci JJ emphasized the "significant differences" between interprovincial and international contexts and warned of the likelihood of a future need to re-examine the scope of available defences in an appropriate case. The real and substantial connection test was described by Binnie and Iacobucci JJ as "a framework" and cautioned that the court should not be "overly rigid" in formulating available defences.[128] LeBel J, also dissenting, formulated enhanced defences.[129]

The majority refers to the defences of fraud, public policy, and natural justice as sufficient to balance the interests of plaintiffs and defendants consistently with order and fairness within the principle of

---

124 See *Teck Cominco*, above note 7 at paras. 21–31.

125 *Ibid.* at paras. 39–40.

126 *Beals*, above note 5 at paras. 28, 84, and 135.

127 *Ibid.* at para. 41.

128 *Ibid.* at para. 85–86.

129 LeBel J suggested several sources of protection to Canadian defendants. First, he reformulated the real and substantial connection analysis to include more explicitly what would normally be factors within a *forum non conveniens* analysis, especially insofar as the fairness to the defendant in forcing him or her to litigate in a foreign jurisdiction should be considered. Second, LeBel J suggested that plaintiffs should have to establish that the judgment was from a fair judicial system. Third, he proposed expansions to all of the existing defences. *Ibid.* at paras. 182, 195, and 219–45.

comity.[130] Other established categories are penal and taxation law.[131] The possible defence denying enforcement of the "other public law" of the originating jurisdiction was not discussed.[132] It may therefore not be recognized, a position that has been suggested elsewhere.[133] It does, however, present a dimension relevant to any area of administrative regulation and tribunal determination, including these dimensions within telecommunications. A public law defence presents a different focus from that of pure public policy. It reflects a state policy similar to taxation or penal law. By seeking extraterritorial enforcement, the foreign government is seen to be projecting itself extraterritorially in promotion of its public law or policy cause. Recovery of environmental site restoration costs has been considered under this category and enforced.[134] A national attempt to utilize specifically enacted legislation to recover artifacts of indigenous citizens extraterritorially has also provoked comment.[135]

Involvement of a foreign government as a plaintiff may sharpen the perspective of public law and discourage recognition or enforcement. It is suggested this should not be a decisive feature. The projection of public law or public policy objectives can be just as readily presented in a dispute between private persons. Two examples illustrate this position. First, consider the potential of enforcement in Canada of civil claims in the United States under the US *Patriot Act*[136] against persons responsible for injuries to US citizens worldwide.[137] This presents an expansion of US governmental interests beyond the United States itself, but the proceeding is essentially a private claim. Conversely, consider potential US recognition and enforcement of a Canadian *ex juris* pecuniary

---

130 *Ibid.* at para. 40.

131 Canadian courts have long refused to enforce foreign penal or revenue laws. See Jean-Gabriel Castel & Janet Walker, *Canadian Conflict of Laws*, 6th ed., looseleaf (Markham, ON: LexisNexis/Butterworths, 2005–), ss. 8(3)–8(4).

132 Only LeBel J (in dissent) mentioned the public law defence, writing: "Other potential defences, such as the foreign public law exception to enforceability in Canada, which might apply, for example, to a tax claim, are not implicated by the facts of this case." *Beals*, above note 5 at para. 210. See also text accompanying note 129, above in this chapter.

133 See *United States of America v. Ivey* (1995), 130 D.L.R. (4th) 674 (Ont. Ct. Gen. Div.), aff'd (1996), 30 O.R. (3d) 370 (C.A.), leave to appeal to S.C.C. refused (1996), 218 N.R. 159 [*Ivey*].

134 *Ibid.*

135 See *Attorney-General of New Zealand v. Ortiz*, [1984] A.C. 1 (H.L.).

136 *Uniting and Strengthening America by Providing Appropriate Tools Required to Intercept and Obstruct Terrorism (USA PATRIOT) Act of 2001*, Pub. L. No. 107-56, 115 Stat. 272 (2001) [US *Patriot Act*].

137 *Ibid.*, Title 6.

award against US satellite broadcasters for enabling Canadian viewers to receive in Canada their program transmissions when such receipt is contrary to Canadian broadcasting policy and an infringement of Canadian regulatory authority.[138] Should this be any less enforceable than what in *form* is a private claim under US patriot legislation? Indeed, the Canadian regulatory policy in this context is not seeking any extraterritorial application (it applies strictly in Canada), whereas the US patriot initiative is an extension of US policy extraterritorially.

Administrative tariffs affording remuneration to copyright owners for works or subject matter communicated on the Internet might similarly be seen as an extraterritorial expansion of a public law or policy category. The tariffs are set under the *Copyright Act*[139] by the Copyright Board of Canada and administered through a well-established system of collective societies.[140] It is certainly far from an application of private law, yet perhaps the substantial transnational usage and recognition of this system[141] will ensure international policy acceptance of the tariffs in the same manner as the now widely utilized environmental site restoration procedure.[142] The 2004 determination by the Supreme Court allowing the application of such tariffs on musical works transmitted from sources hosted outside of Canada, so long as the transmissions have a real and substantial connection with Canada,[143] may provide the opportunity to test such recognition and enforcement by foreign jurisdictions. A targeting of the Canadian market or supplying a Canadian user would be likely to meet the real and substantial connection with Canada in this context.

Use of a real and substantial connection test for territorial jurisdiction for enforcement of Canadian copyright law invites a comparison with application of this test in conflict of laws. Commentators Leong and Saw[144] make this comparison in the context of finding the *most* real and substantial connection, as between the test of a server located in Canada (the "host server" test formulated by LeBel J) and that of

---

138 Chapter 2, text accompanying notes 241–62 and 341–43.

139 *Copyright Act*, above note 52.

140 See *ibid.*, Part VII. See also Daniel Gervais, ed., *Collective Management of Copyright and Related Rights* (Alphen aan den Rijn, The Netherlands: Kluwer Law International, 2006) c. 9.

141 See Ysolde Gendreau, ed., *Copyright Administrative Institutions* (Cowansville, QC: Éditions Yvon Blais, 2002), especially Claire Kusy, "Comparative Study on Copyright Adminstrative Institutions" at 639.

142 *Ivey*, above note 133.

143 *Tariff 22*, above note 1 at paras. 60 and 77.

144 Susanna H.S. Leong & Cheng Lim Saw, "Copyright Infringement in a Borderless World — Does Territoriality Matter?" (2007) 15 Int'l. J.L. & I.T. 38, n. 12.

real and substantial connection of the majority. This essentially utilizes a *forum non conveniens* analysis and presents a sensible approach. However, it may not reflect the approach in conflict of laws, where real and substantial connection is likely to be focused on simply jurisdiction *simpliciter*.[145] Consistently, territorial competence for copyright enforcement depends on jurisdiction *simpliciter* enabling *any* (rather than the *most* or a *more*) real and substantial connection to be sufficient.

The scope and application of policy defences to enforcement are determined by the private international law of the enforcing jurisdiction. The Canadian approach requires more than a mere legal or policy difference. The foreign law must be repugnant to Canadian concepts of basic morality or "the fundamental morality of the Canadian legal system."[146] Breach of financial and securities disclosure requirements to investors has been held to be fundamental.[147] Foreign government confiscation of property consequent upon illegal warfare is similarly repugnant.[148] The scope of constitutionally protected free speech[149] has not been tested in this context in Canada but was utilized at first instance in the United States as a reason to deny enforcement of an order by a French court that the US-based Internet service provider Yahoo! Inc. render inaccessible in France websites conducting auctions of German National Socialist (Nazi) memorabilia, contrary to French law.[150] Such a determination necessarily asks how far constitutional infringement *per se* should be interpreted as preventing enforcement. For example, would a Canadian judgment in defamation awarded to a public figure, permitted under Canadian law, be unenforceable in the United States by reason of the US constitutional inability of public figures to maintain such proceedings?[151] In effect, does constitutional infringement in itself present a violation of "fundamental morality"?

---

145   See text accompanying notes 96–105, above in this chapter.

146   *Beals*, above note 5 at para. 72.

147   *Society of Lloyd's v. Saunders* (2001), 55 O.R. (3d) 688, 210 D.L.R. (4th) 519 at para. 65 (C.A.). However, in all the circumstances of this case, the foreign judgment was enforced.

148   *Kuwait Airways Corpn v. Iraqi Airways Co (Nos 4 and 5)*, [2002] 2 A.C. 883, [2002] UKHL 19.

149   *Charter*, above note 61, s. 2(b).

150   *Yahoo! Inc. v. LICRA*, 145 F. Supp. 1168 (N.D. Cal. 2001). The result in this case was reversed. The Ninth Circuit (*en banc*) found that the case was not ripe: *Yahoo! Inc. v. LICRA*, 433 F.3d 1199 (9th Cir. 2006). Additionally, Yahoo! Inc. had substantially complied with the order of the French court, which may, in any event, have been penal and not a "final" order.

151   See *Hill v. Church of Scientology*, [1995] 2 S.C.R. 1130.

Differences of this nature reinforce the significant divergences between interprovincial and international contexts in jurisdiction, recognition, and enforcement. It also reflects the limited meaning of reciprocity, as a basis for recognition and enforcement, discussed by LeBel J in *Beals*. Reciprocity does not mean states enforcing each other's court judgments on equal terms. Rather, it is a willingness to recognize and enforce a foreign judgment if the enforcing court would have taken jurisdiction if placed similarly to the foreign court.[152]

This also reflects the significant difference between non-pecuniary and pecuniary orders. A foreign *pecuniary* judgment is enforced at common law (or civil code) as a debt owing upon the judgment, independently of the proceeding that produced the judgment. It is a simple theory of recovery. Non-pecuniary orders, however, are necessarily imbued with a governmental intrusiveness that necessitates the exercise of discretion with respect to issuance. In addition, there may be need for continuing supervision by the court over allocation of judicial resources by the enforcing jurisdiction. In *Pro Swing*, the Supreme Court acknowledged that recognition and enforcement can, in principle, include foreign non-pecuniary judicial orders. The door is therefore open in Canada to proceed in this direction. However, the majority of the Court declined to accord to such orders the simplicity that has attended liberalized recognition and enforcement of foreign pecuniary orders. Non-pecuniary foreign orders were found to involve elements that necessitate an exercise of independent discretion by an enforcing Canadian court, in a manner similar to the discretion that a Canadian court would have exercised if the merits were before the Canadian court.[153] Such principles will need to be developed in future enforcement cases.

Non-pecuniary judicial orders are common in a telecommunications context, particularly with respect to the entry of signals into the jurisdiction of another state. The signals may be lawful in the state of transmission but unlawful, or containing content that will constitute an illegality, in the state of receipt. Examples include the Internet transmission of television signals containing infringing copyright,[154] or a signal that utilizes products or processes that constitute a patent

---

152 *Beals*, above note 5 at para. 202.
153 See comments from *Pro Swing*, above note 6 at paras. 30–31 (Deschamps J for the majority) and 80–84 (McLachlin CJ dissenting). See also Vaughan Black, "Enforcement of Foreign Non-Money Judgments: *Pro Swing v. ELTA*" (2006), 42 Can. Bus. L.J. 81 at 83, 88, and 96.
154 See Chapter 5, Section B(5). See also *Twentieth Century Fox Film Corporation v. iCraveTV*, 2000 WL 255989 (W.D. Pa. 2000) regarding issuance of an injunction

infringement in the state of receipt.[155] In such Internet-related instances, a non-pecuniary order would be effective only if enforceable in the jurisdiction of the host server. Presumably any such order would have to be drawn so as to require the prevention of extraterritorial transmission to the receiving state. If drawn more widely, to prevent all transmission, it would be an attempt by a foreign court to enforce non-existent rights. This was recognized by the majority of the Supreme Court in *Pro Swing* involving US-registered trademarks, which afford rights and exclusivity only within the territory of grant, in this case within the United States.[156] A transmission outside of the United States cannot be proscribed by US-registered trademark law even if a US-registered trademark is included in the transmission. Such rights do not have universal application. In *Pro Swing*, the majority in giving express recognition to this can be seen to have looked behind the judgment of the issuing court, perhaps with respect to a matter regarding the merits (the non-existence of intellectual property rights (IPRs)). To do otherwise, however, would have lent judicial aid to a severe and apparent jurisdictional fiction of the issuing court, brought to light only by the nature of such rights in their recent inclusion in conflict of laws theory and analysis. Such a position ought logically to apply also to *in personam* pecuniary foreign judgments involving IPRs, or is the distinguishing feature of *Pro Swing* the recognition of some broader discretionary factors in enforcement of non-pecuniary orders?

Common law provinces have no legislative measures dealing with recognition and enforcement of foreign non-pecuniary orders in international contexts. Article 3155 of the *Civil Code of Québec* does provide for such recognition and enforcement, interprovincially and internationally. However, in response to the constitutional requirements of *Morguard* and *Hunt*,[157] legislation developed by the Uniform Law

---

for copyright infringement of American content by Canadian Internet broadcasts.

155 An example can be seen in the alleged infringement of a US patent by Canadian-based RIM (Research in Motion) with respect to RIM's BlackBerry e-mail device. Had this matter not been settled, US patent rights would have taken effect for any infringement with respect to US transmissions from the device. See Associated Press, *Settlement Reached in Blackberry Case*, online: www.msnbc.msn.com/id/11659304/#storyContinued.

156 *Pro Swing*, above note 6 at paras. 52–58. McLachlin CJC dissented on this point (at paras. 116–19), reasoning: "Except in cases of fraud or where a judgment is contrary to natural justice or public policy, the court considering the issue of the enforcement of a foreign judgment cannot look behind its terms" (at para. 119).

157 See text accompanying notes 21–26, above in this chapter.

Conference has afforded all provinces with a legislative model of inter-provincial recognition and enforcement of both pecuniary and non-pecuniary orders of Canadian courts.[158] In British Columbia, this is the *Enforcement of Canadian Judgments and Decrees Act*.[159]

In addition to common law (or *Civil Code*) enforcement procedures, both interprovincial and international pecuniary orders may utilize an alternative means of enforcement if available in the province. This involves registration of a foreign *in personam* pecuniary judgment under reciprocal enforcement legislation. In British Columbia, this is the *Court Order Enforcement Act*,[160] in Ontario, the *Reciprocal Enforcement of Foreign Judgments Act*.[161] The benefits of legislation in these respects is limited to judgments from jurisdictions that are actual parties to the scheme of reciprocity reflected in the legislation. Registration enables the foreign judgment to be enforceable as if it were a judgment of the superior court of the enforcing jurisdiction. The requirements of the legislation limit their scope to the traditional recognition and enforcement criteria of presence, attornment, or consent to the extraterritorial order,[162] rather than to the *Morguard* and *Beals* real and substantial connection dimension. However, the interprovincial constitutional requirements of *Morguard* do not render such legislation invalid. It is seen simply as an alternative process to that of enforcement at common law.[163] As such it may be granted on such terms as a province desires.

E. CHOICE OF LAW

Choice of law by a Canadian court is determined by Canadian private international law or conflict of laws theory as the law of the forum. Any statutory provisions, perhaps implementing a treaty or convention, are the primary determinant. In Quebec, the *Civil Code*, Articles 3117, 3128, 3132, and 3133 perform this function. Otherwise, it is a matter of common law. The first step is to characterize the legal nature

---

158 See text accompanying notes 27–28, above in this chapter.

159 *Enforcement of Canadian Judgments and Decrees Act*, above note 28.

160 *Court Order Enforcement Act*, R.S.B.C. 1996, c. 78.

161 *Reciprocal Enforcement of Foreign Judgments Act*, R.S.O. 1990, c. R.5. UK judgments are governed by specific legislation: *Reciprocal Enforcement of Foreign Judgments (U.K.) Act*, R.S.O. 1990, c. R.6.

162 See *Reciprocal Enforcement of Foreign Judgments Act*, ibid., s. 3; *Court Order Enforcement Act*, above note 160, s. 29.

163 *Morguard*, above note 2 at 1110–11 (S.C.R.).

of the issues as choice of law rules differ between categories.[164] Applicable laws available to a court include the law of the forum (*lex fori*); the law of the location of any property, immovable (land) or movable, including intangible interests (*lex situs*); and the law of the place where the wrong occurred (*lex loci delicti*). Other situations of private international law may invoke the law of the place of a person's domicile (*lex domicili*) or of a person's "ordinary residence." In a contractual context, establishing the "proper law" of the particular contract is required. An overall transaction will often invoke several categories. For instance, a motor vehicle accident will involve a tort as to the incident itself, issues of property with respect to ownership of the vehicles, and issues of contract in relation to any rental agreement. Contextually in this chapter, the focus is on tort or delict.

With respect to tort or delict, in 1994 the Supreme Court revised Canadian private international law by stipulating *lex loci delicti* as a mandatory choice of law interprovincially and presumptively in international situations, reserving in the latter context an extraordinary possibility of *lex fori*.[165] The determination is not of constitutional dimension, but the Court noted that a *lex loci delicti* rule would meet interprovincial constitutional requirements, suggesting that any legislative rule to the contrary could give rise to a constitutional evaluation.[166] The determination replaced the English common law rule of double accountability[167] that required a tort to be both a civil wrong in the forum (*lex fori*) and "not justified" in the place of occurrence.[168]

Two features are relevant: first, the legal determination of the *situs* of a tort; and second, an interpretation of the technology and other factual material to identify the precise events that are tortious and where those events occur. Determining the location of a tort for choice of law purposes is essentially the same as determining location for jurisdictional purposes and has already been discussed.[169] The current focus

---

164 See *Kent Trade and Finance Inc. v. JP Morgan Chase Bank*, [2009] 4 F.C.R 109 at para. 16ff. (C.A.), explaining this general approach.

165 *Tolofson*, above note 4 at para. 70. Sopinka and Major JJ preferred to retain a similar discretion to allow *lex fori* even interprovincially and on this issue dissented. *Tolfson*, *ibid.* at paras. 105–7.

166 *Ibid.* at para. 71.

167 See *Phillips v. Eyre* (1870), L.R. 6 Q.B. 1 (Ex. Ct.); and *Chaplin v. Boys*, [1971] A.C. 356 (H.L.) [*Chaplin*].

168 Since May 1996, this rule has not been of general application in the United Kingdom as a result of *Private International Law (Miscellaneous Provisions) Act 1995* (U.K.), 1995, c. 42, s. 10. Significantly, the rule is preserved in respect of defamation proceedings. See *ibid.*, s. 13.

169 See jurisdiction *simpliciter* discussion in Section D, above in this chapter.

attempts to emphasize choice of law elements. Internet-related defamation affords a difficult analysis. Defamation (or libel or slander) protects
reputation in every jurisdiction where there is publication. Publication is the disclosure to any one person other than the plaintiff him or
herself.[170] An Internet uploading of a defamatory publication therefore
presents the prospect of not only multiple jurisdictional liability but
multiple choice of law options. Such duplication of resources is not
in the interest of the public or the parties. Applying *Moran*, the place
of uploading is the "place of the acting," where the publication was
created and made accessible. If mere uploading constitutes publication
and if the tort is complete on publication without any requirement of
damage, as is the position with the tort of libel, though not of slander,[171]
the defamation would be complete at the place of uploading, invoking
the law of that jurisdiction as *lex loci delicti*.[172] However, comparatively
with the communication right in copyright,[173] no publication would
occur without an accessing, creating both a supplier and a receiver.[174]
Merely posting a hypertext to a third party's defamatory source without evidence of accessing by others is not publication.[175]

Defamatory publication on the Internet, being substantially permanent, would fall within the category of libel if not otherwise provided
by statute. Provincial statutes reforming the law of libel and slander
address various situations, for example, broadcasting and news print
media.[176] Most injury to reputation is in the place of business or resi-

---

170 Patrick Milmo *et al.*, *Gatley on Libel and Slander* (London: Sweet & Maxwell,
2004) at 141.

171 *Ibid.* at 79. Libel is committed when defamatory matter is published in a
"permanent" form, whereas defamation published by spoken word or some
other transitory form is slander. Under the Alberta *Defamation Act*, R.S.A. 2000,
c. D-7, s. 2(2), damages are presumed in all defamation actions. However, the
Ontario *Libel and Slander Act*, R.S.O. 1990, c. L.12 acknowledges the distinction between libel and slander: any defamatory words published in a newspaper
or broadcast constitute libel (s. 2), while slander requires "words calculated to
disparage" (s. 16). Applicable legislative provisions must be considered in every
province. See also *Moran*, above note 36 at 398.

172 See *Bangoura*, above note 79 at para. 27 (S.C.J.) rev'd on other grounds. See
also *Wiebe v. Bouchard* (2005), 46 B.C.L.R. (4th) 278 at para. 21 (S.C.), where
uploading was considered to be publication "nationwide."

173 Chapter 5, text accompanying notes 147–52.

174 See *Crookes v. Holloway*, 2007 BCSC 1325, aff'd 2008 BCCA 165. Without evidence of accessing, the element of "publication" was not established.

175 *Crookes v. Wikimedia Foundation Inc.*, 2008 BCSC 1424, 88 B.C.L.R. (4th) 395.

176 Using British Columbia as an example, see *Libel and Slander Act*, R.S.B.C. 1996,
c. 263, ss. 1, 2, and 18. The definition of "broadcast" (s. 1) relates to television
and radio communications.

dence of the plaintiff. This was recognized in *Tolofson*[177] and has been so held in other proceedings, supporting both the taking of jurisdiction and the application of the law of that jurisdiction, thereby avoiding any defence in the place of uploading.[178]

A similar analysis applies to any violation by way of disclosure of privacy interests, whether statutory, common law, or civil code.[179] The law of the place of "disclosure" is likely to be the location of the tort, but the difficulty is similar to that of publication. Is a mere uploading sufficient? Or must there be accessing? Logically, it is the disclosure to the accessor that violates the privacy, and this occurs at the place of receipt. A violation of privacy may, however, be defined so that the law of the enacting jurisdiction is the only applicable law. For example, under the Canadian federal *Personal Information Protection and Electronic Documents Act* (PIPEDA),[180] a breach occurs only upon an *unauthorized release*[181] by a holder of personal information and this would occur upon mere release from containment, ordinarily at the place of collection and storage. A release outside of Canada is also remedial in Canada as *PIPEDA* includes extraterritorial disclosures.[182]

Any relief that might be developed for tortious intrusions or interferences with electronic media or sources would ordinarily occur at the location of the interference and would be subject to the law of that location.[183]

Intellectual property rights should be divided into three categories. First are matters presented at common law or civil law, being rights established by judge made law or interpretation. Second are rights established by a sovereign grant of exclusivity involving an application and examination before grant within the sovereign territory. These include patents, registered trademarks, and registered industrial designs. The third category is copyright protection, involving no sovereign grant and

---

177 *Tolofson*, above note 4 at para. 28.
178 See *Direct Energy Marketing Ltd. v. Hillson*, 1999 ABQB 455, 72 Alta. L.R. (3d) 140 at para. 56; and *Bangoura*, above note 79 at para. 30 (S.C.J.), rev'd on other grounds. In Australia, see *Dow Jones*, above note 50 at paras. 134–35.
179 See Chapter 4, regarding privacy.
180 *Personal Information Protection and Electronic Documents Act*, R.S.C. 2000, c. 5 [*PIPEDA*].
181 *Ibid.*, Sch. 1, s. 4(7)(1).
182 *Ibid.*, Sch. 1, ss. 4(1)(3) and 4(8), as interpreted in *PIPEDA* Case Summary #2006-333: "[The Act] requires organizations to be transparent about their personal information handling practices and to protect customer personal information in the hands of foreign-based service providers to the extent possible by contractual means," online: www.priv.gc.ca/cf-dc/2006/333_20060511_e.cfm.
183 Chapter 3, Section D.

affording a measure of universality of protection throughout countries party to relevant treaties and conventions. Although Article 5(2) of the *Berne Convention* stipulates that author's rights "shall be governed exclusively by the laws of the country where the protection is claimed," the English Court of Appeal has noted this to not preclude an application of choice of laws theory as the reference to "the laws of the country" would include that country's rules of private international law.[184]

The first category will invoke *lex loci delicti*, being at the place where the defendant's misrepresentation causes a foreseeable likelihood of public confusion over the source of the item or service to which the mark or indicia relates. Canadian common law is interpreted broadly to encompass reputation extending to Canada from an extraterritorial source.[185] The reputational "spill over" to Canada is business "goodwill," or property,[186] in Canada.

The second category of intellectual property rights can exist and can be infringed only within the territory of grant. As noted earlier, this has been recognized by a majority of the Supreme Court in *Pro Swing*.[187] The appropriate choice of law is therefore *lex situs*, and the prevailing opinion retains exclusive law and jurisdiction to that territory.[188] Although a separation of issues of infringement from those pertaining to grant has been suggested,[189] the difficulty remains that infringement itself may necessitate an interpretation of the *scope* of the statutory grant, even though its validity is not at issue. Indeed, although incorporeal in nature, these rights are similar to land or immovable

---

184 *Berne Convention for the Protection of Literary and Artistic Works*, 9 September 1886, 828 U.N.T.S. 221, as last rev'd by the *Paris Act*, 24 July 1971, 1161 U.N.T.S. 3, online: www.wipo.int/treaties/en/ip/berne/trtdocs_wo001.html [*Berne Convention*]; *Pearce v. Ove Arup Partnership Ltd.*, [2000] 3 W.L.R. 332, [1999] 1 All E.R. 769 at 801 (C.A.) [*Pearce*].

185 The leading Canadian case is *Orkin Exterminating Co. v. Pestco Co. of Canada Ltd.* (1985), 50 O.R. (2d) 726, 19 D.L.R. (4th) 90 (C.A.), redefining business goodwill to include simply business reputation in the jurisdiction. See also *Walt Disney Productions v. Triple Five Corp.* (1994), 113 D.L.R. (4th) 229, 53 C.P.R. (3d) 129 (Alta. C.A.), leave to appeal to S.C.C. refused, [1994] S.C.C.A. No. 204.

186 *AG Spalding & Bros. v. AW Gamage Ltd.*, [1915] 32 R.P.C. 273 (H.L.) established business goodwill as the proprietary concept in the context of passing off proceedings.

187 See text accompanying note 156, above in this chapter.

188 Hague Conference, above note 12, art. 12.

189 *Ibid.*; see Haines, above note 12 at 69, n. 112. See also *Lucasfilm Ltd. v. Ainsworth*, [2008] EWHC 1878, [2009] FSR 2 at paras. 190–91 (Ch.), probably now overruled in this respect by the conclusion the Court of Appeal with respect to use of foreign law in an IP context. See *Lucasfilm Ltd. v. Ainsworth*, [2009] EWCA Civ 1328, [2009] 3 W.L.R. 333 [*Lucasfilm* (C.A.)].

property, given the sovereign nature of the grant and the territorial limitation. They can be analogized with land and the exclusive jurisdiction and choice of law to the jurisdiction of location for issues of title, possession and damages for trespass.[190] Despite considerable criticism of the scope of this rule, the House of Lords recently declined to reconsider its application,[191] although elsewhere issues concerning *in personam* activity connected with the land[192] have been distinguished from trespass or issues of title to the land. The interpretation of the scope of intellectual property rights in this category is closely linked with the grant itself and is therefore comparable to a title inquiry.[193]

The third category, copyright, is more diverse and has been analyzed in the context of jurisdiction.[194] Both Canadian and United States copyright law are formally territorial.[195] However, United States copyright has been held to apply to acts of extraterritorial infringement, if there is an act of infringement in the United States that is linked sufficiently with the extraterritorial events.[196] Classic examples include the reproduction in the United States of negatives of a cinematographic work subsequently exhibited extraterritorially, enabling US copyright law to apply not only to the reproduction but also to the extraterritorial exhibition or performance;[197] and the partial manufacture in the United States of sound tapes that were utilized extraterritorially in the manufacture of phonographic recordings, enabling US copyright

---

190 *British South Africa Co. v. Companhia de Moçambique*, [1893] A.C. 602 (H.L.) [*Moçambique*].

191 See *Hesperides Hotels Ltd. v. Muftizade*, [1979] A.C. 508, [1978] 2 All E.R. 1168 (H.L.) citing, but declining to apply considerable academic opinion against *Moçambique, ibid.*, and invoking the H.L. Practice Direction of 1966, (*Practice Statement (Judicial Precedent), [1966] 1 W.L.R. 1234 to overturn it. See also Duke v. Andler*, [1932] S.C.R. 734, refusing to enforce a US order concerning title to land in British Columbia.

192 See, for example, *Ward v. Coffin* (1972), 27 D.L.R. (3d) 58 (N.B.S.C. (A.D.)), enforcing an agreement for specific performance with respect to land.

193 See *Itar-Tass Russian News Agency v. Russian Kurier, Inc.*, 153 F.3d 82 (2d Cir. 1998).

194 See text accompanying notes 51–55, above in this chapter.

195 *Copyright Act*, above note 52, s. 5(1): "[C]opyright shall subsist *in Canada* . . . ." [emphasis added]. For a discussion of the territorial limitations of the US *Copyright Act*, see Melville B. Nimmer & David Nimmer, *Nimmer on Copyright*, looseleaf, vol. 3 (New York: Matthew Bender, 1996) § 17.02.

196 See Nimmer & Nimmer, *ibid.*, § 17.03; and Robert G. Howell, "Intellectual Property, Private International Law, and Issues of Territoriality" (1997) 13 C.I.P.R. 209 at 219–21.

197 *Sheldon v. Metro-Goldwyn Pictures Corp.*, 106 F.3d 45 at 52 (2d Cir. 1939), aff'd 309 U.S. 390 (1940).

law to cover the extraterritorial (infringing) manufacture.[198] If applied in an Internet context, an accessing from Canada of a website in the United States might be said to involve infringing elements at the source of the transmission (in the United States) that are sufficiently linked to an infringement in Canada, thereby allowing US copyright law to apply to the whole communication. The move by the Supreme Court to recognize territorial competence upon a real and substantial connection test[199] may reflect some broad comparison with this trend in the United States. There is doubt, however, with respect to *authorization* of infringement.[200] In the United States, the relevant territorial focus is the location where the direct act of infringement occurred. No action will lie in the territory of authorization for a direct infringement elsewhere.[201] This reflects that an act of "authorization" is culpable only if a direct infringement results.[202] Authorization cannot, therefore, constitute an antecedent infringement within the territory. Yet once the direct infringement has occurred in the forum territory, why should the extraterritorial authorization not be remedial in the forum so long as there is a sufficient real and substantial connection between the territory and the authorization?

Ironically, US law has reached this outcome, not through the statutory authorization right but through the tort principles of contributory infringement and vicarious liability. If foreign authorizers "knew or should have known" of the likely copyright infringement in the United States, these tort theories will apply.[203] Today, contributory infringement is the primary remedy in the United States for third party or indirect liability for copyright infringement.[204] The analysis it presents is, in essence, the real and substantial connection analysis of tort conflict of laws. Applying tort analysis frees the forum court from the strict territorial restraint of forum statutory copyright.

---

198 *Famous Music Corp. v. Seeco Records, Inc.*, 201 F. Supp. 560 at 568–69 (S.D.N.Y. 1961).

199 See text accompanying notes 21ff., above in this chapter.

200 *Copyright Act*, above note 52, ss. 3(1) ("works"), 15(1), 18(1), 21(1), and 26(1) ("other subject matter") in Canada.

201 *Subafilms, Ltd v. MGM Pathe Communications Co.*, 24 F.3d 1088 (9th Cir. 1994), recently followed in *Armstrong v. Virgin Records, Ltd.*, 91 F. Supp. 2d 628 at 634 (S.D.N.Y. 2000) [*Armstrong*].

202 Nimmer & Nimmer, above note 195, s. 12.4[A][3] and 12.4[D][2].

203 *Armstrong*, above note 201 at 635.

204 Nimmer & Nimmer, above note 195, § 12.4.

F. AN ALTERNATIVE COPYRIGHT CHOICE OF LAW THEORY

An innovative development in the United States, consistent with a limited consensus at the Hague Conference on Private International Law,[205] might afford even greater ability and flexibility to enforce copyright in a context of Internet communications.[206] The approach involves a court appropriately having personal jurisdiction then applying foreign copyright law upon a choice of law of *lex loci deliciti*. For example, a Canadian court with personal jurisdiction over a defendant might deal with an infringement that occurred in France by applying French copyright law.

Despite a fledgling but debated recognition to this effect in English law,[207] the option was rejected by the Court of Appeal in 2009 in *Lucasfilm Ltd. v Ainsworth*.[208] Any application in Canada would therefore need to focus primarily on a North American context, reflecting the interconnections of trade and commerce between Canada and the United States and the developments in Canadian private international law in jurisdiction, recognition, and enforcement procedures now closer to those prevailing in the United States[209] than those in England and the Commonwealth. This may in turn support a greater integration of the principles of copyright law enforcement contextually with these developments.

Lucasfilm in its precise facts, along with hypothetical modification, affords an Internet-related transaction that enables Canadian and English perspectives to private international law to be compared and contrasted within the embrace of new media. The English Court of Appeal finds appropriately that legal principles should not be Internet or technology specific.[210] Yet an Internet-related transaction will present nuances and perspectives that can occur so readily only within that medium. The defendant was domiciled in the United Kingdom and

---

205 Hague Conference, above note 12 at 69–70.

206 Paul E. Geller, "Conflicts of Laws in Cyberspace: Rethinking International Copyright in a Digitally Networked World" (1996) 20 Colum.-V.L.A J. L. & Arts 571.

207 *Pearce*, above note 184. Contrast *Tyburn Productions Ltd. v. Conan Doyle*, [1990] 1 All E.R. 909, [1991] Ch. 75.

208 *Lucasfilm* (C.A.), above note 189. The court (at para. 157) referred to a New Zealand High Court decision in support of this denial. See *Atkinson Footware v. Hodgskin International Services* (1994), 31 I.P.R. 186 at 189–92 (H.C.N.Z.).

209 See above note 8.

210 *Lucasfilm* (C.A.), above note 189 at paras. 193 & 194.

operated a web business there, from which sale of products were made within both the United Kingdom and the United States. The products did not infringe UK copyright but did infringe US copyright law in respect of sales to the United States from the United Kingdom. A default judgment had been obtained in the United States but was unenforceable in the United Kingdom within the traditional scope of recognition and enforcement: consent or attainment or agreement to US jurisdiction. These were not met. Chancery (trial) sought to overcome this by applying US law for the US violations and enforcing it through the personal jurisdiction it had over the UK defendant. The rejection of this approach in the Court of Appeal left the plaintiff without relief for the US infringements. In Canada, the US default judgment would probably be enforceable under *Beals*.[211] The Canadian court would be saved from considering the potential of applying US copyright law on a choice of law theory. Yet when changing the situation hypothetically to one that might involve infringement in both Canada and the United States, an additional perspective must be considered. Without either the Canadian or US court determining foreign copyright law, two proceedings would be necessary, one in Canada for Canadian infringement and the other in the United States for US-related infringement. Given that both arise from the single Internet source, is this not a duplicatory waste of judicial and other trial-related resources that is avoidable upon merely utilizing the choice of law theory?

The development has been explored by commentators in the United States[212] and in Canada.[213] The leading US authority is *London Film Productions Ltd. v. Intercontinental Communications, Inc.*.[214] The plaintiff was a British corporation. The defendant, a New York corporation, had allegedly infringed the plaintiff's copyright in Chile and other areas of South America. The suit was before the Federal District Court in New York, and personal jurisdiction over the defendant was established.[215]

---

211 See text accompanying note 111ff., above in this chapter.

212 See Jane C. Ginsburg, "Global Use/Territorial Rights: Private International Law Questions of the Global Information Infrastructure" (1995) 42 J. Copyright Soc'y 318; Jane C. Ginsburg, "United States of America" in Marcel Dellebeke, ed., *Copyright in Cyberspace: Copyright and the Global Information Infrastructure* (Amsterdam: Otto Cramwinckel, 1997) at 324–37; and Geller, above note 206.

213 Robert G. Howell, "Canada" in Marcel Dellebeke, ed., *ibid.*, at 269–89; *Howell*, above note 196; and Barry Sookman, "Copyright and the Information Highway: Some Issues to Think About (Part II)" (1997) 11 I.P.J. 265 at 287–94.

214 *London Film Productions Ltd. v. Intercontinental Communications, Inc.*, 580 F. Supp. 47 (S.D.N.Y. 1984) [*London Film*].

215 *Ibid.* at 48. Issues with respect to the constitutionality of US federal court jurisdiction to determine copyright proceedings not involving US copyright

The principles of national treatment would protect the plaintiff's copyright in Chile to the extent provided by Chilean law. Ordinarily, the proceeding would have to be brought in Chile. In ruling that proceedings could be brought in New York with the choice of law being Chilean copyright law, the District Court noted several features.[216] First, copyright, more than other matters of intellectual property, is suited to such adjudication because it is "a transitory cause of action," meaning that "it has no *situs* apart from the domicile of [the] proprietor."[217] Both the United Kingdom and Chile were members of the *Berne Convention*. The plaintiff's copyright would, therefore, be protected in both countries without the need for formalities such as registration in either country. Second, the absence in copyright of any "grant" from government to confer protection excluded any likelihood of a forum court ruling upon the validity of any foreign governmental activity or "act of state."[218] Third, the only issue before the US court was the factual issue of infringement; the court did not have to consider whether copyright existed and whether it was valid. This was seen to lessen any prospect of a court of another jurisdiction being faced with accepting or rejecting an interpretation by the US court of foreign copyright law. Fourth, general policy factors favoured the taking of jurisdiction by a US court because there was no other forum having personal jurisdiction over the defendant, which, without the intervention of the US court, would leave the plaintiff without a forum in which to proceed to protect its copyright.

London Film has received subsequent support[219] and is consistent with a similar, but more difficult, analysis in the context of trademark[220]

---

law have been raised. See Nimmer & Nimmer, above note 195, s. 17.03, n. 11. In this instance, the jurisdiction (*vis-à-vis* state courts) was established on other grounds.

216   *London Film, ibid.* at 48–50.

217   *Ibid.* at 49 citing Nimmer & Nimmer, above note 195, § 12.01[C] .

218   Any governmental or administrative action of a foreign government is not justiciable in this context in the courts of another country. For example, if a matter involves the infringement of a patent, but the defendant introduces, by way of defence, a challenge to the validity of the grant of the patent, the matter could not proceed in the courts of another jurisdiction. Likewise, a court will decline jurisdiction if to take it would cause an "unseemly conflict" with a judgment in another country.

219   See *Armstrong*, above note 201 at 636–38, providing an extensive discussion in 2000. See also *Frink America, Inc. v. Champion Road Machinery Ltd.*, 961 F. Supp. 398 (N.D.N.Y. 1997); *Carell v. Shubert Organization, Inc.*, 104 F. Supp. 2d 236 (S.D.N.Y. 2000); *Well-Made Toy Mfg. Corp. v. Lotus Onda Indus Co., Ltd.*, 2003 WL 42001 (S.D.N.Y. 2003).

220   *Vanity Fair Mills, Inc. v. The T. Eaton Co. Ltd.*, 234 F.2d 633 (2d Cir. 1956).

and patent[221] infringement. The nature of these rights, involving grants from foreign governments, would now be more problematic within a choice of law theory,[222] but if pursued it would be simply on the issue of infringement without any consideration of the validity of an intellectual property right granted by a foreign sovereign.[223]

There is also some possibility of a registration of copyright, even if not required. Voluntary registration will ordinarily provide presumptions and evidentiary advantages.[224] More significantly, however, the presence of a registration may be seen as providing the copyright with a *situs* and thereby removing the conception of copyright as "transitory" and raising the possibility of *lex situs* as choice of law.[225] Nimmer, in support of *London Film*, explains correctly that the imposition of administrative formalities is precluded by the *Berne Convention*.[226] However, this does not necessarily mean that any voluntary registration is of no effect in any choice of laws analysis. The potential implications of administrative formalities was considered in *ITSI T.V. Productions Inc. v. California Authority of Racing Fairs*, where the court rejected the approach taken in *London Film*. [227]

The potential of any adoption in Canada of this principle is entirely speculative. There is no historical support in Commonwealth jurisprudence,[228] but there are examples of enforcement in proceedings involving extraterritorial issues that were not expressly analyzed.[229]

---

221 *Ortman v. Stanray Corporation*, 371 F.2d 154 (7th Cir. 1967); *Packard Instrument Company, Inc. v. Beckman Instruments, Inc.*, 346 F. Supp. 408 (N.D. Ill. 1972).

222 Hague Conference, above note 12 at 69–70.

223 See *Jose Armando Bermudez & Co v. Bermudez Intern.*, 2000 WL 1225792 at paras 4–6 (S.D.N.Y. 2000); and *New Name, Inc. v. Walt Disney Co.*, 2007 WL 5061697 at para. 5 (C.D. Cal. 2007) finding no challenge to any sovereign acts in Canada in the context of infringement *simpliciter* of Canadian trademarks and copyright. The court also distinguishes copyright from trademarks on the basis of a lack of a grant and formalities for copyright.

224 See, for example, *Copyright Act*, above note 52, s. 53, setting out presumptions flowing from registration.

225 See Howell, above note 196 at 223. Registration may be seen to be an administrative or governmental act giving the copyright a location and removing its "transitory" nature.

226 Nimmer & Nimmer, above note 195, § 17.03, n. 9.

227 *ITSI T.V. Productions Inc. v. California Authority of Racing Fairs*, 785 F. Supp. 854 at 866 including n. 19 (E.D. Cal. 1993), rev'd in part on other grounds, 3 F.3d 1289 (C.A. Cal. 1993).

228 See *Potter v. Broken Hill Pty. Co. Ltd.* (1906), 3 C.L.R. 479 (H.C.A.); and *Norbert Steinhardt & Son Ltd. v. Meth Patents Pty Ltd.* (1960), 34 A.L.J.R. 372 at 374 (H.C.A.), rejecting jurisdiction for extraterritorial enforcement of a patent.

229 See *Baschet v. London Illustrated Standard Company* (1989), [1900] 1 Ch. 73 (Ch.); *Jonathan Cape Ltd. v. Consolidated Press Ltd.*, [1954] 1 W.L.R. 1313 (Q.B.);

The approach has been endorsed by English commentators[230] and was relevant in proceedings before the Federal Court in Canada, and would have required resolution had the court not decided against the plaintiff on the facts.[231] It is also consistent with the decision in *Tolofson* by the Supreme Court, determining choice of law in tort to be *lex loci delicti.*[232]

In Canada, consideration must also be given to the scope of section 89 of the *Copyright Act* to the effect that no "copyright or any similar right" can exist except under the Act.[233] This provision, however, concerns Canadian or territorial copyright law. It does not address any development of recognizing foreign law in a context of private international law. When enacted in 1921 (effective 1924), the primary purposes were the abolition of common law copyright (for unpublished works) and the consolidation of copyright from earlier Imperial and Dominion enactments.[234]

Although the English Court of Appeal has now denied, as contrary to policy, the application in an English court of a foreign copyright law,[235] the essential issue for any Canadian court considering this option, beyond a pure policy determination, is whether a distinction can be made between copyright on the one hand and patent and trademark rights on the other. If a distinction can be made upon the matters set out earlier,[236] should copyright be seen as a "transitory" right, not

---

and *Campbell Connelly & Co. Ltd. v. Noble* (1962), [1963] 1 W.L.R. 252 (Ch.).

230 See Stephen M. Stewart, *International Copyright and Neighbouring Rights*, 2d ed. (London: Butterworths, 1989) at para. 3(28). The possibility of such a proceeding under conflict of laws principles is acknowledged in Walter Arthur Copinger, *Copinger and Skone James on Copyright*, 12th ed. (London: Sweet and Maxwell, 1980) at para. 619, but denied in the 13th ed. (1991) at para. 11(31). These commentaries utilize the English rule in *Chaplin*, above note 167, establishing jurisdiction *lex fori* where the alleged conduct would be a wrong in the forum (when there is also personal jurisdiction over the defendant) had it occurred in the forum and is not justified under the law of the territory where it occurred, *lex loci delicti.*

231 *Preston v. 20th Century Fox Canada Ltd.* (1990), 33 C.P.R. (3d) 242 (F.C.T.D.), aff'd (1994), 53 C.P.R. (3d) 407 (F.C.A.). See Howell, above note 196 at 212, pointing out that any infringement by reproduction in *Preston* would have occurred in the United States. Infringement by way of public performance in Canada would be remedial under Canadian law.

232 See text accompanying above note 165.

233 *Copyright Act*, above note 52, s. 89.

234 *Copyright Act, 1921*, S.C. 1921, 11–12 Geo. V, c. 24, s. 44 (now s. 89). Common law copyright was preserved for unpublished works in *Donaldson v. Beckett* (1774), 2 Bro. 129, 1 E.R. 837 (H.L.).

235 *Lucasfilm* (C.A.), above note 189.

236 See text accompanying notes 212–27, above in this chapter.

linked exclusively to a forum of particular territory, in a manner similar to trespass to land within a territory and thereby to be free from the restraints of the choice of law rule in *Moçambique*?[237] In its policy determination, the English Court of Appeal has applied *Moçambique* to copyright upon a territorial limitation in both forum and law.[238]

G. SUMMATION AND PROGNOSIS

Transborder social and commercial activities that characterize today's environment will inevitably increase the demands on private international law (conflict of laws) as transactions increasingly present "a foreign element." Telecommunications technologies are a substantial contributing factor to the globalizing of trade and business, which itself reflects greater personal mobility, freer trading arrangements, and growth in the financial and service industries. The medium of the decentralized Internet as the optimal transactional medium not only adds to *jurisdictional* and *enforcement* demands but presents subject areas — such as intellectual property rights and regulatory measures — that have historically had little influence in conflict of laws theory and practice.

To date, the concepts of private international law have accommodated this new environment, yet changes are likely. An examination of *Lucasfilm* in the United Kingdom illustrates the point. The English Court of Appeal's rejection of the ability of an English court to apply US copyright law upon a choice of law theory to give enforceable relief in the United Kingdom against the UK defendant for sales into the United States, while at the same time denying recognition and enforcement of the US judgment by retaining the traditional limited recognition and enforcement mechanism — presence, consent, or attornment of a defendant — is difficult to justify. By contrast, in Canada, if the foreign court has exercised an appropriately restrained jurisdiction upon a minimum contacts theory that may, for present purposes, be seen as the real and substantial connection test, the US judgment would probably have been recognized and enforced. This reflects that Internet targeting of sales into the United States of items infringing US copyright law is likely to be a sufficiently real and substantial connection for Canadian courts to recognize appropriate jurisdiction in the US court.

---

237 *Moçambique*, above note 190.
238 *Lucasfilm* (C.A.), above note 189.

The Canadian approach of liberalizing recognition and enforcement of foreign judgments is applicable to all *in personam* pecuniary and, in a developing and discretionary context, non-pecuniary, awards. As such, the Canadian reforms have a broader impact than any choice of law innovation attempted by Chancery (trial) in *Lucasfilm*. The position as to recognition and enforcement in Canada is, indeed, much closer to that in the United States and may well encourage and enhance cross-border and other international trade and commerce. Perhaps this means that Canadian courts need not embark on a choice of law theory, yet such would be beneficial in allocation of scarce judicial resources in instances of infringing sales in both Canada and the United States The need for two proceedings, one for Canadian infringement and one for US infringement, would be avoided. This seems to be logical and consistent with the broadening developments that have occurred to date.

Yet some safeguard might be necessary. In this respect, it is unfortunate that the majority of the Supreme Court in *Beals* was unenthusiastic about a corresponding review of the narrow defences available in recognition and enforcement, while not ruling this approach out at some future time. Narrow grounds of defence are axiomatic with narrow grounds of recognition and enforcement. To change one without considering the other is to risk inconsistency and logic with the potential for injustice. The perspective of the dissenting judges that the defences will at some stage require re-evaluation[239] is prophetic.

Universality in recognition and enforcement with limited defences is reflected in the *Civil Code of Québec* and has engendered some debate in that province. The two contentions in the interpretation of the enforcement of foreign judgments under the *Civil Code* have focused on allowing or denying the influence of factors in the nature of *forum non conveniens* to be considered in determining whether the foreign court has exercised an appropriately restrained jurisdiction. The Supreme Court of Canada in *Canada Post Corporation v. Lépine* rejected use of provisions of the code that reflected these factors, a position seemingly consistent with that at common law.[240] This consequence presents several questions for the common law provinces. Overall, the interpretation of provincial legislation will be paramount. Legislation that distinguishes provisions between jurisdiction *simpliciter* and *forum non conveniens*, as for instance in the widely adopted Uniform Law Conference recommendations in the *Court Jurisdiction and Proceedings Transfer* enactments, may be subject to a similar interpretation as that given

---

239 See text accompanying notes 128–29, above in this chapter.
240 See text accompanying notes 99–104, above in this chapter.

by the Supreme Court to the separate articles of the *Civil Code*. As with the *Civil Code*, the provisions equating with jurisdiction *simpliciter* and those of *forum non conveniens* are separately expressed. If, then, enforcement depends simply on factors of jurisdiction *simpliciter*, whether statutory or at common law, applied to enforcement through reciprocity, further matters must be addressed.

First, within the real and substantial connection test, *how substantial* must the connection be and is this of a greater measure internationally than interprovincially? The need for *significant* substantiality was emphasized by the Supreme Court in *Beals* and systemic uniformity and consistency is widely acknowledged interprovincially, but not necessarily internationally. Yet no divergence between these contexts has evolved to date in the formulations of the real and substantial connection test. It is suggested that such a distinction ought to be considered. Second, the potential of new defences as formulated by LeBel J — that really reflect factors of *conveniens*[241] but without disturbing the normality of the principle *forum non conveniens* being considered only by the originating court — might be revisited. The recognition of factors of fairness to the parties within the real and substantial connection test may also assist in this context. Third, if the enforcing jurisdiction has earlier issued an anti-suit injunction that was not followed but that necessarily has involved an assessment of the relative or *conveniens* factors, should a resulting foreign judgment be enforced? It is suggested that to do so would be incongruous unless the merits so required. Fourth, the determination by the Supreme Court in *Teck Cominco Metals Ltd. v. Lloyds Underwriters* in 2009 that parallel Canadian and foreign proceedings ought not to require a stay of the Canadian proceedings recognizes relative or *conveniens* factors, and the Court was expressly cognizant of the potential future difficulties of enforcement.[242]

Recognition and enforcement of non-pecuniary international orders presents a further significant expansion, but one balanced by a discretionary element that in itself looks behind the foreign judgment, something that was not done historically, in the much more confined recognition and enforcement constraint. The involvement of an intellectual property right providing a *territorial* right also necessitates the discretion to look behind the judgment to ensure the scope of the judgment is limited to the territory of the right itself. This avoids *de facto* universality being accorded to the intellectual property right and is logically also applicable to pecuniary judgments involving such a right.

---

241 See text accompanying note 129, above in this chapter.
242 See text accompanying notes 123–25, above in this chapter.

Perhaps this will encourage some overall re-evaluation of expanded enforcement, with appropriate discretionary balancing for recognition and enforcement. It is suggested that a consideration of both aspects will accord greater enhancement of international trade and commerce.

Overall, federal or provincial legislative measures may also be desirable to give greater certainty and a more holistic perspective to the issues discussed in this chapter. Judicial reform is necessarily less comprehensive. The difficulty in an international context, however, is a failure or absence of any real consensus between jurisdictions. This may encourage a continuation of fluidity and correspondingly discourage legislative measures as being too difficult to change and often lacking in the flexibility that ordinarily attends judicial reform.

SELECTED
FURTHER READINGS

BROADCASTING AND TELECOMMUNICATIONS

BABE, ROBERT E. *Telecommunications in Canada: Technology, Industry, and Government* (Toronto: University of Toronto Press, 1993)

BLACK, SHARON. *Telecommunications Law in the Internet Age* (San Francisco: Morgan Kauffman, 2002)

BRECHER, JAY ET AL. *Media and Postal Communications*, Halsbury's Laws of Canada (Markham, ON: LexisNexis, 2007–)

GRANT, PETER S. ET AL. *Canadian Broadcasting Regulatory Handbook, 2002*, 7th ed. (Toronto: McCarthy Tétrault, 2004)

HANDA, SUNNY. *Communications Law in Canada*, looseleaf (Toronto: Butterworths, 2000–)

HANDA, SUNNY ET AL. *Communications*, Halsbury's Laws of Canada (Markham, ON: LexisNexis, 2007–)

RYAN, MICHAEL H. *Canadian Telecommunications Law and Regulation*, looseleaf (Scarborough, ON: Carswell, 1993–)

SALTER, LIORA ET AL. *The CRTC and Broadcasting Regulation in Canada* (Toronto: Thomson/Carswell, 2008)

CONFLICT OF LAWS

FAWCETT, JAMES, & PAUL TORREMANS. *Intellectual Property and Private International Law* (Oxford: Oxford University Press, 1998)

KRUGER, THALIA. *Civil Jurisdiction Rules of the EU and Their Impact on Third States* (Oxford: Oxford University Press, 2008)

RAFFERTY, NICHOLAS ET AL. *Private International Law in Common Law Canada: Cases, Text, and Materials*, 3d ed. (Toronto: Emond Montgomery, 2010)

SVANTESSON, DAN J. *Private International Law and the Internet* (Alphen aan den Rijn: Kluwer International, 2007)

WALKER, JANET. *Castel and Walker Canadian Conflict of Laws*, 6th ed., looseleaf (Markham, ON: LexisNexis Canada, 2005–)

———. *CONFLICT OF LAWS*, Halsbury's Laws of Canada (Markham, ON: LexisNexis, 2006–)

COPYRIGHT

APLIN, TANYA. *Copyright Law in the Digital Society: The Challenges of Multimedia* (Oxford: Hart, 2005)

DIMOCK, RONALD. *Intellectual Property Disputes: Resolutions and Remedies*, looseleaf (Toronto: Carswell, 2002–)

GARNETT, K.M., & GILLIAN DAVIES, *Copinger and Skone James on Copyright*, 15th ed. (London: Sweet & Maxwell, 2005)

GEIST, MICHAEL. *In the Public Interest: The Future of Canadian Copyright Law* (Toronto: Irwin Law, 2005)

GELLER, PAUL EDWARD. *International Copyright Law and Practice*, looseleaf (New York: Mathew Bender, 1988–)

HANDA, SUNNY. *Copyright Law in Canada* (Markham, ON: Butterworths, 2002)

HARRIS, LESLEY ELLEN. *Canadian Copyright Law*, 3d ed. (Toronto: McGraw-Hill Ryerson, 2001)

HUGHES, ROGER. *Copyright Legislation and Commentary*, 2006/2007 ed. (Markham, ON: LexisNexis Butterworths, 2006)

McKEOWN, JOHN. *Fox on Canadian Law of Copyright and Industrial Designs*, 4th ed., looseleaf (Toronto: Carswell, 2003–)

NIMMER, MELVILLE, & DAVID NIMMER, *Nimmer on Copyright*, looseleaf (New York: Matthew Bender, 1997–)

TAMARO, NORMAND. *Annotated Copyright Act, 2009* (Toronto: Carswell, 2008)

VAVER, DAVID. *Copyright Law* (Toronto: Irwin Law, 2000)

VAVER, DAVID. *Intellectual Property Law: Copyright, Patents, Trademarks* (Toronto: Irwin Law, 1997)

WALTER, MICHEL, & SILKE VON LEWINSKI. *European Copyright Law: A Commentary* (Oxford: Oxford University Press, 2010)

PRIVACY LAW

DRAPEAU, MICHEL W. ET AL. *Protection of Privacy in the Canadian Private and Health Sectors*, 3d ed. (Toronto: Thomson/Carswell, 2007)

FRASER, DAVID ET AL. *Privacy Law in the Private Sector: An Annotation of the Legislation in Canada*, looseleaf (Aurora, ON: Canada Law Book, 2002–)

KENYON, ANDREW, & MEGAN RICHARDSON. *New Dimensions in Privacy Law: International and Comparative Perspectives* (Cambridge: Cambridge University Press, 2006)

LEVIN, AVNER, & MARY JO NICHOLSON. "Privacy Law in the United States, EU and Canada: The Allure of the Middle Ground" (2005) 2:2 University of Ottawa Law & Technology Journal 357

McISAAC, BARBARA, RICK SHIELDS, & KRIS KLEIN. *The Law of Privacy in Canada* (Toronto: Carswell, 2000)

POWER, E. MICHAEL. *Access to Information and Privacy*, Halsbury's Laws of Canada (Markham, ON: LexisNexis, 2006–)

TRADEMARK, DOMAIN NAMES AND INTERFERENCE

BENTLY, LIONEL, & BRAD SHERMAN. *Intellectual Property Law*, 2d ed. (Oxford: Oxford University Press, 2004)

CORNISH, WILLIAM RODOLPH. *Intellectual Property: Omnipresent, Distracting, Irrelevant?* (Oxford: Oxford University Press, 2004)

CORNISH, WILLIAM RODOLPH, & DAVID LLEWELYN. *Intellectual Property: Patents, Copyright, Trade Marks and Allied Rights*, 5th ed. (London: Sweet & Maxwell, 2003)

HUGHES, ROGER. *Trade-Marks Act and Commentary*, 2009 ed. (Markham, ON: LexisNexis Butterworths, 2009)

HUGHES, ROGER ET AL. *Trade-marks, Passing Off and Unfair Competition*, Halsbury's Laws of Canada (Markham, ON: LexisNexis, 2007–)

JOLLIFFE, R. SCOTT, & KELLY A. GILL. *Fox on Canadian Law of Trademarks and Unfair Competition*, 4th ed., looseleaf (Toronto, ON: Carswell, 2002–)

WILLOUGHBY, TONY, & SALLY ABEL. *Domain Law Practice: An International Handbook* (Oxford: Oxford University Press, 2005)

TECHNOLOGY LAW

COLLINS, MATTHEW. *The Law of Defamation and the Internet*, 2d ed. (Oxford: Oxford University Press, 2005)

GEIST, MICHAEL. *Internet Law in Canada*, 3d ed. (Concord, ON: Captus Press, 2002)

HARRIS, LESLEY ELLEN. *Digital Property: Currency of the 21st Century* (Toronto: McGraw-Hill Ryerson/Trade, 1998)

SCASSA, TERESA, & MICHAEL DETURBIDE. *Electronic Commerce and Internet Law in Canada* (Toronto, ON: CCH Canadian, 2004)

SOOKMAN, BARRY. *Computer, Internet and Electronic Commerce Law*, 2d ed., looseleaf (Toronto: Carswell, 1991–)

TAKACH, GEORGE. *Computer Law*, 2d ed. (Toronto: Irwin Law, 2003)

TABLE OF CASES

TABLE OF STATUTES AND OTHER AUTHORITIES

Agreement Implementation Act, S.C. 1994, c. 47

An Act respecting the protection of personal information in the private sector, S.Q. 1993, c. 17

An Act respecting the protection of personal information in the private sector, R.S.Q., c. P-39(1)

An Act to amend the Copyright Act, 2d Sess., 39th Parl., 2008

An Act to Amend the Copyright Act, S.C. 2002, c. 26

An Act to Amend the Telecommunications Act and The Teleglobe Canada Reorganization and Divestiture Act, S.C. 1998, c. 8

Anticybersquatting Consumer Protection Act, 15 U.S.C. § 1125(d) (1999)

Berne Convention for the Protection of Literary and Artistic Works, 9 September 1886, 828 U.N.T.S. 221, as last rev'd by *Paris Act*, 24 July 1971, 1161 U.N.T.S. 3

Bill C-2, *An Act to Amend the Radiocommunication Act*, 3d Sess., 37th Parl., 2004

Bill C-27, *Electronic Commerce Protection Act*, 2d Sess., 40th Parl., 2009

Bill C-32, *An Act to amend the Copyright Act*, 3rd Sess., 40th Parl., 2010

Bill C-60 *An Act to amend the Copyright Act*, 1st Sess., 38th Parl, 2005

Broadcasting Act, R.S.C. 1970, c. B-11

Broadcasting Act, R.S.C. 1985, c. B-9

Broadcasting Act, S.C. 1991, c. 11

Canada–United States Free Trade Agreement Implementation Act, S.C. 1988, c. 65

Canadian Broadcasting Act, S.C. 1936, c. 24

Canadian Environmental Protection Act, R.S.C. 1985 (4th Supp.), c. 16

Canadian Radio Broadcasting Act, S.C. 1932, c. 51

Canadian Radio-television Telecommunications Commission Act, S.C. 1974-75-76, c. 49

Child Online Protection Act, 47 U.S.C. § 231 (1998)

Competition Act, R.S.C. 1985, c. C-34

Constitution Act, 1867 (U.K.), 30 & 31 Vict., c. 3, reprinted in R.S.C. 1985, App. II, No. 5

Constitution Act, 1982, being Schedule B to the *Canada Act 1982* (U.K.), 1982, c. 11

Consumer Protection Act, C.C.S.M. c. 200

Controlling the Assault of Non-Solicited Pornography and Marketing Act of 2003, Pub. L. No. 108-187, 117 Stat. 2699

Copyright Act 1968 (Cth.), as am. by *Copyright Amendment (Digital Agenda Act) 2000* (Cth.)

Copyright Act 1994 (N.Z.), 1994

Copyright Act of 1976, Pub. L. No. 94-553, 90 Stat. 2541, codified at 17 U.S.C.

Copyright Act, 1921, S.C. 1921, 11–12 Geo. V, c. 24

Copyright Act, R.S.C. 1970, c. C-30

Copyright Act, R.S.C. 1985, c. C-42

Copyright Act, U.S.C. tit. 17 inserted by *Digital Millennium Copyright Act*, Pub. L. No. 105-304, 112 Stat. 2860 (1998)

Copyright Amendment (Digital Agenda Act) 2000 (Cth.)

Copyright Amendment Act, R.S.C. 1985 (4th Supp.), c. 10

Copyright Amendment Act, S.C. 1931 (21–22 Geo. V.), c. 8

Radiocommunication Act, R.S.C. 1985, c. R-2, as am. by S.C. 1989, c. 17

Radiotelegraph Act, S.C. 1913, c. 43

Railway Amendment Act, S.C. 1908, c. 61

Reciprocal Enforcement of Judgments (U.K.) Act, R.S.O. 1990, c. R.6

Reciprocal Enforcement Judgments Act, R.S.O. 1990, c. R.5

Sale of Goods Act, R.S.B.C. 1996, c. 410

Spam Act 2003 (Cth.)

Telecommunications Act, S.C. 1993, c. 38

Telecommunications Amendment Act 2005 (N.Z.), 2005/70

Telesat Canada Act, S.C. 1969, c. 51

Telesat Canada Reorganization and Divestiture Act, S.C. 1991, c. 52

Terrorism (USA PATRIOT) Act of 2001, Pub. L. No. 107-56, 115 Stat. 272 (2001)

Trademark Act of 1946, 15 U.S.C. 1051

Trade-marks Act, R.S.C. 1985, c. T-13

Transfer Act, S.B.C. 2003 c. 28

Transport Act, S.C. 1938, c. 53

Uniting and Strengthening America by Providing Appropriate Tools Required to Intercept and Obstruct Terrorism (USA PATRIOT) Act of 2001, Pub. L. No. 107-56, 115 Stat. 272 (2001), renewed *USA PATRIOT Improvement and Reauthorization Act of 2005*, Pub. L. No. 109-177, 120 Stat. 192 (2006)

Visual Artists Rights Act of 1990, 17 U.S.C. (1990)

Wireless Telegraphy Act, S.C. 1905, c. 49

INDEX

ABOUT THE AUTHOR

Robert Howell has taught in the Faculty of Law at the University of Victoria, British Columbia, since 1980. He has taught property in the first-year program since that time, but in 1985 he focused his research and primarily taught intellectual property law and policy. The impact of technological change led him to expand his specialization into telecommunications law and policy, and to private international law, initially its linkage with technology and intellectual property but, since 2003, across all dimensions of this subject. Professor Howell has also done research on and taught courses in managing intellectual property and he has presented summer term programs in intellectual property law, including the International Intellectual Property Summer Program from 2002 to 2007, alternating in venue between Victoria and Oxford.

Professor Howell has published nationally and internationally in his areas of specialization and has organized and participated in national and international conferences and seminars. In 1999 he co-authored (with Linda Vincent and Michael Manson) a national coursebook — *Intellectual Property Law, Cases and Materials*; and in 1998 and 2002 he completed *Reports on Database Protection and Canadian Laws* for Industry Canada and Canadian Heritage. In 2008, Professor Howell was appointed for a five-year term on the Board of the British Columbia Law Institute, the principal law reform entity in British Columbia.

RECYCLED
Paper made from
recycled material
FSC® C021757

Marquis Book Printing Inc.

Québec, Canada
2011

Printed on Silva Enviro 100% post-consumer EcoLogo certified paper,
processed chlorine free and manufactured using biogas energy.

100%   PERMANENT